THIRTEENTH CENTURY ENGLAND I

PROCEEDINGS OF
THE NEWCASTLE UPON TYNE CONFERENCE
1985

THIRTEENTH CENTURY ENGLAND
I

PROCEEDINGS OF
THE NEWCASTLE UPON TYNE CONFERENCE
1985

Edited by P. R. Coss and S. D. Lloyd

THE BOYDELL PRESS

First published 1986 by The Boydell Press
an imprint of Boydell & Brewer Ltd
PO Box 9, Woodbridge, Suffolk IP12 3DF
and Wolfeboro, New Hampshire 03894-2069, USA

ISBN 0 85115 452 2

British Library Cataloguing in Publication Data

Thirteenth-century England. — 1-
1. Great Britain — History — 13th century
942.03′4 DA225

ISSN 0269-6967
ISBN 0-85115-452-2

Library of Congress Cataloguing in Publication Data

Proceedings of the Newcastle-upon-Tyne conference, 1985.
(Thirteenth-century England, ISSN 0269-6967 ; 1)
Conference sponsored by the University of Newcastle upon Tyne and Newcastle upon Tyne Polytechnic.
1. Great Britain—History—13th century—Congresses. 2. England—Civilization—Medieval period, 1066 – 1485—Congresses. I. Coss, Peter R. II. Lloyd, S.D. (Simon D.) III. Conference on Thirteenth Century England (1st : 1985 : Newcastle upon Tyne) IV. University of Newcastle upon Tyne. V. Newcastle upon Tyne Polytechnic. VI. Series: Thirteenth-century England (series) ; 1.
DA225.P76 1986 942.03′4 86-24442
ISBN 0-85115-452-2

ISSN 0269-6967

Printed in Great Britain by
St Edmundsbury Press, Bury St Edmunds, Suffolk

CONTENTS

PREFACE

The first Conference on Thirteenth Century England was held at Newcastle upon Tyne in September 1985. The contents of this volume are based upon the proceedings at that gathering, comprising the four main papers (from Drs. Carpenter, Maddicott, Miller and Prestwich) together with a large proportion of the shorter communications. Some of these contributions have been modified since they were first read.

Like the Conference itself, the papers printed here are not limited to the study of any one particular theme, although a focus is provided by studies of the relationship between the Crown and its subjects, the relationship between central and local government, and aspects of contemporary society. Collectively, the papers illustrate many of the trends in current research, combining a critical re-examination of standard interpretations, with the exploration of neglected or underused sources, and the formulation of new approaches. They are one manifestation of the renewed interest in the history of thirteenth century England after many years of comparative neglect. It is hoped that further conferences, and the publication of their proceedings, will help to sustain this interest as well as providing a regular forum for discussion and debate.

The editors would like to take this opportunity to thank the University of Newcastle upon Tyne and Newcastle upon Tyne Polytechnic for hosting the Conference and to acknowledge with gratitude the work of all those who helped make it a success. Special thanks are due to the Warden and staff of Henderson Hall of Residence and the staff of Coach Lane Campus for creating a congenial atmosphere for the Conference, and to the Vice-Chancellor of the University for his generous contribution to the reception.

Newcastle upon Tyne
1986

Peter Coss
Simon Lloyd

ABBREVIATIONS

Ann. Mon.	*Annales Monastici*, ed. H. R. Luard, 4 vols. (*RS*, 1864 – 9)
BIHR	*Bulletin of the Institute of Historical Research*
BL	British Library
BN	Bibliothèque Nationale
CCR	*Calendar of Close Rolls*
CChR	*Calendar of Charter Rolls*
CDRI	*Calendar of Documents relating to Ireland, 1171 – 1307*, ed. H. S. Sweetman, G. F. Handcock, 5 vols. (London, 1877 – 86)
CDRS	*Calendar of Documents relating to Scotland*, ed. J. Bain, 4 vols. (Edinburgh, 1881 – 8)
CFR	*Calendar of Fine Rolls*
CIMisc.	*Calendar of Inquisitions Miscellaneous*
CIPM	*Calendar of Inquisitions Post Mortem*
CLR	*Calendar of Liberate Rolls*
CPR	*Calendar of Patent Rolls*
CR	*Close Rolls*
CRR	*Curia Regis Rolls*
DBM	*Documents of the Baronial Movement of Reform and Rebellion, 1258 – 1267*, selected R. F. Treharne, ed. I. J. Sanders (Oxford, 1973)
DNB	*Dictionary of National Biography*
EcHR	*Economic History Review*
EETS	*Early English Text Society*
EHD,ii	*English Historical Documents, II 1042 – 1189*, ed. D. C. Douglas (2nd edn., London, 1981)
EHD,iii	*English Historical Documents, III 1189 – 1327*, ed. H. Rothwell (London, 1975)
EHR	*English Historical Review*
Fees	*Liber Feudorum: The Book of Fees commonly called Testa de Nevill 1198 – 1293*, 2 vols. in 3 (London, 1920 – 31)
Foedera	*Foedera, conventiones, litterae et cuiuscunque generis acta publica . . .*, ed. T. Rymer (new edn., ed. A. Clarke *et al.*, 4 vols., London, 1816 – 69)

GEC	*Complete Peerage of England, Scotland, Ireland, Great Britain and the United Kingdom*, 13 vols. in 14 (London, 1910 – 59)
Journ.	Journal
m.	marks
n.s.	New series
Paris	Matthew Paris, *Chronica majora*, ed. H. R. Luard, 7 vols. (*RS*, 1872 – 83)
PRO	Public Record Office
Procs.	Proceedings
Rec. Soc.	Record Society
RLC	*Rotuli Litterarum Clausarum in Turri Londinensi asservati, 1204 – 27*, ed. T. D. Hardy, 2 vols. (London, 1833 – 44)
RLP	*Rotuli Litterarum Patentium in Turri Londinensi asservati, 1201 – 16*, ed. T. D. Hardy (London, 1835)
Rot. Parl.	*Rotuli Parliamentorum*, 6 vols. (London, 1783 – 1832[])
Royal Letters	*Royal and other Historical Letters illustrative of the Reign of Henry III*, ed. W. W. Shirley, 2 vols. (*RS*, 1862 – 6)
RS	Rolls Series (London, 1858 – 96)
ser.	series
Soc.	Society
Trans.	Transactions
TRHS	*Transactions of the Royal Historical Society*
VCH	*Victoria County History*

Edward I and the Lessons of Baronial Reform: Local Government, 1258 – 80

J. R. Maddicott

Edward I returned from the Holy Land in 1274 to a kingdom that was far from settled. It was less than a decade since Simon de Montfort had been killed at Evesham and only seven years since his disinherited followers had been finally brought to terms. The political and tenurial grievances of the Montfortians, part cause and part effect of a bitter civil war, had not been subdued by Henry III's success. Despite the work of the papal legate Ottobuono, the attempt at a land settlement in the Dictum of Kenilworth, and the reforms conceded in the Statute of Marlborough, Henry's authority in his last years had rested less upon the consent of his people than upon their acquiescence in what many may have seen as a royalist *révanche*. It was not until his son's reign that the gains of military victory were legitimised in 20 years of acceptable royal rule: one of those rare periods in English medieval history when political harmony owed more to good government than to successful foreign warfare.

Behind this achievement lay Edward's skill in learning from the mistakes of his father. Like another Edward who followed another Henry in the fifteenth century, Edward I had to be in all things his predecessor's opposite if he was to restore the position of the Crown. Where Henry III's authority had been shattered in 1258 by competing factions at his court,[1] Edward I gave ear and favour to a broad circle of magnates. Where Henry had made public policy in private, Edward sought consent through parliament. Where Henry had lived from hand to mouth, borrowed haphazardly, and borne heavily upon his subjects, Edward drew a steady income from the customs, borrowed systematically from Italian merchants, and taxed lightly. Finally, where Henry had antagonised the gentry and freeholders of the localities through fiscal exploitation and oppressive officials, Edward set out to conciliate groups which had emerged in 1258 as vociferous critics of his father's government. That he did so without compromising on the essentials of royal authority was a mark of his political acumen and practical intelligence. How he did so is the subject of what follows.

Edward's reforms must be set against a background of febrile uncertainties and political danger. The years before his effective accession in 1274 had been characterised by a pervading sense of apprehensiveness on the part of those in power. About March 1270 Archbishop Walter Giffard of York had cited the

[1] D. A. Carpenter, 'What happened in 1258?', in *War and Government in the Middle Ages: Essays in Honour of J. O. Prestwich*, ed. J. B. Gillingham, J. C. Holt (Woodbridge, 1984), 112 – 14; idem, 'King, Magnates, and Society: the Personal Rule of King Henry III, 1234 – 1258', *Speculum*, lx (1985), 57 – 9. Unless otherwise stated, all manuscript references are to documents in the PRO.

current *turbatio regni* as the reason for his inability to visit the pope,[2] and in August of the same year Henry's fears for his kingdom's safety had prevented him from accompanying his son on crusade.[3] Something of their justification may be seen in the projected rising of the London *populares* against the aldermen which was intended to coincide with Henry's death and which, had it occurred, might easily have returned the city to the factional conflicts of the early 1260s.[4]

These forebodings did not only spring from the partial demise of royal power during the years of Edward's absence. We may suspect more easily than we can prove that behind them stood many of the forces and interests which had come to life in the Montfortian period. Those who had been rebels were now sometimes criminals. Roger Godberd of Nottinghamshire, for example, that prototype Robin Hood, had joined Montfort in the war of 1264 – 5, but had then taken to the woods, where he remained at large, living by banditry, until his capture in 1272.[5] Others had acquired a wartime taste for disorder which could be exploited more deliberately by those with a cause to maintain. When the prior of Norwich fell out violently with the men of the city in August 1272, just before Henry's death, he summoned to his aid 'a great multitude of *malivoli* who, when the kingdom was disturbed, had been thieves, plunderers and malefactors'.[6] More alarming still was the possibility that former rebels might move beyond mere crime to a new rebellion. A rumour reported to Walter Merton, the chancellor, probably in August 1273, spoke of other *malivoli* who were gathering together and conspiring to break the peace in Essex, Leicestershire and elsewhere. This was especially significant, for Leicestershire had been the Montfortian heartland, the *pays* of some of Montfort's most loyal baronial supporters, and the county of the intrepid villagers of Great Peatling, who, in a famous episode, had attacked the king's men in the days after Evesham for 'going against the welfare of the commonalty of the realm and against the barons'.[7] Here, if anywhere, trouble was to be expected. So it was, too, at Ely, the last stronghold of the disinherited in 1267, where a hostile occupation of the isle seems to have been expected in July 1272 and again in May 1274.[8] Nervous and uncertain, Edward's regents looked to the old seats of rebellion for its recurrence.

In part the restlessness of the early 1270s was no more than the magnification of commonplace criminality. With the country so disturbed, it is easy to see why, in June 1273, the sheriffs should have been forbidden to outlaw those who had been indicted before the justices in the recent eyres.[9] Rather than create more desperate men, driven from their communities and into a life of

[2] *The Register of Archbishop Walter Giffard, 1266 – 79*, ed. W. Brown (Surtees Soc., cix, 1904), 158, 244.
[3] *Foedera*, I,i. 483 – 5; F. M. Powicke, *King Henry III and the Lord Edward* (Oxford, 1947), ii. 582.
[4] *De Antiquis Legibus Liber: Cronica Maiorum et Vicecomitum Londoniarum*, ed. T. Stapleton (Camden Soc., old ser., 1846), 152; G. A. Williams, *Medieval London: From Commune to Capital* (London, 1963), 243 – 4.
[5] J. C. Holt, *Robin Hood* (London, 1982), 97 – 9.
[6] *De Antiquis Legibus Liber*, 145.
[7] SC 1/1/179; *CI Misc. 1219 – 1307*, nos. 769 – 72; *Select Cases of Procedure without Writ under Henry III*, ed. H. G. Richardson, G. O. Sayles (Selden Soc., lx, 1941), 43.
[8] *CPR 1266 – 72*, 667; *CPR 1272 – 81*, 52.
[9] *CCR 1272 – 9*, 48.

crime, the government was prepared to modify the rigours of the law. Other orders to the sheriffs for the preservation of the peace, issued a few weeks later in August, suggested that the problem was already great enough. Malefactors were committing robberies and homicides throughout the counties, sheriffs and bailiffs of liberties were conniving at their misdeeds, the courts of liberties and the county courts were failing to maintain order.[10] In October the help of the Church was invoked to the same end, and in a solemn ceremony in Westminster Hall the new archbishop, Robert Kilwardby, and eight of his suffragans excommunicated all disturbers of the peace.[11] It is unlikely that this attempt to impose something like the peace of God had much effect. The commissioning of Henry Lacy, earl of Lincoln, in April 1274 to take charge of the county posses of Yorkshire and Nottinghamshire, and to pursue malefactors in those counties, points to the government's continuing distrust of the sheriffs and to local disorders so serious that only the extraordinary appointment of an earl might be expected to quell them.[12]

Violence and the threat of violence, the ineffectiveness of the peace-keeping machinery, and, most of all, the shadow of rebellion, thus made the years of Edward's absence an unquiet time. But the threat of political stability came also from two other and more precisely definable directions: from aristocratic feuding and from continuing discontent among the gentry at the misgovernment of the counties. Like much of the local disorder, both were legacies of the reforming period. Feuding began at the top, with the relations between the new king and his cousins, the surviving children of Simon de Montfort. The murder of Henry of Almain in church at Viterbo in March 1271 by Guy de Montfort and the young Simon, in revenge for their father's death at Evesham, had shown the depth and savagery of the conflicts engendered by the barons' war.[13] Edward, in turn, had reacted sharply when Stephen de Bersted, bishop of Chichester and ex-Montfortian, proposed to bring back Montfort's third son, Amaury, to England in 1273. Writing in indignation from Gascony, the king forbade the bishop's entry and ordered the confiscation of his temporalities. When he was eventually able to lay hands on Amaury in 1275, he kept him in prison for nearly six years.[14]

Even in the early 1270s, however, the danger that the Montfortian name might serve to rally dissent was probably only a limited one, and Edward's actions owed more to hatred than to fear. More ominous was the continuation of the magnate conflicts of the civil war, for these both threatened the peace and kept old wounds open. In 1273 Robert de Ferrers, dispossessed after the civil war of his earldom of Derby by Edmund of Lancaster, had seized his former manor and castle of Chartley in Staffordshire from their holder, Roger Lestrange, only to be violently ousted in his turn by his successor, Edmund. That Edmund was supported in his attack by another earl, Henry Lacy, and a somewhat reluctant council, but opposed by Gilbert de Clare, earl of

[10] *CCR 1272–9*, 25.
[11] *De Antiquis Legibus Liber*, 161; *Councils and Synods, II (1265–1313)*, ed. F. M. Powicke, C. R. Cheney (Oxford, 1964), ii. 807–9.
[12] *CPR 1272–81*, 67.
[13] F. M. Powicke, 'Guy de Montfort (1265–71)', *TRHS*, 4th ser., xviii (1935), 16–20; see also Tout's article on Henry of Almain in *DNB*.
[14] *De Antiquis Legibus Liber*, 158–9; *CFR 1272–1307*, 6; L. E. Boyle, 'E cathena et carcere: The Imprisonment of Amaury de Montfort, 1276', in *Medieval Learning and Literature: Essays presented to R. W. Hunt*, ed. J. J. G. Alexander, M. Gibson (Oxford, 1976), 379–97.

Gloucester, shows how quarrels arising directly from the war might continue to divide the aristocracy.[15] If Ferrers was the most prominent loser from the royalist victory of 1265, other minor barons had comparable grievances against their dispossessors. In Yorkshire during 1273, for example, Thomas de Furnivall, a leading wartime royalist, set upon Ingram de Oldcotes, a minor member of the gentry, who had himself attacked Furnivall's manor and castle of Sheffield in the disturbed months after Evesham.[16] At Edward's return the trenches and barbicans of Sandwich in Kent, constructed during the war and still to be seen in 1275, stood as symbols of the continuing barriers to peace.[17]

Feuds among the baronage were only one manifestation of resentments which were widespread throughout political society in the years around 1270. They were implicit too in the flourishing cult of Simon de Montfort, which the Dictum of Kenilworth had vainly attempted to suppress. Some 190 miracle stories survive from the period 1265 – 80, almost all of them associated with the earl's tomb at Evesham.[18] Unfortunately, only 15 are dated by the year, but of these three came from 1269, one from 1272 and two each from 1273 and 1274; so clearly Montfort's shrine was attracting pilgrims at just this time. Equally significant was the diversity of the *miraculés*, who represented many social groups and occupations. Among them were the abbot of Dale in Derbyshire, the dean of Warrington in Lancashire, a monk of Winchcombe, five knights, including Sir Simon de Pateshull (a former Montfortian sheriff and one of the disinherited[19]), the steward of Bishop Cantilupe of Hereford, a carpenter, a miller and a fisherman. They journeyed to Evesham from distant parts. A majority lived more than 40 miles from the shrine, many came from counties as far away as Kent and Derbyshire, some lived in villages such as Brill in Buckinghamshire which are known to have sympathised with the rebellion. There were many reasons why they should have sought healing at Montfort's tomb, but at the least their search implied some belief in Montfort's sanctity and some sympathy for his cause. That men of such diverse backgrounds came to the tomb from so many different localities hints at a continuing attachment to reform and a country unreconciled to the restoration of royal power.

These discontents were fuelled by financial loss, the abandonment of reform, and, in the counties, by an apparent return to the political *status quo ante bellum*. Many of Montfort's erstwhile followers found themselves heavily in debt. Not only did they have to buy back the king's favour,[20] but the Dictum

[15] *Chronicles of the Reigns of Stephen, Henry II and Richard I*, ed. R. Howlett (*RS*, 1884 – 9), ii. 564; SC 1/7/85; SC 1/22/26; *CCR 1272 – 79*, 12, 17 – 18, 316; *CPR 1281 – 92*, 53; *CIMisc. 1219 – 1307*, no. 966; *Select Cases in the Court of King's Bench*, I, ed. G. O. Sayles, (Selden Soc., lv, 1936), 20 – 1; H. Le Strange, *Le Strange Records* (London, 1916), 140 – 1, 145 – 6, 198 – 9; E. F. Jacob, *Studies in the Period of Baronial Reform and Rebellion, 1258 – 67* (Oxford, 1925), 388 – 94; R. Somerville, *History of the Duchy of Lancaster*, I (London, 1953), 5.

[16] P. A. Brand, 'Oldcotes v. Darcy', in *Medieval Legal Records*, ed. R. F. Hunnisett, J. B. Post (London, 1978), 67 – 8. For other similar feuds, see *Select Cases*, ed. Sayles, III, cx – cxi.

[17] *Select Cases*, ed. Sayles, I, 13 – 14.

[18] *DBM*, 322 – 3; 'Miracula Symonis de Montfort', *Rishanger's Chronicle*, ed. J. O. Halliwell (Camden Soc., old ser., 1840), 67 – 110; R. C. Finucane, *Miracles and Pilgrims* (London, 1977), 131 – 5, 169 – 70.

[19] C. H. Knowles, 'The Resettlement of England after the Barons' War, 1264 – 67', *TRHS*, 5th ser., xxxii (1982), 37.

[20] 'Chronicon Thomae Wykes', in *Ann. Mon.*, iv. 220.

of Kenilworth forced them to pay heavily to redeem their lands. Just though the Dictum was by comparison with the executions and attainders which were to punctuate the civil wars of the fifteenth century, it set in train legal proceedings which were to last for years and which committed many of the defeated to payments still unmet at Edward I's accession. The special eyre set up in 1267 to deal with cases arising from the Dictum was suspended in 1272, but a trickle of cases continued to come before the King's Bench throughout the 1270s: 13 in Michaelmas term 1273, five as late as Easter 1279.[21] The sums still outstanding were often large and sometimes diminished only slowly. John d'Eyvill, the leader of the Ely rebels in 1266–7, still owed 380 *m.* of his 900 *m.* redemption fine in 1272; Nicholas de Segrave still owed 200 *m.* in 1289.[22] Such debts often meant resort to the Jews and, in the long term, the alienation of lands to monied royalists, such as Walter de Merton and Adam de Stratton, who could afford to redeem them.[23]

Montfortian diehards, however, had never been more than a minority among the gentry and minor baronage, and by 1272 those whose lands were unredeemed were probably no more than a minority of that minority. The apparent failure of reform, and a return to the old order in local government, are likely to have been much more general grievances. Those who had backed the major reforms of 1258–60 (the Provisions of Oxford and Westminster, the Ordinance of Sheriffs, the baronial eyres), had comprised a much wider section of local society than the enthusiasts and desperadoes who had fought at Evesham or held out in the Fens in the years which followed. It is true that the Statute of Marlborough had seemed to perpetuate much of the reformers' work. The restrictions which it imposed on the lord's right to suit of court, the sheriff's tourn, and abuses in the eyre, for example, were substantially those of the Provisions of Westminster. Yet the signs are that the statute was not widely observed. In Essex and elsewhere complaints against recent and illicit exactions of the murdrum fine, the beaupleder fine, and the sheriff's misuse of his tourn were all common in the Hundred Roll enquiries of 1274–5, although the statute had regulated all these matters.[24] On the central issue raised by the counties in 1258–9, the character and terms of office of the sheriff, there was a loud silence. The post-war settlement ignored the demands of the reforming period for local sheriffs, acting for one year only, who would do justice to rich and poor alike, take no bribes or wrongful exactions, demand no excessive hospitality, and serve as custodians, receiving an allowance rather than paying an excessive farm to the Exchequer.[25] The limits of conciliation, hardly liberal ones, were represented by the Statute of Marlborough.

The terms on which the sheriffs held office represented a particular denial of local aspirations. After 1265 the sheriffs had once again to pay the Exchequer, over and above their farms, those increments which before 1258 had

[21] Knowles, 32; *Select Cases*, ed. Sayles, II, cxxii.

[22] Knowles, 35; Powicke, *Henry III*, 554.

[23] Knowles, 35; *The Early Rolls of Merton College, Oxford*, ed. J. R. L. Highfield (Oxford Historical Soc., n.s., xviii, 1964), 28.

[24] *Statutes of the Realm*, I (Record Commission, 1810), 22, 25; H. M. Cam, *Studies in the Hundred Rolls* (Oxford, 1921), 152–5, 161–3; Cam, *The Hundred and the Hundred Rolls* (repr., London, 1963), 119.

[25] *DBM*, 109, 118–23.

been seen as a prime cause of corruption and extortion.[26] Henry's government was not so imprudent or so impractical as to demand payments at the very high levels of the mid-1250s; but nevertheless increments were not light, and their very existence ran counter to reforming objectives. In Northumberland, for example, the increments of 1241 – 2, 1256 – 7, and of the years around 1270, were £20, £64 and £50 respectively; in Northamptonshire the comparable figures were 100 *m.*, 180 *m.* and 100 *m.*; in Yorkshire, 200 *m.*, 470 *m.* and 300 *m.*; in Norfolk and Suffolk, 200 *m.*, 400 *m.* and 200 *m.*; in Shropshire and Staffordshire, 90 *m.*, 190 *m.* and 166 *m.*[27] In general, the increments of Henry's last years were set either at the figure fixed in 1241, when they had been reimposed by the Exchequer after a period of desuetude, or at a point between the merely burdensome increments of 1241 – 2 and the grossly extortionate ones of 1257 – 8. In this modest relaxation of demands there was undoubtedly a measure of concession. But it should be remembered that the civil war had thoroughly disrupted the collection of Crown revenues in the counties, a disruption from which there was little recovery before Edward I's early years.[28] Even moderate increments, therefore, may have been difficult to raise without the heavy shrieval pressure which had characterised the years before 1258. This is indeed what the Hundred Roll enquiries suggest. If they throw little direct light on the farming of the shires, they show, on the other hand, that the farming of the hundreds at extortionate rates was an almost universal grievance throughout the counties.[29] It meant that bailiffs had to bear down heavily on the men of the hundreds in order to meet the farms imposed by the sheriffs. The linkage between high shire increments, high farms for the hundreds and extortion had been pointed out by the reformers of 1258,[30] and it is likely to have been as marked in the early 1270s as it had been 20 years before. Here again, little had changed.

The sheriffs themselves were a mixed group, about whom it is difficult to generalise. But it is clear that they were often *curiales* and professional administrators and, even if local men, were by no means uncorrupt. In some counties the unsparing sheriffs of the pre-reform period were reinstated. In Shropshire and Staffordshire, for example, the office was held from 1265 to 1267 by Thomas Corbet of Caus, previously sheriff from 1248 to 1250, when he had been notorious for oppressive government. His two successors seem to have been local men, but from 1270 to 1274 the office was held by a succession of prominent Marcher barons, all closely connected with the Lord Edward.[31] In Oxfordshire the sheriff of 1270 – 1, William de Lisle, had twice held the

[26] *DBM*, 274 – 5; D. A. Carpenter, 'The Decline of the Curial Sheriff in England, 1194 – 1258', *EHR*, xci (1976), 21 – 31.

[27] The pre-1258 figures for all counties mentioned above, except Northumberland, are given by Carpenter, 'Decline of the Curial Sheriff', 22. Those for Northumberland are given in J. Hodgson, *A History of Northumberland*, III, iii (Newcastle, 1835), 194 – 299. The post-1258 figures are given in the Pipe Rolls, E 372/113 – 18. Not all the counties appear on the Pipe Roll for 1270 – 1 and so the figures have been collected from the roll for the nearest available year. From *c.*1265 until 1270 and beyond the increments remained unchanged.

[28] M. Mills, '"Adventus Vicecomitum", 1258 – 72', *EHR*, xxxvi (1921), 494 – 5; Jacob, 248 – 75; below, 29.

[29] Cam, *The Hundred*, 93 – 4.

[30] *DBM*, 82 – 3, 120 – 1, 274 – 5.

[31] *VCH Shropshire*, III, ed. G. C. Baugh (Oxford, 1979), 15 – 16; *The Roll of the Shropshire Eyre of 1256*, ed. A. Harding (Selden Soc., xcvi, 1980), xxi – ii.

same office in Northamptonshire during the 1250s, when he had acquired a reputation even more unfavourable than that of Corbet.[32] In Wiltshire the sheriff from 1267 to 1270 was William le Dun, a local man, but from 1270 to 1274 the shrievalty passed to two outsiders, both of them officials of the central government.[33] In 1268 – 9 all the counties were apparently given to Edward, by a grant which was never enrolled but which has left many traces in the records.[34] The right of appointment thus given to him facilitated the subsequent nomination both of Edward's own associates, as in Shropshire and Staffordshire, and of other *curiales*. Their promotion probably owed much to the need for security and tight control during Edward's absence on crusade.[35] These arrangements left little room for the local initiatives in the appointment of sheriffs which had been such a prominent feature of the reforming period.

The results of the Hundred Roll enquiries of 1274 – 5 provide a comprehensive survey of the grievances provoked by the sheriffs of these years. The returns for almost any county could be cited to show the unpopularity of the post-Evesham sheriffs. In Wiltshire there were many complaints against the *curialis* Walter de Stirchley, who had just left office, and some against the local man, William le Dun. In Norfolk and Suffolk none of the five sheriffs who had held office since 1265 escaped unscathed, and against the most unpopular, Robert de Norton (1267 – 70), there were almost a hundred separate charges.[36] But more revealing and unusual than the monotonous record of the Hundred Rolls is the petition submitted to the government by the knights and freeholders of Devon against their sheriff, Roger de Pridias, in 1272.[37] Pridias had been nominated as sheriff of the county in February 1271 by Richard of Cornwall, whose Cornish tenant and bailiff he almost certainly was.[38] He had transgressed in ways which could have been paralleled in many counties before 1258. Since he was a stranger and held no land in the county, the petitioners said, he had overburdened the *patria* with his demands for hospitality. He had imprisoned rich and law-worthy men in order to extort money from them, amerced the poor at will and without the judgement of the county, induced imprisoned thieves to appeal against the rich and faithful men of the county, held his tourn contrary to the county's charter from King John, and distrained men to pay their debts to the Exchequer twice over. They ended by asking for his replacement by a knight of the county. Their petition, with its complaints about the sheriff's tourn and his exactions and its demand for a local man, echoed not only the reforming legislation of 1258 but also earlier local aspirations which stretched back to the reign of John. Both in its formulation and in its recurrent references to the county and its court, it witnessed to the solidarity of the local community in the face of oppressive government.

32 *List of Sheriffs for England and Wales* (PRO Lists and Indexes, ix, 1898), 92, 107; Cam, *The Hundred*, 63; J. R. Maddicott, 'Magna Carta and the Local Community, 1215 – 59', *Past and Present*, cii (1984), 45.

33 *VCH Wiltshire*, V, ed. R. B. Pugh (Oxford, 1957), 12 – 13.

34 *List of Sheriffs*, 1, 43, 122, 144, 152; *CLR 1267 – 72*, 128; N. Denholm-Young, *Richard of Cornwall* (Oxford, 1947), 144 – 6; *VCH Shropshire*, iii. 17.

35 Carpenter, 'Decline of the Curial Sheriff', 31 – 2.

36 *Rotuli Hundredorum* (Record Commission, 1812 – 18), i. 440 – 514; ii. 149 – 81, 243 – 76.

37 Bodleian Library, Oxford, MS Dodsworth 76, f.33; *CPR 1272 – 81*, 32; *Rot. Hundred.*, i. 67 – 8; Cam, *The Hundred*, 16, 42, 72.

38 *CPR 1266 – 72*, 515; *Rot. Hundred.*, i. 67; C. Moor, *Knights of Edward I*, IV (Harleian Soc., 1931), 102.

Those in power were not unresponsive to such demands. In the case of the Devon shrievalty, Edward's deputies ordered an enquiry into Pridias's doings, summoned him to answer before the Exchequer, and, in October 1273, replaced him with the local knight, Sir Thomas Pyn.[39] Local pressure could clearly bring results. So it could too in other matters of interest to the counties. When it was proposed to hold an eyre in Lincolnshire in 1269, the summons was subsequently revoked because seven years had not yet elapsed since the previous eyre: another clear echo of the disputes of the reforming period, when the despatch of the eyres of 1262 – 3 had led to widespread protests, for similar reasons, in the counties.[40] In January 1273, two months after Henry's death, the current eyre visitation was altogether suspended in circumstances designed to give this 'judicious bid for popularity' the widest publicity. The eyre's termination was announced in a parliament at Westminster attended not only by the magnates but by the knights from the counties and burgesses from the boroughs.[41] No doubt these measures were an aspect of the general nervousness of the government during these years: the threat of disorder created the need for concessions. But the concessions made, few and piecemeal, did not go far to satisfy demand or to re-establish the new order of 1258 – 9. Systematic reform had to await Edward's return.

In addition to the proximity of disorder and rebellion, the grievances of the ex-Montfortians and the wider discontents of the counties, three further and related factors contributed to the general unease. Firstly, the prolonged absence of the ruler was itself a danger. It removed the heart of government, the source of patronage and political initiative, and the embodiment of power and authority. In 1273 the rumour that Edward would never return apparently set off an obscure armed rising in the North, and comparable lawlessness was to occur at many other times during the late thirteenth and fourteenth centuries when the king was overseas.[42] Secondly, those who governed in Edward's name were not strong men. The professional element in the regency council was provided by Merton and Burnel, the chancellor and treasurer, but they had neither the personal authority nor the social weight needed to prevent disorder and (what might amount to the same thing) to hold the nobility in check. When armed men prevented the extending of two Herefordshire manors in the early months of 1273, in defiance of the king's writ, the bishop of Hereford wrote forcefully to Merton, reminding him of the impropriety of tolerating such disobedience.[43] Neither Merton nor Burnel was able to stop Edmund of Lancaster seizing Chartley castle from Robert de Ferrers in 1273, despite Gloucester's admonition to them to do so.[44] Nor could Merton induce Edmund to punish his sheriff and bailiffs of Lancashire when they were

[39] *CPR 1272 – 81*, 32; Moor, 68 – 9.

[40] R. F. Treharne, *The Baronial Plan of Reform* (Manchester, 1932), 259 – 60, 398 – 406; *CR 1268 – 72*, 37 – 9. D. Crook, *Records of the General Eyre* (HMSO, 1982), 134, states that the Lincolnshire eyre was abandoned because of a complaint from the county to the king. Although this is very likely it is not stated in the records.

[41] 'Annales de Wintonia' in *Ann. Mon.*, ii. 113; 'Annales de Waverleia' in *Ann. Mon*, ii. 379; 'Annales de Wigornia' in *Ann. Mon.*, iv. 462; Cam, *Studies*, 29.

[42] *Flores Historiarum*, ed. H. R. Luard (*RS*, 1890), iii. 31 – 2; J. Bellamy, *Crime and Public Order in England in the Later Middle Ages* (London, Toronto, 1973), 10 – 12.

[43] J. G. Edwards, *Calendar of Ancient Correspondence concerning Wales* (Cardiff, 1935), 38 – 9.

[44] SC 1/22/26; above, 3 – 4.

accused of despoiling Sir Nicholas de la Huse of his goods and chattels.[45] Against the king's brother the king's chancellor was able to do little.

Thirdly, and as these last examples suggest, the nobility were able to defy the government with something like impunity. If the Chartley affair demonstrated the impotence of the king's representatives in the face of aristocratic feuding, perhaps more serious in the long term was baronial defiance of royal officials and baronial usurpation of royal rights. When, about January 1273, the sub-escheator of Dorset attempted to take for the king two manors belonging to deceased tenants-in-chief, he was forcibly ejected by gangs claiming the protection of Thomas de Clare, younger brother of the earl of Gloucester, and of Roger Mortimer, a member of the governing council.[46] Richard of Cornwall's steward of the liberty of Wallingford was accused of usurping the jurisdiction of the Oxfordshire county court; and we have already noticed the government's concern at the protection given to malefactors by seigneurial courts and bailiffs.[47] In the prevailing state of unease, attacks on royal rights or on franchises conceded by the king came to be seen as part of a wider pattern of disorder. 'In the uncertainty within the realm', wrote Burnel to Merton in 1272 or 1273, 'it is essential to protect as strongly as possible the privileges accorded by kings and to defend them, so that an occasion for offending may be removed from those who desire to promote dissension'.[48] Hence perhaps the decision in January 1274 to hold inquiries into the withdrawal and alienation of royal rights in 11 southern counties.[49] The dissipation of the Crown's resources, by grant or usurpation, had been a consistent feature of the previous reign, gathering pace during the reforming period and remaining unchecked at its conclusion. Now, with the king away and royal power in partial abeyance, there was little to prevent such men as the earl of Gloucester, the chief offender in many counties, from continuing to encroach on the king's rights.[50] He and his peers were the real beneficiaries from Edward's absence.

When Edward returned to England in 1274 he was thus by no means secure. He was the ruler of a country still suffering from the disorderly aftermath of civil war and of subjects whose reforming hopes had been dashed by the royalist victory at Evesham. In the years which followed he mixed conciliation with firm rule in order to re-establish the position of the Crown. By bringing back the Montfortians into public life,[51] distributing patronage equitably, maintaining the loyalty of his household,[52] and winning the support of the counties, he gained not merely power but also authority. The state of his finances, initially very weak, meant that he could not afford to give much away. From his father he had inherited large debts, reflecting both the decline of the Crown's resources during and after the troubles and also

45 SC 1/7/86.

46 SC 1/7/78.

47 *CCR 1272–9*, above, 3.

48 SC 1/7/211. Cf. G. O. Sayles, *The King's Parliament of England* (London, 1975), where, however, the letter is wrongly ascribed to Philip Basset and dated to 1261–3.

49 *CPR 1272–81*, 65; Cam, *Studies*, 123–4.

50 Carpenter, 'King, Magnates', 44–52; *DBM*, 212–13, 220–3. See *Rot. Hundred.*, ii. 118–24, for Gloucester's usurpations in Somerset, as revealed by the 1274 enquiry.

51 Knowles, 38–41.

52 M. C. Prestwich, *The Three Edwards* (London, 1980), 7–8.

Henry's continuingly lavish expenditure on such projects as Westminster Abbey.[53] His own debts, too, were considerable. The Riccardi had advanced some £23,400 for the financing of his crusade and a further £7700 to Burnel for the government of England.[54] In these circumstances some measures which might have won him support were not feasible. There was no move, for example, to reduce the increments demanded by the Exchequer from the sheriffs, which remained throughout the 1270s at the levels set in Henry's last years.[55] In conciliating without necessarily conceding Edward was to show his political skills.

Financial debility, local resentments and magnate aggrandisement thus provided the background to Edward's reform of local government. To restore the standing of the Crown he needed both to re-establish royal rights and to root out the corruption among local officials which had for long been a subject of grievance. These objectives were, of course, closely connected, for extortion and peculation by royal ministers threatened the interests of both king and subjects. Edward made clear his intentions almost from the moment of his return. At his coronation, according to the Furness chronicler, he ordered justice to be maintained everywhere, the guilty, even knights and great men, to be hanged, and justices, bailiffs and sheriffs to take no bribes.[56] In a more widely recorded scene on the same occasion he put aside his crown, saying that he would never take it up again until he had restored the lands alienated by his father to the English nobility and to aliens.[57] This announcement of what was to be the political programme of the next four years was almost immediately followed up. Within two months of the coronation the escheators had been ordered to repossess all lands wrongfully alienated from the royal demesne since the civil war, new sheriffs had been appointed in 32 counties, and enquiries had begun into both royal rights and the behaviour of local officials.[58]

If the ensuing measures marked the start of a new and systematic attempt to reform local government, they also drew substantially upon the precedents established by the baronial reformers of 1258 – 60. In both periods there was an essentially similar sequence of events: local enquiry and the reception of complaints, national legislation, and a return to the localities to redress old grievances and enforce new laws through the eyre. In 1258 commissions of knights had been appointed in every county to investigate complaints against officials and to lay them before parliament. The justiciar, Hugh Bigod, had toured the counties to deal with these and other grievances. An invitation to use the informal *querela* or plaint had encouraged the aggrieved to come forward; and extensive legislation, culminating in the Provisions of Westminster of October 1259, had been devised to reform the law and to restrain both royal

53 Henry spent *c.*£3000 on Westminster Abbey, 1269 – 72. This amounted to about three-fifths of all the cash delivered by the sheriffs to the Exchequer during the same period: see R. A. Brown, H. M. Colvin and A. J. Taylor, *The History of the King's Works*, I (HMSO, 1963), 150; Mills, 494.

54 *CPR 1272 – 81*, 131 – 2.

55 E 372/114 – 24.

56 *Chronicles of . . . Stephen, Henry II and Richard I*, ii. 567.

57 *Chronicles of the Reigns of Edward I and Edward II*, ed. W. Stubbs (*RS*, 1883), ii. cxvii (Barlings chronicle); W. Stubbs, *The Constitutional History of England*, (3rd edn., Oxford, 1887), ii. 109, n.2 (Hagnaby chronicle, and chronicle in Bodleian MS Rawlinson B.414); Bodleian MS Laud Misc. 529, f.74 (Evesham chronicle).

58 *CFR 1272 – 1307*, 28 – 9, 30 – 5; *CPR 1272 – 81*, 59.

and baronial officials. Finally, the eyres of 1260 had been sent out to publicise and enforce the Provisions of Westminster and to make more widely available the redress which the justiciar had earlier been able to provide for only a few counties.[59] Through an integrated programme of enquiry, plaint, legislation and law enforcement, popular opinion had been given both a voice and the means to reform.

Both in broad outline and in detail Edward I followed a similar course. Between October 1274 and March 1275 the Hundred Roll enquiries took commissioners through the counties to investigate royal rights and ministerial misdoings. The returns were then submitted to the king, and the abuses which they revealed were legislated against in the first Statute of Westminster, published in the parliament of April 1275. Edward's original intention had been to follow this up by despatching justices in 1276 or 1277 to deal with the complaints recorded in the Hundred Rolls and to enforce the new statutes, but the Welsh war supervened, and it was not until 1278 that an eyre was commissioned to cover the whole country in two circuits. Its job was both to try the offences recorded in 1274 – 5 and to implement the new legislation, as well as to determine claims to liberties and to undertake the eyre's traditional judicial and administrative tasks.[60] No doubt this sequence of enquiry, legislation and law enforcement was in part a necessary one, with distant antecedents. It had been followed, for example, in the amendment and working out of Magna Carta between 1215 and 1218.[61] How else could kings discover and redress the grievances of their subjects? But it seems inconceivable that Edward did not have closely in mind the nearer precedents provided by the baronial reforms. If he was in part doing what came naturally, he was also stealing the clothes of the Whigs.

Three particular aspects of the Hundred Roll enquiries point more precisely to the parallels between Edward's activities and those of the earlier reformers: the articles of the enquiry, the submission of *querelae*, and the occasional use of juries of knights. The articles put to the hundred juries both by the county panel of knights in 1258 and by the royal commissioners of 1274 had a general similarity of direction: they were designed to reveal official misdeeds, to ascertain the king's rights, both feudal and landed, and to disclose their usurpation. Both sets had developed from the articles of the eyre, and some matters of enquiry were common to the articles of 1274, 1258 and to those used in the eyres of 1246 – 9, the last extant set before the reform movement.[62] The taking of bribes by royal officials to exempt men from jury service and from knighthood, for example, was investigated on all three occasions. More interesting, however, were those articles of 1274 which found parallels only in 1258. The abuse of the sheriff's tourn and the taking of bribes to allow felons to go free were both investigated in 1274 and 1258, but not, apparently, before. Both were matters of great popular concern.[63] Still more remarkable was the application of the 1274 articles, not just to royal officials but also to

[59] Treharne, 108 – 204, *passim*.
[60] Cam, *Studies*, 30 – 9, 41 – 62; Cam, *The Hundred*, 225 – 32.
[61] J. C. Holt, *Magna Carta* (Cambridge, 1965), 274; Maddicott, 30.
[62] The articles of 1274 are given in Cam, *The Hundred*, 248 – 57; those of 1258 in *Paris*, vi. 397 – 400; and those of 1246 – 9 in *Crown Pleas of the Wiltshire Eyre, 1249*, ed. C. A. F. Meekings (Wilts. Arch. and Nat. Hist. Soc., Rec. Branch, xvi, 1961), 27 – 33.
[63] *DBM*, 84 – 5, 126 – 9, 140 – 2, 298 – 9; Cam, *The Hundred*, 67 – 74, 118 – 28.

'the lords and bailiffs of all liberties whatsoever'. The principle enunciated here reflected not only the enquiries made in 1258 into the misdeeds of seigneurial bailiffs but the whole thrust of baronial reform, which had set out to place the officials of king and magnates under the same law. It was consistent, too, with Edward's statement at his coronation that the guilty should be punished, even though they were knights and magnates.[64] The profession of impartial justice was to be one of the props of the new régime.

The parallels between the articles of 1274 and 1258 were not, of course, exact, and there was one important divergence of emphasis. In 1274 the matter of the Crown's rights predominated over the redress offered to its subjects. The first 14 articles dealt with such abuses as the withdrawal of suit to the local courts, the misuse of franchises and the obstruction of the king's orders; and nine separate articles were given to the activities of the escheators, the officials most concerned with the custody of the Crown's lands and feudal rights. In 1258 one general article had been thought sufficient for the escheators, and much more stress had been laid on the offences of officials against the king's subjects rather than against the king. But if this order of priorities was reversed in 1274, the later articles resembled the earlier closely enough to suggest that the similarities were not accidental.

The most novel feature of the eyres of 1258 – 60 had been the extensive use of the *querela*, the informal complaint, sometimes made orally, which gave the poor man access to justice without the expense of procedure by writ or criminal appeal. Although complaints without writ were not unknown in earlier eyres, they had been few in number and limited in scope; it was Bigod's eyre of 1258 which first brought their wholesale expansion, often as a means of bringing accusations against local officials.[65] The same procedures were followed, at least sporadically, in 1274 – 5. In some counties, notably in Essex and Cambridgeshire but also in Devon, the commissioners are known to have received *querelae*, and it is probable that they were deliberately solicited. Other plaints, made in the first instance to the hundred juries rather than to the commissioners, may lie disguised in the juries' presentments. Those that we can recognise were directed most frequently against sheriffs and hundred bailiffs, as in 1258.[66] By thus taking up the precedents of the reforming period, Edward was preparing the way for the much wider use of the *querela*, at the centre as well as in the provinces, which was to come in the next few years.[67]

In at least one of the commissioners' circuits, that covering Essex, Hertfordshire, Norfolk and Suffolk, use was made of juries of knights to present evidence against offenders.[68] Here was another reminiscence of 1258. Then, as we have seen, four knights in each county had collected grievances, first for presentation to the October parliament and then for determination by the justiciar on his eyre. In 1274 it was only in little Hertfordshire that a jury of knights spoke for the whole county. In the other three larger counties the knights either collected oral plaints for presentation to the commissioners or else they spoke for groups of hundreds: a more practical scheme than that devised in 1258. In both periods the use made of knights reflected not just their

[64] Above, 10.
[65] Crook, 41; Jacob, 65 – 70; Treharne, 112 – 13.
[66] *Rot. Hundred.*, i. 68, 136 – 8, 144; Cam, *Studies*, 133 – 8.
[67] Below, 23 – 5, 28.
[68] Cam, *Studies*, 128 – 32.

leadership of county society, but their likely effectiveness in revealing the misdeeds of those in authority. Sheriffs and petty tyrants, before whose offences the small man kept silent, might yet be vulnerable to the more resolute prosecution of their peers or social superiors.

In both their aims and their methods the Hundred Roll enquiries thus drew upon the reforms of local government instituted between 1258 and 1260. But they also provided precedents for the future. The task of the Hundred Roll commissioners had been limited to the collection of evidence, and they had done nothing to punish offenders, whether royal ministers or others. This was left to the countrywide eyre which began in 1278 and which stood as a direct sequel to the earlier enquiries. Its articles incorporated all those put before the hundred juries in 1274 – 5, and its justices were specifically empowered to hear and determine *querelae* against both the ministers of the king and of others.[69] Henceforth the resulting plaints began to be included as separate sections in the eyre rolls.[70] Some of the new articles which the eyre administered expressed in concrete terms the principle embodied both in the reception of plaints and in the application of the 1274 – 5 enquiries to magnate officials as well as royal ones: that seigneurial offences were no more to be tolerated than those of royal officials. Questions on 'those who are amerced without reasonable cause . . . and not by their peers', on distraint outside the fee and on the attempts by magnates to draw cases into their own courts, marked the first moves towards the practical limitation of common seigneurial abuses since the Provisions of Westminster and its concomitant eyre in 1259 – 60.[71]

Finally, knightly juries of presentment were for the first time brought into the eyre's proceedings to speak for their counties. Between 1281 and 1289 they feature in the eyre rolls for six counties,[72] reporting most frequently on cases involving great men or their servants whom the ordinary juries of presentment might have left unscathed: the misdeeds of the earl of Surrey's officials, for example, or the murder of his mistress by the master mason of Abingdon Abbey, concealed both by the abbot and by the town jury.[73] In all these ways the eyres inaugurated in 1278 adopted on a more general scale some of the precedents set in 1274 and in 1258 – 60.

The reforms of local government which began with the Hundred Roll enquiries brought the Crown much popularity; that indeed was partly their purpose. By giving the aggrieved the chance to complain and the prospect of redress, they played an essential part in the king's bid for the support of his provincial subjects, on which his own authority ultimately depended. Contemporaries regarded the enquiries not as an investigation of royal rights, which was probably their primary purpose, but solely as an attempt to limit the misconduct of officials. *Inquisitores* were sent throughout the counties, says the Furness chronicler, to enquire about justices, sheriffs, bailiffs and all kinds of malefactors; and when they reached Lancaster, on 20 November 1274, many came before them to complain of their losses and injuries. An identical

69 Cam, *Studies*, 61, 94 – 8.

70 Crook, 41, 146 ff. A few separate 'plaint' membranes had already appeared among the eyre rolls for 1261 – 2. See Crook, 32.

71 *Statutes of the Realm*, i. 237; Cam, *Studies*, 98 – 100; Carpenter, 'King, Magnates', 45.

72 Crook, 32, 163 – 5, 169 – 70; *The Eyre of Northamptonshire, 1329 – 30*, I, ed. D. W. Sutherland (Selden Soc., xcvii, 1983), xxvii, n.2.

73 JUST 1/924, m.72d. (Sussex, 1288); JUST 1/44, m.2d. (Berks., 1284).

note was struck by the Dunstable annalist, who wrote that 'the king sent his inquisitors everywhere to find out how the sheriffs and other bailiffs had behaved themselves'; though he adds, in tones of world-weary realism, 'but no good came of it'.[74] In the long term this may have been true, but in 1275 men saw a new attempt to ensure fair government in the localities, the only precedent for which lay in the popular baronial reforms of 1258 – 60.

The measure of Edward's aims and achievements can best be judged from the first Statute of Westminster of 1275. The statute stood midway between the Hundred Roll enquiries of 1274 – 5 and the eyres of 1278, prohibiting many of the practices revealed earlier and providing the basis for the articles of the later eyres sent out to suppress those practices. As the first step towards action it added to the respect which Edward had gained from the preceding enquiries. Its 51 clauses set out to remedy a diversity of abuses in a legislative cornucopia which may itself have been a legacy of the baronial reform movement. The nearest comparison lay with the 24 clauses of the Provisions of Westminster, many of them reiterated in the Statute of Marlborough, and the very possibility of such large-scale and miscellaneous changes in the law was one first revealed by the reforming legislation of 1258 – 9. We have to go back to the Statute of Merton and Magna Carta to find even inadequate parallels.[75]

Three themes underlay the statute's apparent heterogeneity. Firstly, it contained measures for the better maintenance of the peace. Its preamble referred to 'the peace less kept than it ought to be and the laws abused and malefactors less punished', and clause 9 attempted to ensure the common pursuit of malefactors by the county posse, their exclusion from the refuge provided by magnates' liberties, and severe punishment for sheriffs and other bailiffs who connived at felonies. These measures were largely directed at causes of disorder especially prevalent during Edward's absence, as we have seen.[76] Secondly, the statute imposed other limitations on the magnates. The articles of the 1278 eyre concerning amercements, distraint and the extent of seigneurial jurisdiction were all derived from restrictions imposed in the statute. That on distraint outside the fee derived ultimately from the Provisions of Westminster.[77] Thirdly, the longest section of the statute, some 16 clauses, dealt with local administration and derived, more directly than the remainder of the statute, from the returns to the Hundred Roll enquiries. In regulating such matters as the claims of sheriffs and other royal bailiffs to hospitality, their taking of prises, their freeing of malefactors on bail, and their unlawful disseisins, the drafters of the statute were responding to local grievances and to pressure from below.[78]

That Edward intended these new measures, formulated in response to popular grievances, to be made widely known is suggested by the arrangements made for their publication. They were promulgated in Edward's first

[74] *Chronicles of . . . Stephen, Henry II and Richard I*, ii. 567; 'Annales de Dunstaplia' in *Ann. Mon.*, iii. 263.

[75] P. A. Brand, *The Contribution of the Period of Baronial Reform (1258 – 67) to the Development of the Common Law in England* (Oxford University D.Phil. thesis, 1975), 366.

[76] Above, 2 – 3.

[77] cl.11: *DBM*, 144 – 5. Westminster I, cls. 6, 16, 35: *Statutes of the Realm*, i. 28, 31, 35.

[78] cls. 1, 7, 15, 24, 32: *Statutes of the Realm*, i. 27 – 8, 30, 33, 34. Cf. G. L. Harriss, 'The Formation of Parliament, 1272 – 1377', in *The English Parliament in the Middle Ages*, ed. R. G. Davies, J. H. Denton (Manchester, 1981), 45 – 6.

parliament and in the presence of numerous representatives of the shires and boroughs. Just how numerous those representatives were has not always been realised. Writs to the sheriffs ordered the attendance of four knights from each county and of four or six burgesses from every city, borough and market town.[79] The few returns which survive show that burgesses were returned from towns which were never again represented in parliament during the middle ages: such insignificant places as Biggleswade, Shefford and Odell in Bedfordshire; Nuneaton, Coleshill and Alcester in Warwickshire; and Uxbridge and Staines in Middlesex. 'If the fragmentary lists which remain to us may be taken as typical of the returns made throughout the country', writes Professor McKisack, 'more towns must have been represented in this parliament of 1275 than in any subsequent parliament before 1500'.[80] It is not impossible that we should envisage an assembly of some 148 knights and perhaps 600 burgesses, making a total of 700 – 800 representatives of the Commons:[81] far more, for example, than the 280 representatives who appeared in the Good Parliament of 1376.[82] It is usually asserted that the projected imposition of new customs duties on wool and hides in this parliament explains the government's desire for the large-scale representation of those whom these levies might concern.[83] *Prima facie* this seems implausible: how many wool-exporting merchants lived in Biggleswade? It is more probable that their presence was intended to ensure that the reforms to be considered in parliament had as large an audience as possible.

Edward's awareness of the need for publicity was shown in a complementary way by the extraordinarily elaborate scheme devised for the statute's dissemination in the localities: possibly the most elaborate for any medieval statute. The instructions for publication were enrolled on the Patent Rolls, in itself an unusually scrupulous procedure.[84] Although the language of these instructions is not always clear, they point to more than the customary methods of publication. The statute was to be proclaimed both in county and hundred courts, in cities, boroughs and market towns, and wherever else seemed expedient. It was then to be transcribed and delivered to the sheriff and other royal bailiffs and to two or four of the 'more faithful and worthy' knights of the county, with the assent of the whole county community. This scheme was clearly intended to ensure that the statute should be made widely known, that sheriffs and other royal officials should be made aware of the new restrictions

[79] C. H. Jenkinson, 'The First Parliament of Edward I', *EHR*, xxv (1910), 231 – 6. Jenkinson argues, p. 233, that the 'villa mercatoria' of the writ of summons is best translated as 'town of merchants'. This seems unlikely since the same phrase is used in the instructions for the proclamation of the Statute of Westminster, where it clearly has a much more general meaning, and since it is hard to see how the very minor places from which burgesses were returned can have been regarded as 'towns of merchants'.

[80] Jenkinson, 234; M. McKisack, *The Parliamentary Representation of the English Boroughs during the Middle Ages* (Oxford, 1932), 5.

[81] Four knights from each of 37 counties = 148 knights. The surviving returns for the towns show three in Bedfordshire, each returning four men, two in Middlesex, and eight in Warwickshire. If we assume that four towns per county each returned four representatives, we reach a total of 592 town representatives. We do not, of course, know how many of those elected actually appeared.

[82] Harriss, 38.

[83] Jenkinson, 233; McKisack, 5.

[84] *CPR 1272 – 81*, 104, printed in full in *Statutes of the Realm*, i. 39. Cf. H. G. Richardson and G. O. Sayles, 'The Early Statutes', *Law Quarterly Review*, l (1934), 545 and n.22.

which it imposed on them, and that the senior knights of the counties should be in some sense the guardians of the statute. Although the parallel cannot be pressed too far, we are inevitably reminded of the panels of four knights set up in each county in 1259 to receive *querelae* and to supervise the conduct of sheriffs and bailiffs under the terms of the Provisions of Westminster.[85]

The king's success in obtaining both publicity and approbation for the statute may be judged from the reactions of the chroniclers. The first Statute of Westminster was more widely reported than any other piece of Edwardian legislation,[86] and in terms which were universally favourable.[87] The fullest and most perceptive comment came from Thomas Wykes, an especially valuable witness since he was probably living in London at this time and his chronicle is contemporary with the events which it describes.[88] The king, says Wykes, desired as was proper to please the people and to revive and reform the feeble laws which had long slumbered through the impotence of his predecessors, the disturbance of the realm and their own misuse. The new statutes which he drew up, consonant with right and also very necessary for the whole kingdom, bound the hearts of the people to him with an inestimable love.

Wykes implies that the statute was intended to win back support for the Crown after a long period of debility and dissension, and here he was almost certainly correct. We should regard it as Edward's coronation charter, designed, like the coronation charters of Henry I and Stephen, to strengthen the Crown at a moment of initial weakness by the promise of good government and the renunciation of the excesses of the previous reign. The difference was that in Edward's case the support which the king sought through legislative reform was not only, or even mainly, that of the great 'interest groups' of the twelfth century, the baronage and the church. He was more concerned with men below baronial status: knights, freeholders and perhaps the inhabitants of small country towns, whose grievances against royal and baronial ministers had been a central issue in his father's reign. Those grievances he now proposed to remedy by an act for which he sought almost unprecedented publicity.

The Statute of Westminster, promulgated in a crowded parliament, marked the growing importance of that assembly as a focal point for reform and for contact between king and subjects. From this time onwards it normally met twice a year, at Easter and Michaelmas: an annual rhythm lasting until the start of Edward's long absence in 1286.[89] It was a rhythm which echoed, without quite conceding, the demand of the Provisions of Oxford for thrice-yearly parliaments. The presence of the Commons, apparently only occasional, may have been much more frequent that the records allow us to detect.

[85] *DBM*, 150–5; Treharne, 187.

[86] A statement based on a survey of 15 of the main printed chronicles. Westminster I is mentioned in 13, Westminster II in 11, Mortmain in 10, the Statute of Jewry in 9, Winchester in 4, Gloucester in 3.

[87] *Flores Hist.*, iii. 45; *Ann. Wigorn.*, 467; *Ann. Dunstaple*, 265; *The Chronicle of Walter of Guisborough*, ed. H. Rothwell (Camden Soc., lxxix, 1957), 213; *Ann. Winton.*, 119; *Ann. Waverley*, 384; *Chronicles of . . . Stephen, Henry II and Richard I*, ii. 568; *Chronicon Petroburgense*, ed. T. Stapleton (Camden Soc., old ser., 1849), 21.

[88] *Chron. Wykes*, 263; N. Denholm-Young, 'Thomas de Wykes and his Chronicle', in his *Collected Papers* (Cardiff, 1969), 263, 265.

[89] H. G. Richardson and G. O. Sayles, 'The English Parliaments of Edward I', *BIHR*, v (1928), 133–5.

That knights and burgesses attended the assembly of 1273 is known only from one chronicle reference; their attendance at the Easter parliament of 1275 was disclosed only when some fragmentary returns came to light about 1912; and the summoning of the knights alone to the Michaelmas parliament of the same year is revealed only by one surviving writ to the sheriff of Kent.[90] When we read later, in the preamble to the Statute of Gloucester of 1278, that the king had summoned to the parliament there 'the more discreet persons of his kingdom, as well the greater as the less', it is reasonable to surmise that they included the Commons.[91] The growth of petitioning and the probability that petitions were delivered in parliament, discussed below, strengthens the supposition that through parliament Edward had more frequent contacts with his provincial subjects that we can know of. Given his awareness of the need for local reforms, it would be surprising if this were not so.

In the year following the Easter parliament of 1275 parliament continued to be the forum for legislation and royal *acta* which worked very much to the interests of the formerly disaffected men of the shires. At the Michaelmas parliament, to which knights were summoned, Edward was granted a fifteenth on moveables for the payment of his debts and gave in his turn the Statute of Jewry. This measure placed important limitations on the moneylending activities of the Jews and was in part a concession to the gentry and minor baronage, especially of those ex-Montfortians who had fallen into Jewish hands through borrowing money to pay redemption fines incurred under the Dictum of Kenilworth.[92] That it was widely welcomed is clear from the chroniclers. Some saw it as a continuation of the reforms already instituted in the Easter parliament;[93] one connected it directly with the grant of the fifteenth to the king, making the tax appear as a *quid pro quo* for the statute;[94] and another noted the unanimous consent which was given to the grant.[95] The concession of a tax was in a sense the first fruits of the king's new policy. It marked the practical benefits to be derived not only from limitations on the Jews but from the more wholesale reforms undertaken earlier in the year.

Conciliatory measures were taken up again at the Easter parliament of 1276. This parliament saw some final act of peacemaking with the dissidents of the previous reign. According to the Waverley annals, 'the king conceded his peace to the disinherited', and the *Flores Historiarum* broadened the ranks of the beneficiaries to include all those who had formerly disturbed the peace. No official record survives of what was done, but the occasional pardons to former rebels occurring on the Patent and Memoranda Rolls during the next few months support the chronicles.[96] This was evidently a part of a more general pacification, for in the same parliament Edward confirmed both

[90] *Ann. Winton.*, 113; Jenkinson, 231; Stubbs, ii. 234, n.5; above, 8, 14 – 15.

[91] *Statutes of the Realm*, i. 45.

[92] *Statutes of the Realm*, i. 220 – 1; C. Roth, *A History of the Jews in England* (3rd edn., Oxford, 1964), 70 – 3; above, 4 – 5.

[93] *Chronicles of . . . Stephen, Henry II and Richard I*, ii. 571; *Ann. Dunstaple*, 265; *Flores Hist.*, iii. 45.

[94] *Historiae Anglicanae Scriptores Varii*, ed. J. Sparke (London, 1723), 120 (Robert of Boston's chronicle).

[95] *Chronicles of . . . Stephen, Henry II and Richard I*, ii. 571.

[96] *Ann. Waverley*, 386; *Flores Hist.*, iii. 47; *Ann. Wigorn.*, 470; *CPR 1272 – 81*, 138, 140, 151; E 159/50, m.7d.

Magna Carta and the Charter of the Forest, and in March of the following year confirmation of the Forest Charter was followed up by orders for the perambulation of the forests.[97] This was of particular interest to the localities. The forest had been a major topic of grievance in 1258, but one which had apparently been left unreformed.[98] In providing for a general perambulation, the first since the 1220s, Edward took a popular step and one regarded in the counties as long overdue.

In part, of course, these undertakings were a tactical exercise in public relations, and both on Jewish debts and on disafforestation more was promised than was carried through.[99] Nevertheless, Edward was prepared to make concessions to local interests, even when these involved some sacrifice of royal rights or income. When the community of Worcestershire told him in 1275 that it would be greatly harmed if the fines and amercements imposed in the late eyre were collected forthwith, as the king had ordered, Edward agreed to moderate his terms, 'wishing to show grace to the community'. And when the community of Shropshire approached him in November 1277 to request the pardoning of debts already paid to the Exchequer, but for which the former debtors had lost their tallies of receipt, he again gave ground.[100] By concessions of this sort, given in response to petitions from county communities, Edward sought to appease local grievances which were more specific and less general than those which needed a legislative remedy.

But neither the general changes brought by the Statute of Westminster, nor the concessions to particular groups (the disinherited, the indebted, the men of the forests), nor the Crown's piecemeal responses to particular requests, constituted in themselves a secure guarantee of reform for the localities. Even if the new statute could be effectively enforced through the eyre, this was an essentially punitive response to wrongs already committed. None of these reforms faced directly the issue which was as prominent in the 1270s as it had been in the 1250s: the role and character of the sheriff. In 1258 the sheriff's oppressive government had lain at the heart of local protests and had set in train welcome reforms. The Provisions of Oxford had laid down that the sheriff should be a local landowner, appointed annually and paid a salary by the king, so that he would not have to live by bribery and extortion.[101] Local men, it was believed, would be more susceptible than outsiders to the social constraints of neighbours and neighbourhood in the way in which they went about their business. Their livelihood in their counties would mean that they would not have to demand hospitality for themselves and their staffs;[102] and a yearly term of office would remind them of the need to account for their stewardship in the near future.[103]

The protest of the Devonians against their sheriff in 1273 had shown that

[97] *Ann Wigorn.*, 469; *Ann. Waverley*, 386; *Ann. Winton.*, 120; *CPR 1272–81*, 237. For an instance of the enforcement of Magna Carta in Bedfordshire at this time, in response to a royal writ, see F. Thompson, *The First Century of Magna Carta* (Minnesota, 1925), 48.

[98] *DBM*, 80–1, 154–5; Treharne, 182; Maddicott, 36–40.

[99] Roth, 70, n.3; M. L. Bazeley, 'The Extent of the English Forest in the Thirteenth Century', *TRHS*, 4th ser., iv (1921), 152–7.

[100] *CCR 1272–9*, 211, 433.

[101] *DBM*, 108–9.

[102] *DBM*, 120–1.

[103] *DBM*, 262–3.

these ideals remained very much alive,[104] yet Edward could by no means concede them in full. King and locals had a common objective in rooting out shrieval corruption, but after that their interests diverged. The king could not afford to make financial concessions and, as we have seen, shire increments were maintained at a moderately high level. The Exchequer must have been aware of the declining revenues from the counties brought about between 1258 and 1260 in part by the abolition of increments and the introduction of salaried sheriffs.[105] Nor could he afford to give the office wholly into the hands of local knights. As Henry III had found, local sheriffs, often relatively small men, 'lacked the financial resources, and the prestige and power derived from attachment to the court, to keep the magnates in check and uphold royal interests against them in the localities'.[106] The massive usurpations of royal rights with which Edward had to contend were not only the result of civil war but also of the ineffectiveness of the sheriffs, who, both before and after 1258, had been complaisant before magnate power. If Edward was to regain lost rights he seemingly needed to appoint powerful men, *curiales* and royal administrators able to stand up to the great. Yet this was not at all what the counties wanted. Edward's twin policies, to conciliate local interests and to restore the lands and liberties of the Crown, were apparently in conflict.

What was Edward to do? His first actions were to dismiss the sheriffs, to appoint new ones and to impose on them a new oath. Between 13 October and 27 December 1274 the shrievalties of 32 counties, including the justiciarship of Cheshire, changed hands and 22 new appointments were made. With the exception of Middlesex, the only counties to retain their sheriffs were those five held in fee by magnates (Cornwall, Lancashire, Rutland, Westmorland and Worcestershire) over which Edward had no control.[107] Most of the changes were made in the second half of October, and they were in part a necessary preliminary to the Hundred Roll enquiries which began in the following month.[108] In just such a way there had been wholesale changes in the shrievalties in October and November 1258, during Hugh Bigod's eyre, and the object in both periods was almost certainly the same: to encourage complaint against the most prominent of the Crown's local officials, whose continuance in office might have deterred it. Edward was probably also concerned to turn out those who had ruled the shires so ineffectively in his absence, failing to control disorder or to prevent magnate aggrandisement, and to demonstrate his good intentions to his subjects. The virtually clean sweep of the shrievalties, the first since 1258–9, signalised a new start and a new style of government.

Yet at this stage Edward went no further, and there was certainly no wholesale promotion of local men. Of those sheriffs who can be categorised, there were ten *curiales* in office before the changes and eight afterwards. Some five of the outgoing sheriffs, and about eight of the newcomers, were primarily local landowners, with their main personal interests in the counties of their shrievalties.[109]

104 Above, 7–8.
105 Above, 5–6; Mills, 494; Treharne, 361–2.
106 Carpenter, 'King, Magnates', 66; *DBM*, 220–3.
107 *CFR 1272–1307*, 30–8.
108 Cam, *Studies*, 125, 140–1.
109 These figures are deduced from the biographical data in Moor, *Knights of Edward I.* Unless otherwise stated, biographical information about the sheriffs in the following paragraphs comes from the same source.

So there was perhaps a slight tendency towards the appointment of local men, but no more than that. Among the new appointees were such Edwardian loyalists as Thomas de Sandwich (Essex), who had accompanied Edward to the Holy Land, and professional administrators such as Walter de Stirchley (Nottingham and Derby) and Walter de Schelfhangre (Cambridge and Huntingdon), who held successive shrievalties in different counties. The Dunstable chronicler, who was to comment perceptively on the much more significant changes in 1278, merely noted those of 1274 without remark.[110]

The new oath imposed on the incoming sheriffs similarly suggests that Edward's priorities at this stage lay with the protection of his own rights rather than the conciliation of local interests. Found on the opening membrane of the 1274–5 Memoranda Roll, the oath stresses forcefully the sheriff's duties towards the Crown. He was to serve the king loyally, maintain the rights of the Crown and not assent to their diminution or concealment. When he knew of rights concealed or withdrawn, whether in lands, rents, franchises or suits of court, he was to try to regain them. If he could not do so, he was to report to the king or to those of the council whom he knew would tell the king (and the note of suspicion here is revealing). He was not to respite the king's debts for fear or favour. He was to return and to execute the king's writs, appoint local bailiffs for whom he was willing to answer, and impose on them the same oath. By comparison with this long statement of obligations towards the king, his obligations towards the king's subjects were noted with brevity. He was to treat the people justly, do right to both rich and poor, harm no one for gifts, promises or favour, and acquit men who had paid their debts to the king.[111] This was a statement of principle but it was hardly specific. The oath of 1258, by contrast, had said virtually nothing of the king's rights but had gone into elaborate detail about the sheriff's duty to his constituents, forbidding him to take anything other than food and drink, limiting his claims to hospitality and the size of his staff, and forbidding him to farm the hundreds.

Neither the type of men whom Edward appointed in 1274, then, nor the oath which he imposed on them suggests that his main concern was to meet local demands. Attentive though he was to those demands, the Crown's rights took precedence, both in the articles for the Hundred Roll enquiries and in the sheriff's oath. The changing of both escheators in September points to the same urgent concern with rights.[112] Yet by itself the new oath was hardly an effective restraint on the sheriffs. Marginated 'Sacramentum Vicecomitum' on the Memoranda Roll, some humorist in the Exchequer has added the unofficial heading 'Periurium Vicecomitum', suggesting no great expectations of reform. The contrast between oath and perjury was the contrast between good intentions and likely results.

During the next few years, however, steps were taken to reduce the sheriff's power and to reform the office, preparing the way for the more far-reaching

110 *Ann. Dunstaple*, 263.

111 E 159/49, mm.1d,2d. Although the sheriff's oath certainly existed at an earlier date, this appears to be the first known example; it was unknown to W. A. Morris, *The Medieval English Sheriff* (Manchester, 1927), 176. That it was new in form is suggested by its enrolment on the Memoranda Roll. It continued to provide the standard form of oath until at least the reign of Edward II. See T. Madox, *The History and Antiquities of the Exchequer* (London, 1769), ii. 149, n.kk; and *CCR 1307–13*, 441.

112 *CFR 1272–1307*, 15.

changes in the shrievalties which came in 1278.[113] What were those steps? Firstly, and most obviously, came the Hundred Roll enquiries, the ensuing legislation and the executive action embodied in the articles for the 1278 eyre. Secondly came new limitations on the sheriff's legal jurisdiction, which Dr. Palmer has described.[114] In essence, new means were provided for removing cases from the local courts, primarily the county, where the sheriff presided, to the central court of Common Pleas. Before 1275 the writ *recordari* had been used to transfer to the higher court cases initiated by writ in the county; but cases brought by plaint could not be so removed, thus allowing sheriffs and their deputies to influence their course. From Michaelmas 1275, however, the *recordari* was made available for cases brought by plaint as well as by writ, thus allowing the litigant to circumvent the sheriff's jurisdiction. This resulted in a multitude of cases going forward to the Common Pleas which would formerly have been settled in the counties. In a parallel and concurrent development, the use of the writ *pone* was greatly extended to take other cases from the county and from seigneurial courts to the central court, often on grounds of bias on the part of the sheriff or other presiding officer of the lower court. The effect of these changes was to limit the scope for shrieval misbehaviour, to give litigants better access to the court of Common Pleas and to take business from the county to London. So popular were the new measures that already in 1278 steps had to be taken to curb the flood of new business now being drawn into Common Pleas.

Thirdly, the sheriff was placed under a new form of supervision as part of a radical attempt to manage the Crown's lands and feudal rights more efficiently. On 3 November 1275 the two escheators north and south of Trent were dismissed, and with them, presumably, their local deputies, the county sub-escheators who had everyday control of the king's escheats, wardships and lands. Within each county the sheriff was now given charge of wards and escheats. Very significantly, the only exceptions made to these new arrangements were for the five counties held in fee by magnates, where the wards and escheats were delivered to the sheriffs of neighbouring counties. Edward evidently placed more trust in those sheriffs whom he had appointed in the previous year than in the nominees of magnates who might constitute a major threat to royal rights.[115] The dismemberment of the old escheatries was completed a few days later when three men, soon to be known as the king's stewards, were appointed to take charge of the royal lands and escheats in three groups of counties. Ralph Sandwich was assigned 14 counties in the south, the west, and the west midlands. Kent, where Sandwich himself was an important landholder, was given to Thomas de Normanvill, together with seven other counties in the north and north midlands. The third group, comprising the 14 remaining counties in the east and east midlands, was delivered to Richard de Holebrok. Sandwich had been a prominent Montfortian in the civil war, but was serving as a royal minister again from 1273,[116] while

[113] Below, 26–7.
[114] R. C. Palmer, *The County Courts of Medieval England, 1150–1350* (Princeton, N.J., 1982), 228–42, 261.
[115] *CFR 1272–1307*, 37, 55; E. R. Stevenson, 'The Escheator', in *The English Government at Work*, II, ed. W. A. Morris, J. R. Strayer (Cambridge, Mass., 1947), 116.
[116] Knowles, 39.

Normanvill and Holebrok, so far as can be seen, came from minor knightly families in Rutland and East Anglia respectively and had not previously held office. Each was now given the very considerable salary of £50 a year, presumably to reduce the temptation of corruption and illicit profit.[117]

These changes were confirmed and elaborated in the Statutes of the Exchequer, drafted in the same month.[118] Their net effect was to do away with the separate office of county sub-escheator, make the sheriff responsible for wards and escheats under the supervision of the stewards, and give the stewards responsibility for the royal lands formerly managed by the escheators and their deputies. The intention was to preserve and improve the profitability of the king's feudal and landed rights. The abolition of the escheators both reduced the numbers of local officials (in itself likely to be a popular measure) and removed a class of minister whose opportunities for profiteering at the king's expense had been fully demonstrated in the Hundred Roll enquiries. The sheriffs who took over some of their duties, strictly supervised and accountable at the Exchequer, had little room for independent action. Real power now lay with the stewards, men whom the king could trust and who exercised a new degree of centralised control.

During the next few years the stewards became the most influential of all the Crown's local officials, exercising a wide supervision over lands, forests and wardships, taking inquisitions into the value of lands and often serving as commissioners of oyer and terminer. In doing so they made further gains at the expense of the sheriffs. Despite the latter's local responsibility for escheats, the stewards were increasingly regarded both as escheators and as custodians of castles.[119] Potentially more significant still was the power given to them to hear complaints against royal ministers, including the sheriffs. In November 1276 all three stewards were commissioned to hear complaints against the taxers and collectors of the fifteenth granted in the previous year.[120] Then, in December, they were commissioned to hear and determine complaints, *querelae*, concerning trespasses committed by sheriffs and other royal officials active in their respective bailiwicks from the time of the stewards' appointment.[121]

It is difficult to know how much importance to attach to this. The three stewards may have been intended to constitute a permanent tribunal, each in his own area, to which complaints against local officials could be addressed. But it is perhaps more likely that they were intended temporarily to replace the judicial commission probably appointed in the autumn of 1276 to tour the country and to hear and determine complaints against officials. This commission, the sequel to the Hundred Roll enquiries and the Statute of Westminster, had been abandoned when it became plain, in the November parliament, that war with Wales was imminent.[122] There is no evidence that the stewards ever acted, but clearly Edward's wish was to make it possible for complaints to be

[117] *CFR 1272–1307*, 55–6; *CPR 1272–81*, 112.

[118] *Statutes of the Realm*, i. 197–8; Stevenson, 119. For the date, see Cam, *Studies*, 37–8.

[119] Stevenson, 118; *CFR 1272–1307*, 56, 76.

[120] *CPR 1272–81*, 183.

[121] *CPR 1272–81*, 236. A few more details may be gleaned from the original enrolment: C 66/96, m.27d.

[122] *Statutes of the Realm*, i. 44; Cam, *Studies*, 41–2, 54; R. E. Latham and C. A. F. Meekings, 'The Veredictum of Chippenham Hundred, 1281', *Collectanea*, ed. N. J. Williams (Wiltshire Arch. and Nat. Hist. Soc., Rec. Branch, xii, 1956), 51.

heard against the sheriffs and others, whether before the justices or the stewards. Thus he hoped, in the words of the order setting up the judicial commission, to provide for 'the relief of the people and the hastening of justice'.

In the mid-1270s, then, the establishment of the three stewards gave the sheriff a more closely defined and restricted role. If he now had a novel responsibility for wardships and escheats, it was one clearly limited by the stewards' superiority, by their responsibility for royal lands, which gave them a footing in every county, and perhaps by their power to receive complaints against shrieval misconduct. The Crown gained both through the abolition of one layer of local administration, the escheators and sub-escheators, and through a more reliable and more strictly controlled hierarchy of command. Ultimately, however, the stewardships proved to be no more than an experiment, which found no permanent place among the institutions of English local government. It may have been because their holders had become too overburdened to work effectively that in 1283 they were abandoned and the two escheatorships north and south of Trent re-established.[123]

The stewardships were not the only means used by the Crown to supervise officials and to review their behaviour. In the mid-1270s Edward's personal interest in these matters was several times demonstrated by the hearing of plaints *coram rege* against ministers: most notably in April 1277 when the King's Bench visited Norwich and heard some 23 *querelae* from the people of Norfolk and Suffolk, almost all of them against the sheriff and his staff.[124] Neither plaints in the King's Bench nor, of course, plaints against officials were new,[125] but their combination on so substantial a scale was a novelty. There were other enquiries of an *ad hoc* kind, such as that undertaken in April 1278 into the misdeeds of the coroners of Buckinghamshire since the last eyre.[126] To some extent a substitute for the eyre, these devices were superseded in November 1278 when the eyres themselves got underway. Not only did these provide for a full review of official misconduct, as we have seen, but their two circuits may have been intended to function as 'permanent eyre courts', exercising a more regular control over provincial administration and justice than past eyres. Such at least is the implication of the fixed annual salaries now paid, by a new arrangement, to the eyre justices as well as to the justices of the two central courts.[127] The new eyres, more permanent in their constitution and more comprehensive in their business than their predecessors, may have seemed likely to mitigate the effects of abolishing the stewardships in 1283. All these experiments emphasised the resourceful and inventive quality of Edwardian government in its approach to a perennial problem.

They emphasised, too, the growing reliance placed by Edward on the plaint. First developed by the baronial reformers as a means of encouraging local action against peccant officials, the use of the plaint had widened considerably in the 1270s. The entertainment of plaints by the Hundred Roll commissioners, the stewards, Common Pleas, King's Bench and eyre, bore witness to

123 *CFR 1272–1307*, 174; Stevenson, 118; SC 1/10/159.
124 JUST 1/1233, mm.3–5; Cam, *Studies*, 53, n.1; *Select Cases*, ed. Sayles, IV (Selden Soc., lxxiv, 1957), lii.
125 Sayles, *Procedure without Writ*, xiv–xvi.
126 JUST 2/255/1B; R. F. Hunnisett, *The Medieval Coroner* (Cambridge, 1961), 119, 123–4.
127 *CCR 1272–9*, 503–4; Crook, 7.

its burgeoning potential as a means of prosecuting the delinquent and, more generally, of giving voice to local grievances. Once the king's subjects had thus gained access to the king's justices, sheriffs and other royal bailiffs had to tread more warily. Yet it remained all too easy for such men to intimidate the aggrieved and to obstruct their grievances, as the Hundred Roll enquiries had shown.[128] What was needed was the means to complain at the centre, in the presence of the king himself or his chief ministers, and away from local influences and pressures. In the 1270s that means came to hand with the emergence of the petition delivered in parliament. It has been argued elsewhere that this variety of *querela* developed in the 1270s, very probably as a result of direct encouragement from the king and as a means of offering redress against dishonest officials.[129] Of course, in parliament, as in the counties, only a proportion of plaints concerned officials; nor was access to the king restricted to meetings of parliament, for he might be approached directly as he travelled around the countryside. So it was in Essex in 1281, when complaints were put before Edward by 'divers men of the county' against an honorial bailiff.[130] The early medieval tradition of the personal dispensation of justice by the king died hard. But from 1275 it was parliament which provided an occasion for the delivery of petitions to the king more regular and predictable than the haphazard provincial halts and sojourns of the royal household.

In one particular respect the argument can be taken further. From 1275 we can see a growing convergence between the sessions of parliament, the delivery of plaints, and the issuing of commissions of oyer and terminer, often to hear and determine the grievances enumerated in those plaints. Commissions of oyer and terminer first become numerous in May 1275[131] and for the next few years there is a close correlation between the meetings of parliament and the subsequent drafting of oyer and terminer commissions. As the accompanying table shows, only four oyer and terminer commissions were issued in the first three months of 1275. But in May, after the Easter parliament, nine were issued, and in November, after the Michaelmas parliament, a further seven. The commissions issued during these two months account for more than half those issued during the year. The same pattern was repeated during the next three years, though the commissions sometimes spread over the month of parliament's meeting and the two following months.

Just over a third of these commissions are said to have issued in response to plaints, and in other cases we may often suspect that this was so, even though no plaint is mentioned. Naturally, the misconduct of officials did not form the subject either of most early petitions to parliament or of most commissions.[132] Nevertheless, a substantial number of commissions did deal with the type of offences and offenders investigated both by the Hundred Roll enquiries and by the later eyres. Of the nine issued in May 1275, for example, we find one sent out to deal with 'trespasses and excesses' by the ministers of Edmund, the

[128] Cam, *Studies*, 146, 191; Cam, *The Hundred*, 43–4.

[129] J. R. Maddicott, 'Parliament and the Constituencies, 1272–1377', in *The English Parliament*, ed. Davies, Denton, 62–8.

[130] *CPR 1272–81*, 473–4.

[131] R. W. Kaeuper, 'Law and Order in Fourteenth-Century England: the Evidence of Special Commissions of Oyer and Terminer', *Speculum*, liv (1979), 740–3. The commissions are found on the Patent Rolls, usually, but not invariably, on the dorse.

[132] For the figures, see Maddicott, 'Parliament', 64.

Parliament, plaints and oyer and terminer commissions

		1275		1276		1277
January		1		–		–
February		2		4(4)		–
March		1		1		3(1)
April	X	–		–	X	5
May		9(4)	X	7(3)		8(5)
June		2(2)		5(1)		1
July		1(1)		14(7)		1(1)
August		4(1)		1		–
September		2		5(2)	X	4(2)
October	X	1(1)	X	2(1)		8
November		7(4)		8(2)		1
December		–		5(1)		–
Totals		30(13)		52(21)		31(9)

Note: Figures indicate the number of oyer and terminer commissions issued per month. Figures in brackets are for those stated to have been initiated by plaint. 'X' indicates the month in which a parliament began.

king's brother, 'on complaint before the king', and another to deal with a complaint by Walter de Wylton that a former sheriff of Wiltshire had withdrawn the toll of malt paid by certain men at his mill. Of the two commissions issued in June 1275, one arose from a complaint by 'many persons of the barony of Kendal' about the behaviour of the sheriff of Westmorland whose serjeants, more numerous than was customary, had demanded excessive hospitality, extorted money and extended the use of the sheriff's tourn.[133] Those assigned to try these cases were usually professional justices, trustworthy men close to the king. Between 1275 and 1277, for instance, those holding commissions most frequently were William de Northburgh, Roger Loveday, Guichard de Charron, John Lovetot and John Mettingham, all royal justices.

What was the significance of these changes? Firstly, the issuing from May 1275 of commissions of oyer and terminer, usually after the conclusion of a parliament and often in response to plaints, strengthens the case for believing that petitions to parliament in effect begin with the Easter parliament of 1275, momentous in so many other ways. So abrupt an innovation strengthens the case, too, for believing that an invitation to deliver *querelae* was probably sent out to the counties before that parliament and, more speculatively, that at least some of the very large number of representatives summoned to parliament brought with them the petitions of their constituents. Secondly, the simultaneous development of the parliamentary petition — the *querela* delivered at the centre — and of commissions of oyer and terminer added one more to the restrictions by which the position of the sheriff and other local officials was now circumscribed. Through the use of the plaint and the redress offered in response by the king and his ministers, local opinion could be invoked against local officials.

133 *CPR 1272–81*, 118–19, 121.

Between 1275 and 1278 the independence of the sheriff was thus considerably reduced. The extended range of the writs *pone* and *recordari* deprived him of much jurisdiction. Stewards, occasional commissions of oyer and terminer, and the novel eyres instituted in 1278 checked and supervised him more closely; the expansion in the use of the *querela*, both in the provinces and at the centre, gave a voice to protest and the possibility of redress to the aggrieved. At the same time these reforms did much to meet the Crown's main concern for the preservation of its rights. The abolition of the escheators, the devolution of some of their functions to the sheriffs, and the control exercised by the stewards made it easier to superintend royal rights and limited the opportunities for local officials to connive with magnates in their usurpation. In addition, it must have been thought that the encouragement of complaint would help to impose on the sheriffs a standard of conduct from which the king would benefit as much as his subjects. More specific were the measures laid down by the Statute of Gloucester of 1278, which empowered the forthcoming eyre to judge claims to franchises in the counties.[134] The Quo Warranto proceedings which ensued made it clear that magnates would no longer be able to appropriate royal rights with impunity, as they had done under Henry III and during the years of Edward's absence. The heyday of the expanding franchise was over.

These developments lay behind the significant changes in the shrievalties which took place in the autumn of 1278. On 25 October 1278, 16 sheriffs were replaced in 23 counties, and in November and December a further five sheriffs were appointed for nine counties.[135] This was in part the preliminary to the general eyre commissioned in August:[136] as in 1258 and 1274, it was doubtless thought that complaints would be more readily forthcoming if their likely targets were out of office and power. Altogether more remarkable was the change in the type of man appointed. 'The king removed all the sheriffs, namely clerks and foreigners, and replaced them with knights from their own counties', says the Dunstable chronicler.[137] Here he was substantially right: professional administrators and *curiales* went out, local men came in. So far as can be seen, in at least five cases a local man replaced a *curialis* and in no case was the reverse true. Of those leaving office, four held or would hold shrievalties in other counties, suggesting their status as professional administrators. Of those entering office, none was so placed. In Buckinghamshire and Bedfordshire, to give some examples, the retiring sheriff, Hugh de Stapleford, was a Nottinghamshire man and former keeper of the honour of Peverel; the new sheriff, John de Cheyney, was a local knight and landowner of no great social importance. In Nottinghamshire and Derbyshire the professional administrator Walter de Stirchley, former sheriff of Wiltshire, was replaced by Gervase de Wilford, lord of Clifton and Wilford in Nottinghamshire and knight of the shire for his county in the parliament of 1295. Apart from the five magnate sheriffs the only man to retain office was Hildebrand of London, sheriff of Wiltshire, and he, significantly, came from a family long settled in the county.[138]

134 D. W. Sutherland, *Quo Warranto Proceedings in the Reign of Edward I, 1278–94* (Oxford, 1963), 26–7.
135 *CFR 1272–1307*, 102–5.
136 Crook, 144–5, 158.
137 *Ann. Dunstaple*, 279.
138 *VCH Wiltshire*, v. 13.

The comments of the Dunstable chronicler suggest that there was deliberate policy behind these changes and that they were recognised for what they were: a revolution in county government. They gave the counties all that they wanted. After a long period of experimentation, and for the first time since 1258 – 9, local men had been restored to the shrievalties. It was a change which was to prove permanent. Although occasional intruders were still placed over the counties, for the most part the sheriffs who held office from 1278 onwards were the 'loyal men and sound landholders', each of them 'a vavasour of that same county', whom the Provisions of Oxford had demanded.[139] The 'decline of the curial sheriff', evident in the 20 years prior to 1258,[140] had been confirmed in a forceful reassertion of the principles of the Provisions. What had made this necessary was Edward's need to win over the local communities of knights and substantial freeholders so prominent in the politics of his father's reign. What had made it possible were the steps taken between 1275 and 1278 to supervise the sheriffs more effectively, to reduce their powers and to limit the expansion of magnate authority in the localities at the expense of the Crown. With the eyre set up to challenge franchises, the *curialis/* administrator, able to prevent the misuse of magnate power through his social weight and court connections, became less necessary. Edward's reforms had squared the circle: the counties could now be conciliated without the risks previously entailed by the appointment to the shrievalties of the local middle-rankers whom provincial opinion wanted.

The 1270s were a time of reconstruction in the aftermath of civil war, resembling the first decade of Henry II's reign or of Henry III's. In each period the Crown faced the need to restore lost rights, reconcile the defeated to a new régime and rebuild support without making damaging concessions. Edward's problems were more acute than those of his predecessors because the *tempus turbationis* of 1258 – 65 had been both more revolutionary and more violent than that of Stephen's reign or John's. It had ended in a bloody battle, large-scale tenurial disturbances, the disruption of the Crown's revenue-gathering activities and the restoration of an unpopular political order which, in the localities at least, was not markedly different from that overthrown in 1258. Edward's own past compounded these difficulties. Even before the reforming period, his lawlessness and cruelty had provoked forebodings about his future behaviour as king,[141] forebodings which must have been deepened by his own self-seeking duplicity during the troubles. In his early years on the throne he had to show not only that he could reconcile his father's opponents to his own rule but that he could provide the equitable and just government which his past career gave his subjects no good reason to expect. His reforms were not only a vindication of royal government but of his own character as well.

It would be foolish to pretend that in his reforming methods and policies Edward was guided solely by the precedents of 1258 – 60. Much of what he did

[139] *VCH Wiltshire*. v. 13; *VCH Shropshire*, iii. 17; G. Templeman, *The Sheriffs of Warwickshire in the Thirteenth Century* (Dugdale Soc., Occasional Paper, vii, 1948), 41 – 9. Cambridgeshire and Huntingdonshire seem to have gone against the trend. See H. M. Cam, *Liberties and Communities in Medieval England* (London, 1963), 45 – 8.

[140] Carpenter, 'Decline of the Curial Sheriff', *passim*.

[141] *Paris*, v. 598; *The Song of Lewes*, ed. C. L. Kingsford (Oxford, 1890), 14 – 15, 89 – 90.

drew upon the long traditions of administrative enquiry, itinerant justice and centralised supervision of ministerial and provincial government which had first come together in Angevin England. The ancestor of the Hundred Roll enquiries was the Inquest of Sheriffs of 1170; the ancestors of the *querelae* were the plaints which appear sporadically in the earliest surviving plea and eyre rolls of the 1190s and which lay behind even the most formal of judicial writs;[142] while the eyre had long concerned itself with royal rights and official misconduct. Yet what happened in the 1270s was more than simply the expansion and culmination of ancient practice: it was closely grounded on the immediate past. Edward's whole campaign for the reform of local government reflected a central part of the baronial programme. The procedures which he adopted — enquiry, legislation, enforcement through the eyre — reflected with considerable precision the procedures of 1259–60. The legislation of the Statute of Westminster, both in its form and to some extent in its content, paralleled that of the Provisions of Westminster. The attention paid to publicity matched one of the most notable features of the earlier reforming years. Finally, the use of the plaint to articulate popular protest and to bring the dishonest to book was taken over and extended by Edward's government. It became a means by which the poor and uninfluential, as well as their superiors, could make themselves heard, not only on matters of injustice in the localities, but on all manner of topics and at the very centre of government, before the king and council in parliament.

The means by which the baronial reforms were transmitted and developed from the 1250s to the 1270s can only be a matter of speculation. Much of what had been done no doubt remained common knowledge, and Edward himself had lived on the fringes of the reform movement during its years of greatest activity. But more significant may have been the role of the justices and of one of them in particular: Ralph Hengham. At the start of the baronial reform movement Hengham had been the clerk of Giles de Erdington, Bench justice from 1251 to 1255 and a man prominent among the judicial supporters of the barons.[143] Erdington had been one of the 24 commissioned to negotiate an aid for the king in 1258, had sat with the justiciar at Bermondsey and Canterbury in the eyre of 1258–9, and had possibly acted as baronial sheriff of Cambridgeshire and Huntingdonshire in 1261.[144] As Erdington's clerk, it is likely that Hengham observed both the reception of plaints and the work of the eyre. He himself emerges as an eyre justice in 1271 and was promoted to the Chief Justiceship of King's Bench in Michaelmas Term 1274. That this appointment followed close on Edward's return to England may suggest the king's interest in his career. As chief justice, he can hardly have avoided a share in the drafting of the first Statute of Westminster; we have Wykes to vouch for the prominent role of the justices in its making, and we know for certain that Hengham was responsible for drafting parts of Westminster II in 1285.[145] The case cannot be pressed further, but there is at least circumstantial evidence to suggest that the two major periods of reform were united by the public career of Ralph Hengham.

142 Sayles, *Procedure without Writ*, xxii, liv.

143 C. A. F. Meekings, 'More about Robert Carpenter of Hareslade', *EHR*, lxii (1957), 262.

144 *DBM*, 104–7; Treharne, 146, 187, 268.

145 *Radulphi de Hengham Summae*, ed. W. H. Dunham (Cambridge, 1932), xlvi–vii; *Select Cases*, ed. Sayles, I. liii; *Chron. Wykes*, 263; T. F. T. Plucknett, *Statutes and their Interpretation in the First Half of the Fourteenth Century* (Cambridge, 1922), 49–52.

It would be easy to assume that the measures of the 1270s merely marked the temporary reburbishment of a system of local government whose structural weaknesses denied the possibility of permanent reform. *Sub specie eternitatis*, the cynic may think, the Dunstable chronicler was right, and his gloomy judgement on the Hundred Roll enquiries, 'No good came of it', may stand as a comment on the whole enterprise. It is true that the English tradition of farming the counties and of reliance on unpaid local officials, whether *curiales*, professional administrators or county vavasours, encouraged both corruption and partiality in local government. It is true too that Edward's reforms contained the seeds of their own failure. The eyre, its work enormously increased by the new articles of 1278, faltered and died before the burdens placed upon it; the commissions of oyer and terminer, initially linked to the plaint and dominated by royal justices, became subject to pressure from magnates and from petitioners who were often allowed to nominate the justices whom they wanted;[146] and local sheriffs too, far from being the just administrators and joint servants of king and community whom the shires wanted, often became caught up in the affinities and aspirations of competing magnates. In the later middle ages it was not so much baronial franchises which threatened the Crown's rights and powers in the localities, but the remorseless extension of magnate influence over the institutions and personnel of local government and local justice.[147] In the long term Edward's measures weakened central control and strengthened the very forces which he sought to check.

Such a verdict rests perhaps on the wrong criteria. Edward's reforms, however flawed in their consequences, served their main purpose at the time: to assist that restoration of confidence in royal government which was the keynote of the 1270s. In their different ways both the apparent failing of Montfort's cult in the late 1270s and the conquest of Wales, achieved without internal dissent or constitutional crisis, marked Edward's success in rallying support for the Crown. To that success the reform of local government made a powerful contribution by placating those whose support the Crown now needed. The large and steady increase in the monies paid by the sheriffs into the Exchequer between 1274 and 1287 suggests a comparable success in reasserting crown control over local officials and royal rights.[148] And in an institutional sense, too, Edward's work achieved some permanent and positive results. The Easter parliament of 1275, well attended, legislatively productive, its results broadcast to the counties through statutes and proclamations, foreshadowed and encapsulated many later parliamentary developments. For example, the link then forged, with apparent suddenness, between petitioning and parliament, became the means to most of the legislation of the later middle ages. If any parliament can be regarded as a model, it was this one.

Edward's administration in these years was extraordinarily fertile and productive in new ideas. The experiments with the stewards, the diversion of county business to the central courts, the commissions of oyer and terminer, the growth of petitioning, and the scale of new legislation, all testify to the

146 Kaeuper, 753, 758–63.

147 Carpenter, 'King, Magnates', 69.

148 Mills, '"Adventus Vicecomitum", 1258–72', 494; idem, '"Adventus Vicecomitum", 1272–1307', *EHR*, xxxviii (1923), 336; idem, 'Exchequer Agenda and Estimates of Revenue, Easter Term 1284', *EHR*, xl (1925), 231.

thought now being given to the ways in which the country might be more equitably and more profitably managed. We would have to go back to the middle years of Henry II, between 1166 and 1176, to find a comparable period of innovation in government. But Edward faced problems rather different from those of Henry; nor could he work entirely by Henry's methods and for Henry's ends. To rebuild royal authority it was no longer sufficient to restore royal rights, provide justice and supervise the lay and ecclesiastical aristocracy. The reforms and disturbances of 1258 – 65 had given a new political prominence to the middling men of the localities whose exigent concern for good government and honest officials the king now had to recognise. Their emergence, as holders of local offices, petitioners for reform and representatives of their communities in parliament, was also the emergence of the late medieval English polity. In the direction of that nascent polity during the 1270s, whatever his later attitudes, Edward preferred not masterfulness but the arts of political management.[149] That was a main reason for his success.

[149] Cf. K. B. McFarlane, *The Nobility of Later Medieval England* (Oxford, 1973), 267.

Edward I and the Judges: the 'State Trials' of 1289–93

Paul A. Brand

I

Edward I landed at Dover on 12 August 1289 after having spent over three years out of England. For the senior members of the judiciary who had run the main royal courts during Edward's absence, the year which followed his return proved to be traumatic. Four of the five justices of the Bench were dismissed from their posts. Its chief justice, Thomas Weyland, subsequently abjured all the territories under Edward I's rule and went into exile in France; the others were imprisoned in the Tower and then began the payment of large fines to the king for wrongdoing. All three judges of King's Bench were dismissed, and two similarly imprisoned and made to begin payment of substantial fines. One former justice of King's Bench agreed to pay a considerable sum to obtain a royal pardon. Death had already removed three of the five men who had served on a regular basis between 1286 and 1289 as justices of the 'Northern' eyre circuit; of the two survivors, one was imprisoned and fined in 1290, though the other survived unscathed. All four surviving regular justices of the 'Southern' eyre circuit were imprisoned and started paying large fines for misconduct.

This purge of senior royal judges and of their clerks was not an entirely isolated phenomenon. Complaints of misconduct during the king's absence were made at the same time against certain other senior royal officials and at least two of them (Adam of Stratton, one of the chamberlains of the Exchequer, and Master Henry de Bray, escheator south of the Trent) were dismissed from office and punished for wrongdoing. A large number of local officials were also the subject of complaints, and between 1290 and 1293 about 40 of these were imprisoned and made to pay fines for their misconduct.

The dismissal and punishment of individual royal officials, even quite senior ones, for misconduct was by no means unknown prior to 1289; and investigations into, and punishment of, the misdeeds of local officials had a long history stretching back at least as far as the Inquest of Sheriffs of 1170. But the making of complaints against so many royal judges and the punishment of so many of them was quite unprecedented. Henry of Bath, the senior justice of the court of King's Bench, had been dismissed and punished for misconduct in 1251, but he was the only judge to be disgraced at this time.[1] Master William of

[1] This episode is discussed by the late C. A. F. Meekings, *King's Bench Justices, 1239–1258*, scheduled for publication in the Selden Society's supplementary series. Unless otherwise stated, all manuscript references are to documents in the PRO.

Watford, a justice of the Jews, had been dismissed and convicted of misconduct in 1272 and subsequently outlawed, when he failed to surrender to his bail; but again he was the only justice directly implicated in wrongdoing.[2] The closest precedent to the events of 1289 – 90 lies in the disgrace of Hamon Hautayn and Robert of Ludham in 1286 for misconduct in the running of the Exchequer of the Jews. But the justices of the Jews can hardly be counted as members of the higher judiciary and again the scandal was confined to a single court.[3]

The downfall of so many royal judges certainly made a considerable impression on contemporaries. All the chroniclers mention it. It inspired a biblical parody, the 'Story of the Passion of the Justices' (*Narracio de Passione Justiciarorum*) and a short poem.[4] It is also something mentioned in almost all modern textbooks on the period as well as in some more specialised works on the history of English law and legal institutions. There is, however, only one detailed 'modern' account of this episode, that by Tout and Johnstone.[5] A reappraisal of all the relevant evidence, including some material not known to Tout and Johnstone, indicates that much of their account is in need of revision. In this paper I will try to indicate some of the more serious errors in this standard account and sketch out the main outlines of a revised interpretation of the whole episode.

II

'For three years', wrote Tout and Johnstone, 'the country had been free from [Edward I's] personal supervision' and,

> from his justices and officials of trust, down to the humblest of his subordinates, all apparently had seized the opportunity of their master's absence to extort money, pervert justice, use their official position to serve their private ends.

It was hardly surprising, therefore, that a 'universal outcry' had 'greeted him on his return'. The king's response had been the appointment in mid-October 1289 of a group of commissioners, headed by John de Pontoise, bishop of Winchester, 'ad audiendum gravamina et injurias si que per ministros illata fuerint quibuscunque personis regni'. These commissioners, the *auditores querelarum*, had then been at work at Westminster for the next three years, and a record of their proceedings still survived in two plea rolls now in the Public Record Office (JUST 1/541A and 541B). It had been as an 'immediate result' of their work that there had occurred the 'gradual removal of the

[2] The relevant records are printed and discussed in Brand, 'The Exchequer of the Jews, 1265 – 90', to appear as the introduction to Vol. VI of the Jewish Historical Society's edition of the Plea Rolls of the Exchequer of the Jews.
[3] *Select Cases in the Court of King's Bench*, I ed. G. O. Sayles (Selden Soc., lv, 1936), clv – lix.
[4] *State Trials of the Reign of Edward the First, 1289 – 1293*, ed. T. F. Tout, H. Johnstone (Camden Soc., 3rd ser., ix, 1906), 95 – 9. There is a second version of the poem in BL MS Stowe 386, f.201v.
[5] *State Trials*, introduction.

greatest offenders'. Thomas Weyland, 'the first to suffer', had been 'starved into submission after an ignominious flight, and finally by his own choice abjured the realm'. Ralph de Hengham, William of Brompton, John de Lovetot, and others 'were imprisoned and fined'. The 'permanent character of [Thomas Weyland's] punishment', his 'notable disgrace and banishment', indicated that he had been 'more deeply involved than his colleagues' in wrongdoing; and the 'enormous sum of 7,000 marks reported as the amount of [Hengham's] fine would seem to imply serious guilt' on his part as well. In both cases the punishment imposed reflected a general judgment on the extent and nature of each man's wrongdoing, but some of the fines paid by the other judges were, Tout and Johnstone suggested, of an entirely different character. Once the worst offenders had been punished, the king's rigour could 'abate for a money consideration'. In their cases, the fine was no more, in effect, than a bribe to the king to pardon their offences.[6]

A first important correction concerns the downfall of Thomas Weyland. The precipitating cause of Weyland's downfall was a murder which took place in July 1289. Within two months justices had been appointed to enquire into the killing, and by mid-September 1289 Weyland had been indicted for having harboured the two killers. He was subsequently arrested but managed to escape and take refuge at the Franciscan friary at Babwell. It was while he was still a fugitive that he was suspended from office, and that suspension was a direct consequence of his indictment and flight. Eventually Weyland was starved out and taken under safe-conduct to London. Although a number of complaints of official misconduct had by then been made against him, the only charges he faced at his trial were those of having been an accessory after the fact to murder and of prison breach (for having escaped from custody). In advance of the trial Weyland was offered a choice between ordinary jury trial on these charges, perpetual imprisonment and abjuration. He chose the latter. Arraignment was, therefore, merely the formal prelude to Weyland's admission of guilt and his abjuration. The *auditores querelarum* played no part in Weyland's downfall. His indictment preceded their appointment by almost a month, and it was this indictment which led to his arrest and flight and his consequent suspension (and eventual dismissal) from office. His 'trial' was before three specially appointed justices of gaol delivery, none of whom was an *auditor querelarum*. Weyland's eventual abjuration was the 'punishment' for two specific offences of felony, neither of which had any connection with his duties as a royal justice. It was not the consequence of any general judgment of just how deeply Weyland had been involved in official wrongdoing while the king had been abroad.[7]

It is doubtful whether the *auditores querelarum* really were, as Tout and Johnstone supposed, appointed in response to a stream of complaints received by Edward I on his return to England. Admittedly, this is what the Dunstable annalist tells us, and John of Oxnead even suggests that they were appointed because of the many complaints the king had received while he was still abroad. The Osney annalist, however, is equally clear that it was the

[6] *State Trials*, xiii, xxix – xxx.

[7] Thomas Weyland's downfall is discussed in greater detail with full references in Brand, 'Chief Justice and Felon : The Career of Thomas Weyland, Chief Justice of the Bench, 1278 – 89', in the Proceedings of the 1985 English Legal History Conference (forthcoming).

appointment of the commission which provoked the complaints and not *vice versa*; and the wording of the writ notifying sheriffs of the appointment of the *auditores* and ordering them to publicise it gives as the king's motive for so doing his 'heartfelt desire for the tranquillity of our kingdom and people' and speaks only of 'any complaints . . . there might be'. This does not sound like a king reacting to a stream of complaints already received.[8] Moreover, an eyewitness present at Westminster on 12 November 1289, the day and place appointed for the receiving of complaints, tells us that only a few people actually brought complaints on that day; and other evidence suggests that many of the complaints against the judges, and against others too, were only submitted later: in the judges' cases, probably only *after* their dismissal and punishment.[9]

The timing of the appointment of the *auditores querelarum* suggests that it could have been a reaction to the news of the indictment and flight of Thomas Weyland. Edward I might have begun to wonder whether others of his senior judges and officials had been involved in serious wrongdoing during his absence. Inviting those with grievances against them to submit complaints was one way of discovering the truth. But the timing may well have been fortuitous. The wording of the writ to sheriffs telling them of the establishment of the *auditores querelarum* does not suggest any particular concern with the misdeeds of senior royal officials or judges, and may well indicate that when it was drafted it was expected that it would be local officials who would be the main, and perhaps the only, object of complaints. The appointment of the *auditores querelarum* should, then, perhaps be seen as yet another Edwardian expedient for dealing with the persistent problem of misconduct by local officials — in succession to the Hundred Rolls enquiry of 1274 – 5, the abortive plans for special justices set out in the statute of Ragman and the delegation to the justices in eyre (as from 1278) of powers to hear complaints against local officials. This time the king and his advisers were trying a centralized solution, deputing the receipt of complaints and the holding of preliminary hearings into them to what amounted to a subcommittee of the king's council, but reserving to the council itself the giving of judgment on them. Edward certainly had good reasons for embarking on a fresh attack on the problem of local government corruption. He was short of money.[10] Almost inevitably some, quite possibly many, of his local officials would be convicted of misconduct in any fresh enquiry and would then be compelled to make fine with him for their offences. Encouraging such complaints, and redressing the grievances of the complainants, might also turn out to be helpful when he came to seek the consent of parliament to taxation. On this hypothesis, it was no part of the original plan to provide a forum for complaints against senior royal officials and justices. It was largely a matter of chance that the remit of the commissioners was sufficiently wide to allow them to entertain such complaints as well as those against local officials.

Tout and Johnstone were, in any case, wrong to suppose that it was the *auditores querelarum* appointed in mid-October 1289 who remained at work for the next three years. The original *auditores* were specifically commissioned

[8] *Ann. Mon.*, iii. 356; *Chronica Johannis de Oxenedes*, ed. H. Ellis (*RS*, 1859), 274; *Ann. Mon.*, iv. 319; *Foedera*, I, ii. 715.

[9] *HMC Report on MSS in Various Collections*, vol. i (1901), 256 – 7.

[10] M. C. Prestwich, *War, Politics and Finance under Edward I* (London, 1972), 202.

to receive complaints and to report on them to the next session of parliament; it was the king's council itself that was then to give judgment on them. Their work and their existence came to an end at the Hilary parliament of 1290.[11] What the two surviving plea rolls (JUST 1/541A and 541B) identified by Tout and Johnstone as a record of proceedings before the original group of *auditores* actually record, for the most part, are proceedings subsequent to the Hilary parliament of 1290 before two separate groups of *auditores* with jurisdiction over greater and lesser offenders respectively, and with power to give judgment on the complaints that were made to them. These two separate, though not wholly independent, groups seem to have been appointed at the same parliament. That which dealt with great offenders was again led by the bishop of Winchester and contained five of the original seven *auditores*; that which dealt with lesser offenders was led by Master Thomas of Scarning. The appointment of these two separate groups was presumably a reaction to the volume of complaints that had by then been received against the great offenders. After Michaelmas term 1291, these two groups in turn seem to have been merged under a single new head, Peter of Leicester.

Tout and Johnstone give the impression that it was the *auditores querelarum* who alone conducted all the 'State Trials' of 1289 – 93, and alone imposed punishment on the major offenders. They seem, however, to have played only a very limited part in the proceedings which led to the imprisonment and fining of the judges. Weyland's colleagues were convicted of misconduct in proceedings initiated by a complaint which seems to have been submitted directly to the king's council at the Hilary parliament of 1290; and judgment on it was certainly given by the council during the course of that parliament. The complaint seems to have been directed solely against Thomas Weyland. It was only during the course of the proceedings that it was decided that the alleged misconduct of the chief justice also implicated the court's chief clerk and all of Weyland's colleagues in the Bench, other than Beckingham.[12] Solomon of Rochester and his colleagues of the 'Southern' eyre circuit seem likewise to have been convicted of wrongdoing as the result of a complaint made directly to the king's council at this parliament and in this case, too, judgment seems to have been given by the council itself during the course of the parliament.[13] The original group of *auditores querelarum* did at least process the complaint which eventually led to the downfall of Ralph de Hengham, but again the actual judgment in the case seems to have been given by the king's council in the Hilary parliament of 1290.[14] Hengham's colleague, William of Saham, seems also to have been convicted of wrongdoing as a result of the same complaint, but the judgment against him was probably given by the 'great offenders' group of *auditores querelarum*.[15] He seems to have been the only justice whose initial conviction was before this group. Other justices were brought before these commissioners to answer complaints against them, but only after their initial convictions for wrongdoing. In several cases complainants did succeed in securing redress as a result of their complaints against

[11] *Foedera*, I, ii. 715.
[12] CP 40/81, m.102.
[13] SC 8/263, no. 13125; *Rot. Parl.*, i. 56; KB 27/124, mm.42d – 43.
[14] *State Trials*, 27 – 40.
[15] *State Trials*, 27 – 40.

justices being heard by the commissioners, but in only one do the commissioners seem to have given a further judgment against a royal justice, ordering his renewed imprisonment pending his agreement to pay a second fine to the king.[16]

And what of the supposed shift in the king's attitude towards offenders during the course of the 'State Trials'? Weyland's 'punishment', as we have seen, was not imposed for judicial corruption, and its apparent harshness merely reflects the seriousness of his offence. The other judges were, with one exception, all treated in much the same way: a brief period of imprisonment preceding the agreement of the offender to pay a sizable fine to the king. The imprisonment was analagous to that suffered by defendants in ordinary civil litigation when they had been convicted of a trespass, not a punishment in itself but simply a way of ensuring that the defendant consented to pay a sum 'agreed' with the king for his release and found adequate sureties to do so. The amount of the fine must in all cases have reflected the offender's ability to pay rather than any considered judgment on the extent and gravity of his wrongdoing, since it was fixed while other charges of wrongdoing were still pending and did not subsequently increase even when the offender obtained a royal pardon of all wrongdoing committed while in the king's service or was again convicted of wrongdoing.[17] It seems clear that Hengham's fine was so large not because he was the worst offender but because he was the wealthiest. Only in the single case of Nicholas of Stapleton is it possible to see any softening of the king's attitude, for Nicholas was allowed to pay his fine for a pardon before he had been convicted of any wrongdoing.[18] But this hardly amounts to a major shift in royal policy.

It is also clear that Tout and Johnstone were wrong in asserting that *all* of the king's justices had taken advantage of the king's absence to 'extort money, pervert justice and use their official position to serve their private ends'. This is not to deny that there is some fairly substantial evidence of judicial corruption during the period the king was out of the country. In his complaint against Thomas Weyland, Hugh of Gosbeck alleged that the chief justice had been responsible for the alteration of part of an entry on his plea roll, the main official record of all business done in the court, to Hugh's detriment. The roll had originally recorded Hugh as denying the claim of a demandant to be the rightful heir of the relative on whose seisin he had based his title to a rent-charge in two Suffolk villages and the submission of this issue to a jury. Weyland had erased this part of the entry and substituted for it a passage recording that judgment had been given against Hugh on the grounds that he had left the court before the conclusion of the hearings in contempt of court. Weyland's plea roll has indeed been erased at the relevant point, and after his

[16] *State Trials*, 5 – 11; but there is no evidence that Boyland paid a second fine. He had previously been convicted of wrongdoing with Rochester and the other members of the 'Southern' eyre circuit.

[17] There is only one piece of evidence to suggest that fines might have been increased after their initial 'agreement'. A schedule to one of the membranes of JUST 1/541B (printed at *State Trials*, 39) puts Hengham's fine at 8000 *m*., though he is known to have paid well over 9000 *m*. and perhaps as much as 10,000 *m*. Only John de Lovetot is known to have been made to pay a second fine for wrongdoing, and he is known to have protested vigorously at being made to do so; E 159/66, m.26. It may not have been for wrongdoing while in the king's service.

[18] *CPR 1281 – 92*, 389; *CFR 1272 – 1307*, 284; *State Trials*, 84.

fall he is to be found in possession of a rent-charge in the two villages concerned of exactly the same value as that at stake in the litigation. Presumably he had been given some sort of interest in it as the price of his assistance.[19] It also seems certain that Henry Gerard of Guildford, the clerk of John de Lovetot, had received a bribe from Gilbert of Dunmow for his assistance in procuring a favourable jury at a gaol delivery session to acquit him of a charge of homicide, and quite possible that part of the bribe was destined for Henry's master. In the course of proceedings before the *auditores querelarum* both Gilbert and Henry admitted the transaction.[20] There is also fairly strong circumstantial evidence of wrongdoing by Nicholas of Stapleton and William of Brompton.[21] It should be noted, however, that in the case of each of these justices convincing evidence of corrupt behaviour exists only for a handful of cases at the most, a minute proportion of the total number of cases which the justices had heard during these years, and this notwithstanding the fact that the appointment of the *auditores querelarum* and the downfall of the justices gave those with grievances against corrupt justices an excellent opportunity to seek redress. If there was corruption it seems to have been on a much smaller scale than Tout and Johnstone seem to imply.

Moreover, as we have already seen, at least two of the justices who had served the king during this period survived the 'State Trials' entirely unscathed; one (Ellis of Beckingham) retaining his position as a justice of the Bench, the other (John of Mettingham) becoming chief justice of the same court.[22] It also seems probable that a further three justices who were convicted of wrongdoing in 1290 were not in fact guilty of any serious misconduct. Roger of Leicester, one of the justices of the Bench, was only convicted of wrongdoing in a single set of proceedings. The complaint appears to have been directed solely against Weyland, and it seems to have been the king's council which concluded that Leicester and all of Weyland's other colleagues (apart from Ellis of Beckingham, who only escaped responsibility because for the one term in question he was not sitting in the Bench) were guilty of misconduct simply because the plea rolls made for them were in agreement with the chief justice's plea roll in their recording of the case. This was harsh treatment because in so doing they were simply following the established practice of the court, under which the rolls of the other justices 'followed' that of the chief justice and were copied from it, probably some time after it was written. It looks even harsher when we remember that it may well be that it was only Weyland himself who actually knew what had really happened in the case.[23] Leicester was only involved in one other set of proceedings: those arising out of a complaint made against Richard of Boyland in his role as an assize justice for Cambridgeshire. In the course of these proceedings Boyland requested that Leicester be summoned to answer with him as his fellow justice in hearing the assize. Both men seem to have been cleared of any wrongdoing in the matter.[24] Walter of Hopton, one

19 CP 40/73, m.86d; E 372/139, m.8d.

20 *State Trials*, 53–61.

21 I hope to discuss this in detail elsewhere.

22 It should, however, be noted that Mettingham did become involved in several of the proceedings against his colleagues.

23 CP 40/81, m.102; JUST 1/541B, mm.5,10d,12,24d,33; *Bartholomaei de Cotton Historia Anglicana*, ed. H .R. Luard (*RS*, 1859), 173; *CR 1251–3*, 372.

24 JUST 1/540B, m.5d.

of the justices of the 'Southern' eyre circuit, was also convicted of wrongdoing only in a single case. In a subsequent petition he made out a convincing case for exoneration from all responsibility. The petition was initially rejected, but it may ultimately have been successful for there is no trace of the fine being paid or of measures being taken to make him pay it.[25] There are no other complaints alleging misconduct by him. Master Thomas of Siddington was convicted of misconduct in the same proceedings. He was not able to make a similarly convincing case for escaping liability but his responsibility was probably only formal and does not reflect any real culpability on his part. In any case, for him too, this seems to have been the only set of proceedings in which he was involved.

There was, then, certainly some corruption during the king's absence, though by no means all the justices were involved in it, and the actual extent of it may have been comparatively small. It does not follow that even this small amount of corruption was in any way facilitated by the king's absence. There is no real reason to suppose that when he was in the country the king was able to exercise so tight a control over his judges or other royal officials as to exclude entirely all possibility of corruption on their part. It may well be that the amount of corruption revealed by the 'State Trials' of 1289 – 93 did not differ greatly from that which was normal when the king was in the country; and it may well be that all that was exceptional in 1289 – 93 was that the king created the most favourable conditions possible for individuals wronged by corrupt justices to complain of their grievances.

Tout and Johnstone put a specific figure on only four of the fines which the judges were induced to agree to pay: those of Hengham, Brompton, Rochester and Saham, amounting in all to some 20,000 *m.*[26] In fact fines for misconduct, or in Stapleton's case for a pardon, were made by a total of some ten justices; and, although we cannot be certain of the exact amount in every case, the total seems to have been in excess of 30,000 *m*. Tout and Johnstone also tabulated the amounts actually paid by eight of the judges, a grand total of just under £15,000.[27] Unfortunately their figures are incomplete, for they do not take into account any payments made after Hilary term 1294. The total actually paid by or on behalf of the eight judges was in excess of £19,127 6s. 8d. and to this figure should be added the £200 paid by a ninth judge, Nicholas of Stapleton. To reach a total for the profits made from the trials of the judges by the king we must also add in the £350 received by the king from the forfeiture of the chattels of Thomas Weyland and from one year's profits from his lands.[28] The king's total profit from the trials thus came to just under £20,000, not much under one year's normal Crown income.

Tout and Johnstone noted only one instance of the rehabilitation of one of the disgraced justices: that of Ralph de Hengham, appointed a member of the king's council in 1300 and as chief justice of the Bench in 1301.[29] But Hengham was not the only one. By 1300 William of Brompton had sufficiently regained the king's confidence to be employed overseas on negotiations concerning the

[25] SC 8/263, no.13125; *Rot. Parl.*, i. 56.
[26] *State Trials*, xxix – xxxii.
[27] *State Trials*, xxxviii.
[28] E 372/139, mm.8d,5d. Most of his chattels and most of the profits from his lands went to the prior of Ely and the abbot of Bury St. Edmund's.
[29] *State Trials*, xxx.

dower of the king's daughter Elizabeth, countess of Holland, and in 1302 he was appointed a justice of the Cornish eyre.[30] Master Thomas of Siddington was sent on the king's service to Scotland in 1298 but died the following year.[31] Most of the other judges did not survive long enough to be rehabilitated. The earliest to die was William of Saham. By 1296 Boyland, Lovetot and Stapleton were dead as well.[32] The only justices to live beyond 1300 and not be rehabilitated were Hopton and Leicester. Even Thomas Weyland enjoyed a measure of rehabilitation. In 1292, while in Paris, he was one of the legal experts consulted by an emissary of Edward I about the Scottish succession question, and later he was given a pardon allowing him to come home to England, so that it was in Essex that he died early in 1298.[33]

III

In this paper I have followed conventional usage in referring to the various proceedings involving judges, clerks and other royal officials heard between 1289 and 1293 as 'State Trials'. The term is a convenient and, in some respects at least, an apt one. The defendants were all royal officials, and in most cases what was being alleged against them was misconduct in an official capacity. In certain other respects, however, the term is misleading. As we have already seen, Thomas Weyland's indictment and trial were for wrongdoing wholly unconnected with his official duties, and the same seems also to have been true of the two trials of Adam of Stratton.[34] More importantly, there is little trace, even in those proceedings where official misconduct was alleged, of the proceedings being seen as 'state trials'. There was no use of the procedures of presentment or indictment characteristic of legal proceedings concerned with offences against the king or the public interest, no use other than in one wholly exceptional case of criminal appeal procedure.[35] Nor was there even an attempt to maintain the theory that complainants were suing in the name of the king, or in the king's name as well as their own.[36] Judicial corruption and other forms of official wrongdoing were treated simply as matters of private grievance, of concern only to those who had directly suffered as a result of

30 *CPR 1292–1301*, 102; *Records of Antony Bek, Bishop and Patriarch, 1283–1311*, ed. C. M. Fraser (Surtees Soc., clxii, 1953), 76–8,85; *CPR 1292–1301*, 494; *CPR 1301–07*, 57,64.

31 *Documents Illustrating the Crisis of 1297–98 in England*, ed. M. C. Prestwich (Camden Soc., 4th ser., xxiv, 1980), 157,158,n.1; CP 40/124, m.38; *CIPM*., iii. no. 551.

32 E 159/65, m.15d; *CIMisc*., iii. no. 365; *CIPM*, iii. no. 207; City of London Record Office, Hustings Deeds and Wills, Roll 22, no. 2.

33 Above, n. 7.

34 Stratton's first conviction early in 1290 was for felony and he was probably tried like Weyland before specially appointed commissioners. No records of this trial have so far been discovered. His second conviction for the forgery of charters was in proceedings in the Exchequer early in 1291; E 368/62, m.12.

35 *State Trials*, 40–5.

36 Except in the proceedings brought against Nicholas of Stapleton by Thomas of Goldington and his wife, where the fiction that they had been suing on the king's behalf was invoked when Stapleton acquired a royal pardon after the joinder of issue to halt further proceedings: *State Trials*, 81–4. But this was only possible because the original proceedings in which the alleged miscarriage of justice had occurred were themselves conducted at the king's suit.

them. Complainants were, therefore, free to withdraw from their complaints as they saw fit and so be able to make out of court settlements with those they accused. Admittedly, the king did receive fines from offenders on conviction; but even this, as we have already noticed, was also characteristic of other purely private types of litigation. It could well be argued that one of the most interesting aspects of the whole episode, though one which has been obscured by the label conventionally attached to these proceedings, is that in certain important respects these were not 'State Trials' at all.

Royal Patronage under Edward I

Michael Prestwich

Patronage is one of the most important political arts, but it has not received much attention in the case of Edward I's reign. Its efficient operation is much better illustrated, perhaps, by Henry I's rule, elegantly described by Sir Richard Southern, and the results of its mismanagement are well demonstrated by the events of Richard II's reign, ably analysed by J. A. Tuck.[1] In a memorable and much quoted phrase K. B. McFarlane relegated the question of patronage under Edward I, arguing that the king 'preferred masterfulness to the art of political management.'[2] McFarlane was not the first to take the view that Edward lacked generosity. The chronicler Pierre Langtoft considered that the war in Wales of 1294 – 5 was prolonged because the king failed to grant conquered lands to his magnates as he should have done, and made a similar criticism with regard to Scotland. He also thought that the failure of the earls to accompany Edward to Flanders in 1297 was the result of the fact that 'he had given too little'.[3] Yet although Langtoft provides contemporary warrant for McFarlane's view that Edward 'showed no great belief in the virtues of largesse', the topic of patronage is not one that can be lightly dismissed.[4] Even an ungenerous king could not rule without making some appointments and gifts: patronage was an essential lubricant of political society.

At some points in his career Edward showed that he was well aware that men's allegiance could be acquired by means of judicious gifts and promises. Before he came to the throne, his dealings with the Marcher lords in the course of the Barons' Wars showed this very plainly.[5] In 1297, according to the Evesham chronicle, the earl of Warwick was detached from the opposition cause by means of bribery.[6] M. G. A. Vale has argued in a discussion of the king's relationship with the Gascon nobility 'that he was far from unaware of the political advantages that would accrue from the exercise of largesse.'[7] In Scotland, it not Wales, Edward did make some lavish grants. With regard to

[1] R. W. Southern, *Medieval Humanism and Other Studies* (Oxford, 1970), 206 – 33; J. A. Tuck, *Richard II and the English Nobility* (London, 1973). Unless otherwise stated, all manuscript references are to documents in the PRO.

[2] K. B. McFarlane, *The Nobility of Later Medieval England* (Oxford, 1973), 267.

[3] *The Chronicle of Pierre de Langtoft*, ed. T. Wright (*RS*, 1868), ii. 216, 296, 328.

[4] McFarlane, 267.

[5] *Ann. Mon.*, iii. 225.

[6] J. H. Denton, 'The Crisis of 1297 from the Evesham Chronicle', *EHR*, xciii (1978), 576.

[7] M. G. A. Vale, 'The Gascon Nobility and the Anglo-French War', in *War and Government in the Middle Ages: Essays in Honour of J. O. Prestwich*, ed. J. B. Gillingham, J. C. Holt (Woodbridge, 1984), 146.

the church, royal policy was in part directed towards increasing Crown patronage. It is not possible to examine the whole range of royal patronage under Edward in one short paper, but some general points can be made from studying the way in which a few specific individuals benefited from serving the king, and from the study of one particular type of evidence of royal patronage, the accounts for gifts made through the royal wardrobe.

The case of two families closely involved with Edward from his early days is illuminating. The names of Clifford and Leyburn recur with unremitting regularity thoughout his career, from the heady days of 1259 to the grim struggle against the Scots at the end of the reign. The Cliffords achieved a notable increase in power and influence, emerging rapidly as the major family in the West March towards Scotland. Roger de Leyburn was Edward's steward in the 1260s, and his son William was a knight of the royal household for most of his active career. Such men were the type that would surely have gained much from royal patronage.

Both Roger de Leyburn and Roger Clifford benefited very greatly from the royalist triumph at Evesham in 1265. Not only did they obtain much land from former rebels, but also they were granted the marriages of the heiresses of Robert de Vipont for their sons, so acquiring major interests in the North West.[8] Vipont had been a Montfortian, and the grant made excellent sense in terms of reinforcing royalist strength after the civil war. Yet moving on into Edward's reign, this picture of loyal followers being well-rewarded changes and darkens. Roger de Leyburn had acquired Leeds castle, Kent, in 1268. He died in 1271, and in 1278 Leeds was made over to the Crown by his son William. The background to this transaction was one of heavy debts to Jewish moneylenders which were then acquired by Queen Eleanor, who obtained the castle in payment.[9] In a sense the queen was assisting William, but the change in the position of the Leyburns in a decade is a striking one. William did receive benefits from the Crown: he was granted some minor wardships, and the marriage of the son and heir of William de Say for his daughter. His debts to the Crown were pardoned at the queen's request. He received grants, such as that of the custody of Pevensey Castle in 1294, but although he succeeded in building up the family estates, this was not by means of any major permanent grants of land from the king.[10] He was, of course, a knight and then a banneret of the household, receiving in the latter capacity annual fees and robes worth 36 *m.* a year, but William, for all his importance, stands as an example of the limited character of Edward's patronage.

It was William de Leyburn's younger brother Roger who married the Vipont heiresss Idonea, but he died in 1284, and the way was left relatively clear for the Cliffords to expand their interests in the North. Three generations of Cliffords served Edward. The elder Roger was a supporter of his from the late 1250s, and played an important part in Welsh affairs until his capture by Prince Dafydd at Hawarden in 1282. His son Roger was one of those drowned in the disaster at the Menai bridge in 1282. The Cliffords did not therefore benefit from the territorial settlement that followed the second Welsh war.

[8] *CR 1264–68*, 325.
[9] R. A. Brown, H. M Colvin, A. J .Taylor, *The History of the King's Works* (London, 1963), ii. 695; *CCR 1272–9*, 221; *CPR 1272–81*, 335.
[10] William's career is summarised in *GEC*, vii. 634–7.

Robert Clifford, son of the younger Roger, served the king in the Scottish wars as loyally as his father and grandfather had done in the Welsh. He received various posts and commissions from Edward: constable of Nottingham castle from 1298, justice of the forests north of the Trent, keeper of the palatinate of Durham. More permanent rewards were hard to come by. He received the manor of Hert, and then the manor of Hartlepool, both in Durham, in 1306. He was also granted the Cumberland lands of Christopher Seton, the Englishman who went over to the Scots. In Scotland, Clifford was granted Caerlaverock castle. The building up of Clifford power in north-western England was founded upon royal patronage in the form of the grant of the Vipont marriage, but thereafter it owed little to the king's generosity. Nor did it become fully apparent until early in Edward II's reign, when Robert Clifford acquired the other half of the Vipont inheritance from his aunt Idonea and her second husband, John de Cromwell.[11]

The Cliffords and Leyburns were families of some standing in their own right and it is not perhaps surprising that royal patronage in such cases was of a limited and cautious character. There were men in Edward's household who did rise from relatively humble origin to baronial status: did they receive more from the king? Eustace de l'Hacche was one such, first serving Edward in 1274, and having the rank of sergeant at the outset of the first Welsh war. By the end of the reign he was a banneret in receipt of an individual summons to parliament. He was more than a solider; for part of his career he was attached to the queen's household, and he was in charge of the royal princesses during Edward's stay in Gascony, 1286–89. Yet for all Eustace's success, grants, particularly of land, did not come his way on the scale that might be expected. He held a couple of manors at will, one for only 12 years. In Hatch, Wiltshire, he had a grant of free warren and one of the proceeds of the view of frankpledge. Wardships and marriages often came the way of household knights, and among others he was granted the marriage of John de Hardreshull's heir, and bought that of John de la Hide's heir. The limited nature of Edward's generosity towards him is indicated by the fact that at the end of his life he was still not a tenant-in-chief. He had, however, accumulated land from other lords. He held a manor from Isabella de Forz, and by the late 1290s had estates in 11 counties. Even so, Eustace was not a rich man at the time of his death, for his executors were forced to petition in parliament for payment of the crown's debts to him so that his legacies to the Holy Land might be paid.[12]

One example of greater generosity on the king's part is worth consideration, partly as it was not included by McFarlane in his discussion of the earldoms under Edward I. John of Brittany, second son of Duke John of Brittany, was brought up in Edward's household, and accounts testify to the king's generosity in paying for his upkeep, including such items as his costs in going to

[11] *CFR 1272–1307*, 401; *CChR 1300–26*, 69, 77; *CPR 1292–1301*, 355; Bodleian Library, Dodsworth MS 70, f.64.

[12] E 101/3/13; E 101/3/30; E 101/4/1; J. C. Parsons, *The Court and Household of Eleanor of Castile in 1290* (Toronto, 1977), 63n.; *GEC*, vi. 387–9; *Rot. Parl.*, i. 199; SC 8/1556, 1557, 1558. In *Records of the Wardrobe and Household 1285–1286*, ed. B. F. and C. R. Byerley (London, 1977), xxxvii, n.3, the editors state that they can find no evidence that Eustace became a banneret. Of the many pieces of evidence showing this, it is not necessary to cite more than *Liber Quotidianus Contrarotulatoris Garderobiae*, ed. J. Topham *et al.* (London, 1787), 188.

tournaments. His father adhered to the French during the war of 1294 – 7, but John's loyalty to Edward was unaffected. Despite his lack of experience and youth, he was given command in Gascony in 1294, a decision which did not prove to be a wise one. Though wardships and marriages came his way, he did not receive any major grants until 1299, when he was allocated the substantial sum of £1000 for his maintenance. Some of this was received in the form of lands in England which had belonged to John Balliol. Then in 1305 John was appointed as Edward's lieutenant in Scotland with a salary of 3000 *m.* a year. The final accolade, which John hardly seems to have deserved, came in the following year, when he was granted the earldom of Richmond. This had, of course, been held by his father, who had died in 1305, but Edward clearly made a positive decision to ignore the claims of the elder brother, Arthur.[13] This was not a case of the 'passive acceptance' of a new earl, as McFarlane argued was the case with the earldom of Arundel in about 1289.[14] It should be noted, though, that while Edward was generous to a man whom he treated almost as his own son, he did not diminish the Crown's stock of lands by granting any royal estates in perpetuity to him.

If Edward was lacking in generosity as far as grants of lands were concerned, did he perhaps make up for this in other ways? In the twelfth century it seems that the granting of gifts (*dona*) as well as payment of wages was used by the Crown as a means of rewarding household knights.[15] There is, by Edward I's reign, a great deal of evidence in the Wardrobe accounts for the gifts made by the king. There is certainly no impression of great generosity on Edward's behalf. The most substantial presents were those given for diplomatic purposes, notably to members of the papal curia, notorious for their demands. Thus, in 1287, Cardinal James of Colonna was given £125, and, in 1290, 6000 florins, almost £730. On the latter occasion Benedict Gaetani received 4000 florins, and two other cardinals 1000 and 800 florins respectively. At the end of the reign Walter Langton, the treasurer, was allocated 20,000 florins to make presents to Clement V after his elevation to the papal throne.[16] Such presents were of a very different order to the normal gifts given by the king and should perhaps be compared with the great subsidies paid to foreign allies during the Anglo-French war of the 1290s, rather than with the normal items of the *dona* accounts.

Members of Edward's own family were obvious recipients of his generosity. New Year's Day gifts of gold buckles and the like were largely confined to the king's children and grandchildren, but no large sums were involved, the most expensive in 1306 costing no more than 10 *m.* The king's daughters were generously treated. In 1304 – 5 Elizabeth received £98 for robes, and in the following year £109. She also had £50 for a new carriage when she was in France, and Edward paid off her debts in Holland, which arose from her first marriage to John, count of Holland. Eleanor de Clare, the king's granddaughter, was given almost £29 to buy jewellery prior to her marriage to Hugh Despenser in 1306, along with £10 for robes for her maidservants. Joan de

[13] John's career is fully discussed by I. Lubimenko, *Jean de Bretagne, comte de Richmond. Sa vie et son activité en Angleterre, en Écosse et en France (1266 – 1334)* (Lille, 1908). See also royal Wardrobe accounts, eg. E 36/201, f.13; E 101/352/21, for his youth in Edward's household.
[14] McFarlane, 267.
[15] J. O. Prestwich, 'The Military Household of the Norman Kings', *EHR*, xcvi (1981), 7.
[16] E 36/201, f.56; E 101/352/21; E 101/369/11, f.95.

Bar, another granddaughter, was paid almost £170 for the costs of robes, coffers, horses and carriages in the same year.[17]

Foreigners were often well-treated, even when there can have been little expectation that they would serve Edward in the future. An Italian esquire leaving the king's service and returning home was given £40; a household knight, Jordan de Lubeck, received £10. Two ladies of Queen Margaret's household returning to France were given £78 6s. 8d. between them. Gifts to Jaime de Gerica and Pascual de Valencia in 1305 had a slightly different character, however, for they received £200 and £100 respectively, on condition that they ceased making any further demands upon the king when they departed for their native Spain.[18]

The bulk of the payments for gifts do not suggest any systematic patronage policy, but rather the giving of *ad hoc* rewards for special services. Some gifts related to the wars. Two archers who discovered the postern-gate at Stirling castle in 1304 were given 4s. Thomas de Greenfield, the engineer in charge of the construction of the great siege engine there, the Warwolf, was given £40, and his workmen 10s. in addition to their wages. In the same campaign a Scot, John of Musselburgh, received 10s. for his services in guiding John de Segrave and other magnates when they were in pursuit of Simon Fraser, the former household knight who had deserted Edward to fight for the Scots. It was perhaps more profitable to tell the king about some military triumph than actually to perform a notable deed. Simon Fraser's capture was worth £10 to each of the messengers to tell the king about it, and the man who brought the news of the capture of the earl of Atholl received 13 *m.*[19] Bad news was not well received: the man who told the king early in January 1300 that Stirling castle had fallen to the Scots received only ½ *m.* for his expenses. Family news was particularly well received: so delighted was Edward on hearing of the birth of Thomas of Brotherton, his first son by Queen Margaret, that he promised the messenger 200 *m.*[20]

The great men at court do not appear to have received royal gifts on any scale. The typical acts of generosity were those to the relatively humble. Minstrels and other entertainers often feature on the *dona* accounts, receiving perhaps £2 or £3 if their performance was particularly good. Boy bishops on St Nicholas' day were usually given £2. In Gascony, a poor English scholar singing in a church received £1.[21] A man who recovered a lost royal falcon obtained £2 as his reward. Sometimes the king showed considerable generosity to members of his household, as when his chamber valet Edmund of Cornwall was given 200 *m.* on the occasion of his marriage in 1304, but such grants were not common.[22] As for the magnates, they seem to have found it necessary to give the king presents, rather than receive gifts from him. In 1301 Anthony Bek gave Edward six hunting dogs, a palfrey and a mule. The archbishop of York gave a warhorse and a palfrey.[23] Gifts of falcons and hawks were common. Near the end of the reign Aymer de Valence, William de Braose, Hugh

[17] E 101/568, f.6; E 101/369/11, ff. 95, 104v – 105.

[18] E 101/552/21; C 47/4/5, f.45v., E 101/366/17; BL Add. MS 7966a, f.69v.

[19] BL Add. MS 8835, ff.43, 44v; BL Add. MS 35292, f.33v.; E 101/369/11, ff.97v., 98.

[20] *Liber Quotidianus Contrarotulatoris Garderobiae*, 157, 182.

[21] E36/201, f.54.

[22] E 101/369/11, f.95v.; BL Add. MS 8835, f.45.

[23] BL Add. MS 7966a, f.67.

de St Philibert and John of Berwick all presented birds to the king, as did his son, the Prince of Wales. The names of some of the birds in the royal mews (Clinton, Strathbogie, Droxford and d'Engayne) testified to the fact that they had been given to Edward.[24] Patronage in the form of gift-giving was not a one-way process.

The accounts of *dona* suggest that Edward I was rather less generous than his son. John Botetourt was not rewarded for his services as admiral with a gift of £500 by Edward I, as he was by Edward II. Five of the queen's ladies received 10 *m.* from Edward I when they dragged him from his bed one Easter Monday morning, but three knights who did the same to Edward II were paid £20. John de St John was not assisted in the payment of his ransom to the French after his capture in 1297 with a gift of 1000 *m.* in the way that the earl of Hereford was after he was taken at Bannockburn.[25] The contrast is not an extreme one, but it helps to show that Edward I did not rely on largesse to any great extent to get his way.

Patronage on an extensive scale was only possible if the Crown had an ample supply of lands to grant out. This Edward certainly had. At the same time, there were constraints upon him. He apparently promised at his coronation that he would recover for the Crown all that his father had lost, and there was on his part a clear desire to increase the landed endowment of the Crown rather than a readiness to dissipate it. Even before Edward returned to England at the outset of the reign, a deal was struck whereby John de Burgh effectively made the king his heir, receiving in exchange the custody of the Tower of London and Colchester castle. Lands which de Burgh subsequently sold without royal permission were taken into the royal demesne, the most important manor being Banstead, Surrey. The bulk of the de Burgh lands, on John's death, went to the queen.[26] This deal was perhaps the prototype for those more famous acquisitions of land which McFarlane discussed: those of the estates of Aveline de Forz and her mother Isabel de Redvers, the earldom of Cornwall on the death of Earl Edmund in 1300, and the Bigod lands on the earl of Norfolk's death in 1306.[27] Very little was granted out in perpetuity from these various estates. Skipton, an important part of the de Forz inheritance, was eventually granted along with Cockermouth to John de St John, but only for life and only because he could not lay his hands on the 1000 *m.* worth of land which the king had promised him in Galloway.[28] Edward's policy of retaining land as far as possible in his own hands was a severe constraint upon his exercise of patronage.

Edward was much more prepared to make grants of lands in his overseas dominions, Wales, and Scotland than he was in England. He chose to promote the career of his friend Thomas de Clare with the grant of Thomond in Ireland in 1276. This was to form the basis of a massive lordship, thanks to Thomas's energy and military skill.[29] Otto de Grandson, the king's great Savoyard friend

[24] E 101/369/11, f.157 *et seq.*

[25] C47/4/1, f.27v.; BL Cotton. MS Nero C VIII, f.86; Society of Antiquaries MS 121, p. 63.

[26] *Cronica Maiorum et Vicecomitum Londoniarum*, ed. T. Stapleton (Camden Soc., old ser., 1846), 163; *CFR 1272–1307*, 7, 18, 36, 41, 46; *CPR 1272–81*, 41.

[27] McFarlane, 256–9, 262, 265.

[28] *CPR 1292–1301*, 537–8.

[29] *CChR 1257–1300*, 198; M. Altschul, *A Baronial Family in Medieval England: the Clares, 1217–1314* (Baltimore, 1965), 191–3.

and councillor, was chiefly rewarded with lands in Ireland and the custody of the Channel Isles.[30] It should be noted, however, that by the later years of the reign the king and his justiciar, John Wogan, were displaying a territorial acquisitiveness comparable to that which marked the Crown's policy in England. In Wales, the conclusion of the second Welsh war was marked by grants to some of the leading magnates. The main beneficiaries were the earl of Lincoln, Earl Warenne and Reginald de Grey, with some rewards going to the Mortimers and to John Giffard of Brimpsfield. The bulk of the knights of the household and of the others who fought in the king's armies received no grants in Wales, though Lincoln and the other beneficiaries of the king's generosity naturally brought their own followers in to their new Marcher estates.[31]

In Scotland the situation was more complex. In 1298, before the battle of Falkirk, Edward declared that he would expropriate his Scottish enemies and redistribute their lands. After the battle, at Carlisle, such a redistribution did take place, though the surviving documentation provides only a partial picture of what was done. Edward then adopted a policy of granting lands to his supporters in advance of conquest. Thus Bothwell was promised to Aymer de Valence in 1301, a month before the castle actually fell. By 1302 some 50 Englishmen were listed as possessing lands in Scotland, with the earl of Warwick, the earl of Lincoln, Aymer de Valence and John de St John being the leading recipients of grants. The collapse of Scottish resistance in 1304 presented Edward with the difficult problem of how to satisfy the demands of his own men for rewards, on the one hand, with the request by the Scots that those who surrendered should have full hereditary enjoyment of their lands and goods, on the other. In 1305 a settlement reminiscent of the Dictum of Kenilworth provided a system whereby the Scots who had lost their lands might redeem them. In the case of the earl of Lincoln, this meant that the king had to promise him £4000 out of forthcoming ecclesiastical vacancies, wardships and marriages, in compensation for the loss of lands in Scotland which now had to be restored to their former owners. The problem was far from settled by the time that Bruce rebelled.

The renewal of war in Scotland in 1306 meant that Edward could once again begin rewarding his men with grants there. It was clearly necessary to engage in more active persuasion to get men to fight in Scotland than had been the case in Wales, and it is interesting to note that, in granting out lands, Edward does not appear to have made any distinction between those who were fighting at their own expense and those who were serving at wages. Edward showed no reluctance to hand out comital titles in Scotland. Hastings became earl of Menteith, Percy earl of Carrick, and Monthermer earl of Atholl, though this latter title had to be surrendered shortly as the former holder's son proved to be loyal to Edward. On Edward's slow and painful journey north in 1306 he was presented with many petitions requesting lands in Scotland, but most were not successful. Edward promised that he would issue an ordinance dealing with the matter, but this was never forthcoming. The problem of how to reward his own supporters adequately while not alienating potential backing in

[30] *CChR 1257–1300*, 254; *CPR 1272–81*, 125. Otto de Grandson's career is described at length by E. R. Clifford, *A Knight of Great Renown* (Chicago, 1961).

[31] *Calendar of Chancery Rolls Various 1277–1326*, 223, 240–1; R. R. Davies, 'Colonial Wales', *Past and Present*, lxv (1974), 3–23.

Scotland was an extremely difficult one, never properly resolved.[32]

It is interesting that Edward did not grant his lieutenant, John of Brittany, lands in Scotland. There may have been a deliberate policy by the later years of the reign of not giving those entrusted with high command estates in the land they controlled. Earlier, Jean de Grailly in Gascony had been treated fairly lavishly, and his personal interests as a landowner may have conflicted with his duties as seneschal, contributing to his fall.[33] Equally, there were problems when John de Vescy, a major landowner, was appointed justiciar in Ireland in 1290. John Wogan, justiciar from 1295, was in contrast not granted much land in Ireland by Edward I; he only began to build up his personal territorial position there under Edward II.[34]

The exercise of secular patronage by its very nature detracted from the power of the Crown in one sense. Although the king might hope to benefit from his generosity in terms of the services he received from those on whom he bestowed lands, the fund of royal resources was inevitably diminished with every grant. Ecclesiastical patronage, on the other hand, cannot be viewed in the same way. Any increase in royal influence over church appointments served to augment royal power. At the highest level, Edward's ecclesiastical policy was not successful. He failed to instal Robert Burnell in the see of Canterbury, and in Archbishops Pecham and Winchelsey he was confronted by redoubtable advocates of the liberties of the church. In more general terms, however, royal policies with regard to ecclesiastical appointments were aggressive and successful. The later years of the reign in particular witnessed a very considerable extension of royal patronage, as Edward exploited his rights to make appointments when livings became vacant during episcopal vacancies and during royal custody of the lands of tenants-in-chief. This process has been most ably demonstrated by P. C. Saunders' researches.[35] The most notable example of Edward's aggressive attitude was his demand that his clerk and notary John Bouhs be appointed to a sacristship in York minster along with the living associated with it. Archbishop Greenfield wanted the position for James de Segrave, but he could not find any lawyer prepared to speak on his behalf. When he addressed the court himself, the dressing-down he received was so severe that, according to Guisborough's chronicle, he went away in such sadness that he became ill and died shortly afterwards.[36] The hard-headed and ambitious clerks in the royal administration were the obvious chief beneficiaries of the king's policy and were, indeed, probably the authors of it. The techniques employed were ingenious, making use, for example, of the doctrine that time could not run against the king, to make presentations by reason of an episcopal vacancy long after that vacancy had ended. John

[32] I intend to set out the evidence for Scotland more fully in 'Colonial Scotland: the English in Scotland under Edward I', in a forthcoming volume, *Scotland and England: Twelve Essays*, ed. R. A. Mason.

[33] J-P. Trabut-Cussac, *L'administration anglaise en Gascogne sous Henry III et Edouard I de 1254 à 1307* (Paris, Geneva, 1972), 142 n.

[34] J. Otway-Ruthven, *A History of Medieval Ireland* (London, 1968), 209 – 11; G. J. Hand, *English Law in Ireland, 1290 – 1324* (Cambridge, 1967), 21 – 6.

[35] P. C. Saunders, 'Royal Ecclesiastical Patronage in England 1199 – 1351' (University of Oxford D.Phil. thesis, 1978).

[36] *The Chronicle of Walter of Guisborough*, ed. H. Rothwell (Camden Soc., 3rd ser., lxxxix, 1957), 358 – 9; Saunders, 324; *Select Cases in the Court of King's Bench under Edward I*, ed. G. O. Sayles, iii (Selden Soc., lviii, 1939), 136 – 7.

Droxford, keeper of the Wardrobe, obtained the living of Nassington in 1305, though the vacancy in Lincoln had come to an end in 1300.[37] There could be unseemly competition for positions. The controversial appointment of Edward's clerk Walter Bedwin to the treasurership of St Peter's, York was not merely contested on behalf of the papal nominee Francesco Gaetani, but also by John Droxford, who threatened to take it for his brother 'by force of his lordship'.[38] In many cases Edward himself took no part: just as his officials were given discretion to sell small wardships, so the chancellor was fully empowered to act without consultation in the case of livings worth less than 20 *m.*[39]

Another way in which the church served Edward as a fund of patronage was his demand for corrodies from monasteries for his servants in their old age. At the start of the reign he abandoned Henry III's practice of using Exchequer pensions for this purpose: corrodies cost the Crown nothing. In one month, March 1293, the king demanded no less than seven corrodies from seven different religious houses. There might be problems, as in 1303 when the monks of Bury St Edmunds objected to providing for Roger le Usher with two horses and two grooms, on the grounds that they were already looking after another former royal servant. Edward's response was to order them to accept Roger, but with only one horse and groom.[40]

It would be wrong to credit all exercise of royal patronage to Edward's own personal policy and initiative. The impetus for many grants came from below, not from above. Near the end of the reign Walter Langton wrote to the king suggesting that it would be to his profit should Isabel de Clare hold certain lands until her brother Gilbert came of age. Edward gave his consent, but he plainly did not initiate the grant.[41] On a more important matter, the appointment of Isabella de Vescy to the custody of Bamburgh castle, Edward was quite ready to go along with Langton's suggestion that she should have the position, but he did his best to distance himself from the whole business.[42] The granting of commissions of oyer and terminer was a form of patronage, and here pressure certainly came from below, as in the case of Margaret de Hardreshull, who wrote to John Langton, the chancellor, to say that she did not want Hengham to act as justice in a case she had against Philip Marmion, and suggested other names.[43] It may be, indeed, that Edward had a certain distaste for the whole business of patronage. After the siege of Stirling in 1304 the question of how to reward those who had fought in the army was put to a committee, not decided by the king, and the delay in answering petitions for lands to be granted in Scotland suggests that the matter was not one to which Edward gave any priority.[44] In one instance the king agreed to a petition in parliament from one of his chancery clerks, Geoffrey de Welleford, for a suitable living, and the chancellor was ordered to present him 'in the king's

37 *CPR 1301–7*, 380.
38 E 101/368/18/61.
39 Saunders, 217; E 159/59, m.22v.
40 *CCR 1296–1302*, 122–3, 127; *CCR 1302–7*, 104.
41 SC 1/61, 37.
42 M. C. Prestwich, 'Isabella de Vescy and the Custody of Bamburgh Castle', *BIHR*, xliv (1971), 148–52.
43 SC 1/26, 38.
44 *Documents and Records illustrating the History of Scotland*, ed. F. Palgrave (London, 1831), i. 274–5.

name without speaking to the king concerning this or announcing it to him.'[45]

Edward's use of patronage was certainly limited in comparison with that of many rulers. Yet this did not mean that he found it hard to find men willing to serve him. A letter to the chancellor John Langton from Katherine Paynel, who died in 1296, shows that positions at court were eagerly sought yet hard to obtain, even though they might well not prove lucrative. She asked for Langton's assistance in placing her son Stephen in the royal household, 'where he could learn good sense and manners', and she promised to cover all his expenses as far as she was able. In the event, her plea seems to have been unsuccessful and Stephen failed to obtain the polish his mother hoped he would acquire.[46] At a higher level, those who were successful in the king's service were obviously able to exploit their positions in the king's favour to build up their wealth, not by obtaining grants from the king but by such methods as the acquisition of land by a judicious use of statute merchant, a technique at which Walter Langton was a past-master. The evidence of enrolled recognisances shows how clerks such as William Hamilton built up their fortunes.[47] The lists of household knights in the Wardrobe accounts show that Edward had little difficulty in attracting men to his service, particularly in the militarily and politically successful decade of the 1280s.[48] On occasion, too, Edward was certainly able to bully men into serving him, the best-known example being the way in which he persuaded the earl of Arundel and various other magnates to serve in Gascony in 1295, by threatening to collect all the debts that they owed to the Crown.[49] Officials were frequently threatened with serious consequences should they be lax in the execution of their duties, but Edward was also capable of flattery. In 1306 he congratulated Walter Langton, the treasurer, and the chancellor on the way they had conducted some business, stating that,

> he holds them for prophets, for they have ordered the things as well as if St Chrysostom had said them . . . it seems to the king that the things could not have been better done.'[50]

The limited scale of Edward I's patronage meant that he avoided the kind of criticism that had been directed at his father, or that was to be levied against his son. Under Henry III the favours accorded to the Poitevins and Savoyards had been a major issue, but Edward I's reliance on aliens, such as Otto de Grandson or the Italian bankers, was never regarded in the same light. There was certainly none of the extreme unpopularity of royal favourites that characterised Edward II's rule, nor the frequent demands for the resumption of royal lands. Yet there were dangers in Edward I's policies. Edward's lack of generosity towards his magnates was a contributory factor in the crisis of 1297:

45 *CCR 1302 – 7*, 352.

46 K. Edwards, 'The Social Origins and Provenance of the English Bishops during the Reign of Edward II', *TRHS*, 5th ser., ix (1959), 63 – 4, 78 – 9.

47 A. Beardwood, 'The Trial of Walter Langton, Bishop of Lichfield, 1307 – 1312', *Trans. American Philosophical Soc.*, new ser., liv (1964), 10 – 36; R. H. Bowers, 'From Rolls to Riches: King's Clerks and Moneylending in Thirteenth-Century England', *Speculum*, lviii (1983), 60 – 71.

48 M. C. Prestwich, *War, Politics and Finance under Edward I* (London, 1972), 46 – 7.

49 *Book of Prests of the King's Wardrobe for 1294 – 5*, ed. E. B. Fryde (Oxford, 1962), xlviii.

50 *Calendar of Chancery Warrants 1244 – 1326*, 255.

the earl of Arundel in particular made it very clear that he simply could not afford to go to fight overseas for the king again.[51] Roger Bigod's hostility towards Edward owed much to the way that he had been pressed over many years to pay off the debts that he owed to the Crown.[52] In 1298 a serious row took place after the battle of Falkirk, when Bohun and Bigod protested vigorously that they had not been consulted as was their right over the grant of the isle of Arran to Thomas Bisset. As a result the two earls withdrew from the campaign in Scotland, and Edward was unable to follow up his victory as intended. Some lands, notably in Annandale and Galloway, were not granted out by Edward for fear of further infuriating the earls, but Edward had no further co-operation from Bigod.[53] Brian FitzAlan's refusal of command in Scotland on the grounds of his poverty shows that it was not always easy for Edward to persuade men to serve him, given his lack of generosity.[54] Yet, with the obvious and important exception of 1297, Edward did in general obtain the support of his subjects in his enterprises. Some of the foreigners in his service were clearly discontented at their lack of rewards: Jean de Lamouilly, who used gunpowder to make Greek fire for use at the siege of Stirling, was eventually to kidnap the earl of Pembroke, so angry was he with the way in which he was treated by the English Crown.[55]

It was perhaps Edward's failure to reward those Welsh and Scots who supported him that had the gravest consequences. Prince Dafydd backed Edward in the first Welsh war, but his subsequent treatment and, very probably, the limited scale of his rewards were a major factor in the outbreak of the second Welsh war. Rhys ap Maredudd, the Welsh rebel of 1287, was another who was aggrieved by the scant rewards for his earlier service in Edward's cause. If more of the Welsh had been treated as favourably as was Gruffydd ap Gwenwynwyn, then the English might have found the task of conquest a much easier one. In Scotland, Langtoft suggests, the failure of Ralph Manton, cofferer of the Wardrobe, to pay wages promptly and in full contributed to Simon Fraser's decision to desert Edward's service: he had been a household knight.[56] Most serious of all was the case of Robert Bruce. His decision to join the English cause in the winter of 1301 – 2 brought him little benefit. Edward was not, it seems, prepared to reward a Scottish supporter with lands in the way that he was treating the English magnates. Instead, Bruce found his franchisal rights in Annandale questioned, and he had some problems in recovering estates lost during the period when he had opposed the English king.[57] How important such factors were in Bruce's decision to rebel in 1306 cannot be determined, but it may well be, had he been better treated by Edward, that the English might have been able to maintain their hold on Scotland for longer than was in fact the case.

[51] *Documents Illustrating the Crisis of 1297 – 8 in England*, ed. M. C. Prestwich (Camden Soc., 4th ser., xxiv 1980), 141 – 2.

[52] Prestwich, *War, Politics and Finance*, 237; E 159/40, m.19; E 159/66, m.33.

[53] *Chronicle of Walter of Guisborough*, 329. Bohun, of course, died later in 1298.

[54] *Documents illustrative of the History of Scotland, 1286 – 1306*, ed. J. Stevenson (Edinburgh, 1870), ii. 222 – 4.

[55] BL Add. MS 8835, f.44v.; *Documents*, ed. Stevenson, ii. 480; J. R. S. Phillips, *Aymer de Valence, earl of Pembroke 1307 – 1324* (Oxford, 1972), 111 – 13.

[56] *The Chronicle of Pierre de Langtoft*, ii. 344.

[57] *CDRS*, ii. nos. 1657, 1588, 1604.

There are obvious dangers in generalising too much from a narrow selection of evidence and in assuming that Edward I had a coherent policy. Yet some patterns can be seen in royal patronage in his reign. There was an obvious difference in the king's attitude towards members of his own family, and others. The career of John of Brittany is one example of several. Maurice de Craon, Edward's cousin, no doubt owed his position as royal lieutenant in Gascony in 1289 to his relationship to the king, and also his lavish allocation of 10,000 *livres tournois* a year.[58] Amadeus of Savoy was another of the king's influential foreign relations: the promise made to him in 1299 of 1000 *m.* a year out of wardships and vacancies proved to be a heavy burden in the final impecunious years of the reign.[59] The need to provide for his immediate family was a motive for Edward's policy of accumulating land, though it should be noted that his endowment of his son Edward of Caernarfon in 1301 was not as generous as that which he had himself received in 1254 from Henry III. It may be that the promises of substantial lands for his children by his second marriage was the result more of diplomatic pressure from the French than of Edward's own policies.[60] A concern for his family, however, was certainly a major element in Edward's patronage policies.

Examination of Edward's relations with his magnates, and of his treatment of his household knights, brings out the limited scale of patronage in this period. The great men were certainly rewarded for service in Wales, and more so in Scotland, with grants of lands, but the king was careful not to make hereditary grants of estates in England. Even those household knights who rose from relatively humble origins in the course of the reign received relatively little from the Crown, though they were obviously able to profit very considerably from their position to build up their estates. The one area where royal patronage was considerably extended under Edward was that of the church. There was a substantial increase in the number of livings granted by the king, and it appears that the clerks in royal service gained much more than the laymen did. For all that Edward may have preferred to act masterfully, patronage and political management were essential elements in his style of kingship. Rishanger commented on the skill with which he dealt with a feud between the earl of Warwick and Walter de Beauchamp in 1300, and described the way in which he engaged in individual persuasion in order to try to obtain a grant of taxation in the same year.[61] The royal propaganda of 1297, and the way in which Edward tried to divide the ranks of his opponents, shows that he was well aware of the political arts. The nature of medieval society was such that patronage in the form of grants of offices, wardships and marriages, ecclesiastical livings and so forth was an essential element of government. The fact that Edward I did not engage in the excesses of his father or his son does not mean that the question of patronage was unimportant in his reign. The honours accorded to John of Brittany, the church livings accumulated by royal clerks, and even the gifts to men of humble rank, just as much as the failure to reward Robert Bruce, were all important elements in Edward's kingship.

[58] *Rôles Gascons*, iii, ed. C. Bémont (Paris, 1906), i – lii. In England, however, Maurice appears to have been the subject of the king's acquisitiveness, with his lands in Surrey going first to Robert Burnell and then to the king in a deal whose implications are far from clear. See *CCR 1279 – 88*, 180 – 1.
[59] *CPR 1292 – 1301*, 425; *CPR 1301 – 7*, 46.
[60] *Foedera*, I, ii. 998.
[61] *Willelmi Rishanger, Chronica et Annales*, ed. H. T. Riley (*RS*, 1865), 404 – 6.

The Fiscal Uses of Royal Wardships in the Reign of Edward I

S. L. Waugh

Although historians have generally treated royal wardships and marriages as economic commodities, the precise role of those rights in royal finances is far from clear. It is sometimes assumed, for instance, that the king offered most wardships and marriages for sale to the highest bidder in an open market, thereby generating income for the treasury as part of its 'ordinary' revenue.[1] Yet, not only have investigations of royal income failed to detect a significant cash contribution from these sources, but it is also obvious that many wardships were never 'sold' at all and were instead granted freely as royal patronage.[2] What, then, was the primary value of these prerogative resources to the Crown, and how could it exploit them to its best advantage? The purpose of this article is to clarify these issues by analyzing Edward I's use of royal wardships and marriages.

Edward's reign is ideal for this purpose for two reasons, First, the financial health of the monarchy changed dramatically over the course of his reign, producing corresponding changes in the use of wardships and marriages. As Dr. Prestwich has demonstrated, the pressures of war in the later years of Edward's reign forced the government to undertake various expedients to raise money, one of which was an effort to squeeze greater profits out of the king's rights as a landlord.[3] Edward's reign can thus be divided into two periods, before and after 1296, in which his exercise of feudal lordship differed significantly.

In the second place, Edward proved to be an exacting landlord. His determination in that respect is best known in the Quo Warranto proceedings, but he was no less demanding in his treatment of reliefs, wardships, marriages, widows' marriages, alienations and escheats. As soon as he returned to England in 1274, he demonstrated his interest in these rights in the hundred inquests, which were designed in part to inform him about his estate and tenantry and how well his officers had managed them in his absence. Shortly thereafter he undertook an ambitious administrative reorganization which was intended to simplify and centralize his seigneurial authority by eliminating the escheatorships, turning the routine management of wardships and escheats

[1] See, eg. B. Lyon, *A Constitutional and Legal History of Medieval England* (2nd edn., New York, 1980), 132. Unless otherwise stated, all manuscript references are to documents in the PRO.
[2] G. L. Harriss, *King, Parliament, and Public Finance in Medieval England to 1369* (Oxford, 1975), 136–41; J. R. Strayer, 'Introduction', *The English Government at Work, 1327–1336*, II (Cambridge, Mass., 1947), 4–5, 22–7; E. R. Stevenson, 'The Escheator', *English Government at Work*, 136–56.
[3] M. C. Prestwich, *War, Politics and Finance Under Edward I* (London, 1972), 151–223.

over to the sheriffs, and investing authority over feudal rights and royal demesnes in three stewards.[4] Although the experiment fell apart by late 1282 and Edward restored the traditional escheatorships the following year, he built on the precedent by gradually expanding the scope of the escheator's duties, a process that accelerated after 1296. Finally, any thoughts his tenants-in-chief may have harboured that Edward was an easy landlord were quickly dispelled in 1285 when he seized the lands of both Hugh Despenser and his wife Isabel, widow of Patrick de Chaworth, and kept them in custody nearly a year because she had married Hugh without Edward's permission. The seizure raised nearly £600 or 56% of the total income from the escheatorships that year, along with another £400 from the sale of Hugh's goods. Edward also charged the couple 2000 *m.* for their trespass but later pardoned the fine.[5]

Though Edward was a demanding landlord, he was not a foolhardy one. He largely respected the limitations that had been imposed on royal lordship over previous generations. His feudal resources were, after all, the lands, children, and widows of his tenants-in-chief, so that his lordship affected the families and economic interests of the most powerful men in the realm. The barons had forcibly reminded the king in 1215 and again during the period of baronial reform in the middle of the century that, as landlord, he had the responsibility to keep inheritances intact and unharmed, that he had to support the heir, and that he could not pressure widows or heiresses into marriages they did not want. Throughout Henry III's reign, moreover, the barons had complained that Henry misused his rights, bestowing them on unworthy individuals, failing to raise sufficient revenues from them, and arranging unsuitable marriages for wards.[6] As one who had been involved in the political struggles of his father's reign, Edward must have understood that there were limits to what he could extract economically from royal lordship and that if he demanded too much, his tenants would react against it.

His feudal resources, however, were tempting. As is well known, when a tenant-in-chief died leaving behind a minor heir or heirs, the Crown, in many cases, exercised the right of prerogative wardship, which meant that it assumed all of the powers of lordship over the estate and heir.[7] The king acquired custody of all the tenant's lands regardless of whom they were held, the right of marriage of the heir, any advowsons that became available, the right of wardship over military sub-tenants, and custody of any lands held in dower out of the estate as widows died. He could sell non-essential goods, tallage unfree tenants and collect feudal dues. He exercised similar powers over the lands of idiots, whether incapacitated temporarily or from birth, and over the property of felons. He gained additional wardships during ecclesiastical vacancies when military tenants died leaving minor heirs. Even if the heir of a tenant-in-chief was not a minor, the right of primer seisin gave the king the

[4] Stevenson, 116–19.

[5] E 372/141 m.23 (account of Henry de Bray, escheator south of the Trent, 14 Edward I; the lands were in custody from 21 December 1285 to 30 November 1286); E 401/106; E 159/60 m.16.

[6] S. L. Waugh, 'Marriage, Class, and Royal Lordship in England Under Henry III', *Viator*, xvi (1985), 198–206.

[7] 'Introduction', *Prerogativa Regis: Tertia Lectura Roberti Constable de Lyncolnis Inne Anno 11 H. 7*, ed. S. E. Thorne (New Haven, 1949), xiv–xlvi; F. Pollock and F. W. Maitland, *The History of English Law Before the Time of Edward I* (2nd edn., Cambridge, 1968), i. 307–29; J. M. W. Bean, *The Decline of English Feudalism, 1215–1540* (Manchester, 1968), 7–20.

right to collect rents, revenues, recognitions, and amercements from the estate and its tenants before he turned it over to the proper heir.

The monetary value of these rights could be realized in several ways. A wardship or marriage could be 'sold' for a fine, or the lands could be farmed or rented to one or more individuals, or the Crown could retain custody and collect the issues itself. Even a grant quit of any fine or rent represented an indirect contribution to the Exchequer on the expenditure side, since it reduced the outflow from the Treasury for patronage or other expenses.

Although the incidence of these benefits was unpredictable, depending as it did on the accidents of births and deaths among tenants-in-chief, Edward was steadily supplied with wardships. Altogether, more than 455 wards and their lands came into royal custody over Edward's reign, excluding the lands of idiots and felons.[8] The wardships varied enormously in value, but of the minors, 83 were the heirs of baronies or portions of baronies, while another 150 belonged to knightly families, some of which were substantial landholders, like the Audeleys, Bassets of Drayton, Colevilles or Tanys.[9] These baronial or knightly wardships were considerably more valuable to the Crown than those of lesser tenants-in-chief. In the year beginning Michaelmas 1304, for example, the escheator north of the Trent accounted for a net income of slightly more than £500, but of this sum, £321. 4s. 9¼d., or 64%, was raised after 19 April 1305 from the lands of the earl Warenne.[10] To summarize the incidence of wardships in crude averages: Edward received approximately 13 wardships a year, of which half were likely to involve the lands of baronial or knightly families.

How, then, did Edward employ these resources? In the period down to 1296 he allocated most of them as patronage while simultaneously improving the efficiency of his administration to increase the cash receipts from feudal lordship. This policy can best be explained by comparing it to Henry III's, for they differed in several respects. To begin with, Edward extended the time that lands in wardship were in the custody of royal officials before granting them out. The average length of time between the issuance of the writ *diem clausit extremum* and the grant of a wardship was eight months for Henry's reign and 18 for Edward's, giving Edward's officials more time to collect revenues from the lands.[11] The shorter custodies of Henry's reign can be attributed to the fact that by 1258 he had promised virtually all future wardships to favourites or officials in place of the fees that they received at the Exchequer. As a result, there was a queue of royal clients waiting to snatch up wardships as soon as

[8] This figure is compiled from grants of wardships and/or marriages recorded in the Chancery rolls, Exchequer memoranda rolls or the escheators' accounts. There are inquisitions post mortem for only 258 of these 455 wards, while another 97 wards for whom there are inquests cannot be traced either as royal wards or as not pertaining to the Crown.

[9] The baronies have been identified from I. J. Sanders, *English Baronies* (Oxford, 1960), and knightly families from C. Moor, *Knights of Edward I* (Harleian Soc., lxxx – lxxxiv, 1929 – 32); *Records of the Wardrobe and Household, 1285 – 1286*, ed. B. F. and C. R. Byerly (London, 1977); and from statements in the records of the wardships.

[10] E 372/150 m.33.

[11] These figures are calculated from the dates of the writs given in the inquisitions post mortem and the dates of the Chancery enrolments of the grants. Only those in which there are clear dates for both have been used. They should be treated with caution, however, because those for Henry's reign are based on a sample of only 111 compared to 232 for Edward's.

they came into royal hands.[12] In contrast, Edward made fewer promises so that there was less urgency to give up the wardships. Escheators, therefore, retained some lands and heirs in custody for years, collecting the issues in the meantime.

Furthermore, Edward modified his father's practice regarding the sale of wardships and marriages. Between 1227 and 1271, fines averaged 1333.6 *m.* a year, while in the period from 1272 to 1296, they averaged only 809 *m.* a year. And if one massive fine of 7000 *m.*, charged to Edmund of Cornwall in 1282 for the wardship of the Wake estate, is deducted, then the annual average falls to 529 *m.*[13] Edmund's fine alone accounted for 33% of the total amount that Edward charged in these years. Edward granted out as many wardships as his father had, but he was more generous in the sense that recipients had to pay less for the privilege than they had in his father's reign. For example, deducting large fines over 500 *m.* from the totals, the average fine in Henry's reign was 103 *m.* and only 74 *m.* in the first half of Edward's reign.[14] Most of Edward's fines were levied on 'minor' wardships, those valued at £20 a year or less, and Edward gave his local agents greater discretion over these wardships than that exercised by his father's officials. Henry had distinguished between major and minor wardships in defining the authority of his lieutenants in England while he was in Gascony in 1242, and the reformers used the distinction in 1258 to circumscribe royal authority.[15] Edward, however, made it a standard practice and directed his escheators and stewards to sell or farm wardships valued at £20 or less a year.[16] John de London, the escheator south of the Trent in the first four years of the reign, thus accounted for £1,380 from such fines.[17] The escheator decided whether to sell, lease or retain custody of the lands of smaller landholders, and how to dispose of the marriages of their heirs. It was a sensible policy since the purchasers of minor wardships would most likely be found in the neighbourhood in which the tenant-in-chief held his lands, that is, in the escheator's or sub-escheator's bailiwick.

Edward made up for the loss of fines in other ways. For example, he leased more wardships than Henry had. In 45 cases, or 12% of all his grants in these years, the grantee had to pay a rent for the custody of the lands. The government usually levied the rent at the appraised value of the lands recorded in the inquisition post mortem, which almost certainly underestimated their real value, and in only a few instances compensated for this bias by charging an increment to the assessed value.[18] The rents, therefore, benefited both the

[12] Between 1247 and 1258, Henry promised approximately 90 men wardships totalling 8354.5 *m.*, a figure compiled from *CPR 1247–58*.

[13] The figures are compiled from the amounts stated in the Originalia or Fine Rolls and from actual payments. They underestimate the true total levied because in some cases the rolls note that a fine was charged without giving the amount. The total, moreover, is the amount *levied*, not the amount the Exchequer or Wardrobe actually collected. Edmund's fine is noted in *CPR 1281–92*, 35, 163.

[14] Between 1227 and 1271, fines offered by 246 individuals totalled 60,013 *m.*, of which 27 were 500 *m.* or more apiece, totalling 37,500 *m.* (62%). Between 1272 and 1296, 89 offered fines totalling 20,223 *m*, of which six were large fines, totalling 14,050 *m.* (69%). This last figure includes Edmund's fine.

[15] *CPR 1232–47*, 290; *DBM*, 102–03; *CPR 1258–66*, 29.

[16] *CPR 1272–81*, 77, 314; *CPR 1281–92*, 30; E 159/59 m.22d.

[17] E 372/122 m.1d; *CFR 1272–1307*, 47, 49.

[18] Eg., Edward farmed one manor in 1273 for the extended value of £7. 8s. 10d. plus an

government and the recipient, who could anticipate making a profit over and above the rent.

Edward's changes in administrative practice may have modestly increased revenues from the escheatorship, though because of differences in accounting procedures it is impossible to compare precisely the income from feudal sources under Henry III and Edward I. Between 1258 and 1274 the escheatorships produced more than £4100, or about £256 a year.[19] In the years 1283 – 92 for which accounts for both escheatorships survive, proceeds rose to more than £6907, or about £863 a year.[20] That is substantially more than the £533. 6s. 8d. Exchequer officials in 1284 estimated escheats and primer seisin would produce, though their estimate was limited to lands retained in royal custody.[21] In fact, receipts in the Exchequer from feudal sources in the year after Easter, 1285, totalled nearly £730, excluding the windfall of £400 from the sale of Hugh Despenser's goods.[22] Compared to taxes, customs and county farms, however, wardships and marriages did not constitute a significant source of income.

Royal lordship in these years did not generate greater revenues because Edward distributed most of his feudal incidents as patronage to strengthen the solidarity of his court and administration. The vast bulk of this wealth, 312 of 377 grants or 83%, went to members of the royal family (39), household knights (50), the queen's servants (5), and to royal servants, yeomen and clerks (214 or 57%). The list of recipients reads in part like a household account: Robert fitz John, household steward received 4 wardships; Eustace de Hacche, household knight, 4 wardships; William Latimer 2 wardships, and so on. The wardships that men of this rank obtained, moreover, were usually commensurate with their status, and Edward seldom charged them anything for grants. The single most conspicuous recipient was Queen Eleanor. She received at least 16 wardships or marriages before her death in 1290, as well as the fines or farms from three granted to other individuals, and Edward specifically intended that some of the wardships would be used to defray her household expenses.[23] A distinct policy regarding the use of wardships and marriages thus seems to have taken shape between 1272 and 1296: the government profited from minor wardships through sales, leases, and direct receipts, while it used major wardships largely as patronage to reward service and to secure the adherence of lords, knights, and officials around the king.

---

increment of 60s. or 41% of the value. See *CPR 1272 – 81*, 30. In some cases he levied the rent in round numbers, which may indicate that an increment had been added, as in 1288 when he charged a rent of £14 a year for a manor which had been valued at £12. 2s. 4¼d. See *CFR 1272 – 1307*, 255; C 133/5, no. 5, the total *de claro*, less dower.

19 The total is calculated from the escheators' accounts in E 372/105 mm.20d – 21; E 372/106 m.21; E 372/112 m.2; E 372/114 m.19; E 372/115 m.11d; E 372/117 m.7; E372/120 mm.24 – 24d; E 372/124 mm.19 – 22; E 372/127 m.2; and E 136/1/1, 2. Some of the accounts are incomplete and some overlap.

20 E 372/128 mm.34 – 34d; E 372/133, mm.30d, 31 – 31d; E 372/141 mm.23 – 23d, 24, 26; E 372/136 mm.24d, 25. I have not found an account for south of the Trent for 18 Edward I. Part of the increase in revenues from the escheators is due to the sales of minor wardships. For the most part, in the reign of Henry III escheators did not account for fines.

21 M. H. Mills, 'Exchequer Agenda and Estimate of Revenue, Easter Term 1284', *EHR*, xl (1925), 229 – 34.

22 E 401/104; E 401/106. The total does not include any receipts from the escheatorship south of the Trent, besides the £400.

23 SC 1/16/207.

The subtleties of feudal patronage, however, were no match for the crushing fiscal needs of the Crown after 1296, and the policy that had been fashioned in the 1280s was quickly demolished in the following decade. Edward needed all of his resources to pay for war, and those of feudal lordship were no exception. The turning point seems to coincide with Edward's letter to the Exchequer in 1296 asking them to raise money from every source, after which the Exchequer and escheators searched out and exploited all kinds of seigneurial dues.[24] They made a more vigorous effort, for example, to collect reliefs, dragging heirs before the treasurer and barons in larger numbers than before to show why they had not paid. Escheators held lands in custody longer, and the Crown increased the fines for the wardships and marriages that it sold. Widows could also anticipate losing their lands for a time if they were rash enough to marry without licence. Following Joan of Acre's unauthorized marriage to Ralph de Monthermer, for example, Edward seized her lands and held them for more than three years, during which they produced nearly £2000.[25]

There was, moreover, a new drive to enforce the king's prohibition on alienations by tenants-in-chief without royal licence. Henry III's proclamation in 1256 enunciating the principle had been vague, simply prohibiting entry into a lay fee held in chief without specifying the types of alienation or the amounts of land alienated, and enforcement had been lax.[26] Though Edward seems to have made a modest effort to tighten-up enforcement in the first two decades of his reign, the Chancery issued only a few licences and pardons while escheators took few lands into custody as a result of unauthorized alienations.[27] That situation changed between 1294 and 1298. Licences increased beginning in 1294, and after 1296 escheators seized a larger number of lands *ex officio* and held them in custody longer, while possible offenders were attached, brought before the Exchequer to defend their alienation, and fined for the trespass, if convicted.[28] Furthermore, the Exchequer interpreted the prohibition as widely as possible to cover any kind of alienation. The 'articles of the escheator', as well as their accounts, show that escheators enforced the measure against leases or life grants, grants of rent-charges or annuities, and the manumission of villeins, alongside more obvious actions such as gifts or sales of land, appropriations contrary to the Statute of Mortmain, or entry by an heir into a fee before performing homage.[29] Any infraction resulted in the seizure of the property, and the escheator held it and collected the income until a fine was paid, which could be several years. Between 28 February 1283 and 29 September 1285, Master Henry de Bray accounted for only five tenements alienated by two tenants-in-chief south of the Trent, which produced about £10. Fifteen years later, Walter de Gloucester accounted for 25 tenements

[24] E 159/69 m.11d, cited by Prestwich, 94, n. 3.

[25] E 372/149 mm.32d – 33; E 136/1/18; E 136/1/19A. The lands were in custody 3 May 1298 – 16 November 1301.

[26] *CR 1254 – 56*, 429, and Bean, 66 – 79, 85 – 103, esp. Table II, p. 72.

[27] E 372/117 m.7; E 372/122 m.1d; E 372/124 m.21.

[28] Evidence for the change can be found in Exchequer and escheators' material, as well as in the Chancery rolls: Bean, 72; E 153/10 nos. 1 – 3, /49 nos. 1 – 6; E 143/4/2 nos. 9, 10, 13, 18; E 143/4/4 nos. 6, 7; E 143/4/6 nos. 1, 4, 7; E 136/1/20; E 136/3/10; E 136/3/11; E 372/149 mm.30d – 31d; E 159/69 m.11d; E 159/72 mm.10, 10d, 11(2), 21, 43d, 53, 71. For a different interpretation of this change, see Bean, 75 – 9.

[29] *Statutes of the Realm*, ed. A. Luders *et al.* (London, 1810), i.238 – 41; E 372/155B mm.8 – 16; E 372/154 m.53; E 136/3/11.

alienated without licence in the same bailiwick in a single year, 1299 – 1300. Yet they were only small parcels and produced £12. 10s., or an average of 10s. apiece.[30] The government was scraping the bottom of the barrel, and the policy, in effect, was as punitive as it was fiscal.

As a result of these changes in policy, the direct cash receipts from the escheatorships increased significantly. Down to 1296, receipts averaged £262 per year north of the Trent and £894 in the south, but after 1296 the annual averages jumped to £344 and £1700 respectively. Fines offered for wardships and marriages also increased, from an average of 809 (or 529) *m.* to 1156 *m.* a year. Finally, Exchequer receipts from all feudal sources totalled nearly £2100 in the year following Easter 1298. These figures demonstrate an impressive ability on the part of Edward's government to marshal all of the Crown's resources for a specific policy.

Royal lordship, moreover, was swept up into the system of wardrobe finance and used to pay wages, debts and expenses. The Crown had granted wardships for these purposes before, but never on the scale that it did in the later years of Edward's reign. The government signalled this new emphasis in 1297 when Edward granted the lands of Adam de Bavent to John de Cobeham in order to repay John's loan to Edward of 500 *m.* to expedite the king's 'urgent business.'[31] In the following years, Edward allotted groups of wardships to the repayment of large loans. In 1298 and 1299, for example, Walter of Gloucester turned nine wardships and marriages, valued at about £835, over to Henry, count of Bar to help pay the king's debt of £1916 to Henry.[32] Edward similarly granted wardships to several individuals who had paid sums to Italian merchants on behalf of Queen Margaret and made a number of grants to Margaret herself to help pay debts.[33] Yet, though deep in debt to the Italians himself, Edward granted few wardships or feudal revenues directly to foreign merchants.[34] He learned from his father's mistakes and kept wardships out of 'alien' hands.

The most impressive example of this use of feudal resources was Edward's grant in 1298 to repay Edmund of Cornwall's loans totalling 9840½ *m.* and 10¼d.[35] Edmund received 39 of the 48 wardships and marriages granted that year, while the recipients of 5 of the remaining 9 paid him their fines or farms. In addition, Edmund received reliefs, fines from widows for the right to marry, and amercements for marrying without licence. The account of Edmund's executors for the debt and repayment in 1304 revealed that these sources produced 11,760 *m.*, nearly 2000 *m.* more than the king had owed.[36] As it turned out, Edmund had loaned another 3300 *m.* to the Wardrobe of which only a portion had been repaid, so that the executors did not have much

30 E 372/133 mm.31 – 31d; E 372/149 mm.30d – 31d.
31 *CIPM*, iii.75; E 159/71 m.9, 6 November.
32 E 372/149 m.30; *CPR 1292 – 1301*, 399.
33 *CPR 1301 – 07*, 60, 238, 368, 369, 372, 374 – 5, 410; E 372/149 mm.37d – 38.
34 *CPR 1292 – 1301*, 77, 158, and *CPR 1301 – 07*, 142 – 3 are the only examples I have found.
35 The order for the delivery of wardships can be found in *CPR 1292 – 1301*, 326, 440. The wards, marriages, fines, farms and widows that Edmund actually received are listed in the account by his executors to the Exchequer: E 101/506/6, 7, 8. (Nos. 6 and 7 are drafts of the audit, and no. 8 is a clean copy listing lands and fines in the same order.) Additional information about the grants to Edmund is in E 372/149 m.37d; E 159/71 m.66.
36 E 372/149 mm.27 – 27d, 29; *CPR 1301 – 07*, 463.

to pay back. Their account, moreover, underscores just how valuable the king's feudal lordship could be. The wardships accumulated in a single year or so produced nearly 12,000 *m.* over five years, and, after the audit, the executors had to restore several wards that were still in their custody. Indeed, Edmund probably received even more from the wardships, since the Exchequer calculated the repayment from the values given in the inquisitions post mortem rather than on the actual receipts.

In the final years of Edward's reign, escheators frequently handed their receipts directly to the Wardrobe or its creditors. The tone of the writs to escheators becomes more urgent as the government struggled to pay for the war with Scotland.[37] Creditors, armed with Wardrobe debentures, applied to the escheators for payment. Walter of Gloucester himself sent four squires to Scotland at royal pay, which, with the cost of horses, amounted to £63 20d., for which he received a Wardrobe debenture.[38]

The measures taken in the years after 1296 confirm Dr. Prestwich's picture of a government besieged by the costs of its own policies. They provide an indication of how pervasive Wardrobe financing had become and the degree to which it influenced the operation of offices outside the household. More generally, Edward's use of royal wardships also demonstrates an important characteristic of thirteenth-century government. Contrary to the modern, statist assumptions cited at the outset of this piece, the king was not interested *solely* in maximizing his cash receipts from feudal sources. Edward certainly did that in the later years of his reign, but it is also clear that he prized the adaptability of royal lordship which allowed him to adjust his use of these resources according to changes in policy. Even at the end of the reign, when the bulk of the wardships went to creditors like Edmund of Cornwall, Edward still distributed some as rewards to those who had served him in Scotland, Flanders or Gascony.[39] At the end of the thirteenth century, in other words, royal wardship remained the personal prerogative of the king, responsive to his will and needs.[40]

[37] E 153/5/4 – 17, 23 – 6; E 136/249/1.

[38] E 136/249/1 no. 6.

[39] *CPR 1292 – 1301*, 257, 336; *CPR 1301 – 07*, 247, 257, 500.

[40] Research for this article was made possible by a grant from the American Philosophical Society.

The Gold Treasure of King Henry III

D. A. Carpenter

English medieval kings frequently strove to build up reserves of treasure. King Henry I, for example, in the words of the Anglo-Saxon chronicle, 'gathered a great amount of treasure — gold and silver — and no good to his soul was done with it'. The reasons for coveting a treasure are obvious. It gave the means to hire soldiers, buy support and meet emergencies, both foreign and domestic. Much of King Stephen's success, in the first years of his reign, was due to the possession of Henry's treasure. Once it was spent, his troubles began.[1]

The question of whether, in the years of his personal rule, King Henry III accumulated a financial reserve, has received little attention. In general, historians seem agreed that he lacked the necessary discipline and foresight.[2] But in fact, as this paper will show, between 1243 and 1258 Henry worked with success to build up a store of treasure. That treasure, for reasons which we will investigate, was in gold. By the 1250s, collection of gold had become central to the king's financial activities. The whole process throws new light on Henry's projected crusade, the Sicilian enterprise, the gold coinage of 1257, the Crown's financial predicament before the crisis of 1258, and, more generally, on the king's ability to save and live within his means in the period after 1237, when parliament denied him extraordinary taxation on moveable property. Henry's treasure is also relevant to a consideration of what has been called the 'European gold famine'. This meant that until the thirteenth century the currencies of Western Europe were in silver, whilst those of the East, where there was a dearth of silver, were largely in gold. During the course of the thirteenth century the situation was reversed. Whilst the East began to mint silver coinages, probably with silver coming from the West, gold, probably released by the East, moved westwards. The result was seen in western gold coinages. In 1232 came Frederick II's augustales. Twenty years later both Florence and Genoa minted successful gold currencies, and

> touched off 'one of the greatest chain reactions in monetary history'. This was to end with the victory of gold in almost every

[1] *EHD*, ii.199; J. O. Prestwich, 'War and Finance in the Anglo-Norman State', *TRHS*, 5th ser., iv (1954), 39–41.

[2] Sir J. H. Ramsay, *A History of the Revenues of the Kings of England* (Oxford, 1925), i.262–365, see p. 359; idem, *The Dawn of the Constitution* (Oxford, 1908), 298; F. M. Powicke, *King Henry III and The Lord Edward* (Oxford, 1947), i.303–5; S. K. Mitchell, *Studies in Taxation under John and Henry III* (New Haven, 1914), 345; R. F. Treharne, *The Baronial Plan of Reform* (Manchester, 1932), 49–51.

part of Europe by the middle of the fourteenth century.[3]

Was Henry III's ability to collect gold, and his gold coinage, testimony to the waning of the gold famine in England?

In uncovering Henry's gold treasure two major sources have been utilised, the first being the accounts of the king's Wardrobe enrolled on the Pipe Rolls. Henry's gold was largely collected in the Wardrobe, and its steady accumulation is revealed by the section of the accounts which detailed the amounts of gold, silver plate and jewels coming each year into the Wardrobe. These accounts are not in print, and have been little used by historians; this is why the existence of Henry's gold treasure has hitherto been unknown. The second major source is the Fine Rolls. A considerable part of Henry's gold came in the form of fines which individuals and institutions made with the king for favours and concessions. From September 1251 onwards these were recorded on the Fine Rolls and thus we can see from whom Henry's treasure was obtained.

The story of Henry III's gold treasure begins on his return from Gascony in September 1243. Before that, the Wardrobe only acquired gold to fund the king's pious oblations.[4] Thereafter, Henry saved two separate gold treasures. The first, accumulated between 1243 and 1253, was spent financing the 1253 – 4 Gascon campaign. The second, gathered between the king's return to England at the end of 1254 and the political revolution of 1258, was largely sold in France in 1259 – 60 and in London in 1261. We will look at the two treasures in turn.

I

Between 1241 and his death in 1254, the whole period covered by the first gold treasure, the keeper of the Wardrobe was Peter Chaceporc. The appendix, on pp. 83 – 8, is based upon his annual Wardrobe accounts, and upon the special account which he rendered in June 1253 for all the gold which he had collected since 1242 – 3. The table shows the amount of gold received by the Wardrobe in each regnal year, the amount of that gold expended during the year, and the amount remaining at the end of it. Chaceporc's accounts for these 'remains' in June 1253 show that they were all kept. Together, they formed the whole of the Wardrobe gold treasure which, in June 1253, prior to the king's departure for Gascony, Chaceporc delivered to the treasurer and chamberlains of the Exchequer for deposit in the king's Treasury at Westminster.

According to the figure given in the accounts, the total amount of gold collected in the Wardrobe by 30 May 1253 was 2110 *mg.* 4*sg.*; that is, as we will

[3] A. M. Watson, 'Back to Gold — and Silver', *EcHR*, 2nd ser., xx (1967), 7. The quotation is from R. S. Lopez, 'Back to Gold, 1252', *EcHR*, 2nd ser., ix (1956 – 7), 219.

[4] For the Wardrobe accounts prior to 1242 – 3, see E 372/79, m.21d; E 372/81, m.28; E 372/83, m.13. The numerous references to the acquisition of gold in the Liberate and Close Rolls before 1242 – 3 are concerned with the king's oblations. All manuscript references in this paper are to documents in the PRO.

see, the weight in pure gold of 2110 *m.* 4*s.* of silver.[5] There are grounds for thinking, however, that by June 1253 Henry's treasure was considerably larger than the 2110 *mg.* collected in the Wardrobe. In June 1254, in Gascony, the king received 1632 *mg.* 5 *dg.* of treasure sent from England.[6] Before that, in return for loans in July 1253 and March 1254 of respectively 6000 *m.* and 4000 *m.*, 1207½ *mg.* had been pledged to Richard, earl of Cornwall. Since these loans were never repaid, this 1207½ *mg.* must have been separate from the money sent to Gascony. Although the king did not formally ratify the delivery of the gold to Richard until November 1256, from the start it had been placed in the latter's keeping.[7] If, then, we add together the sum sent to Gascony and the sum given to Richard, it makes the total gold treasure of 2839 *mg.* 7 *sg.* 1 *dg.* Since there is no evidence that gold was stored after 30 May 1253, all this was probably collected before that date.[8] The likelihood is that the 729 *mg.* 3 *sg.* 1 *dg.*, over and above the 2110 *mg.* 4 *sg.* of Chaceporc's Wardrobe treasure, came from a fund which the king had built up outside the Wardrobe. At 2839 *mg.*, Henry's gold weighed around 650 *kg.*, a little under two-thirds of a tonne, the equal of some 51 of the 28 lb. (avoirdupois) bars in which gold is currently stored in the vaults of the Bank of England. In terms of value, as we will see later, the treasure was the rough equivalent of some 28,390 *m.* of silver.

But at this point the reader may be sceptical. Did Henry's gold really exist or was gold perhaps a mere term of account? Anxieties on this score can be removed: there is no doubt that Henry's gold *was* gold. In Chaceporc's accounts the different forms in which the gold was received were often expressed. It was both in leaf, ingots and dust, (*in folio, cunio et palliola*),[9] and in various types of money: Byzantine bezants, a few of Frederick II's augustales and *oboli* and *denarii* of musc, the latter being the dinars and double-dinars of the Almohade dynasty in Spain and North Africa (1130 – 1269).[10] Admittedly, in some years (1242 – 3, 1244 – 5, 1246 – 51) gold in money was distinguished from gold said simply to be in so many marks, but

[5] The total is given in *CLR 1251 – 60*, 134, and see *CR 1251 – 3*, 386. Throughout this paper *mg.* = marks of gold, *sg.* = shillings of gold, and *dg.* = pennies of gold.

[6] Francisque-Michel, *Rôles Gascons* (Paris, 1885), i. no. 3874; *CPR 1247 – 58*, 314.

[7] *CPR 1247 – 58*, 236, 364, 373, 528; C 66/71, m.17; *CLR 1251 – 60*, 147; N. Denholm-Young, *Richard of Cornwall* (Oxford, 1947), 159.

[8] The Fine Rolls show that gold was still being received into the Wardrobe after 30 May. By the king's delayed departure in August, it amounted to some 61½ *mg.* 248 bezants; see C 60/50, m.8 onwards. Probably this gold was taken with the king to Gascony. (There are no Wardrobe accounts for the period 30 May 1253 – 10 Jan. 1255.) After the king's departure, fines of gold virtually disappear from the Fine Rolls kept by the government in England, August 1253 – Dec. 1254; C 60/50, mm.3 – 1; C 60/51; C 60/52, mm.13, 12.

[9] *Aurum in palliola* is variously translated as gold dust, gold in spangles, and gold in ingots and satchels; for it see Lopez, 227.

[10] For the bezant, which may be identified with the hyperpyron of the Byzantine empire or with the hyperpyron of the Byzantine successor state at Nicaea, see P. Grierson, *Byzantine Coins* (London, 1982), 10 – 12, 215, 239 – 41. (Mr Grierson has kindly helped me with questions concerning the bezant.) For money of musc, see P. Grierson, '*Oboli de Musc*', *EHR*, lxvi (1951), 75 – 81; idem, 'Muslim coins in thirteenth century England', in *Near Eastern Numismatics. Studies in Honor of G. S. Miles*, ed. D. K. Kouymjian (Beirut, 1974), 387 – 91. Both papers are reprinted in P. Grierson, *Later Medieval Numismatics* (London, 1979). The king can be found buying bezants at between 22d. and 26d. each, and *oboli* of musc at between 14d. and 16d. each; see *CLR 1226 – 40*, 255, 478; *CLR 1240 – 50*, 113 – 14. See also below, n. 112.

the accounts for 1243 – 4, 1245 – 6 and 1251 – 3 suggest the latter was made up of gold in leaf, or in leaf, ingots and dust.

How much then was Henry's treasure worth? It is clear that in both Chaceporc's accounts and the Fine Rolls, gold described as being of so many marks, shillings or pennies was pure gold to the weight of that number of marks, shillings or pence in silver.[11] When the king received gold which was impure a compensation was made for the degree of debasement. Thus, in Chaceporc's accounts 62 bezants were said to 'make' 1 *mg.*[12] If that was a calculation simply by weight then the bezant weighed 3.71 gm.[13] In fact, it weighed 4.5 gm., but because the bezant was a debased coin it took more than a mark's weight of bezants to make up a mark of pure gold.[14] Since, then, Henry's treasure was expressed in terms of pure gold, we can make a rough estimate of its value.[15] Although occasionally it did a little better, the most usual rate at which silver bought pure gold in this period was 10:1, that is 10 *m.* of silver bought 1 *mg.*[16] This ratio between gold and silver was also employed by the king when he priced fines in gold, when he received silver in place of gold which was owed him and when he fixed the value of his gold coinage in 1257.[17] This did not mean, of course, that Henry would necessarily find anyone to buy his gold at 10:1 if he suddenly wished to turn a large part of it back into silver, but if we take that ratio as a rough rule of thumb, then the Wardrobe treasure was the equivalent of some 21,110 *m.* of silver, and the treasure as a whole some 28,390 *m.* of silver.

Where did Henry's first gold treasure come from? Why did the King collect it? And what light does it throw on his financial situation?

It seems highly probably that initial contributions to the treasure — to the 65 *mg.*, whose source is not indicated, and the 198 *mg. de donis, finibus et perquisitis* saved in the years 1242 – 3 and 1243 – 4 — came from welcome-home presents to the king on his return from Gascony in September 1243. Both Matthew Paris and the Dunstable annalist refer to these.[18] Since the regnal year ended on 27 October, such gifts could have got into the accounts for both 1242 – 3 and 1243 – 4. Also important were gifts and fines from the Jews: the Jews had always been a source of gold for the king.[19] But a heading of

[11] In the Fine Rolls, when a fine in *mg.* was paid underweight, it was said to be underweight by so many (silver) pennies; C 60/49, m.3; C 60/54, m.5.

[12] See below, n. 112.

[13] I make this and other calculations on the basis that the mark used in London was 230 grammes, though it may have been a little more; see Grierson, '*Oboli de Musc*', 78.

[14] See Grierson, *Byzantine Coins*, 215, 241. It is equally clear that when in the accounts (see below, n. 112) 14 augustales were said to 'weigh' 3s. 6d. that was the weight of their gold content, not their gross weight.

[15] I assume that in the years, in Chaceporc's accounts, where totals were given in so many marks of leaf and money, a conversion into pure gold in respect, where necessary, of the money, has already taken place.

[16] For evidence of silver buying gold, including gold in *oboli* and *denarii* of musc, *aurum combustum* and gold in leaf at 10:1, see *CLR 1226 – 40*, 478; *CLR 1240 – 5*, 121; *CR 1247 – 51*, 418; *CR 1254 – 6*, 46, 76; C 60/52, m.11; and see *Cronica Maiorum et Vicecomitum Londoniarum*, ed. T. S. Stapleton (Camden Soc., old ser., 1846), 29 – 30, and below n. 36. For gold being bought a little cheaper, see *CLR 1240 – 5*, 273 – 4; and below, 73. Money of musc was certainly pure gold or nearly so; Lopez, 225 – 7; Grierson, '*Oboli of Musc*', 75 – 81.

[17] *CR 1242 – 7*, 219, and see below, 77 – 8.

[18] *Ann. Mon.*, iii. 162; *Paris*, iv. 255, 260.

[19] See, eg., *Ann. Mon.*, iii. 66.

Matthew Paris, 'not a little gold extorted from the Jews', suggests that it was now being demanded from them on a new scale. The king was also, of course, keeping what he obtained. Paris adds that although the king allowed silver from the Jews to be collected on his behalf by others, he received the gold 'with his own hand', a clear indication that it came into the Wardrobe.[20]

After 1243 – 4, it will be seen that the rate of gold accumulation drops sharply for two years before beginning a steady ascent until, at 180 *mg.* in 1249 – 50, it is not far below the 1243 – 4 level. There is scattered evidence that much of this gold was still coming from Jewish gifts, fines and tallages.[21] In September 1249 the king was also employing a policy, which he was to develop more fully a little later, of using silver to buy gold; 380 *m.* of a Jewish tallage were set aside for that purpose.[22] It may also be that numbers of ecclesiastics and laymen were making fines of gold with the king. If these were paid cash down into the Wardrobe they would not need to appear on the Fine Rolls, whose chief purpose was to provide the basis for the Originalia Rolls which informed the Exchequer of money owed to the king.

Turning next to the period between 1250 – 1 and the end of May 1253, it will be seen that there was a sharp increase in the gold saved by the Wardrobe. Whereas 725 *mg.* were added to the treasure in the eight years between 1242 – 3 and 1249 – 50, the following two years and seven months, down to the end of May 1253, saw the collection of 1382 *mg.*

In 1250 – 1 itself some 434 *mg.* were added to the Wardrobe treasure. Of this, the 123 *mg.* 14 *dg.*, 339 bezants, 32 *denarii* and 13 *oboli* of musc *de donis, finibus et perquisitis*, probably came, as before, from the Jews and from unrecorded fines of ecclesiastics and laymen. The other major item in this year was the 288 *mg.* 3 *sg.* 4½ *dg.* 'bought with money received from the Treasury'. We know that 1299 *m.* 4s. 8d. of this money, which bought gold at almost exactly 10:1, stemmed from a royal order of January 1250 assigning to two Jews various issues from the Exchequer of the Jews to purchase gold 'as the king enjoined them'.[23]

After 1250 – 1 the Wardrobe accounts indicate no further subventions from gold bought with money 'from the Treasury'. This does not mean that the king had given up using silver to buy gold. Rather, the gold thus purchased made up the 729 *mg.* which, we have suggested, were collected outside the Wardrobe.[24] As for the Wardrobe treasure, Chaceporc's accounts show that the large sums — the 447 *mg.* of 1251 – 2 and the 501 *mg.* of the seven months of 1252 – 3 —

20 *Paris*, iv. 260; *CR 1242 – 7*, 130, 135, 156; and note the 12 augustales in the Wardrobe in 1243 – 4 of the gift of Aaron of York.

21 Eg., *CR 1242 – 7*, 307, 317, 371; *CR 1247 – 51*, 249, 316; *CLR 1245 – 51*, 272; C 60/41, m.5; C 60/43 m.15; C 60/46, m.10.

22 C 60/46, m.3. I have assumed that the new tallage, as well as the old, was to be used to buy gold although the wording is not quite precise on this point. For earlier purchased gold, see *CR 1242 – 7*, 277.

23 *CR 1247 – 51*, 255 – 6, 418; *CLR 1245 – 51*, 338. For other orders between Oct. 1250 and July 1251 assigning money from the Jews for the purchase of gold, see *CR 1247 – 51*, 339, 374, 387, 425, 434, 473, and below, 72.

24 For purchased gold which probably went to the treasure outside the Wardrobe, see *CLR 1251 – 60*, 48, 63; *CR 1251 – 3*, 70. After 1250 – 1, the only 'bought gold' contributing to the Wardrobe treasure came from fines in silver being used to buy gold. Between 28 Oct. 1251 and 30 May 1253, the Fine Rolls show some 306 *m.* earmarked in this way, nearly all from fines for quittance of jury service or for charters granting free warrens, markets and fairs.

came chiefly from fines of gold paid directly into the Wardrobe. In order to inform the Exchequer about the treasure, these fines now appeared on the Fine and Originalia Rolls.[25] They were still paid very quickly, either cash down or at least before the despatch of the Originalia Rolls where the payment into the Wardrobe was already noted.[26] Many of these fines were for the purchase of liberties. Chaceporc's accounts show that, between 18 February 1251 and 30 May 1253, 231 *mg.* 8 *sg.* 5½ *dg.* in leaf and money came from diverse people buying warrens, markets, fairs, respite of knighthood, 'writs' and 'other liberties'. The cost of a charter granting a free warren, or a market and fair, varied between ½ *mg.* and 2 *mg.*, with 1 *mg.* being the most common sum. The Fine Rolls show that, between 28 October 1251 and 30 May 1253, around 116 *mg.* 279 bezants came from 123 fines for warrens, markets and fairs, 25 being made by ecclesiastics, 97 by laymen and one by a town.[27] Chaceporc's headings of 'other liberties' and 'writs' probably included fines for exemption from jury service. The usual price for this liberty, frequently linked with exemption from office holding, was ½ *mg.* or 1 *mg.* Between 28 October 1251 and 30 May 1253, 115 of these fines brought in around 59 *mg.* 355 bezants and 10 talents. Much less lucrative were the 36 fines for respite of knighthood which produced, in the same period, around 3 *mg.* 4 *sg.* 3 *dg.*, 240 bezants, 20 *oboli* of musc and 12 talents.[28]

Kings had, of course, long made concessions of these kinds. Two things now were new. In the first place, Henry III was mounting a deliberate selling campaign. Matthew Paris commented, in 1252, that the king

> caused it to be openly proclaimed in public places, namely markets, that those who wished to have warrens should speak to him, and, money having been given, they would be benignly heard.

This, Paris adds, 'many did'.[29] Probably, even before 1252, the king had encouraged people to come forward for such grants, since their number had been increasing before that year, as Table I indicates. (There was no similar increase in the grants of markets and fairs.) It is probable that the king adopted a similar policy of proclamation and encouragement in respect of grants of quittance of jury service. There were 14 of these on the Patent Rolls in 1249–50 and 121 in 1251–2.[30]

In the second place, of course, Henry increasingly insisted that these concessions should be paid for in gold. The insistence was not absolute. As Table I makes plain, considerable numbers of charters for free warrens, markets and

25 The relevant Fine Rolls are C 60/49 (1251–2), and C 60/50 (1252–3). Excerpts from them (containing some fines of gold) are in *Excerpta e Rotulis Finium 1216–72*, ed. C. Roberts (London, 1835–6), ii. 120–74.

26 The Originalia Rolls corresponding to C 60/49 and C 60/50 are E 371/17 and E 371/18.

27 These, and subsequent figures, are based on all the fines made between 28 Oct. 1251–30 May 1253 and stated to have been paid, provided that the payment was not attermed to a date outside the time span covered by the table. In fact nearly all this money would have come in after 17 Feb. 1252, for which division see below, n. 112.

28 For exemptions and respites in Henry III's reign, see S. L. Waugh, 'Reluctant Knights and Jurors: Respites, Exemptions, and Public Obligations in the Reign of Henry III', *Speculum*, lviii (1983), 937–86.

29 *Paris*, v. 356.

30 *CPR 1247–58*, 117–55.

Table I

Regnal Year	A No. of charters granting free warrens in Charter Rolls	B No. of charters granting markets and fairs in Charter Rolls[31]	No. of A & B paid for in gold on Fine Rolls	No. of A & B paid for in silver on Fine Rolls
1247 – 8	27	11	–	14
1248 – 9	17	14	–	3
1250 – 1	52	18	3	33
1251 – 2	76	22	50	15
1251 – 30 May 1253	86	16	73	1

fairs have no corresponding entry on the Fine Rolls. Gold may have been given for some of these grants, but others perhaps were paid for in silver or conceded free. But of the fines on the Fine Rolls, the great majority were made in gold. The same is true of the letters conceding exemptions from jury service and office holding. In 1251 – 2, against the 40 fines in gold for this favour, there were 14 in silver. Next year, down to 30 May, there were 65 fines in gold and none in silver.

It was not, however, only fines for free warrens, exemptions and so forth that Henry was receiving in gold. He also required large numbers of miscellaneous fines, including some for further diverse liberties, to be paid in that medium. Between 28 October 1251 and 30 May 1253 there were, for example, 22 fines made by monastic houses and cathedral chapters for confirmation of their liberties, bringing in over 70 *mg*. Towns, too, gave gold for the confirmation of old liberties or for the concession of new; 10 *mg*., for example, came from the burgesses of Scarborough. Towns also paid for quittance of tallage, 20 *mg*. being given by the Londoners for this, an exaction noted by Matthew Paris.[32] In addition, up to 31 *mg*. were paid by 10 sheriffs for the pardon of various misdemeanours. Other kinds of concessions paid for in gold included pardons of homicide, and judicial favours such as the promise of speedy judgments, the appointment of particular judges, and the moving of cases to the court *coram rege*.[33] The gold from all these sources, together with around 65 *mg*. oz 165 *mg*., 395 bezants, 66 *oboli* of musc, and 26 talents from Jewish fines, contributed to the 568½ *mg*. 2 *sd*. 11½ *dg*. placed in Chaceporc's accounts under the heading 'fines' (at last separated from 'gifts and things acquired') between 18 February 1252 and 20 May 1253.[34]

[31] *CChR 1226 – 57*, 327 – 434. I have included in column A the few charters which conceded free warrens *and* markets and fairs.

[32] *Paris*, v. 333.

[33] The excerpts from the Fine Rolls give some impression of these miscellaneous fines. See *Excerpta Rot. Fin.*, ii. 124 – 67.

[34] In these years two fines of 50 *mg*., from the community of the Jews, are not specifically stated as paid. The money from the liberties mentioned in this paragraph is too large to be included under Chaceporc's heading (1251 – 2) 'other liberties' and must therefore have been included under 'fines'.

Although we cannot be certain, it seems that the actual price charged in gold for concessions was the same as what the price would have been in silver, allowing for a conversion ratio of 10:1. Thus Peter de Roffa, having originally fined in 5 *m.* of silver for respite of knighthood, ultimately paid ½ *mg.* instead.[35] We will suggest later that most people, fining in gold with the king, bought the necessary gold from goldsmiths. That may have been a nuisance, but since there is evidence that even small amounts of gold could be bought on the 10:1 ratio in the 1250s, there was no direct financial loss involved in paying fines to the king in that metal.[36] If there had been, one may doubt whether Henry could have sold liberties on the scale that he did.

In general, therefore, the expansion of the treasure after 1249 – 50 was achieved by the king using silver to buy gold and by him receiving gold in return for the concession of liberties and other miscellaneous favours. The gold in the Fine Rolls came from four main sources: the Jews, ecclesiastics and ecclesiastical institutions, towns, and laymen. Between 28 October 1251 and 30 May 1253 the division was as follows in Table II.

Table II

28 October 1251 to 30 May 1253	Gold paid into the Wardrobe according to the Fine Rolls	
	Amount	No. of fines
Jews	65 *mg.*, 395 bezants, 66 *oboli* of musc, 26 talents and perhaps 100 *mg.*	72
Ecclesiastical	160½ *mg.* 252 bezants	82
Towns	93 *mg.*	25
Laymen	292 *mg.* 1125 bezants, 20 *oboli* of musc, 22 talents[37]	370

Why, then, was this treasure collected, or, more exactly, why was it collected in gold? The only direct comment on this by a contemporary was made by Matthew Paris. Writing of the Christmas festivities of 1250, Matthew declared that Henry III reduced their scale in order to save money for his forthcoming crusade. Paris then added that

> since the king knew that he was to go to the eastern parts where gold is used as money and reward for stipendiaries serving on an

[35] C 60/49, m.21. In Oct. 1256 and Jan. 1257, when there is evidence for some fines of gold being paid in silver, they were paid on the basis of a 10:1 conversion ratio. See C 47/3/7/48; C 47/3/5/14 (for the payments). Compare the fines themselves in C 60/53 and C 60/54.

[36] C 60/49, m.4, Edward of Westminster: 1 *mg.*, though see also m.3; C 60/52, m.11, Gregory le Paumer: 2 *mg.* in leaf etc; *CR 1254 – 6*, 76; the 100*s* in Chaceporc's accounts for 1252 – 3; and see *Cronica Maiorum et Vicecomitum*, 29 – 30.

[37] The amount of gold produced by the fines on the Fine Rolls was considerably less than that indicated as coming from fines in Chaceporc's accounts. Probably some fines were still escaping inclusion on the Fine Rolls.

> expedition, he began to desire to collect gold. . . . Hence those who wished to expedite business at the king's court gave the king gold rather than silver.[38]

Paris's statement reflects exactly the way gold replaced silver in the fines made with the king. The link he makes between gold collection and Henry's crusade receives confirmation from the terms of the king's will made in 1253, before his expedition to Gascony. Here, Henry left all his gold, by now, as we have seen, a considerable sum — 'in subsidium Terrae Sanctae.' It was to be borne there, with the king's Cross, by men chosen by the queen and his executors.[39] Henry III had formally taken the Cross in March 1250. The probability, therefore, is that the great expansion in the gold treasure, seen in Chaceporc's accounts after 1248 – 9, is related to the king's projected crusade. What Henry was doing was exactly what Watson speculates that crusaders did. 'It seems likely', he writes, 'that the crusaders tried to take with them as much *gold* as they could secure, since gold was the basis of all currencies in the Arab East'.[40]

One might wonder, however, whether this policy was still valid in the thirteenth century, when silver coinages were common in the East, and when the banking operations of the Templars and Italians were both reducing the need to transport large sums of specie and facilitating exchange between gold and silver.[41] Yet there are indications that in planning to take gold to the East, Henry was doing nothing unusual. Evidence for the composition of the treasure which accompanied Louis IX on his crusade in 1248 appears wanting.[42] But in 1250, according to Matthew Paris, a great amount of money was sent from France to Louis at Damietta. It consisted of 'gold and silver, namely talents, sterling and approved money of Cologne, and not unsatisfactory money, namely money of Paris and of Tours'.[43] As far as the gold was concerned, this statement cannot be dismissed as a combination of prejudice and hyperbole. An account roll from the same year, 1250, shows that gold worth 1684 pounds 12s. 6d. Tours, together with silver worth 9719 pounds 12s. 11d. Tours was sent *ultra mare* to the crusading Alphonse of Poitiers.[44]

Many contemporaries doubted Henry III's sincerity as a crusader, and some later historians have echoed their scepticism. The story of Henry's gold

[38] *Matthaei Parisiensis Historia Anglorum*, ed. F. Madden (*RS*, 1866 – 9), iii. 99, 320; see also, *Paris*, v. 274.

[39] *Foedera*, I, i. 496, where the will is misdated 1272. The significance of the will in this context was pointed out to me by Dr S. D. Lloyd.

[40] Watson, 7.

[41] Watson, 5 – 6; D. M. Metcalf, 'The Templars as bankers and monetary transfers between West and East in the twelfth century', in *Coinage in the Latin East. The Fourth Oxford Symposium on Coinage and Monetary History*, ed. P. W. Edbury, D. M. Metcalf (BAR International Ser., lxxvii, 1980), 1 – 17. I am grateful to Dr Edbury for discussing with me points arising from this volume. A. Sayous, 'Les mandats de Saint Louis sur son trésor', *Révue Historique*, clxvii (1931), 254 – 304.

[42] Sayous, 'Les mandats de Saint Louis', 262 – 5; see also W. C. Jordan, *Louis IX and the Challenge of the Crusade* (Princeton, 1979), 99 – 100, and ch. 4 as a whole.

[43] *Paris*, v. 116 – 17; Jordan, 99 – 100.

[44] *Layette du Trésor des Chartes*, III, ed. J. de Laborde (Paris, 1875), no. 3911; E. Cartier, 'Or et argent, monnoyés ou non monnoyés, envoyés en Palestine à Alfonse, Comte de Poitiers', *Revue numismatique*, xii (1847), 121 – 50.

treasure proves that the king's commitment was genuine.[45] Indeed, Henry was extremely reluctant to divert his treasure from the Holy Land to finance the unwelcome Gascon expedition of 1253. As we have seen, the treasure was not taken initially to Gascony. Instead, it was deposited in the Treasury and, if used, used at first only as a pledge for a loan from Richard of Cornwall. Plainly the king hoped to keep the treasure intact for his return. If he did not return, his gold and his Cross were to be taken to the Holy Land by others.

The gold treasure after March 1250, therefore, was related to the crusade. But how does one explain the smaller but nonetheless significant amount of gold amassed before that date? There seems little doubt that this treasure was deliberately collected. Between 1234 and 1242 virtually no gold had come into the Wardrobe in the form of gifts and fines. The flow of gifts and fines in gold thereafter must have been at royal instigation.[46] Equally, there can be little doubt that the gold the king received, he wished to retain. Year after year, as we have seen, the 'remains' were husbanded in the Wardrobe. When Henry was short of money in 1245 and 1247, instead of selling his gold, he pledged it to Richard of Cornwall for loans of 2000 *m.*[47] In 1248, when he needed money to finance Simon de Montfort in Gascony, he sold his silver plate rather than his gold.[48]

One reason for this early collection of gold can be ruled out. It had nothing to do with the king's oblations. Gold *de donis, finibus et perquisitis* was not used for these. Instead, the king's 'oblation gold', the bulk of it *oboli* of musc, was separately acquired and accounted for by Chaceporc. The only year in which the accounts were intermingled was 1243–4 and, even here, a separation was made between the *oboli* of musc *de donis* etc., which were all kept, and the *oboli* purchased and used for the king's oblations. What is a possibility, however, is that the beginning of the treasure had something to do with the new feretory of Edward the Confessor. Henry had begun this 'from purest gold' in 1241. Between 1243–4 and 1249–50, almost the only occasions on which gold *de donis* etc. was not stored was when it was given to the feretory.[49] Conceivably therefore, Henry, on his return from Gascony in September 1243, thought enthusiastically of the new feretory and declared that he would like gold for it. In the event, however, the king achieved a vast overshoot. More gold was quickly acquired than could actually be used on the feretory, which perhaps explains the sharp drop in the rate of collection in the years 1244–6. In all, between 1243–4 and 1248–9, while 32 *mg. de donis, finibus et perquisitis* were given to the feretory, 480 *mg.* were stored.[50] This gold, moreover, was not stored for use on the feretory at some future date for, in Henry's will

[45] For the fullest discussion of Henry's crusading vows, which likewise concludes that the crusade was seriously meant, see A. J. Forey, 'The Crusading Vows of the English King Henry III', *Durham University Journ.*, lxv (1973), 229–47.

[46] See *CR 1242–7*, 124.

[47] *CPR 1232–47*, 456; *CLR 1245–51*, 105. I assume that these were two separate loans of 2000 *m.*

[48] E 372/95, mm.12,13; *Paris*, v. 21–2.

[49] *Paris*, iv. 156–7; H. M. Colvin *et al.*, *The History of the King's Works* (London, 1963), i. 147. The only other substantial expenditure was 7 *mg.* used for two images in 1243–4. It is difficult, however, to distinguish gold offerings to the existing feretory (as perhaps in 1242–3) from gold for work on the new one.

[50] It is not suggested, however, that the gold indicated in Chaceporc's accounts was the total going to the feretory in these years.

of 1253, 500 *m.* of silver were thought sufficient to complete the work.[51] The feretory of St. Edward, therefore, may have provided the initial impetus behind the acquisition of gold, but it can scarcely explain why the king continued to save gold on the scale he did.

Perhaps Henry simply wished to have treasure in gold, the most prestigious of metals. We have seen that Henry I's treasure was both in gold and silver, and in 1216 King John probably held 60 *mg.* in Devizes castle.[52] But Henry III may also have had a more tangible purpose, that of helping the crusading cause in the East. His brother, Richard of Cornwall, had gone to the Holy Land in 1241. Louis IX assumed the Cross in December 1244. In the next year, according to Matthew Paris, Henry, explaining the parlous state of his kingdom surrounded by enemies, refused to allow the crusade to be preached in England.[53] But by 1247, although not taking the Cross himself, Henry accepted that there should be an English crusade and tried to secure his half-brother, Guy de Lusignan, as its leader.[54] Perhaps the steady rise in the gold treasure from the year 1246–7 onwards should be seen against this background. Henry was trying to build up funds to support the projected English expedition.

What light, then, does the gold treasure throw on the king's financial situation? The first point to establish is whether gold formed Henry's only treasure. There can be little doubt that it did, at least by 1249–50. By that date there is no evidence that the king either possessed or was accumulating a reserve of silver. Certainly he had none in 1253 when the Gascon expedition was funded by a 6000 *m.* loan from Richard of Cornwall (on the security of 700 *mg.*), a 5000 *m.* subvention from the Jews, and the timely arrival of 7750 *m.* of treasure from Ireland. The 13,060 *m.* which followed in October 1253 were probably the issues of the Michaelmas Exchequer.[55] Of course, the king always hoped that a parliamentary aid might transform his situation; and in April 1250, having taken the Cross, he was granted by the pope a tenth of ecclesiastical revenues for three years. The prospect of this ecclesiastical taxation, however, did not diminish the king's efforts to construct a gold treasure from his own ordinary resources. Henry was able to do this, moreover, without the burden of old debts. In 1250, the king, according to Matthew Paris, 'prudently freed himself from the debts which he owed many merchants', a process which is confirmed by the Liberate Rolls.[56] Thereafter, until the king's departure for Gascony, royal letters were free from the complaints of debt and shortage of money so characteristic of other periods of the reign. After October 1249, therefore, Henry's collection of gold provides an accurate reflection of the surplus revenue which the king could generate without help from extraordinary taxation.

The results which Henry III achieved in these circumstances were respectable. Between 28 October 1249 and 30 May 1253, if we use the 10:1 ratio between gold and silver as a rough guide, the equivalent of 15,620 *m.* of silver

[51] *Foedera*, I, i. 496.

[52] *RLC*, i. 602. For Henry I's gold, see also W. T. Reedy Jr, 'The Origins of the General Eyre in the Reign of Henry I', *Speculum*, xli (1966), 723–4; J. A. Green, '"Praeclarum et Magnificum Antiquitatis Monumentum": The Earliest Surviving Pipe Roll', *BIHR*, lv (1982), 14 and n. 71.

[53] *Paris*, iv. 488–9.

[54] *Les Registres d'Innocent IV*, ed. E. Berger (Paris, 1884), i. no. 4054.

[55] *CPR 1247–58*, 236, 216, 220; *CLR 1251–60*, 147, 150; *CR 1251–3*, 386.

[56] *Paris*, v. 114; *CLR 1245–51*, 279–80, 286, 307–8, 315–21.

were saved in the Wardrobe, a yearly average of 4363 *m*. If we take merely the two years seven months between 28 October 1250 and 30 May 1253, the yearly average rises to 5356 *m*. This, moreover, was only the Wardrobe treasure. If we accept that between 28 October 1249 and the end of May 1253 a further 729 *m*. of pure gold were saved outside the Wardrobe, then the annual rate of collection becomes equal to some 6399 *m*. To save on this scale Henry, according to Matthew Paris, reduced his household expenses in 1250.[57] But he still had money for Westminster Abbey on which 3000 *m*. annually were probably spent after 1245.[58] Had Henry continued to save at the rate of 6399 *m*. a year until June 1256, his projected date of departure, he would have had gold equalling some 47,587 *m*. of silver to take with him to the Holy Land. The gold treasure would, then, have made a contribution to the crusade at least as large as the ecclesiastical taxation granted by the pope, which was expected to raise some 45,900 *m*.[59] Even the sum achieved by May 1253, if the equivalent of 28,390 *m*., was only a little short of the 30,000 *m*. which Henry II is said to have assembled in the Holy Land for his own projected crusade.[60] As it was, the fact that Henry III had 2839 *mg*. to help fund his Gascon expedition in 1253 – 4 goes some way to explaining its relative success.

Powicke, therefore, was correct when he surmised that Henry III's underlying financial situation was sound.[61] Where he and other historians were wrong was in supposing that the king lacked the necessary discipline to take advantage of this. In fact, over some 10 years Henry displayed remarkable self-control in refusing to break into his gold treasure. In 1250, as we have seen, he also reduced the running expenses of his household. Several orders indicate the king's personal interest in the business of the treasure. In July 1251, when the treasurer, together with Edward of Westminster and Philip Lovel, were instructed to buy gold from the issues of the Jewry, the writ added that they were to do so 'as the kingly lately enjoined Philip'. In August 1252, Edward of Westminster was told to send the king 'the document concerning the receipt of gold and treasure during the time of the king, as the king, on his departure, ordered him by word of mouth'.[62] Two months later, by a writ which, incidentally, indicates where the treasure was kept, Edward of Westminster, Chaceporc and Lovel were despatched to the king's chest, *cista*, in the treasury at the New Temple where the royal *regalia* and jewels were deposited. They were to weigh the gold in Chaceporc's custody there, replace it securely and let the king know the weight without delay.[63]

Yet the king's gold treasure also reveals the weakness of his financial situation. First, we should not exaggerate its size. Although the 2839 *mg*. were a

[57] *Paris*, v. 199.
[58] Colvin, i. 134.
[59] I base this figure on the Valuation of Norwich which put the annual value of clerical income in England at around £102,000; W. E. Lunt, *Financial Relations of England with the Papacy to 1327* (Cambridge, Mass., 1939), 260.
[60] H. E. Mayer, 'Henry II of England and the Holy Land', *EHR*, xcvii (1982), 724. Of course, this only represented a portion of the money Henry would have assembled had his crusade taken place. Mr J. O. Prestwich has kindly given me further information about Henry's treasure in the Holy Land.
[61] Powicke, i. 305.
[62] *CR 1247 – 51*, 473; *CR 1251 – 3*, 148.
[63] E 368/27, m.3. For an earlier indication that the gold was kept at the New Temple, see *CR 1242 – 7*, 277, 307.

great help to the king in Gascony, by October 1254 he was borrowing heavily from the archbishop and citizens of Bordeaux, and he returned to England with many debts.[64] Henry's treasure seems small compared to his father's. Over a period of years, John had over 200,000 *m.* 'at call' in his various provincial treasuries.[65] Henry's gold also depended to an appreciable extent on the sale of liberties. Politically if money was obtained without causing discontent that had advantages. On the other hand, such a sale could not go on for ever; as the later 1250s were to show, there was a limit to the number of people who wanted to buy free warrens, and exemptions from jury service. The building up of the treasure was also a slow and painstaking process, averaging at best some 6399 *m.* a year. Although Henry could live within his means in time of peace, he required a long period of saving to build up a sufficient chest if he was to fight a war, or go on a crusade. Essentially, the history of Henry's gold treasure shows that there was no real substitute for extraordinary taxation. This was only partly a matter of size. At the equivalent of 28,390 *m.* of silver, Henry's treasure in May 1253 was dwarfed by the 60,000 *m.* of the fifteenth on moveables of 1225; but it did not compare unfavourably with the 24,750 *m.* of the fortieth of 1232, and the 33,750 *m.* of the thirtieth of 1237. The difference was that the bulk of these taxes came in within a year.[66]

II

When Henry III returned to England at the end of 1254 his gold treasure, nurtured over so many years, was totally expended. The king's reaction was immediate. He began to save gold all over again. The accounts of the new keeper of the Wardrobe, Artald de Saint-Romain, reveal that 390 *mg.* in leaf and money were collected in the Wardrobe between 10 January 1255 and 29 April 1256.[67] Of this sum 162 *mg.* 12 *sg.* 11½ *dg.* 'in leaf and money' were bought with 1583 *m.* of general Wardrobe receipts, a rate between gold and silver of 1:9.71. The second main source was 'gifts and fines', which produced 143 *mg.* 'in leaf', 13½ *mg.* in 'bezants and money', and a further 30 bezants, 4 *denarii* and an *obolus* of musc; a total of some 157 *mg.*[68] The Fine Rolls show that these sums derived, as before, from payments for liberties and other miscellaneous concessions. Thirdly, Saint-Romain's accounts recorded the receipt, besides other smaller items, of 34 *mg.* in leaf and bezants, 4 bezants and 12 *oboli* of musc from Jewish gifts and fines, and 13½ *mg.* in leaf from the issues of the seal.

King Henry's first gold treasure was related to his projected crusade. That crusade was no longer on the immediate agenda when Henry returned to

64 *CPR 1247–58*, 340–1, 344; *Paris*, v. 487–8.

65 J. E. A. Jolliffe, 'The Chamber and the Castle Treasures under King John', in *Studies in Medieval History presented to F. M. Powicke*, ed. R. W. Hunt, W. A. Pantin, R. W. Southern (Oxford, 1948), 135.

66 F. A. Cazel, 'The fifteenth of 1225', *BIHR*, xxxiv (1961), 69–70; *The Red Book of the Exchequer*, ed. H. Hall (*RS*, 1896), iii. 1064.

67 E 372/99, m.30d.

68 The 157 *mg.* from gifts and fines probably included the gold bought with 245 *m.* silver from fines paid into the Wardrobe and designated for the purchase of gold. See C 60/52; C 60/53.

England at the end of 1254. Instead, the king had accepted the papal offer of the throne of Sicily for his second son, Edmund, and was committed to sending an army to wrest the kingdom from its Hohenstaufen rulers. Since gold was the currency in Sicily, Henry's second treasure was presumably designed to fund his Italian army.[69] With this aim in view the king once again saw gold as his main financial reserve beyond what he could obtain from extraordinary taxation. Once again he tackled its collection with vigour. When Henry used silver to buy gold, he waited impatiently for the arrival of his purchases in the Wardrobe. He was also interested in the precise rates of exchange between gold and silver. Thus in April 1255, when he sent his goldsmith William of Gloucester 60 *m.* and ordered him 'to make us have without delay 6 *m.* of good smelted gold [*aurum combustum*]', he added,

> and since we understand that marks of this kind are not worth in all 10 *m.* of silver, make us have as much gold as you can from the excess of the gold [bought] from that money, so that we have the gold this coming Monday in the morning at Merton before we rise from our bed; and this omit to do on no account.[70]

What can Henry's second gold treasure tell us of his financial situation as the great crisis of 1258 approached? Unfortunately there are no Wardrobe accounts between 30 April 1256 and 7 July 1258. This gap makes it impossible to trace with any certainty the accumulation of treasure in this vital period. It is true that between 30 April 1256 and 7 July 1258 the Fine Rolls appear to show that 535 *mg.* 36 besants and 6 talents were paid into the Wardrobe in the form of fines of gold.[71] But we cannot add this 535 *mg.* to the 390 *mg.* retained in the Wardrobe down to 29 April 1256 and say that the gold treasure, when the king bowed to reform at the end of April 1258, approached some 925 *mg.* First, there is evidence that some fines of gold were now being paid in silver.[72] Second, much of the gold coming into the Wardrobe was also going out again. Henry, as we shall see, was breaking into his gold treasure in a major way.

There are, however, some clues to the size of the king's gold treasure as the crisis of 1258 approached. In the summer of 1257 Henry decided to mint his own gold coins. The task was entrusted to William of Gloucester who was sent, in all probability, a large part of the Wardrobe gold treasure. He may have also used gold in his own possession which he had bought with silver. A result of the minting was seen on 27 August 1257. On that day William delivered into the Wardrobe 466 *mg.* in the king's new money, together with a little over 103 *mg.* in bezants and money of musc.[73] In August 1257, therefore,

69 Lopez, 226 – 7.

70 *CR 1254 – 6*, 178.

71 Although many of these fines were attermed, they were all noted as paid either to Artald de Saint-Romain or his successor Peter des Rivaux. Thus there is no doubt that payment had been made by 7 July 1258 when des Rivaux was dismissed; C 60/53; C 60/54; C 60/55; see *Excerpta Rot. Fin.*, ii. 228 – 76, where examples of fines of gold may be found.

72 See above, n. 35. A few fines of gold in C 60/53; C 60/54 are specifically stated to have been paid in silver; see also *Excerpta Rot. Fin.*, ii. 326; C 47/3/5/26. However in 1257, as in March 1256, the Fine Rolls noted that gold proffered in payment of a fine was *debile*; C 60/53, m.15; C 60/54, m.5.

73 *CPR 1247 – 58*, 649 – 50; and see *CR 1256 – 9*, 90.

Henry's gold treasure was worth at least 569 *mg*. But how large was it nine months later, at the time of the political revolution of 1258? This question can be approached by looking at the fate of the treasure after the revolution. Although the evidence may not reveal the dispersal of all Henry's gold, we do know that in August 1258 100 *mg*. were sent as a pledge to the abbot and convent of Beaulieu. In 1259 these 100 *mg*. were used to expedite the king's affairs at the papal court.[74] Further, between 8 July 1258 and 27 October 1260, 529 *mg*. (335 *mg*. 3 *sg*. 10 *dg*. in the king's new money) were received by the keepers of the Wardrobe, much of it probably from the 'store' of the king which is mentioned in their accounts.[75] Taking these 529 *mg*. with the 100 *mg*. at Beaulieu, we have a total of 629 *mg*. If we then subtract from this sum around 130 *mg*., which may be estimated very approximately as current gold receipts between 8 July 1258 and 27 October 1260, it leaves about 500 *mg*.[76] This represents, in all probability, the remains of the treasure which Henry had built up before the crisis of 1258.[77]

Henry III, therefore, was not exactly 'bankrupt' in 1258. At the time of the political revolution he probably held at least 500 *mg*. In addition, there was gold and silver plate in the Wardrobe worth over 1200 *m*. of silver.[78] The king also had no problem in meeting his day-to-day expenses. Although most of the Issue Rolls for Henry III's reign are lost, they survive for the Michaelmas term of 1257 and for the Easter term of 1258, demonstrating that the king's writs of *liberate* were generally honoured.[79] Thus, for all the reformers' condemnation of the king's poverty, and their fierce talk of an act of resumption to cure it, there was no immediate need for them to press ahead with such unpopular schemes, and they did not do so.

If, however, Henry was not 'bankrupt' in 1258, his resources were tiny when set against his ambitions. A treasure worth some 5000 *m*. was negligible beside the cost of an expedition to Sicily or the money owed to the pope. It would not go far even for a campaign in Wales. Perhaps that was one reason why the new government concluded a truce with Llywelyn and claimed that

[74] *CPR 1247–58*, 643–4; *CPR 1258–66*, 15, 17.

[75] E 361/1, mm.1d,2,1; specifically between Oct. 1258 and Oct. 1259, the keepers received 462 *mg*.; 362 *mg*. 3 *sg*. in new money, 75 *mg*. 20 *dg*. in leaf, 30 *mg*. in musc, 24 *mg*. 4*sg*. 4¾ *dg*. in bezants, 7 *mg*. 4 *sg*. 1 *dg*. *in cuneo* and diverse monies; between Oct. 1259 and Oct. 1260 they received 67 *mg*.; 31 *mg*. 3*dg*. in leaf, 13 *mg*. 3 *sg*. ¾ *dg*. in musc, 14 *mg*. in bezants, 9 *mg*. 10 *dg*. in new money, and some small change.

[76] The current receipts included one major windfall. On 27 Oct. 1259 the Wardrobe obtained 85 *mg*. 40 *dg*. from the chattels of a disgraced Jew. See *CR 1256–9*, 459; *CR 1259–61*, 1; *CPR 1258–66*, 48. Some 46 *mg*. from fines of gold appear to have been due to the king between July 1258 and Oct. 1260. Not all of this may have been paid, or paid in gold, but that compensates for our ignorance of the gold which the king received from gifts in this period, and for any fines not on the Chancery Rolls; C 60/55; C 60/56; C 60/57; *Excerpta Rot. Fin*., ii. 318, 332; *CR 1256–9*, 386–7, 357, 448; *CR 1259–61*, 48, 84–5. I have assumed that the gold mentioned in *CLR 1251–60*, 485; E 403/18 came from the treasure saved before the revolution of 1258. It is impossible to say anything useful about either receipts or expenditure between 30 April and 7 July 1258.

[77] It will be noted that the keepers of the Wardrobe received steadily less gold as this reserve was exhausted; see above, n. 75. Between 25 July 1261 and 31 Dec. 1264, little more than 41 *mg*. entered the Wardrobe apart from what was acquired for the king's oblations; E 372/113, m.3d.

[78] E 361/1.

[79] E 403/15A; E 403/3114. The payments here may be compared with the writs of *liberate* for 1257–8 in *CLR 1251–60*.

the king's poverty placed the kingdom in danger if attacked by a neighbouring prince.[80] What is also clear is that by 1258 Henry's attempts to augment his gold treasure had run into the sand. This is reflected by its size in April 1258. Even if it was larger than the 500 *mg.* which we have postulated, equalling perhaps the 569 *mg.* which Henry possessed in August 1257, that still meant the treasure was only around 180 *mg.* larger than the 390 *mg.* in the Wardrobe in April 1256. It is possible to trace how this situation came about.

Henry III had returned from Gascony in 1254 burdened with debts. In the next three years his letters complained of poverty and 'extreme need' in a way they had not between 1250 and 1253.[81] Although Henry began at once to save gold, this was only possible because the household expenses were supported by a 10,000 *m.* loan from Richard of Cornwall.[82] Meanwhile the king faced the necessity of a campaign in Wales. Against this background he largely abandoned the practice of using silver to buy gold. Between April 1256 and April 1258, over 4800 *m.* of silver for this purpose may have been sent to William of Gloucester.[83] But, between November 1256 and July 1257, the king reluctantly instructed William to surrender either 4130 or 4430 *m.* of this sum. The money was now needed, amongst other things, to meet the expenses of the royal household and the costs of the 1257 Welsh expedition.[84]

At the same time as he ran into problems with the purchase of gold, Henry found it more difficult to collect it in the form of fines. As we have seen, there is evidence that some fines of gold were now being paid in silver. Conceivably, those making the fines were experiencing difficulties in obtaining gold. More probably, Henry needed silver to meet immediate household expenses and no longer insisted that payment be in gold. Another difficulty was that the sources from which the first gold treasure derived were drying up. After 10 January 1255 only 60½ *mg.*, 64 bezants and 6 talents came from the Jews.[85] This reflected the fact that in February 1255 the king had assigned the Jews to Richard of Cornwall in part payment of the 10,000 *m.* loan mentioned earlier.[86] In addition, gold acquired through the selling of liberties was no longer so abundant. In the three years and six months between 10 January 1255 and 7 July 1258, according to the Fine Roll figures, fines for warrens,

[80] *DBM*, 91–2.

[81] *Paris*, v. 487–8; *CR 1254–6*, 28,74,88,113,157–61,242,425; *CLR 1251–60*, 271; *CR 1256–9*, 110.

[82] *CPR 1247–58*, 400–1, and 500–1, for the use of gold as a pledge for a loan; and see *Paris*, v. 488.

[83] 2110 *m.* from fines of silver paid into the Wardrobe and earmarked for the purchase of gold, C 60/63, C 60/54, C 60/55; perhaps around 1500 *m.* from general Wardrobe receipts, a tentative conclusion from the perplexing accounts of William's executors in E 372/116, m.32d, partly printed in G. G. Scott, *Gleanings from Westminster Abbey* (Oxford, 1863), 113–14; perhaps 1255 *m.* from the Exchequer (prior to April 1256 William may have received 310 *m.* from this source), *CR1254–6*, 211–12; *CR 1256–9*, 208–9; *CLR 1251–60*, 278, 297, 431, 434; *CLR 1267–72*, no. 2299I; E 403/3114. It may be that further money was sent William of which we have no evidence.

[84] *CR 1256–9*, 6, 26, 38, 68; *CPR 1247–58*, 553, 558, 561, 570, this last involving 2000 *m.* which are given in the accounts of William's executors as only 1700 *m.*; E 372/116, m.32d. The failure of Henry's efforts to see that this money was returned to William is suggested by E 372/101, mm.8, 7d; see, however, *CR 1256–9*, 26; *CLR 1251–60*, 434.

[85] Figures of fines in this paragraph are based on C 60/52 (1254–5); C 60/53 (1255–6); C 60/54 (1256–7); C 60/55 (1257–8).

[86] *CPR 1247–58*, 400–1; *Paris*, v. 487–8.

markets and fairs were worth only 59½ *mg*. 12 bezants, little more than half the sum which they raised in the one year and seven months between October 1251 and May 1253. Similarly, the 52½ *mg*. 38 bezants from fines for quittance of jury service in the second period were less than the 59 *mg*. 355 bezants and 10 talents produced in the first.

For a while the decline in revenue from the sale of these liberties was offset by a vast increase in the fines for respite of knighthood. In the Fine Rolls between April 1256 and 7 July 1258, there were 358 of these fines, producing, in the same period, 256 *mg*. 20 bezants. Even if some of these fines were in fact paid in silver, there was still a striking contrast with the 36 fines made between 27 October 1251 and 30 May 1253 which raised only 3 *mg*. 4 *sg*. 3 *dg*., 240 bezants, 20 *oboli* of musc and 12 talents. The fines for respite of knighthood were produced by the king's order to the sheriffs in April 1256 to distrain all those, holding by military service, with annual incomes of £15 or more, to take up knighthood.[87] Although the king may genuinely have hoped to increase the number of knights, his aim was also to make money. As he anticipated, large numbers of people purchased respites from the doubtful honour. The king now charged ½ *mg*. or, more rarely, 1 *mg*. for such favours, considerably higher prices than those in force in the period of the first treasure when respites were bought for 6 or 12 bezants. Nearly all the fines were now attermed, but only 38 had not been paid in full by 7 July 1258. These fines, then, were lucrative, but they were probably a reason for the unpopularity of the king's government in the shires in 1258. In addition, once they began to run out, Henry found nothing to take their place. Thus, although in 1257 gold was still flowing into the Wardrobe from old fines, the number of new ones was steadily diminishing. Between 28 October 1257 and 30 April 1258, new fines for respite of knighthood totalled only 4 *mg*., new fines for warrens, markets and fairs came to 3½ *mg*., and those for exemption from jury service, 5½ *mg*. During the same period there were few fines in gold for the miscellaneous concessions we have seen earlier. These concessions were still being made, but the fines for them were in silver rather than in gold. As before, we may suspect that this reflected the king's need for silver to meet his immediate expenses.

By July 1257, therefore, as he prepared for his campaign in Wales, Henry's attempt to build up a second substantial gold treasure was beginning to collapse.[88] The situation was further compounded by the decision the king now took to disburse a significant amount of the gold which he had collected since January 1255.

The medium for this disbursement was Henry III's gold coinage. On 16 August 1257, when the king was at Chester, he instructed the sheriff of London to proclaim that the 'gold money of the king' should run in the city and elsewhere throughout the kingdom, each coin being worth 20 silver pennies. This indicated an exchange rate between silver and gold of 10:1, since the coin

87 *CR 1254–6*, 293.

88 However, in April 1258 itself, in three writs of *liberate*, the king ordered 203 *m*. to be given to William of Gloucester for the purchase of gold. The Issue Rolls show that two of these writs were honoured, producing 128 *m*.; *CLR 1251–60*, 431, 434; *CLR 1267–72*, no. 2299; E 403/3114; see also E 372/116, m.32d. The dwindling pace of gold collection prompted measures in 1257–8 to get in unpaid fines of gold, though it was admitted that some of the fines listed might in fact have been paid; an indication of the confusion into which affairs were drifting. See E 371/22, mm.14, 15.

was of pure gold and weighed two silver pennies.[89] In 1247, when Henry launched his new silver coinage, he borrowed the necessary silver from his brother, Richard of Cornwall. No loan was necessary from Richard or anyone else for the issue of 1257. What Henry did was to mint a large part of his gold treasure. If the coinage was launched in August 1257, minting had presumably begun somewhat earlier. We may doubt whether it continued long after the political revolution in April 1258.[90] Probably the 190 *mg*. in new money which William of Gloucester delivered into the Wardrobe in October 1258 had been coined considerably earlier.[91] This delivery, and the earlier one of 466 *mg*. in August 1257, establish a minimum mintage of 52,480 gold pennies.[92] It is not surprising, therefore, that the six surviving coins display the use of four different obverse dies, the minimum life of a die being perhaps 10,000 coins.[93] Just how much royal gold William minted in total can only be a matter for speculation. My own guess is that it was around 1000 *mg*., the equivalent of some 80,000 pennies.

The new money was quickly put into circulation. By November 1257 the mayor and citizens of London were complaining that, in so many hands, it was bringing down the price of gold in leaf. Conceivably some individuals brought gold to William of Gloucester to have it turned into coin. But, if this had happened on any large scale, Henry's new money would have been more successful than it was. More likely, the king himself, having minted a large part of his treasure, put the coinage into circulation by using it to meet various debts and expenditures.[94] Had the Wardrobe accounts survived for this period they would probably show a large outflow of gold, in the form of the new money, to meet various household expenses. As we have seen, later than 7 July 1258, although the evidence may be incomplete, the king is only known to have possessed the 335 *mg*. which the keepers of the Wardrobe received in 1258–60, together with another 100 *mg*. if the sum deposited in Beaulieu Abbey was in new money.[95]

One reason why the king decided to mint his gold was the projected expedition to Sicily. We will suggest later that much of Henry's treasure was probably in leaf, *folium*, that is in thin strips of gold. It was not, therefore, in a particularly usable form. There is evidence that, as early as 1251, Henry reflected that it would be more helpful to have his treasure in coin, and perhaps he would have minted it before leaving on crusade.[96] In 1257 the king

[89] *CR 1256–9*, 88; *Cronica Maiorum et Vicecomitum*, 29–30.

[90] I can find no accounts for the mintage, but see *CPR 1247–58*, 576; *CPR 1258–66*, 4; *CR 1256–9*, 415; E 372/102, mm.9, 27; E 372/104, mm.3d, 4d; E 372/105, mm. 33d, 34d, 39, 40; E 372/107, mm.12, 11d; E 372/116, m.32d; E 372/141, m.19.

[91] *CPR 1258–66*, 4, which also shows that the 190 *mg*. were minted from the king's gold. The delivery formed part of the receipts mentioned above, n. 75.

[92] *CPR 1247–58*, 649–50.

[93] Sir J. Evans, 'The First Gold Coins of England', *The Numismatic Chronicle*, 3rd ser., xx (1900), 220–2, pl. xi; *Spink Coin Auctions Catalogue: the Norweb Collection of English Coins — Part 1* (Spink & Son, 1985), 36–8; D. Selwood, 'Medieval Minting Techniques', *The British Numismatic Journal*, xxxi (1963), 64.

[94] See *CPR 1247–58*, 576.

[95] See above, 75. Some of the money the king still possessed may itself have come back into his hands, having been in circulation. The 100 *mg*. at Beaulieu presumably ended in Italy since they were used to further the king's affairs at the papal court. Two of Henry's gold coins have been found in Italy. See *Spink Coin Auctions Catalogue: the Norweb Collection, Part 1*, 37.

[96] *CR 1247–51*, 509.

was clearly happy with the part of the treasure which was in money. This was why, that August, alongside the new gold pennies, William of Gloucester delivered bezants and musc into the Wardrobe. But it made sense to convert the treasure in leaf into coin. By doing so Henry also informed the Sicilians, aware of Frederick II's impressive augustales, of the power and authority of his own kingship. For Henry's gold coin boasted a new and splendid design. Whereas the silver pennies of 1247 merely presented a crude royal head, the gold coins of 1257 depicted Henry sitting elegantly on his throne, holding orb and sceptre.[97]

If Henry's main reason for collecting gold after 1254 was to fund his Sicilian expedition, why did he break into his precious store in order to launch the gold coinage in England? This was not simply because Henry wanted the English, like the Sicilians, to be struck by the golden aura of his kingship, though that may have been a factor. He also had little choice. By the summer of 1257, with the costs of the Welsh campaign looming, Henry saw no alternative to spending some of his gold treasure. If he had simply sold a large amount of it, he would probably have obtained a price worse than 10:1. It made more sense to mint his own coins, fix their value and insist, as he did, that they be accepted.

Another reason was more ambitious. Henry may have hoped that people would wish to change gold, in leaf and other forms, into his coinage. By charging for the change the king might make a considerable income. From this point of view the gold coinage was an expedient to raise money, an attempt to replace the now diminishing fines for knighthood with a new, and perhaps more permanent, source of income. In the event the king's hopes were dashed, for the coinage proved extremely unpopular.

In November 1257, clearly reacting to complaints, the king summoned the mayor and citizens of London to come before him at the Exchequer at Westminster. He charged them on oath to say whether the gold coinage was 'of use for the common benefit of his kingdom or not'. If Henry was hoping for reassurance he was disapponted. The mayor and citizens replied that the coinage would do 'great damage to his kingdom, and especially to poor people whose chattels were not worth one gold coin.' They then went on to say that the coinage had also reduced the price of gold,

> since the money had become dispersed in so many hands, which is evident from the fact that gold in leaf which always was accustomed to be worth 10 *m.* is now only worth 8 or 9.

After further unspecified reasons had been adduced as to why the coinage was useless, the king announced that he still wished the new money to run. However, no-one was to be compelled to take it and anyone could exchange it at the exchange for 19½d of silver.[98]

The king's concession acknowledged the unpopularity of his coinage and restricted his ability to put it any further into circulation. What had gone wrong? Lopez has suggested that Henry made the mistake of overvaluing his coin. Since, so Lopez avers, the price of gold was falling in the 1250s, by

[97] For the design, *Spink Coin Auctions Catalogue: the Norweb Collection, Part 1*, 36–8; for augustales, see Lopez, 227.
[98] *Cronica Maiorum et Vicecomitum*, 29–30.

sticking to the 10:1 ratio Henry was expecting his coin to fetch more than it was worth.[99] The problem with this theory is that, as far as England is concerned, there is no conclusive proof that the price of gold was falling generally before 1257.[100] What is true, however, is that the sudden appearance of a large amount of gold quickly brought the price down. Consequently Henry found himself holding the value of his coin above what gold in other forms was fetching on the market. This can scarcely have inspired confidence in the new money.

The mayor and citizens pointed out another problem when they told the king that his coinage would harm poor people. They were probably appealing to Henry's celebrated concern for the poor, but it was true that many poor people would have little use for a coin worth as much as 20d. Its circulation was bound to be restricted. However, the chief reason for the failure of Henry's money lay in the fact that foreign gold coins, such as bezants and *oboli* of musc, had not prepared the way through any extensive circulation of their own. Although Henry would probably have preferred his gold in money, there are reasons for thinking that most fines were paid in leaf. According to Chaceporc's particularly informative account for 1243 – 4, gifts and fines produced in money only 110 bezants and 111 *oboli* of musc (less than 3 *mg.*), whereas 193 *mg.* 5 *sg.* 1 *dg.* came in 'leaf, ingots and dust'. The accounts of Artald de Saint-Romain show that between January 1255 and April 1256 gifts and fines brought 143 *mg.* in leaf and only a little over 13½ *mg.* in bezants and money. Elsewhere in Chaceporc's accounts, and most notably between 1251 and 1253, large amounts of gold from fines came both 'in leaf and money'. But that leaf preponderated here is suggested by the fines themselves on the Fine Rolls. Those in money, usually bezants, were both far less numerous and, in total, far less productive than those said simply to be in marks of gold. Two of the latter were specifically stated to have been paid in money, implying that the rest were paid in a different form which, as Chaceporc's accounts indicate, was leaf.[101] Money was regularly proffered only when the king demanded sums of less than ½ *mg.*, for example the 6 or 12 bezants for respite of knighthood. The conclusion is inescapable that large amounts of gold coin were not easy to come by. The situation was thus very different from that 80 years later when Edward III launched his successful gold currency. Then, great numbers of foreign coins were circulating in England.[102]

But if gold money was comparatively scarce in the 1250s, from where did people get the gold they paid the king? It is possible that some ecclesiastical institutions melted down objects whch they possessed in gold. Yet this was a costly process, which lost one the value of the workmanship. Probably those fining in gold bought the necessary amounts from goldsmiths; the gold came in leaf since that was the form in which goldsmiths kept and sold it. No wonder that the mayor and citizens of London, amongst whom there was a strong goldsmith lobby, were concerned when the price of leaf began to come

99 Lopez, 234 – 9.

100 For some of the evidence, see above, 65, 68, 73; *CR 1254 – 6*, 46, 178, 76. C 60/51, m.11, Gregory le Paumer; C 60/54, m.5, Roger of Newcastle.

101 C 60/49, mm.9, 6 (fines of Robert de Ros and of the abbot and convent of de Valle Sancti Salvatoris. For the king's preference for money, see *CR 1247 – 51*, 509.

102 M. Mate, 'The Role of Gold Coinage in the English Economy, 1338 – 1400', *Numismatic Chronicle*, 7th ser., xviii (1978), 127 – 8.

down.[103] They also faced the loss of what had been a roaring trade if men started to pay fines to the king in his own money rather than in leaf bought from goldsmiths. One conclusion from this situation was that a gold coinage was precisely what was required. Another, probably more correct, was that there was simply no need for one. Apart from when they made fines with the king, most people acquired gold only in the form of finished precious objects. Had Henry continued to demand gold on a large scale, that might have gone some way to support his coinage. But the king launched his new money at precisely the time when the demand for gold to buy warrens, exemptions and respites was coming to an end. In that sense the bonanza for the goldsmiths too was already over, whether or not the new coinage succeeded.

King Henry III, therefore, had miscalculated. He had been fooled by his own activity. Only his own hydropsical thirst for gold created the impression that it was in great demand and in wide circulation. The reality was different. Thus, instead of bringing him money, the new coinage was merely the medium for a substantial reduction in his gold treasure. By the end of 1257, spending rather than saving gold, Henry must have been painfully aware that his attempt to build up a treasure to fund the Sicilian enterprise had disintegrated. The stage was set for the crisis of 1258.

III

At the beginning of this paper we wondered whether Henry III's gold treasure was evidence for the easing of the European gold famine. Certainly the ability of English goldsmiths to respond to what must have been a sudden upsurge of demand in the 1250s is impressive. That demand may itself have served to draw gold into the country.[104] Although Henry I had kept gold in his treasury, we may doubt whether he could have collected it on the scale and at the rate of his great-great-grandson. On the other hand, the comparative scarcity of gold coins in England in the 1250s shows that there was still a long way to go before dearth turned to plenty.

As for the financial situation of the monarchy, the history of the gold treasure proves that, during his personal rule, Henry was able, without help from extraordinary taxation, to live within his means and generate a surplus, provided he lived in peace. This was one reason why, for the most part, live in peace was what Henry did. Appropriately, on his new gold coin, the king was portrayed holding not a sword, as on his seal, but a sceptre.

Henry, in collecting his gold, displayed both enthusiasm and self-discipline. But the story of its collection also reflects his misfortunes and miscalculations in the 1250s. Neither treasure was actually used for what it was intended. The first did not fund a crusade; the second did not support an expedition to Sicily. Nor did Henry get the best value from his gold when he did spend it. In acquiring much of his treasure he had accepted a 10:1 ratio between silver and gold. But this did not mean that, if he was forced to turn his gold back into silver, he would necessarily be able to sell it at that rate. Nor did he. We have seen that in

103 G. Williams, *Medieval London* (London, 1963), 60.
104 See *CR 1251–3*, 70.

1253 – 4, 1207 *mg*. raised only 10,000 *m*. of silver from Richard of Cornwall, a rate of under 8.33:1. Similarly, in Paris and elsewhere in France in 1259 – 60, Henry sold 24 bezants and 383 *mg*. 6 *sg*. 6 *dg*. in musc, bezants and new money for only 3271 *m*. 6s. 8½d., a rate slightly worse than 8.5:1. In 1261 in London he secured a rate of just over 9.5:1 when he sold a further 87 *mg*. in leaf, bezants and new money.[105] In effect, Henry obtained much of his treasure at the rate of 10:1 between silver and gold and sold it at between 8.33 and 9.5:1. From that point of view the whole enterprise was a costly mistake. If there was logic in taking gold to the Holy Land or to Sicily, Henry might have done better to have acquired it at a later stage, once departure was certain.

Also open to criticism is Henry's policy of receiving a large amount of his gold in the form of small fines. In effect, this meant that his gold was obtained by numerous individuals making petty purchases. With little bargaining power they could not hope to better the 10:1 ratio and, as we have seen, Henry apparently accepted that ratio in pricing their fines. If, on the other hand, the king had saved his treasure in silver, and acquired his gold by making large bulk purchases, he might have obtained a better rate of exchange. Although other explanations could be offered, this may account for the 9.71:1 rate of exchange when 1583 *m*. of silver bought gold between January 1255 and April 1256. One cannot help wondering, therefore, whether the method by which the king collected his gold lacked wisdom. Did it indeed owe something to Henry's sheer pleasure at seeing the gleaming metal accumulating day after day in the Wardrobe?

As for the gold coinage, here Henry had at least the consolation of being ahead of Louis IX. It was not until 1266, nine years after Henry's effort, that the French king minted his own gold coins, largely, it seems, as tokens of his Christian kingship.[106] But the issue of 1257 did little to enhance the prestige of the English monarch. Henry, majestic on his coins, was snubbed in his own Exchequer by the mayor and citizens of London, a disjunction between aspiration and reality which underlay much of the king's personal rule. The remark of the mayor and citizens that the coinage would do great damage to the kingdom also had a wider significance. Next year a similar charge was brought against Henry's governance as a whole. The days of gold were over.[107]

[105] E 361/1, m.1.

[106] Jordan, 206 – 7, 210 – 13.

[107] This is something compulsive about gold. I would like to thank my colleagues J. L. Bolton and J .B. Gillingham for fielding what must have seemed interminable questions on the subject. I am also most grateful to J. Brand, M. Archibald and Dr B. Cook for extensive help on the numismatic side and to Drs S. D. Lloyd and C. J. Tyerman for giving me considered advice in all matters connected with the crusades.

Appendix: Peter Chaceporc's accounts for Henry III's gold treasure 1242 – 53.

Source: E 372/95, mm.12, 11d. (Chaceporc's account for the gold he received between 28 Oct. 1242 and 17 Feb. 1252); and E 372/96, mm.9d, 10d. (Chaceporc's account for the remains of the gold obtained between the above dates, and for the gold he received between 18 Feb. 1252 and 30 May 1253).
Notes: Each regnal year runs from 28 October to 27 October. The totals remaining at the end of each year I have calculated myself, using the rates of exchange employed in the accounts (see note 112). Small errors seemingly made by the Exchequer in its own calculations are incorporated, but they do not significantly affect the final total. Each total is given to the last whole mark. Throughout the table *mg* = marks of gold, *sg* = shillings of gold, *dg* = pennies of gold, for which see above p. 64.

Year 27
1242 – 3

received
53 *mg*. 10 *sg*.
500 bezants
31 *dg*.
439 *d*. musc

expended

28 *sg*. 2 *dg*. 152 *d*. musc	in oblations of king at feretory St Edward

remaining
51 *mg*. 8 *sg*. 6 *dg*.
500 bezants
31 *dg*.
287 *d*. musc

TOTAL REMAINING
65 *mg*.

Year 28
1243 – 4

received

193 *mg*. 5 *sg*. 1 *dg*. in leaf, ingots and dust[108] 110 bezants 110 ob musc	from gifts, fines and *perquisitis*
8 *mg*. 4*sg*. 1 *dg*. 80 *d*. musc,	from William Hardel
36 pieces of gold,	weight 30s, as in roll of great purchases
215 ob musc,	as in roll of great purchases, year 28
12 augustales,	of gift of Aaron of York

108 *in folio, cunio et palliola.*

expended	
30 *d*. musc,	in oblations of king and queen
36 bezants	to feretory St Edward
8 ob musc	
181 ob musc,	in oblations of king and queen in diverse places *extra capella sua*
36 pieces gold,	in oblations king and queen
6 *mg*.,	to make one image in church of Christ, Canterbury
1 *mg*.,	for an image of St Edward

remaining	
194 *mg*. 9 *sg*. 2 *dg*.	
74 bezants	
50 *d* musc	
12 augustales	
145 ob musc,	of which 34 ob were from the purchased *oboli* and were included next year in the king's oblation gold. The remainder (111 ob comprising all the *oboli*) from fines and *perquisitis* was retained amongst the remains.

TOTAL REMAINING
198 *mg*.

Year 29
1244 – 5

received	(down to 3 July)[109]
21 *mg*.,	from fines and *perquisitis*
150½ bezants	
459 ob musc	from William Hardel
51 ob musc	

expended	
20 *sg*.	
50 bezants	to feretory St Edward
306 ob musc	

remaining
19½ *mg*.
100½ bezants
204 ob musc
28 ob musc

TOTAL REMAINING
23 *mg*.

[109] The account closes on 3 July, apparently because this was when the king set off for his campaign in Wales.

Year 30
1245 – 6

received
34½ *mg.* in money and in leaf — from gifts, fines and *perquisitis*

expended
19 *mg.* — to feretory St Edward

remaining
15½ *mg.*
1 ob musc

TOTAL REMAINING
15 *mg.*

Year 31
1246 – 7

received
54 *mg.* 11 *sg.* 8 *dg.*
12 bezants — from gifts, fines and *perquisitis*

expended
5 *mg.* — to feretory St Edward

remaining
49 *mg.* 11 *sg.* 8 *dg.*
12 bezants

TOTAL REMAINING
50 *mg.*

Year 32
1247 – 8

received
67 *mg.* 3 *sg.* 4 *dg.* — from gifts, fines and *perquisitis*
2 augustales, — of the gift of Abegrattus

expended
nothing

remaining
all

TOTAL REMAINING
67 *mg.*

Year 33
1248 – 9

received

130 *mg.* ½ *dg.* 4 bezants	from gifts, fines and *perquisitis*

expended

the weight of 32 *sg.*,	to feretory St Edward

remaining
127½ *mg.* 16½ *dg.*
4 bezants

TOTAL REMAINING
127 *mg.*

Year 34
1249 – 50

received

183 *mg.* 6 *dg.* 118 bezants 15 ob musc	from gifts, fines and *perquisitis*

expended

3½ *mg.* 26 bezants	to feretory St Edward
12 ob musc,	to feretory St Thomas the Martyr

remaining
179 *mg.*
92 bezants
3 ob musc

TOTAL REMAINING
180 *mg.*

Year 35[110]
1250 – 1

received

123 *mg.* 13 *dg.* 339 bezants 32d musc 13 ob musc	from gifts, fines and *perquisitis*
288 *mg.* 3 *sg.* 4½ *dg.*,	bought from money received from the Treasury

[110] From this year onwards there is no expenditure.

11 *mg.* 27 bezants 4 *d.* musc	bought from money received from the Wardrobe
4 *mg.* 10 *sg.* 14 *d.* musc 1 ob musc	bought from money received from Wibert[111]

remaining
all

TOTAL REMAINING
434 *mg.*

Year 36
1251 – 17 Feb. 1252[112]

received

44½ *mg.* 10 bezants	from gifts and fines
2 *mg.*,	bought from money from issues of the seal

remaining
all

18 Feb. –
27 Oct. 1252

received

273 *mg.* 4 *dg.* in leaf and money	from fines of diverse people
89 *mg.* 1 *dg.* in leaf and money	from diverse people to have warrens, markets, fairs and other liberties
18½ *mg.* 13 *dg.* in leaf, money and dust	from diverse gifts
8 *mg.* in money of musc and bezants	from the issues of the seal by the hand of Wibert
2½ *mg.* 4 *sg.* 7 *dg.* in leaf and money	*perquisitis* of the Justices of Jews

111 Wibert of Kent, the Chancery clerk.

112 The division on 17 Feb. is because, in 1252, Chaceporc accounted for all the gold which he had received between 28 Oct. 1242 and 17 Feb. 1252. In his account, the sum of marks of gold was given as 1178½ *mg.* 22 *dg.* The sum of bezants was given as 1147, which were said to 'make' 18½ *mg.*, 'that is 62 bezants:1 mark'. The sum of *denarii* of musc was given as 418, which were said to 'make' 8 *mg.* and 2 *d.* musc, 'that is 52 *d.* musc:1 mark of gold'. The sum of *oboli* of musc was given as 304, which were said to 'make' 2½ *mg.* and 22 *d.* musc, 'that is 104 ob musc:1 mark'. 'The sum of these sums' was given as 1207½ *mg.*, and 22 *dg.* and 24 *d.* musc, which 'made' 8 *sg.* Thus the final conclusion was 'Sum of all the gold in marks: 1208 *m.* and 16 *denarii* and 14 augustales which weigh 3*s.* 6*d.*'

3 *mg.* 5 *sg.* 1 *dg.* in leaf and money	from diverse people for respite of knighthood
12½ *mg.* 4 *dg.* in leaf and money	from diverse people to have writs
3 *mg.* 22½ *dg.* in bezants and money of musc	purchased
sum (18 Feb. – 27 Oct.)[113] 400½ *mg.* ½ *dg.*	
TOTAL REMAINING 447 *mg.*	

Year 37
1252 – 30 May 1253

received	
295½ *mg.* 2 *sg.* 7½ *dg.*in leaf and money	from fines of diverse people
126½ *mg.* 3 *sg.* 3½ *dg.* in leaf and money	from diverse people to have warrens, markets and fairs, respite of knighthood and writs
42 *mg.* 1 *dg.*	from gifts of diverse people
18½ *mg.* 16 *dg.* in leaf and money	from the issues of the seal
11 *mg.* 4 *sg.* 2 *dg.* in money	*perquisitis* of the Justices of Jews
2 *sg.* 8½ *dg.* in bezants	bought by P. Lovel
4 *mg.* 11 *sg.* 4 *dg.* in leaf	received from 10 cups sold by Henry de Frowick
1 *mg.* 3 *sg.* 7 *dg.* in leaf	from 2 cups sold to the abbess of Shaftesbury
½ *mg.* 3 *sg.* 4 *dg.*	bought from 100s silver received from pannage of the of Buckholt
Sum[114] 501 *mg.* 5 *sg.* 9½ *dg.*	
TOTAL REMAINING 501 *mg.*	

'Sum of preceding sums [from remains from year 27 inclusive] 2110 *m.* 4 *s.* of gold all of which has been delivered to the treasurer and chamberlains to be placed in the Treasury of the king at Westminster by a writ of the king which is *in forulo marescalli inter communia*'.[115]

[113] This is the sum given in the accounts.
[114] This is the sum given in the accounts.
[115] This conclusion is quoted from the accounts. For the writ see, *CLR 1251 – 60*, 134.

The Lord Edward and the Provisions of Oxford (1258): A Study in Faction*

Huw Ridgeway

One of the greatest and most embarrassing threats posed to the reforms promulgated at the Parliament at Oxford in June 1258 must have been the opposition to them of King Henry III's heir, the Lord Edward. Yet the incident remains, perhaps for this very reason, rather obscure; contemporary chroniclers either for the most part omitted to mention it or, if they did, mentioned it briefly and without explanation; even the one apparently eye-witness account, that of the writer of the 'letter from the Oxford Parliament' transcribed into the Burton annals, was tactfully brief in reporting the prince's conduct.[1] R. F. Treharne thus thought that Edward, a harsh landlord, was simply afraid of the Provisions of Oxford which threatened to bring him to book.[2] But there is evidence that Edward's opposition stemmed, in reality, from his alliance at Oxford with his uncles of the house of Lusignan, the king's four hated Poitevin favourites who were the focus for the reforming magnates' wrath. When at the end of July the reformers wrote to the pope with complaints against the Poitevins, they charged them directly with 'infatuating' Edward, and Aymer de Lusignan, the bishop-elect of Winchester, with misleading Edward to oppose the Provisions.[3] Indeed, just after the Lusignans fled from Oxford at the end of June the magnates rushed to prevent what they thought was Edward's wild plan to put almost his entire estates under his uncles' control. Although that was a false alarm it was later discovered that he had actually made Geoffrey de Lusignan Seneschal of Gascony.[4] Perhaps Edward even accompanied the Lusignans in their desperate bid to make a stand at Aymer's castle near Winchester for it was only at Winchester, on 10 July after their resistance had collapsed and they had surrendered before going into exile, that he could be induced to take his oath to the Provisions.[5]

* I should like to thank my research supervisor, Miss Barbara F. Harvey. Unless otherwise stated, all manuscript references are to documents in the PRO.

[1] *Ann. Mon.*, i.164 (Tewkesbury annals); i.445 (Burton annals); ii.97 (Winchester annals); *Paris*, v.697.

[2] R. F. Treharne, *The Baronial Plan of Reform 1258 – 1263* (Manchester, 1932), 77.

[3] *Ann. Mon.*, i.171 – 3 (also in: i.457 – 60; *Paris*, vi.400 – 5) dated by F. M. Powicke, *King Henry III and the Lord Edward* (Oxford, 1947), i.387 n.

[4] *CPR 1247 – 58*, 639 – 41; 664; *CR 1256 – 9*, 319.

[5] For Edward's movements, *CPR 1247 – 58*, 636, 664; *CPR 1258 – 66*, 13. It appears that he withdrew from the Oxford Parliament at least once earlier, for on 23 June he was at Beckley, Oxfordshire. The Lusignans began negotiating with the magnates on 5 July and had evidently come to terms by 10 July. See *CPR 1247 – 58*, 640 – 1. Edward's oath was made on 10 July and his uncles actually left the realm on 14 July. See *Ann. Mon.*, i.445; H. G. Richardson and G. O. Sayles, 'The Provisions of Oxford: A forgotten Document and some Comments', *Bulletin of the John Rylands Library*, xvii (1933), 32.

Now the most startling point about Edward's behaviour at Oxford was that he had formed his attachment to the Lusignans very recently, no more than a few months earlier. His political career had begun, in its own right, in February 1254 when, at the age of fourteen, he was invested with the great appanage of Ireland, Chester, Gascony and the Channel Islands.[6] At first, however, he was extremely cool towards his Lusignan uncles. In November 1254, for instance, he had a lawsuit against William de Valence.[7] From February 1254 – November 1256 he was vigorously obstructing the king's extensive grants of lands and revenues to Guy and Geoffrey de Lusignan which threatened to erode his appanage in Ireland.[8] In spite of their valuable military assistance given to Henry III in pacifying Gascony 1252 – 54, Edward pointedly employed no Poitevins in the duchy after he received seisin of it.[9] Nor did he employ Poitevins in his household before 1258. As recently as November 1256 he put up successful resistance to Henry III's schemes to get him to admit Guy de Lusignan into his council.[10] Edward's attitude only seems to have changed at some point in the following year, probably during the winter of 1257. On 12 December, in a rare departure from his custom, he witnessed a royal grant, a licence to Aymer, the elect of Winchester.[11] In March 1258 he made a grant finally settling his earlier dispute with Geoffrey de Lusignan and by April the Lusignans began to witness his charters.[12] At about the same time he began to mortgage manors to his uncles in return for loans to help him fight the Welsh.[13] Yet it was only at Oxford in June that he really made his feelings public. The magnates could well congratulate themselves, therefore, that they had nipped in the bud a most dangerous alliance between the heir to the throne and the king's evil favourites.

This paper aims to show that Edward's behaviour sheds important new light on the crisis of 1258 and, in particular, on the motives of some of the leading magnates who forced the régime of the Provisions of Oxford on Henry III. Recent research has shown that the 'baronial movement of reform' is a misnomer and that it had its genesis, in fact, in a plot hatched by the Lusignans' enemies at court who were worried by their growing influence over the king.[14] Here it will be argued that the same people had good reason to resent the Lusignans' new friendship with Edward. For among the prime movers of the 1258 revolution were the very people who had hitherto directed Edward's affairs and helped to protect and mould the prince betwen 1239 and 1258: these were Henry III's queen, Eleanor of Provence and her Savoyard

[6] J. R. Studd, 'The Lord Edward and King Henry III', *BIHR*, l (1977), 4 – 6.
[7] *CR 1254 – 6*, 3.
[8] H. S. Snellgrove, *The Lusignans in England 1247 – 58* (Albuquerque, New Mexico, 1950), 48 – 50.
[9] J-P. Trabut-Cussac, *L'Administration Anglaise en Gascogne sous Henry III et Edward I de 1254 à 1307* (Paris, Geneva, 1972), 371ff.
[10] *CR 1256 – 9*, 107.
[11] *CPR 1247 – 58*, 607.
[12] *CCR 1279 – 88*, 180; *CChR 1257 – 1300*, 13; BL, Additional Charter 46918.
[13] *Paris*, v. 679; *CPR 1247 – 58*, 644. This is the only evidence we have that *c.* April 1258 Edward mortgaged Tickhill, Yorkshire, to Aymer the elect of Winchester.
[14] H. W. Ridgeway, 'The Politics of the English Royal Court 1247 – 65 with special reference to the role of Aliens' (Oxford University D. Phil. thesis, 1983), 247 – 314; D. A. Carpenter, 'What happened in 1258?', in *War and Government in the Middle Ages: Essays in Honour of J. O. Prestwich*, ed. J. B. Gillingham, J. C. Holt (Woodbridge, 1984), 106 – 19.

party at court, together with some of King Henry's most senior native courtiers, led by Sir John fitz Geoffrey.

From his birth in 1239, until 1254, Edward's protectors had been his mother, her uncle Peter of Savoy (a member of the royal council from 1241) and their alien followers. Henry III left his son's upbringing to the queen and so Edward was kept at Windsor, her castle, with other royal and noble children under guard of the constable of Windsor, who was always a Savoyard.[15] Important Savoyards were successively custodians of the honour of Eu, which at first supplied the prince's main source of revenue (1244–54): Bernard of Savoy (1244–7), Peter of Geneva (1247–9) and Peter of Savoy himself (1249–54).[16] Even more remarkable is the evidence which suggests that it was thanks only to the foresight of the Savoyards that Edward eventually received an adequate appanage from the king at all. It became Henry III's practice to send copies of important documents recording royal grants and other matters relevant to Edward for safe-keeping to Peter of Savoy's archives.[17] The purpose behind this was to guarantee that the king earmarked estates for the enjoyment of his heir and, indeed, to ensure that he honoured his undertakings. For example, Peter obtained custody of charters recording Henry's 'grant' of Gascony to Edward in 1249 and again in 1252, even though the prince did not receive actual seisin until 1254.[18] These elaborate precautions can be understood as a reflection on the king's weak character and, in particular, on his periodic failures to dominate the various factions in his court. In the early years of Edward's career it was, in fact, essential for his interests to be adopted by the queen's faction to save them from the rival claims of the king's brother, Richard of Cornwall. In 1243 Eleanor and her uncles had to intervene, almost certainly on Edward's behalf, to reverse Henry's rash grant of Gascony to Richard during the Poitou campaign, and when in 1244 (probably in return for the marriage of Sanchia, the queen's sister) Richard agreed to renounce Gascony, only conditionally, he was made to renounce his claims in Ireland.[19] Richard renewed his pressure on the king in the next year and even revived his title of 'count of Poitou' between April and October but was, once more, thwarted by the queen.[20] At the same time, during the Welsh campaign of 1245, the Savoyards advised Henry to refuse Richard the county of Chester, apparently in order to safeguard the interests of Edward or his brother Edmund.[21] Richard was consoled with other grants from the king but these wrangles explain the care with which the queen's faction from the start cut Richard out of the schemes for the regency of England and custody of Edward if he became king while a minor.[22] Even in July 1253, when a regency involving Richard was drawn up while Henry III would be in Gascony, the

[15] T. F. Tout, *Chapters in Mediaeval Administrative History* (Manchester, 1920–33), v. 232–3n.; Ridgeway, table 1, p. 23.

[16] *CPR 1232–47*, 422; *CPR 1247–58*, 52, 272; *CLR 1245–51*, 144; *PRO Lists and Indexes*, xi (London, 1900), 203.

[17] Some still survive, eg., in C 47/9/1.

[18] C 47/9/1; *CChR 1226–57*, 386.

[19] N. Denholm-Young, *Richard of Cornwall* (Oxford, 1947), xvi, 48–51.

[20] C 53/57 mm.1–5; *Paris*, iv. 487.

[21] Denholm-Young, 55–6; C 47/9/1; R. Stewart-Brown, 'The end of the Norman earldom of Chester', *EHR*, xxxv (1920), 52–3.

[22] *CPR 1232–47*, 244, 280, 294.

queen was given sole custody of Edward in the case of the king's death, and the king's letters patent were handed over to Peter of Savoy for safe keeping.[23] But it must not be thought that during these years the Savoyards were merely jealous guardians. They laboured hard with long-term schemes genuinely designed to protect Edward's interests. They were instrumental, for example, in the appointment of their ally Simon de Montfort as governor of Gascony in 1248 in order to strengthen the king's grip on the duchy.[24] From 1249 they also turned their famous diplomatic talents to begin negotiations for Edward's eventual marriage with Eleanor of Castile which led to King Alfonso of Castile's renunciation of his threatening claims on Gascony in 1254.[25]

It is not surprising, therefore, that the queen and the Savoyards continued to play an important part in Edward's affairs even when he had received seisin of his appanage and had no more need of guardians. Peter of Savoy repeatedly witnessed his charters in the years 1254 – 8.[26] The Savoyards were especially vigilant in helping him rule turbulent Gascony: Peter of Savoy and Peter of Aigueblanche, the Savoyard bishop of Hereford, advised him during his first visit to the duchy in 1255, and after this something approaching vice-regal power was, until at least 1257, exercised there by the latter.[27] In 1256 – 7, when the Welsh invaded his estates, Edward immediately turned for loans to the queen, Peter of Savoy and Boniface of Savoy, archbishop of Canterbury.[28]

The Savoyards also played an important part in shaping the composition of Edward's new household. Before 1254 it was merely an extension of the queen's service, but although now nominally independent Edward in practice kept on, until 1258, the men appointed into the leading ranks of his service by the king and queen. It is easy to identify them from the witness lists of Edward's numerous charters. They were from two origins. First, there were some of Eleanor's old servants, such as the knight Stephen Bauzan or the clerk Ralph de Donjon, keeper of Edward's Wardrobe (1255 – 9).[29] Eleanor also secured the advancement of aliens: her kinsman Michael de Fiennes, Edward's first chancellor (1255 – 8) and the Savoyard knights Geoffrey de Joinville and Eubule de Montibus, the prince's constant companion (1251 – 8), chamberlain and, perhaps, steward.[30] The others, by far the more numerous, were a tightly-knit group of some of Henry III's longest-serving councillors and officials, many of whom had already administered, like an embryonic colonial service,

[23] *CPR 1247 – 58*, 206; Denholm-Young, 77.

[24] C. Bémont, *Simon de Montfort* (Paris, 1884), 335 – 7, 341; for de Montfort's links with the Savoyards, see Ridgeway, 58 – 9, 113 – 16.

[25] F. Mugnier, 'Les Savoyards en Angleterre au XIIIe siècle', *Mémoires et Documents publiés par la société Savoisienne*, xix (1890), 229, 256 – 9.

[26] Eg., *Rôles Gascons*, ed. C. Bémont (Paris, 1885 – 1906), I, ii. no. 4554; *CChR 1226 – 57*, 461; *CChR 1257 – 1300*, 7, 13.

[27] Mugnier, 275, 278 – 80; Trabut-Cussac, 9, 161, 253; *CPR 1247 – 58*, 499 – 500, 549; *CR 1256 – 9*, 118 – 19.

[28] *Paris*, v. 612; *CPR 1247 – 58*, 554, 569.

[29] Tout, i. 256n.; *CPR 1247 – 58*, 365; *CLR 1251 – 60*, 27; *CChR 1257 – 1300*, 23 – 4; *CR 1251 – 3*, 491; E 101/349/12 m.1; *Paris*, v. 272, 646; vi. 373; Trabut-Cussac, 372; for other examples, Ridgeway, 174 – 6.

[30] G. P. Cuttino, 'A Chancellor of the Lord Edward', *BIHR*, l (1977), 229 – 32; for Fiennes and the queen, E 101/349/26 mm. 1,2; *CChR 1226 – 57*, 385. G. W. Watson, 'The families of Lacy, Geneva, Joinville and la Marche', *The Genealogist*, n.s., xxi (1904), 12 – 13; *Rôles Gascons*, I, ii. nos. 4324, 4538, 4636; *CChR 1226 – 57*, 453, 461; *CChR 1257 – 1300*, 2, 13, 24; *CR 1251 – 3*, 183; *CR 1254 – 6*, 130. For other Savoyards and Edward, see Ridgeway, 175 – 6.

the various units of Edward's appanage long before he had seisin of them: men such as Alan de la Zouche (justiciar of Chester, 1250 – 6, and then of Ireland, 1256 – 8), Peter de Montfort, a prominent servant of the king on the Welsh March and in Gascony and Edward's councillor from 1254, and John de Grey (justiciar of Chester, 1245 – 50, and seneschal of Gascony 1253) Edward's lieutenant in the mid-Welsh March in 1257.[31] The most important examples of this second type were Sir Geoffrey de Langley, Henry III's former henchman in the forest administration, who became Edward's first estates steward (1254 – 7) and Sir John fitz Geoffrey, who held first place in Edward's council (1255 – 8).[32] Fitz Geoffrey owed his prominence to the fact that he had been a member of Henry III's council since 1237, justiciar of Ireland (1245 – 56) and since 1241 keeper of what was to become Edward's headquarters, Bristol Castle, a post which he retained until his death in 1258.[33] Even the lower ranks of Edward's sevice were recruited from within such well-defined circles. Alan de la Zouche, doubtless, influenced the promotion of his brothers Eudo and William, as well as Edward's *vadlettus* Robert de Beaumes; the Grey family promoted Sir Adam of Jesmond (or Gesimuthe); Peter de Montfort was the patron of Sir John Burdet, and so on.[34] Yet the remarkable point about these men is that many of them, even though not aliens, were in favour with the queen. She was, for example, well-disposed towards Geoffrey de Langley, John fitz Geoffrey, the de la Zouches and probably, thanks to his links with Simon de Montfort, Peter de Montfort.[35] Perhaps she still regarded Edward's household, in some ways, as an extension of her own; when in 1258 she made her new year's distribution of gifts, six of Edward's leading servants were recipients and their names were entered onto her jewel roll indiscriminately alongside those of her own officials.[36]

All this is to say that until 1258 Edward enjoyed the guidance of the most senior and well-established element at court. This harmonious arrangment was shattered at the Oxford Parliament. Just as King Henry III was resisted by his most senior councillors, so Edward, in resisting the Provisions, was at odds with those who had served him since 1254. They were some of the most active supporters of the reforms. Peter of Savoy, John fitz Geoffrey and Peter de Montfort were among the original seven magnates whose sworn conspiracy in

[31] *CChR 1257 – 1300*, 24; *CPR 1247 – 58*, 553, 580; *Rôles Gascons*, I, ii. nos. 4328, 4334; Trabut-Cussac, 372; H. G. Richardson and G. O. Sayles, *The Administration of Medieval Ireland* (Dublin,1963), 77; *The Cartulary of Chester Abbey*, ed. J. Tait (Chetham Soc., n.s., lxxix, 1920), I. v; *GEC*, *sub. nom.*

[32] P. R. Coss, 'Sir Geoffrey de Langley and the crisis of the knightly class in thirteenth century England', *Past and Present*, lxviii (1975), 3 – 5; *Rôles Gascons* I, ii. nos. 4337, 4538, 4554, 4623; *CChR 1226 – 57*, 453, 461; *CChR 1257 – 1300*, 2, 24; CHES. 38/47/1.

[33] Richardson and Sayles, *Administration*, 77 – 8; *Accounts of the Constables of Bristol Castle*, ed. M. Sharp (Bristol Rec. Soc. Publications, xxxiv, 1982), 81, 89.

[34] *GEC*, xii, 932 – 4; R. W. Eyton, *The Antiquities of Shropshire* (London, 1854 – 60), ii. 208, 242; F. W. Dendy 'An Account of Jesmond', *Archaeologia Aeliana*, 3rd ser., i (1904), 39 – 50; Bodleian Library, Oxford, Dugdale MS 13, ff. 256, 501. For these men and Edward, see J-P. Trabut-Cussac, 'Un Rôle de Lettres Patentes du Prince Édouard en 1254', in *Receuil de Travaux offert à M. Clovis Brunel* (Société de l'Ecole des Chartes, Mémoires et Documents no. xii. Paris, 1955), ii. 599 – 615, no. 60; *CPR 1247 – 58*, 513, 603; *CChR 1257 – 1300*, 2, 24; C 61/4m.5.

[35] *CPR 1247 – 58*, 375 – 7, 616; C 47/3/43/6; E 101/349/7; E 101/349/26 m.5; Ridgeway, 418.

[36] E 101/349/26 ml.

April started the revolution and they were, of course, elected onto the reconstituted royal council of fifteen under the Provisions.[37] John de Grey and Roger of Mold (justiciar of Chester, 1257 – 9) were of the twelve chosen to represent the community, and Stephen de Longespée (seneschal of Gascony, 1255 – 7) and Richard de la Rochelle, John fitz Geoffrey's follower and sometime deputy in Ireland, were among those given charge of the royal castles.[38] Edward had acted completely on his own initiative in supporting the Lusignans.

Now there are four reasons, I think, why this happened. First of all, several of these men had good personal reasons to hate the Lusignans. It was, after all, Aymer of Winchester's raid on John fitz Geoffrey's land in the Spring of 1258 which probably sparked off the Poitevins' eventually downfall.[39] Nor could Peter de Montfort take any other course since he was the devoted protégé of Simon de Montfort, who had a bitter dispute with William de Valence.[40] As for the Savoyards, they had quarrelled with the Lusignans long before, in 1252, and after this they began to feel the pinch of their competition for the king's favour.[41] They were at first not under any immediate danger, especially as they had Edward under their thumb, but when he began to get friendly with the Lusignans it was the last straw.

On the other hand, Edward's immediate personal circumstances explain much of his own conduct. He may have been drawn initially to William de Valence, for example, by their mutual frustration with the king and his councillors for the embarrassing failure to handle the Welsh revolt of 1256 – 8. They both held lands which had been prime targets for the Welsh attacks. They also had private quarrels with their fellow Marcher, the all-powerful earl of Gloucester who was one of the king's councillors, and William de Valence even accused Gloucester of treacherously assisting the Welsh.[42] Moreover, as happened with the king, Edward could not wage war without borrowing ready supplies of cash and here again the Welsh war forced the political issue. In 1256 and early 1257, as we have said, Edward borrowed heavily from the Savoyards and Richard of Cornwall but, as luck would have it, they suddenly ran into their own financial difficulties in mid-1257 and so thereafter could provide no further assistance: Richard, the king's leading financier, left the realm in his ruinous pursuit of the Crown of Germany; and the queen and the Savoyards, for their part, had to divert all their resources into paying the enormous ransom of Thomas of Savoy after his capture by the cities of Asti and Turin in 1255.[43] As a result Edward had to turn for loans in 1258 to the ample cash resources of the Lusignans, especially those of the bishop-elect of Winchester. It is little wonder, therefore, that he fell under his uncles' spell. Henry III himself, it may be added, probably fell into a similar trap at the same

[37] Bémont, *Simon de Montfort*, 327; *DBM*, 104 – 5.

[38] *DBM*, 104 – 7, 112 – 13. For la Rochelle: Richardson and Sayles, *The Administration*, 78; Sharp, 81.

[39] Ridgeway, 266 – 8, 289.

[40] Carpenter, 'What happened in 1258?', 115 – 6; Ridgeway, 261 – 3, 268 – 9, 289 – 90.

[41] Ridgeway, esp. chs. 4 – 6.

[42] J. E. Lloyd, *A History of Wales . . . to the Edwardian Conquest* (2 vols. 2nd edn., London, 1912), ii. 714 – 25; M. Altschul, *A Baronial Family in Medieval England; the Clares 1217 – 1314* (Baltimore, 1965), 26, 77 – 9, 83, 127; Ridgeway, 268 – 9, 280 – 1.

[43] Denholm-Young, 86 – 94, 160; Ridgeway, 277; cf. *Paris*, v. 597, 678; *CPR 1247 – 58*, 559.

time; in November 1257, for example, William of Valence lent him 1100 *m.* and in 1258 Aymer of Winchester was rumoured to have promised him vast sums in order to save him from the magnates and the Provisions of Oxford.[44]

A third factor which divided Edward from his councillors in 1258 was that, under the Lusignans' influence, he proposed to break with royal policy defining the relationship of his appanage with the Crown. One of the first actions of the Oxford reformers, as we have said, was to prevent Edward 'illegally' appointing Geoffrey de Lusignan Seneschal of Gascony; at the same time they quashed his 'illegal' grant of the isle of Oléron, strategically placed off the Gascon coast, to Geoffrey's brother, Guy. As J. R. Studd has pointed out, these grants were deemed 'illegal' precisely because they contravened Henry III's charter of 1254 under which Edward had been provided with an appanage 'joined inseparably to the Crown of England': namely, that he could make no grants or appointments therein without the consent of the king.[45] Now this calls for comment. It is hard to believe that in 1258 the reformers were simply responding to the king's anger over Edward's unlicensed grants. One of their principal grievances, after all, was that Henry III was always too ready to listen to his brothers' point of view and to compromise his royal judgement and dignity. Indeed, if Henry now objected to Edward's conduct it would cast a most significant new light on the 1258 crisis and it would even suggest that, for the time being at any rate, he approved of his brothers' downfall and exile. But, in fact, it is more likely that in 1258 we have, under the guise of the Provisions, just one in a long series of interventions by Edward's councillors to frustrate royal indulgence to the Lusignans at the prince's expense; the only difference was that it was now Edward who was, ironically, the originator of the disputed grants. It is worth noting, for instance, what had happened on 28 April 1252 when Henry himself, no less, had granted Guy de Lusignan the Lusignan ancestral lands in Oléron which they had lost to the king in 1226.[46] In 1252 Henry was especially in debt to the Lusignans because only a week earlier Geoffrey de Lusignan had rescued his lieutenant in Gascony from a rebellion.[47] It would appear that Henry's grant was overruled by the intervention of his councillors led perhaps by Peter of Savoy vigilant, as ever, to defend Edward's rights. Guy was allowed only a temporary custody and was forced to give Peter a written declaration that he would restore the land to Edward when the prince was given seisin of Gascony.[48] An even starker illustration of Henry's indulgence was mentioned at the start of this paper when we described the campaign waged 1254–56 to frustrate his grants to the Poitevins from Edward's appanage in Ireland.

These incidents show that the Savoyards and others interpreted 'inseparability from the Crown' as merely another means of assisting — and binding — Henry III to carve out an appanage for his son. From 1247, at any rate, the queen's party were closely associated with schemes for the designation of royal lands as 'inseparable' to this end: Chester in 1247, Gascony and

[44] *CPR 1247–58*, 603; *Ann.Mon.*, i.171.
[45] Studd, 8, 10.
[46] C. Bémont, 'Le Coûtumier de l'Île d'Oléron', *Bulletin Philologique et Historique*, 1917, 274–6.
[47] C. Bémont, *Simon de Montfort*, (English edition, Oxford, 1930), 100–102.
[48] *CPR 1247–58*, 136. Peter of Savoy was at court on that day: C 53/44 m.13–14.

Oléron in 1252 and Stamford and Grantham in 1253; copies of some of these instruments were kept by Peter of Savoy.[49] No doubt it must have been galling, then, when Henry granted Guy land in Oléron in April 1252: it was on the very day that he had proclaimed its 'inseparable' status. Such ideas were in keeping with ideas of the inalienability of the royal demesne which were gaining general acceptance in court circles in the 1250s and were enshrined in the councillors' oath of 1257.[50] They suited a situation where Henry's limited resources in escheated land were now under mounting pressure from his fast-growing family circle.[51] This is why the councillors felt they could resist the prince, and probably the king, in 1258. Moreover, there was a particularly cogent objection that they could level against Edward being allowed a free hand in Gascony in 1258. His grants to the Lusignans threatened to upset diplomatic relations with Louis IX of France at the very juncture when Peter of Savoy was taking a leading part in negotiating the Treaty of Paris. Louis had viewed the Lusignans since the 1240s as dangerous vassals and had striven to cut down their power in Poitou, and so he was unlikely to welcome their sudden aggrandizement.[52] Perhaps Edward did this even to show his opposition to the proposed treaty, the terms of which (especially Gascony's subjection to the overlordship of Louis IX) we know he found so distasteful.[53] But for Peter of Savoy this was the height of irresponsibility for he saw in the treaty the very key to his long-cherished schemes for the peace of the South from which, among other things, Edward's hold on Gascony would be secured.[54] At this sensitive point, then, it was clearly most necessary to keep the headstrong prince under the tight controls of the 1254 charter.

The most dangerous aspect of Edward's new friendship with the Lusignans, however, was that it was an expression of his emergent political personality. By the Oxford Parliament in 1258 he had reached his nineteenth year. Although it is difficult to interpret Edward's behaviour before this date because, as we have shown, he was anything but a free agent, Dr. Studd has pointed to some signs from 1256 of Edward's independence of mind and personal dissatisfaction with the constant interference of Henry III and his councillors in his estates.[55] Moreover, it is hardly surprising that he might come to resent the settlement of 1254, which not only saddled him with councillors and officials not of his own choice but, thanks to the policy of the 'inseparability' of his appanage, denied him the financial independence to reward with lands anyone who did not meet with the approval of the king or — and here was the telling point — the old guard who dominated the councils of the king and prince. Perhaps Edward blamed the veterans such as Geoffrey de Langley, his

[49] *CPR 1232–47*, 501; *CPR 1247–58*, 293; *CChR 1226–57*, 386, 389; C 47/9/1.
[50] G. L. Harriss, *King, Parliament and Public Finance in Medieval England to 1369* (Oxford, 1975), 128–145.
[51] Ridgeway, 191–225 discusses this in detail.
[52] P. Boissonade, 'L'ascension, le déclin et la chute d'un grand état féodal du Centre-Ouest', *Bulletins et Mémoires de la Société archéologique et historique de la Charente* (1935), 212–57; and (1943), 3–49.
[53] P. Chaplais, 'The making of the Treaty of Paris (1259) and the Royal Style', *EHR*, lxvii (1952), 244; *The Historical Works of Gervase of Canterbury*, ed. W. Stubbs (*RS*, 1879–80), ii. 210; *CR 1259–61*, 232.
[54] Ridgeway, 161–70; cf. *CPR 1247–58*, 62, 411, 594, 628, 663; *CR 1254–6*, 195–6; Powicke, i. 239–58.
[55] Studd, 7–8.

steward, for sparking off the disastrous Welsh revolt. It must be significant that when Henry III dismissed Langley for his misrule in 1257 it was the queen, rather than Edward, who in February 1258 petitioned for Langley's pardon.[56]

As any rate, it was exactly during the period 1257–8 that Edward began to recruit into his circle a group of kinsmen and knights who really were his personal choice as followers: the most important figures were his cousin, Henry of Almain, son of Richard of Cornwall, John de Warenne, earl of Surrey, Roger de Clifford, Hamo l'Estrange, John de Vaux and Roger de Leyburn.[57] It so happens that many, though not all, of this group were already connected with the Lusignans; Roger de Leyburn, for example, had been a knight in William de Valence's service whereas John de Warenne was William's brother-in-law and most devoted ally and had recently begun to associate himself with Henry of Almain.[58] We can infer that these men were Edward's personal choice because they had one thing in common, they were the very antithesis of well established courtiers. Indeed, they had no connexion (unlike recruits before 1256) with Edward or Henry III's veterans: they were politically inexperienced or came from the outer fringes of the king's service. Most had their fortunes still to make in every sense.[59] Most, too, were young men like Edward. Henry of Almain and John de Warenne were about four years older. William de Valence and Aymer the elect of Winchester were only in their late twenties and, although admitted since 1251 into the king's council, they had actually taken very little part in its work.[60] Moreover, they shared a very similar outlook with Edward; William de Valence and John de Warenne were violent men, devotees of the tournament which at that time found little favour at court.[61] Edward had much more in common with them than with the peace-loving and 'diplomatic' courtiers of the middle years of Henry III's reign personified by Peter of Savoy.

At first, Edward's new followers were kept in the background by the veterans who probably disliked their links with the Lusignans. But when Edward began to plot early in 1259 before his rebellion, Henry of Almain, John de Warenne, Roger de Leyburn and the others had become his principal advisors.[62] During the following year they and the prince conspired for the return of the Lusignans to England.[63] Later, they were the men who, as is well-known, dominated the prince's service until 1272 and beyond; they fought

[56] *CPR 1247–58*, 616; *Paris*, v. 593; *Ann.Mon.*, iii. 200.

[57] *Paris*, v. 697; *CPR 1247–58*, 601, 607, 659; *CR 1256–9*, 140, 147; *CChR 1257–1300*, 2, 13; Gervase of Canterbury, ii. 220–1.

[58] JUST 1/873 m.18d.; *Paris*, iv. 629; v. 359; *CR 1247–51*, 247, 345; *Ann.Mon.*, i. 444; Denholm-Young, 90–3.

[59] W. Dugdale, *The Baronage of England* (London, 1675–6), i. 77–8, 337, 525–6; H. le Strange, *Le Strange Records* (London, 1916), 100–48; *GEC* and *DNB, sub.nom.* Indebtedness was common among this group. See *Calendar of Jewish Plea Rolls*, ed. J. M. Rigg (London, 1905), i. 15, 22, 48, 68, 102; *CLR 1245–51*, 92; E 159/31m.13d.; E 159/33 m.13; E 163/1/29; E 361/1 m.1; E 368/36 m.16.

[60] Ridgeway, 96–7, 153–9. I know of only two minor instances of John de Warenne and Henry of Almain's formal participation in royal administration before 1258: *CPR 1247–58*, 424, 607, although Warenne witnessed royal charters from 1255.

[61] N. Denholm-Young, 'The Tournament in the Thirteenth Century', in his *Collected Papers* (Cardiff, 1969), 104–17.

[62] *Report on the MSS of Lord Middleton* (Historical Manuscripts Commission, 1911), 67–9; Bémont, *Simon de Montfort* (1930), 173, 287; C 61/4/ mm.1–4.

[63] *CR 1259–61*, 138, 264–5, 283–6; discussed in Ridgeway, 358–61.

alongside Edward at Lewes in 1264 and followed him later on crusade.[64] For his part Edward rewarded their devotion between 1259 and 1264 with large grants of land, often of £100 per annum or more at a time. There could be no better proof for the veterans, who had hitherto received relatively little from the prince for their services, of the fundamental shift in Edward's affections.[65]

For those who had striven so long to dig themselves and their clients into the entourage of the future king these new elements posed an alarming challenge. Edward was displaying the same dangerous independence of mind as the rebellious sons of Henry II a century earlier. It is small wonder, then, that in 1258 the veteran courtiers experimented with shackling him under the Provisions of Oxford with irremovable councillors and officials to administer his castles and estates in his name. Of course, these were all men of the old type, such as John de Grey, Roger de Mold and Stephen de Longespée.[66] Royal castles, furthermore, were placed out of Edward's control, even should he become king in the meantime, for 12 years.[67]

It was to the misfortune of the reformers that Edward was made of sterner stuff than his father. Within months he was exploiting divisions within the new royal council in order to free himself from the settlement of 1258. He achieved brief success through his alliance with Simon de Montfort in 1260.[68] But when Henry overthrew the Provisions in 1261 Edward was once again thrust into subordination, for the king was now firmly under the influence of the Savoyards and other veterans. We read, for instance, that the queen brought about the disgrace and expulsion from court of Roger de Leyburn in 1262.[69] High among the charges against Leyburn was that he had obtained at Paris in November 1260 an illegal grant from the prince of one of his 'inseparable' manors, a grant witnessed, interestingly enough, by the Lusignans.[70] The fall of Leyburn was accompanied by that of Roger de Clifford (perhaps also at the queen's instigation) and, a little later, by that of John de Vaux and Hamo l'Estrange.[71] They promptly joined the party of Simon de Montfort and spearheaded his rebellion in 1263. These were years of rebellion, too, for Henry of Almain and John de Warenne, and of political eclipse for William de Valence, although he was allowed to remain at court.[72] It is his divorce from these men which explains much of Edward's perplexing rootlessness and his exile from the realm in the years 1261 – 3 when he could otherwise have done so much to advance his father's cause. Indeed, when in the Autumn of 1263 he was allowed to woo them back into his sevice, not only did Simon de Montfort

64 *William de Rishanger: Chronica et Annales*, ed. H. T. Riley (*RS*, 1865), 22 – 8; S. D. Lloyd, 'The Lord Edward's Crusade: its setting and significance', in *War and Government*, ed. Gillingham, Holt, 127 – 31.

65 *Rishanger*, 12; *Placita de Quo Warranto Temp.Edw.I,II,III*, (Record Commission, 1818), 429; *CChR 1257 – 1300*, 246; C 61/4m.3; E 368/94 m.47.

66 *DBM*, 94 – 5; Studd, 8 – 9. It is not known why John de Balliol was appointed one of Edward's councillors in 1258. His appointment was untypical and he never took office.

67 Treharne, 99.

68 For what follows in detail, Ridgeway, 336 – 402.

69 *Gervase of Canterbury*, ii. 220 – 1.

70 E 368/94 m.47; E 368/36 m.10.; *CR 1261 – 4*, 117.

71 *Gervase of Canterbury*, ii. 221 – 6; E 368/36, mm.11,15d. *CR 1261 – 4*, 133, 170, 359 – 70; *CPR 1258 – 66*, 378; *CPR 1266 – 72*, 298; *CLR 1260 – 7*, 242.

72 Treharne, 302; Ridgeway, 393 – 4, 400 – 1.

lose some of his most valuable supporters but the court gained some of its most fervent royalists, and in Edward, as is well known, a sorely-needed military leader.[73]

Thus what we see in 1258 is, in many ways, a division in the court of King Henry III between the future generation and the old hands. The political achievement of the Provisions of Oxford was a victory for reactionary forces, for the Provisions were the work of conservative-minded courtiers, native and 'alien', who were afraid of the directions that Henry III and the Lord Edward's policies and affections might take in the future. But with Edward growing into manhood and beginning to think for himself, it is possible to see in the politics of the years 1258 – 65 a very different theme. The veterans discovered that they would have to come to terms with new men, with William de Valence and Roger de Leyburn, and ultimately with the Lord Edward himself.

[73] F. M. Powicke, *The Thirteenth Century* (2nd edn, Oxford, 1962), 170 – 226; Treharne, 301 – 28; L. B. Larking, 'On the heart-shrine in Leybourne Church', *Archaeologia Cantiana*, v (1863), 168 – 76; A. Lewis, 'Roger Leyburn and the pacification of England, 1265 – 7', *EHR*, liv (1939), 193 – 214.

Henry III and the End of the Norman Earldom of Chester

Richard Eales

It seems hardly necessary to argue that the division and redistribution of the estates held by Ranulf earl of Chester which took place in the 1230s was a major event of Henry III's reign. Within the period of Henry's personal rule, between the minority and the aftermath of the civil war in the 1260s, it can be compared only with the division of the great Marshal inheritance in 1245 as a shift in the balance of landed power.

The phrase 'end of the Norman earldom of Chester' was used by R. Stewart-Brown in 1920 as the title of a painstaking article in which he unravelled the details of two linked, though distinct, territorial settlements.[1] On the death of Earl Ranulf 'de Blundeville'[2] in 1232 his far-flung possessions in northern and midland England were divided between his four sisters and their descendants. His nephew John 'the Scot', representing the eldest co-heir, took Cheshire as a single lordship, with some external knights' fees attached to it, and was granted the earldom of Chester. The remaining lands were, notionally at least, split equally between the other three heirs. The second settlement became necessary when Earl John died too without issue in 1237. John also had four sisters, though one had predeceased him leaving no heirs,[3] and the eldest, Margaret, was represented in 1237 by her two daughters and their husbands. From the first it was clear that John's lands held in chief outside Cheshire would be divided among the co-heirs, but before the end of 1237 William de Forz, representing the eldest line of descent, was claiming before the royal court that the *comitatus* of Cheshire was a special case, could not be divided, and should pass in its entirety to him with the title of earl. By the time this plea was rejected *coram rege*, probably late in 1239, the other three heirs had accepted compensation elsewhere in England for their claims on the Chester inheritance. When de Forz did the same in 1241, Cheshire accordingly remained as a single entity, but in the hands of the Crown; eventually to be used, with Ireland and Gascony, for the endowment of the king's eldest son in 1254.[4]

There is much in this sequence of events that could be subjected to renewed

[1] R. Stewart-Brown, 'The end of the Norman Earldom of Chester', *EHR*, xxxv (1920), 26–53. See Table, 113 below.

[2] B. E. Harris, 'Ranulph III earl of Chester', *Journ. of the Chester Archaeological Soc.*, lviii (1975), 100–01, clearly shows that this name is not contemporary.

[3] This was Maud, who married John of Monmouth. See K. J. Stringer, *Earl David of Huntingdon 1152–1219: a study in Anglo-Scottish history* (Edinburgh, 1985), 181, 314 n. 10.

[4] Stewart-Brown, 52–3; J. R. Studd, 'The Lord Edward and King Henry III', *BIHR*, l (1977), 4–19; idem, 'The Lord Edward's lordship of Chester', *Trans. of the Historic Soc. of Lancashire and Cheshire*, cxxviii (1979), 1–25.

examination, and its interest as a precedent is enhanced by the curious parallel with the succession to the throne of Scotland in the 1290s, when the same *dramatis personae* reappear claiming by descent from David earl of Huntingdon.[5] There is also the question of the extent to which Chester was a special case in the patchwork of medieval English government and feudal rights, an indivisible 'county palatine' as William de Forz claimed after 1237. More recent research has helped to refocus this longstanding debate, though there remains a tendency to confuse what are really two distinct issues: first, the practical amount of exempt local power wielded by the earl of Chester before 1237 and unchallenged by the Crown; and second, the more self-contained legal, at times little more than semantic, issue of when the concept of a 'county palatine', described in those words, first evolved.[6]

But the primary concern of this paper is an attempt to describe the political context in which the key decisions about the succession to the earldom of Chester were taken in the 1230s. For this purpose it is important to emphasise that the Chester problem cannot be understood in isolation; it must be seen as one thread in a complex interweaving of events. The period just before and after the death of Ranulf de Blundeville, in which the fate of his inheritance was decided, was also the period of the fall of Hubert de Burgh and the installation of the Poitevin regime of Peter des Roches and his allies, of growing signs that Henry III had lost in 1230 his one real opportunity to recover some of the lands of the lost Angevin empire, of continuing trouble in Wales. Specialist studies of all three of these issues have suggested conclusions at variance with those in the older narrative accounts, and it may be that the Chester case too could contribute to a re-appraisal of these years.[7]

The succession to Ranulf de Blundeville's lands in 1232 was important in the first instance because of the sheer scale of his possessions. Towards the end of his life he held 250 – 300 knights' fees for scutage purposes, about 80 in Cheshire and the rest outside, plus at least another 100 from part of the honour of Richmond and half of the honour of Leicester, both of which he held through Henry III's minority and surrendered only in 1230 and 1231.[8] Succeeding to the earldom of Chester in 1181 and coming of age in 1187, Ranulf had built up his landed power with much skill, and shown great adaptability in surviving the hazards of late-twelfth and early-thirteenth century

[5] The Forz interest in Scotland lapsed in 1246 when William de Forz's first wife Christiana of Galloway died without issue. See B. English, *The Lords of Holderness 1086 – 1260: a study in feudal society* (Oxford, 1979), 50 – 1. On David's nearness to the Scottish throne in his own lifetime, Stringer, 42 – 3.

[6] G. Barraclough, 'The earldom and county palatine of Chester', *Trans. of the Historic Soc. of Lancashire and Cheshire*, ciii (1952), 23 – 57, was the crucial revisionist article. J. W. Alexander, 'New evidence on the Palatinate of Chester', *EHR*, lxxxv (1970), 715 – 29; idem, 'The alleged palatinates of Norman England', *Speculum*, lvi (1981), 17 – 27; idem, 'The English palatinates and Edward I', *Journ. of British Studies*, xxii (1983), 1 – 22, surveys the issue exhaustively. His conclusion that the concept of palatinate status was only fully defined at the end of the thirteenth century rather begs the question of how important it was before it was fully defined. See below, n. 60.

[7] D. Carpenter, 'The fall of Hubert de Burgh', *Journ. of British Studies*, xix (1980), 1 – 17; W. B. Stevenson, 'England and Normandy 1204 – 1259' (University of Leeds Ph.D. thesis, 1974), 229 – 33, 445 – 54; R. F. Walker, 'Hubert de Burgh and Wales', *EHR*, lxxxvii (1972), 465 – 94.

[8] W. Farrer, *Honors and Knights' Fees*, II (London, 1924), 1 – 293; J. W. Alexander, *Ranulf of Chester: a relic of the conquest* (Athens, Georgia, 1983), 105 – 15, 161 – 2. I have not attempted to check Alexander's revised (higher) figure. See below, n. 32 (Richmond) and 34 (Leicester).

politics. The phrase 'a relic of the conquest', which J. W. Alexander extracted from Stubbs and applied to Ranulf in the title of his recent biographical study,[9] hardly bears much relation to the earl's real aims or achievements. If he looked to the past, to family claims and inheritances, to buttress his political ambitions, then so did everyone else. Ranulf had in fact made good many of the hopes entertained by his grandfather Ranulf de Gernons in Stephen's reign, and which his father, Earl Hugh, had so signally failed to realise by his participation in the disastrous revolt of 1173 – 4.[10] He was recognised as earl of Lincoln within a few days of the battle in May 1217; he extended his power steadily in the midlands after the division of the lands of the earls of Leicester in 1204 – 5; in the last years of his life he received a grant of all royal lands between Ribble and Mersey in Lancashire.[11] Chester itself remained an important power base, whatever emphasis is placed on the autonomy of its seigneurial administration. Its strategic significance was hardly diminishing in the 1220s and 1230s, at the height of Llywelyn the Great's power, though there remains something of a question mark over the income it yielded in relation to the contingent costs of its defence. Both Ranulf's so-called Magna Carta of Cheshire, issued in 1215 or 1216, and the terms of the 1232 settlement, make it clear that the county was dependent to some extent on military services rendered from other lordships.[12]

However, it was not just the gross value of Ranulf de Blundeville's holdings but also the part he had played in English politics, which made the distribution of his lands and titles so important. Those who have written about Ranulf's career in the last 50 years have conducted a kind of miniature debate on his motives and attitudes, mirroring the broader one on the political outlook of the aristocracy as a whole, but a key point not taken up by biographical studies so far is the fact that the issue of his succession must have cast a very long shadow before it.[13] Ten years of marriage to Constance of Brittany, widow of Geoffrey Plantagenet, had produced no heir, though the general state of their relationship for much of the period down to their final separation in 1199 makes this hardly surprising. But a rapid second marriage in 1200, to Clemence, daughter of Ralph de Fougères, was no more successful.[14] It is interesting to speculate what arrangements Ranulf had made for the eventuality of his death on crusade when he departed in 1218, though I know of no

[9] See W. Stubbs, *The Constitutional History of England* (3rd edn., London, 1887), ii. 47.

[10] G. White, 'King Stephen, duke Henry and Ranulf de Gernons, earl of Chester', *EHR*, xci (1976), 555 – 65; E. King, 'Mountsorrel and its region in King Stephen's reign', *Huntington Library Quarterly*, xliv (1980), 1 – 10.

[11] *RLC*, i. 308 (23 May 1217); *CChR 1226 – 57*, 101 – 2 (18 October 1229). For the general extension of Ranulf's territorial power, see Harris, 103 – 9; Alexander, *Ranulf*, 1 – 36, 69 – 102.

[12] 'Carta communis Cestrisirie' cl. 15, in *The Chartulary or Register of the Abbey of St. Werburgh Chester*, ed. J. Tait (Chetham Soc., lxxix, 1920), 101 – 9. The 'external' fees owing service to Cheshire were divided in 1232. See Stewart-Brown, 32 – 3. On longer term problems of revenue, see P. H. W. Booth, *The Financial Administration of the Lordship and County of Chester 1272 – 1377* (Chetham Soc., xxviii, 1981).

[13] For Ranulf as a political opportunist, see J. C. Holt, *The Northerners: a study in the reign of King John* (Oxford, 1961), 4, 252; S. Painter, *The Reign of King John* (Baltimore, 1949), 20; idem, *William Marshal* (Baltimore, 1933), 194 – 5. For Ranulf as principled loyalist, see F. M. Powicke, *King Henry III and the Lord Edward* (Oxford, 1947), i. 50 – 1; Alexander, *Ranulf*, 91, quoting R. F. Treharne, *Essays on Thirteenth Century England* (London, 1971), 29. The sceptical approach of Harris, 107 – 14, to these interpretations is salutary.

[14] On these marriages, see Harris, 102 – 3; Alexander, *Ranulf*, 12 – 15.

direct evidence. Perhaps he had already tried to ensure the succession of his nephew John as the next earl of Chester. Certainly, after his return in 1220, and the death of John's father David earl of Huntingdon in 1219, he took over the custody of John, then aged about 15, from Alexander II of Scotland in March 1221 with the permission of the English minority government.[15] In 1222 John was married to Helen, daughter of Llywelyn the Great. This can be regarded as another example of a custodian using his ward as a pawn in his own political schemes, but it might also be seen as a move by Ranulf to bring his heir, who was destined to be a major Anglo-Scottish magnate, more firmly into the orbit of Welsh marcher politics.[16]

If this degree of forward planning could take place, then thought must also have been given to the terms on which the division of Ranulf's lands would eventually be made. John, after all, had the legal right to inherit only as one of a number of equal co-heirs, though as representative of the eldest line he could expect to receive the chief honour and the comital title associated with it. The other co-heirs had to be endowed on an acceptable scale, and this consideration may explain some aspects of Ranulf's acquisitiveness. The lands between the Ribble and Mersey, secured only in 1229, thus went to make up a major part of the allocation to William de Ferrers and his wife after 1232.[17] None of this is intended to be the basis of an argument that an elaborate blueprint for the terms of succession existed long before Ranulf's death. Such projected arrangements, like planned marriage alliances and other family settlements, had to be kept as flexible as possible to cope with unforeseen eventualities. But by 1229 or 1230, when Ranulf was about 60 years old, and must long ago have abandoned hope of a direct heir, tentative plans must have been turning into more substantial expectations. Firm evidence of this can be found towards the end of his life in the extraordinary charter by which he recorded his resignation of the earldom of Lincoln in favour of his sister Hawise. It dates from after August 1231 because it is witnessed by Richard Marshal as earl of Pembroke, but almost certainly it was a product of the earl's last weeks. Such an arrangement would naturally require royal confirmation, which was recorded on the Patent Roll on 27 October 1232, the day after Ranulf's death.[18]

The time of Ranulf's death, of course, could not necessarily have been foreseen. He was still campaigning in France as late as summer 1231, and even in September 1232 was an active participant in the political upheaval which followed the fall of Hubert de Burgh.[19] But when he did die, although no will or Inquisition Post Mortem survives, the sequence of events recorded in the records still strengthens the impression of a pre-planned settlement. On 27 October 1232 Ranulf's lands outside Cheshire only were ordered to be handed over to the escheator Peter des Rivaux. On 21 November 1232 John 'the Scot'

[15] *CPR 1216–25*, 285; *RLC*, i. 455. Alexander, *Ranulf*, 150, n. 64 gives full references to the subsequent custody, which lasted until 1227.

[16] *Annales Cestrienses*, ed. R. C. Christie (Rec. Soc. of Lancashire and Cheshire, xiv, 1887), 50–3; Stringer, 182–3.

[17] Above, n. 11. Stewart-Brown, 31–3, outlines the terms of the division.

[18] Charter text printed in *Topographer and Genealogist*, i (1846), 313–14; for the date, see Alexander, *Ranulf*, 100, 160 n. 47. The royal grant of 27 October, *CPR 1225–32*, 508, was subsequently cancelled when overtaken by the arrangements of 22 November. Below, n. 20.

[19] S. Painter, *The Scourge of the Clergy: Peter of Dreux, Duke of Brittany* (Baltimore, 1937), 74–7; Carpenter, 13; Alexander, *Ranulf*, 99–100.

was given the earldom of Chester; on 22 November Hawise de Quency was allowed to pass on the earldom of Lincoln to her son-in-law John de Lacy, constable of Chester, long-established associate of Earl Ranulf, and the only one of his heirs not already in possession of a comital title. Also on 22 November a provisional allocation of lands was made to the three junior co-heirs, reserving the dower rights of Clemence de Fougères, who was to live until 1253. All were given immediate seisin except Hugh d'Aubigny who was a minor, all paid £50 relief, and all were allowed to appeal against the allocations if they wished, pending an extent and final settlement.[20] This was a rapid and painless series of transactions considering the importance of what was at stake, and the potential legal complications which were swept aside, though in some cases only to resurface a few years later.

If the provisional conclusions reached so far are correct, then one or two questions immediately arise. How could Ranulf hope to secure the enforcement of a planned succession deal? Evidently he could not expect to bind the king by a formal undertaking to override the legal rights of a dissentient heir; at least there is no evidence that he attempted to do so. Such an arrangement could only be made if the king himself were prepared to compensate anyone who suffered because of it. One thinks here of the ill-fated oaths taken by the king on 2 July 1232, probably at the instance of Hubert de Burgh, to uphold all the grants he had made to Hubert himself and a number of leading ministers. Eventually Henry had to extricate himself by papal absolution.[21] Ranulf must have relied instead on private agreements and undertakings, first with the principals directly involved, the heirs, and secondly with those whose influence might be helpful, at court or elsewhere. The charter conceding the earldom of Lincoln to Hawise de Quency was witnessed, among others, by the bishops of Winchester and Coventry, Richard Marshal, William de Ferrers and his son, the justice Stephen de Segrave, Simon de Montfort and William de Cantilupe.[22] In a later plea of 1239, William de Forz argued that John 'the Scot', as heir to the earldom of Chester, had been put in possession even during Ranulf's lifetime.[23] There is no evidence that this was true in any legal sense, but such may well have been the practical situation, as far as the officials and leading tenants of Cheshire were concerned. The county does not seem to have been taken into the king's hands at any stage in 1232.

Ranulf must nevertheless have had many anxieties over the implementation of a settlement in which so many parties were involved. Though he could reach an understanding with Peter des Roches as with Hubert de Burgh — probably more easily — the administrative revolution which followed the justiciar's fall at the end of July 1232 might have been a potential cause for concern, and hence a partial explanation for the willingness of the earl of Chester and other magnates to protect Hubert from the extremes of royal vengeance until it was clear how far the upheaval in the royal household and administration was going to go. Ranulf must have exerted his influence above all to secure the

[20] *Excerpta e Rotulis Finium 1216 – 1272*, ed. C. Roberts (London, 1835), i. 230, for instructions to sheriffs to transfer lands outside Cheshire. *Annales Cestrienses*, 58 – 9, is evidence for John's creation as earl of Chester on 21 November. For grants on 22 November, *CPR 1232 – 47*, 3; *CR 1231 – 34*, 169 – 70; Stewart-Brown, 29 – 33.

[21] Carpenter, 8 – 11.

[22] Text cited in n. 18 above.

[23] *Bracton's Note Book*, ed. F. W. Maitland (London, 1887), iii. 282. See below, n. 60.

appoinment as justiciar of Stephen de Segrave, who according to the Waverley annalist was confirmed in office 'consensu domini regis et magnatum totius regni'.[24] Besides being 'a pliable man' in the opinion of Wendover,[25] Segrave was also a close associate of the earl of Chester and remained closely connected with his heir after 1232. The earls had held lordship over land in Segrave itself since Domesday, and the link had been strengthened more recently by grants from Ranulf to Stephen: all his land in Mountsorrel outside the castle, and Bretby in Derbyshire, a gift confirmed by the king in 1228.[26] Such grants obviously had more to do with Segrave's rising influence in the royal administration than with the original tenurial link between the families.

But a projected settlement of Ranulf of Chester's lands may also be looked at from another point of view: what was in it for the king? Did Henry and his advisers merely wish to cultivate the allegiance of John 'the Scot' and John de Lacy, the most obvious beneficiaries in 1232, or is there evidence that Ranulf and his heirs were providing some sort of *quid pro quo* in the last years of his life? King Henry's dominant concern beteen 1229 and 1232 was evidently his hopes of recovering his father's lands in France, hopes heightened, according to the chroniclers, at the Christmas court of 1228, which was attended by the archbishop of Bordeaux and a number of Norman dissidents, who encouraged Henry in the belief that a well-timed invasion would be met by sympathetic revolts in Normandy and Poitou.[27] Such plans involved the forging and financing of a network of alliances, and also, in the king's view at least, the maintenance of good relations with the papacy. This had obvious implications for domestic politics. It was Hubert de Burgh's lukewarm attitude to the French invasion, combined with his alleged complicity in the attacks on Italian clerks, which eventually brought about his downfall in 1232.[28] Ranulf of Chester was no keener on papal demands than Hubert de Burgh; in 1229 he took the lead in opposing the tenth imposed on the English church and almost certainly prevented it being collected in Cheshire,[29] but he did play a prominent part in the eventual royal campaign in France, taking over sole command of the English forces supporting Peter of Brittany on the death of William Marshal in April 1231 and returning himself only after a three-year truce had been agreed in July. This activity contrasts strongly with Ranulf's relative disengagement from royal policies earlier in the 1220s. John 'the Scot' and John de Lacy also participated in this campaign.[30]

So far evidence of Ranulf's co-operation with royal government in the years preceding 1232 is general in nature, but two specific acts show that he was prepared to dispose of some of his possessions in ways desired by the king,

24 *Ann.Mon.*, ii. 311.
25 *Paris*, iii. 240.
26 Farrer, ii. 71 – 2, 62, 43 – 4; *CChR 1226 – 57*, 85. On Segrave's career in general and association with the earls of Chester, see F. J. West, *The Justiciarship in England 1066 – 1232* (Cambridge, 1966), 265 – 71; R. V. Turner, *The English Justiciary in the Age of Glanville and Bracton, c. 1176 – 1239* (Cambridge, 1985), 225, 240 – 9, 255 – 6; Stringer, 183. Segrave was also brother-in-law of Henry de Hastings, one of the co-heirs of 1237; see Stringer, 315, n. 32.
27 Painter, *Scourge*, 59 – 60.
28 Carpenter, 10 – 17.
29 Alexander, *Ranulf*, 95; *Paris*, iii. 189.
30 For the summons and participation in the campaign, see *CR 1227 – 31*, 248; I. J. Sanders, *Feudal Military Service in England* (Oxford, 1956), 115 – 29. For the course of the campaign, see Painter, *Scourge*, 65 – 77. The king himself was in France only from May to October 1230.

comprehensible only as part of a general settlement. The first of these came in May 1230, when Ranulf agreed to surrender Richmond and his share of the honour of Richmond to Henry's chief ally Peter of Brittany in return for the castle of St. James de Beuvron, once held by his ancestors as viscounts of Avranches.[31] This was a major concession. Peter had been trying to recover all of Richmond since 1217: he was half-promised it when he concluded an English alliance in October 1226, but following one of his many changes of sides, in March 1227, he had lost the honour again, and Ranulf was promised that he could retain it until he recovered his own lands in Normandy.[32] The one castle of St. James was a very token way of meeting this obligation; already in autumn 1230 Henry had to promise Ranulf 1000 *m.* to meet the costs of his continuing campaign in France.[33]

The second of Ranulf's concessions was his agreement that Simon de Montfort should be allowed to succeed to the half of the honour of Leicester which he claimed in the right of his grandfather's wife Amicia de Beaumont. These lands had been in Ranulf's custody, on behalf of the Montfort family with which he was linked through his mother, since 1215, but in 1227 he had had his custody converted into a grant for life, so it was a strong bargaining counter in his hands.[34] Many years later, in 1261 or 1262, Simon gave his own account of what happened in 1230 – 1. Having obtained his brother Amaury's permission, he went to England and petitioned the king for the Leicester inheritance, only to be told that it had already been given to the earl of Chester. Simon broke this deadlock 'the following year' by addressing his plea directly to the earl, who was then in Brittany. After this, it was Ranulf who took the initiative, accepting that de Montfort had a greater right to what had been his father's inheritance, taking him to England 'the following August' (1231) and urging Henry to accept Simon's homage, while renouncing his own claims to 'everything that the king had given him'.[35]

Although this version of events has been taken literally by several historians, including Powicke, who explained Ranulf's behaviour by saying that 'the old

[31] *CR 1227 – 31*, 410 (grant of Richmond, 21 May at Nantes); *Paris*, iii. 3, 198 (castle of St. James fortified by Ranulf).

[32] Painter, *Scourge*, 14 – 17, 41 – 2, 47 – 8, 65; *CPR 1225 – 32*, 124 (grant to Ranulf, 18 May 1227). Having originally lost Richmond on the dissolution of his marriage with Constance of Brittany in 1199, Ranulf had held at least part of the honour by royal grant since 1205. See Alexander, *Ranulf*, 20, 73 – 4, 80 – 1.

[33] *CPR 1225 – 32*, 401.

[34] The two Leicester heiresses of 1204 were Amicia, who married Simon de Montfort II, and Margaret, who married Saer de Quency. For subsequent disputes, confiscations and regrants in John's reign and Henry III's minority, see L. W. Vernon Harcourt, *His Grace the Steward and Trial of Peers* (London, 1907), 74 – 7, 88 – 107; L. Fox, 'The honour and earldom of Leicester: origin and descent, 1066 – 1399', *EHR*, liv (1939), 391 – 4. Earl Hugh of Chester married Bertrada de Montfort, daughter of Simon II: Ranulf of Chester was thus a first cousin of Simon de Montfort earl of Leicester. The grants to Ranulf are printed in Harcourt, 104 (21 July 1215), 107 (18 May 1227).

[35] De Montfort's narration is translated in C. Bémont, *Simon de Montfort, Earl of Leicester 1208 – 1265* (Oxford, 1930), 4 – 5; original text in the earlier French edition, *Simon de Montfort, Comte de Leicester* (Paris, 1884), 332 – 5. It cannot be dated precisely, as it is one of a number of *pièces justicatives* compiled by de Montfort between Henry III's attempt to prosecute him in England in 1260 and the resumption of their dispute before the court of Louis IX in 1262. For differing views, see Bémont (Fr. edn.), 332 – 53, (Eng. edn.) 188 – 9, 196 – 9; *DBM*, 33 – 4, 194 – 211.

man's sense of justice was aroused',[36] there is good reason to echo the scepticism of Bémont about a statement that was specifically designed to rebut the accusation that de Montfort had betrayed the king who had launched his career with a special act of favour.[37] Certainly Simon was disingenuous about his dealings with his elder brother Amaury: negotiations between them continued for years over the terms on which Simon could buy out Amaury's claim, and a formal renunciation in England was only made in 1239.[38] The record evidence also tells rather a different story about the appeal to the earl of Chester. Simon visited Henry in England early in 1230 and obtained a grant of the reversion of the Leicester lands to take effect on the earl of Chester's death; this is recorded in a letter patent of 6 February attested by Hubert de Burgh, Ranulf of Chester, William Marshal, Stephen de Segrave and others. In April 1230, after a messenger from Simon had visited the royal court, this was augmented by a grant of 400 *m.* a year from the Exchequer until the Leicester inheritance fell in. De Montfort thus approached the earl of Chester at St. James de Beuvron 'the following year', later in 1230 or early in 1231, as the king's nominee seeking to make a deal.[39] Exactly what Ranulf conceded and what he hoped to get in return we do not know, but when both of them returned to England in July 1231 and attended court in the first two weeks of August at Painscastle, where Henry's Welsh campaign was currently bogged down, the king accepted de Montfort's homage for the Leicester lands on 13 August and ordered him put into possession.[40] Why Henry was prepared to accept his claim is not so clear; Bémont suggests only that 'the light-hearted extravagant monarch of twenty-four' liked to surround himself with plausible companions.[41] The desire to build up contacts with influential French families, even one represented by a younger brother on the make, is a better explanation of the king's reaction. The subsidies which he continued to lavish on Peter of Brittany until his final desertion in 1234 help to reinforce this point.[42] Meanwhile, in the same few days of early August at Painscastle, Henry also took the homage of Richard Marshal for the earldom of Pembroke, granted his brother Richard of Cornwall the county of Cornwall and other lands in fee, and welcomed back to court the crucial figure of Peter des Roches, for the first time in over three years.[43]

There remains one intriguing aspect of this crucial episode. Both the Tewkesbury annals and the locally-composed *Annales Cestrienses* say that

[36] Powicke, 52.

[37] Bémont (Eng. edn.), 4 – 7.

[38] *CChR 1226 – 57*, 242 (17 April 1239); Harcourt, 78 – 86, 108 – 14, with full text of 1239 confirmation at 114; Bémont (Eng. edn.), 5 – 7; Fox, 394 – 6. The dates assigned to some of Amaury's earlier letters by these writers need re-appraisal; he is unlikely to have been putting forward his own claim to the earldom as late as February 1231.

[39] *CPR 1225 – 32*, 325 (6 February 1230); *CR 1227 – 31*, 316, *Royal Letters*, i. 362 (8 April 1230). It is unnecessary to suppose that Simon visited England as early as 1229 for his meeting with the earl of Chester to be 'the following year': a reckoning of the year from Easter is likely and in any case their meeting could have taken place after 1 January 1231.

[40] *CR 1227 – 31*, 543, *Royal Letters*, i. 401 – 2 (13 August 1231). Harcourt's supposition, 79 – 82, that Ranulf refused to surrender the Leicester lands up to his death is shown to be untenable by Fox, 395 – 6, though there may well have been some difficulties over the transfer.

[41] Bémont (Eng. edn.), 7.

[42] Painter, *Scourge*, 77 – 87.

[43] N. Denholm-Young, *Richard of Cornwall* (Oxford, 1947), 20 – 1; Carpenter, 5 – 6, quoting attestations on the Charter Rolls.

Ranulf then left court in a rage. The Chester annals add that he reached Chester by 21 August, 'but by the command of our lord the king, through Stephen de Segrave, he returned to the king'.[44] J. W. Alexander glosses this by saying that Ranulf had attempted to explain Llywelyn's position, and 'the monarch had reacted petulantly', but neither source supports this.[45] The dispute could well have been about something else: for instance, because Ranulf had not intended that Simon de Montfort should obtain immediate possession of his Leicester lands, or because the king had withheld some concession for which he hoped in return. Following his fifteen months campaigning in France, and the settlements with Peter of Brittany and Simon de Montfort, it must have appeared to Ranulf that he had done a great deal to put himself in favour at court, without much security that his own wishes would be met in the future. In March 1232 he opposed a grant of general taxation to the king on behalf of those who had fought in Brittany, arguing that they should not have to pay as well.[46]

In the event, the projected distribution of Earl Ranulf's lands and titles among his co-heirs passed smoothly into operation on his death. But this state of affairs did not last. By the spring of 1235 the other three heirs had summoned John 'the Scot' by writ to explain *coram rege* why they had not received equal shares of the whole of Ranulf's inheritance, including Chester. The case surfaces on the first roll of William de Ralegh as chief justice *coram rege*, and this may not be entirely coincidental. Segrave's dismissal from office in May 1234 must have increased the chances of pursuing such a suit successfully.[47] John appeared by attorney in April 1235 and argued that as *Dominus Comes* of Chester he did not have to reply to a writ issued outside the county concerning his holdings within it. This held matters up until November 1236, when the objection was turned down, and the earl responded with a series of lesser procedural points.[48] There was by now an obvious danger that the whole succession settlement of 1232 would come apart. The threat also helps to explain Earl John's cautious loyalism in national politics, steering clear both of court factions and of the more local grievances released by Richard Marshal's rebellion in 1233–4.[49] What the king's final decision in the case would have been is unclear; it would probably have been swayed by the political needs of the moment rather than obligations and understandings entered into years before. As it was, John's death shortly before 6 June 1237 caused the plea to be broken off.

Naturally this event too could not have been predicted. Though the earl like his uncle had been long married without producing heirs, there was as yet no real cause for concern; he was little more than thirty. But he was apparently

[44] Tewkesbury annals in *Ann.Mon.*, i. 79; *Annales Cestrienses*, 56–9. On the value of the Chester annals as a source, see Studd, 'Lordship of Chester', 4–5.

[45] Alexander, *Ranulf*, 99.

[46] *Paris*, iii. 212.

[47] *CRR*, xv. 365–6 (case 1423A); *Bracton's Note Book*, iii. 146–7 (case 1127); Stewart-Brown, 34. C. A. F. Meekings discusses the circumstances of Ralegh's appointment and Segrave's dismissal in *CRR*, xv. xxiii–xxxii. Above, n. 26.

[48] The date of April 1235 is a probable inference from the position of the case on the roll: *CRR*, xv. xlviii–ix. It appears with an adjournment (first of many ?) to 25 June 1235. It reappears in the records in about November 1236, with another adjournment allowed until 3 February 1237; *CRR*, xv. lvi–vii, 498–9 (case 1958); *Bracton's Note Book*, iii. 226–7 (case 1213); Stewart-Brown, 34–6.

[49] Stringer, 183.

seriously ill at least for several weeks before the end. On 13 May 1237 Henry de Audley and the bishop of Coventry were sent to Cheshire to keep the peace.[50] When his death was announced, in a letter patent of 6 June 1237, the government's reaction was very different from that in 1232. Cheshire and its castles were taken into the king's hands, and the fealty of the tenants was taken. John Mansel was associated with the administrators sent in to run the county; he, with James de Audley and Walkelin de Arderne, was to report to the king in person.[51] All these arrangements, as Stewart-Brown remarks,

> go far beyond what would have been necessary if only a temporary custody of the county palatine in the king's hand until the recognition of a new earl had been contemplated.[52]

Not surprisingly, William de Forz, John de Balliol and Robert de Brus had all appointed attorneys to make formal claim for their shares in the inheritance by August.[53] It cannot be assumed that there was already a fully-formulated royal plan to take over Cheshire and compensate the co-heirs elsewhere. On 10 July 1237 John de Lacy, earl of Lincoln, was appointed custodian of the county, leasing the demesne for an annual term; his first account, for the year beginning 29 August 1237, appears on the Pipe Roll.[54] Meanwhile, John 'the Scot''s lands outside Cheshire, over which there was no real dispute, were put in the custody of William de Forz, count of Aumâle, father of the claimant William de Forz, by the end of September.[55] But the co-heirs got no joy out of the earldom of Huntingdon, which had been held by John and his father David since 1185 'de feudo regis Scotie'. How, legally, an earldom could be held in this way was unclear, but Alexander II nevertheless reacted quickly to his cousin's death. In mid-June 1237 he was already pleading *coram rege* that the *comitatus* of Huntingdon should pass to him, because it was held from him and he had had custody of its heir, that is between 1219 and 1221. These pleas were all rejected, but the honour of Huntingdon was granted to Alexander by the end of the month anyway; it was not to be diverted from its long-established function of smoothing Anglo-Scottish relations.[56]

By the end of the year it was also becoming clearer that the king and his advisers had now resolved not to let Cheshire slip out of their grasp. The earldom of Chester case, round two, appears *coram rege* in November 1237, with initial pleading on the question of whether, after partition, the co-heirs should each hold directly of the Crown or whether the other three should hold

50 *CPR 1232–47*, 182.
51 *CPR 1232–47*, 184–5 (6 June), 188 (22 June); *CR 1234–37*, 538–9 (22 June).
52 Stewart-Brown, 49.
53 *CR 1234–37*, 540, 563.
54 *CPR 1232–47*, 189, 195; *Cheshire in the Pipe Rolls 1158–1301*, ed. M. H. Mills and R. Stewart-Brown (Rec. Soc. of Lancashire and Cheshire, xcii, 1938), 26–48; Stewart-Brown, 49–50.
55 *CR 1234–37*, 497–8, 507–8.
56 *CRR*, xvi. 6 (case 18); *Bracton's Note Book*, iii. 235–6 (case 1221). The plea was over by 20 June. See *CRR*, xvi. xxviii. Before then Huntingdon lands were being handed over to Alexander's agents. See *CPR 1232–47*, 186 (14 June); *CR 1237–42*, 454 (16 June). Negotiations were already moving towards the Anglo-Scottish treaty concluded at York in September. On the earlier links between Huntingdon and Scotland, see Stringer, 36–7, 53; on the divisions of John's Scottish lands, see Stringer, 185–9.

of William de Forz 'qui habet aesnesciam [the rights of the eldest co-heir] et debet esse comes'.[57] But it is indicative that the king had already, by this time, bought out John de Balliol's claim, by a deal later recorded on the Patent Roll in December. By June 1238 similar arrangements had been made with Robert de Brus and Henry de Hastings, and recorded in the Chancery rolls.[58] All of these were dependent on the resolution of William de Forz's outstanding claim; without that the provisional settlements would lapse and the rights of the co-heirs to pursue their legal claims to shares of the inheritance would revive.

Further progress of the matter is hard to follow because of record losses for the year 1238 – 9, but the final legal resolution of the 'earl of Chester case' is preserved in Bracton's Note Book from a lost curia regis roll. The hearing, probably in the final months of 1239, was before a formidable council of the king, the legate, both archbishops, five bishops, two earls, the durable Stephen de Segrave, now restored to office as chief justice *coram rege*, and many others.[59] William de Forz argued that the county of Cheshire should not be divided because it was a special case, 'cum sit Comitatus Paleys'. But though the other co-heirs put in their pleas, as did William de Ferrers and Hugh d'Aubigny, still pursuing their grievances over the 1232 settlement, de Forz was really up against the Crown and the outcome was predictable. Final judgement was for division, because division had occurred in 1232; whatever the subsequent grievances of the other heirs John 'the Scot' had only received Cheshire as his share of the whole inheritance, not because of its special status. De Forz retained his right to the *caput* of the honour, Chester itself, and the comital title, but this would hardly be supportable on the basis of one half of one third of the honour.[60] His eventual capitulation and acceptance of compensation for his claim followed by October 1241, with a final quitclaim acknowledging the king's tenure 'cum castro, sigillo et libertate gladii' in February 1242.[61] A major territorial shift had taken place, though King Henry seems to have had at first no clear plans for Cheshire. In 1243 it was given to Queen Eleanor for life, as a dower settlement.[62]

[57] *CRR*, xvi. 39 – 40 (case 136C); *Bracton's Note Book*, iii. 242 – 3 (case 1227). The plea is datable to 12 November 1237: *CRR*, xvi. xxx. It was adjourned 'de consensu omnium' to the next term, Hilary 1238, because of general uncertainty over how to decide it: 'omnes dixerunt quod nunquam viderunt talem casum'.

[58] For Balliol, see *CPR 1232 – 47*, 206 (11 December 1237), 209 – 10; *CR 1237 – 42*, 6, 12. For Brus, see *CPR 1232 – 47*, 224 (11 June 1238); *CR 1237 – 42*, 59, 99. For Hastings, see *CPR 1232 – 47*, 224 (11 June 1238); *CR 1237 – 42*, 60, 76. Stewart-Brown, 36 – 9.

[59] *Bracton's Note Book*, iii. 280 – 3 (case 1273), dated tentatively to the period between October 1239 and the early months of 1240 by the list of those present; *CCR*, xvi. xix, xxxvi. The original roll does not survive. There are no Patent Rolls for 23 or 24 Henry III (1238 – 40) and no Close Roll for 23 Henry III (1238 – 9).

[60] Stewart-Brown, 39 – 41, provides a narrative of the plea paraphrased from the record. Much more could be said about it. Alexander, 'Palatinates and Edward I', 6, brushed aside de Forz's claim on the grounds that the case 'was decided without reference to an alleged palatine position'. But given the political circumstances this was hardly surprising; the significant fact is surely that such a claim was made. See above, n. 6.

[61] *CChR 1226 – 57*, 262 (5 October), 263 (16 October); *CR 1237 – 42*, 339 – 40; Stewart-Brown, 43 – 5. After this the other co-heirs began, somewhat haphazardly, to finalise their agreements of 1237 – 8, with an eye to fringe benefits like liberties and privileges, eg. *CChR 1226 – 57*, 262 (16 October 1241, for Isabel de Brus).

[62] *CPR 1232 – 47*, 395 (11 August 1243), confirmed a few years later, 501 (10 May 1247); Stewart-Brown, 52 – 3.

Very different conclusions have been drawn from the eventual outcome of the 1237 succession to the earldom of Chester. For Stewart-Brown,

> the recorded processes of the exchanges were constitutional and legal . . . the whole transaction in the light of the evidence presents the Crown and its advisers in a favourable light. References to the transaction in thirteenth-century Cheshire sources ascribe no hardship.[63]

One is reminded of the observation of J. C. Holt that some thirteenth-century Norman sources gloss over the replacement of John by Philip Augustus as an unexceptionable succession in the duchy.[64] K. B. McFarlane, on the other hand, saw a parallel here with some of Edward's later activities:

> Thus was William de Forz in 1237 denied the earldom of Chester, to which he had an unimpeachable hereditary claim, so that Henry III could annex it for the ultimate benefit of his own eldest son. Edward I owed his valuable palatinate to an act of royal injustice.[65]

Banal as it may be to say so, the truth lies between these two extreme views. Henry III obviously had no need to use coercion in the earldom of Chester settlement when he already held all the crucial cards. Time was on his side: the county and its revenues were in his hands. Even the division of the lands outside Cheshire was postponed in September 1238, taking place at an unknown date between then and June 1241, when the first of the final settlements was enrolled.[66] As the months and years slipped by, the willingness of the co-heirs to sell their claims for the most they could get must have increased. William de Forz, who alone could play for higher stakes, had little hope of judicial remedy, and his abandonment of his claim in October 1241 was clearly influenced by his succession to his father as count of Aumâle in September, and an agreement with the king about the terms on which he could pay off his, and his father's debts at the Exchequer.[67] There is little here to justify a eulogy of the qualities of royal justice. On the other hand, McFarlane's cut-and-dried conclusion seems to ignore the fact that de Forz's claim to an undivided inheritance was at best debatable, and that the rights of collateral heirs were often regarded as negotiable rather than demonstrable in the thirteenth century, not just by Henry III and his son.

[63] Stewart-Brown, 45.

[64] J. C. Holt, 'The end of the Anglo-Norman realm', *Procs. of the British Academy*, lxi (1975), 223 – 4.

[65] K. B. McFarlane, 'Had Edward I a policy towards the earls?', in idem, *The Nobility of Later Medieval England* (Oxford, 1973), 250.

[66] The delay was only for a month or so, see *CR 1237 – 42*, 104. A commission was appointed to make a division in October, see *CPR 1232 – 47*, 234. But there is no evidence of firm settlements until 1241, and as late as 1243 John de Balliol complained that his allocation was still provisional, see Stewart-Brown, 37 – 8.

[67] William de Forz, count of Aumâle died on crusade, perhaps as early as March, in 1241, see *Paris*, iv. 174. But the first evidence of his son being put in possession is on 18 September, see *CPR 1232 – 47*, 258. Possibly the circumstances permitted royal delay. For family debts and other hypothetical reasons for the 1241 Chester settlement, see English, 49 – 51; R. V. Turner, 'William de Forz, count of Aumâle', *Procs. of the American Philosophical Soc.*, cxv (1971), 248 – 9.

One final conclusion I would draw is that 'the end of the Norman earldom of Chester' after 1237 shows the skill and finesse of which royal government could be capable in the early years of Henry's personal rule. This can be argued not just from the diplomatic dealings with the parties, but also from the way the takeover was managed at the local level, to minimise disruption in Cheshire itself.[68] It forms a kind of counterpoint to what I have argued was Ranulf de Blundeville's ingenuity and foresight in securing a planned distribution of his lands and titles on his death in 1232.

[68] Stewart-Brown, 48 – 53; Studd, 'Lordship of Chester', 14 – 19.

Claimants to the earldom of Chester in 1232 and 1237

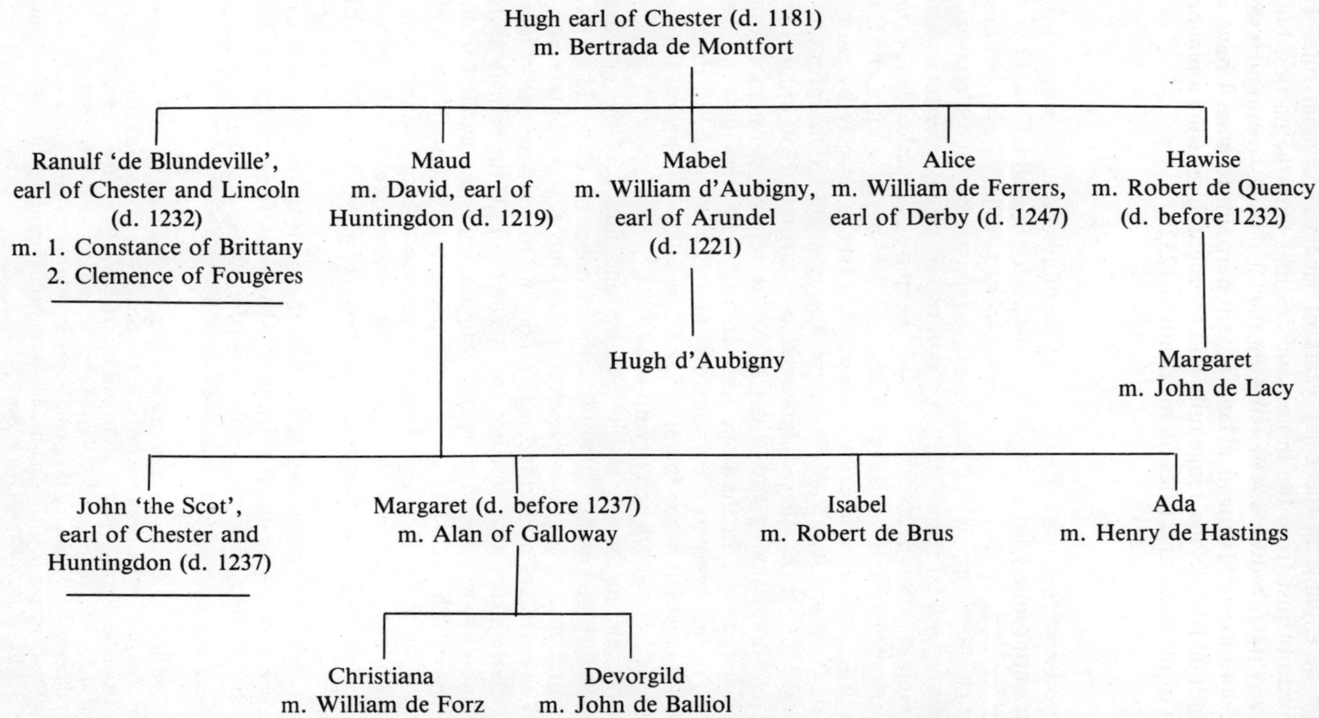

The Number and Distribution of Knights in Thirteenth Century England: The Evidence of the Grand Assize Lists

J. Quick

There are various ways of estimating the number and distribution of knights in thirteenth century England.[1] The most accurate method would be to draw up lists for each county of those men labelled 'miles', 'sire' or 'dominus' (excluding those cases where this last title refers either to ecclesiastics or to non-knightly lords of manors), in such sources as private charters, cartularies and government rolls. However, it would be quite impracticable for one historian to attempt to pursue this line of research for all the counties of England and, therefore, shorter routes must be found. Hence, largely by studying the so-called *Parliamentary Roll*, Denholm-Young suggested that, for any time in the period 1266 – 1322, there might have been around 1250 knights in England.[2] But Denholm-Young was silent as to the relative density of knights in the English counties. In the hope of shedding some new light on these issues, I intend in this essay to use a source hitherto largely ignored, namely the grand assize lists which occur mainly in the eyre rolls. The period I have studied is from the late twelfth century up until 1272.

Although, in theory, all the electors and jurors of the grand assize were supposed to be knights,[3] there is some evidence which could be interpreted to suggest that some grand assize electors and jurors were, in fact, not knights. In 1207 the electors of a grand assize jury in Dorset were put in mercy because they chose jurors who were not knights and in 1303 the bailiffs of the liberty of Richmond were ordered to return four knights in exchange for the four 'servientes' which they had incorrectly presented.[4] Although in both these instances the presence of non-knights was detected, one cannot help wondering in how many other cases such errors were overlooked. In the Wiltshire eyre of 1249, four knights were summoned to elect twelve 'lawful men' for the grand assize.[5]

Yet there are also strong indications that at least the great majority of grand assize knights were indeed knights. Most significantly, perhaps, there were occasions when, owing to an absence of knights, grand assizes simply were not

[1] I would like to thank Dr P. A. Brand and Dr J. R. Maddicott for commenting on earlier drafts of this essay. All manuscript references are to documents in the PRO.

[2] N. Denholm-Young, 'Feudal Society in the Thirteenth Century: The Knights', *History*, xxix (1944), 107 – 19, printed in his *Collected Papers on Medieval Subjects* (Cardiff, 1969), 83 – 94.

[3] See the writ for arraigning the grand assize in *Bracton on the Laws and Customs of England* (hereafter *Bracton*), tr. S. E. Thorne, ed. G. E. Woodbine (London, 1968 – 77), iv. 57.

[4] *CRR 1207 – 9*, 109; CP 40/145 m.86d.

[5] *Civil Pleas of the Wiltshire Eyre, 1249*, ed. M. T. Clanchy (Wilts. Rec. Soc., xxvi, 1970), no. 226, p. 82.

held. It was noted in the Westmorland eyre of 1256 that two parties, after having put themselves on a grand assize, had reached a final concord 'because no knights had come'.[6] In 1253 we hear that in Staffordshire and Middlesex grand assizes had not been held because of a shortage of knights who had not been exempted from local jury duties by the king.[7] The administrators of these three counties had felt it wrong, presumably, to substitute local freemen for knights. Interestingly, the barons in 1258 claimed that grand assizes had not been held 'in many counties' due to the large number of these royal exemptions.[8] But this claim may have been an exaggeration, for no other county appears to have suffered the same problem as Westmorland, Staffordshire and Middlesex and, as the appendix shows, many other counties held numerous grand assizes in the 1250s.[9]

In Westmorland, knights were sometimes drafted in from Cumberland to make up numbers for the grand assize.[10] Similarly in Rutland in 1287 one of the grand assize knights was specified as coming from Northamptonshire, and in Lancashire in 1203 knightly numbers for the grand assize had to be made up with knights from Yorkshire.[11] The same point can be made from these examples as was stated in the previous paragraph: knights rather than freemen appear to have been considered a necessity for a grand assize.

The Crown was clearly anxious to ensure that knights participated in grand assizes. It was the king's justices who amerced the Devon electors for choosing men who were not knights and who detected the presence of mere 'servientes' in the Richmond case of 1303.[12] Following the claim of the barons in 1258 about exempted knights, the Provisions of Westminster made allowance for such exemptions to be overriden in certain circumstances, and this ruling was repeated in the Statute of Marlborough.[13] The Statute of Westminster II mentioned and allowed the practice of using non-local knights in the grand assize so long as they had a tenement in that county.[14] In addition, as we shall see, landless knights do not appear to have been allowed to sit on a grand assize.[15] Presumably justices only permitted men of substance to participate.

There is also the silent testimony of the lists for distraints of knighthood. It is possible to compare some of these lists for the year 1256, when £15 was the level of distraint, with grand assize lists which occur in earlier eyres for the counties of Hampshire,[16] Herefordshire,[17] Leicestershire,[18] Lincolnshire[19] and Surrey.[20] If an elector or juror were to appear in the 1256 distraint lists, then he

[6] JUST 1/979 m.6d.

[7] *CR 1251–3*, 442–3.

[8] *DBM*, 88–9.

[9] As Professor Waugh has said, 'the shortage of (non-exempted) knights was far from crippling to the judicial machinery'; S. L. Waugh 'Reluctant Knights and Jurors: Respites, Exemptions and Public Obligations in the reign of Henry III', *Speculum* lviii (1983), 969.

[10] Eg., JUST 1/981 mm.8d, 13, 13d.

[11] CP 40/68 m.43d (Rutland); CP 40/144 m.184d. (Lancashire).

[12] *CRR 1207–9*, 109; CP 40/145 m.86d.

[13] *DBM*, 142–3; *EHD*, iii. 371.

[14] *EHD* iii. cl. 38, p. 450.

[15] Below, 116.

[16] C 47/1/1 no. 23, JUST 1/778 mm.2, 20d (1256 eyre).

[17] C 47/1/1 no. 29, JUST 1/300C mm.3d, 9 (1255 eyre).

[18] C 47/1/1 no. 3, JUST 1/454 mm.8, 16d, 21 (1247 eyre).

[19] C 47/1/1 no. 15, JUST 1/482 mm.3, 3d, 4d, 5, 6, 6d, 7, 7d, 8d, 10d, 12d, 47 (1245 eyre).

[20] C 47/1/1 nos. 34–5, JUST 1/872 mm.7, 11, 13, 14, 17, 20 (1255 eyre), KB 26/160 m.6 (1258).

could not have been a knight at the time of his earlier service on a grand assize. But, in fact, no such elector or juror occurs in the distraint lists for 1256. The evidence cited above would therefore seem to suggest that, although some non-knights may have participated in grand assizes, the great majority of electors and jurors were indeed knights.

Apart from the difficulty of being sure whether or not knights of the grand assize were actually knights, there are also problems in knowing how many local knights served on grand assizes. Some knights were able to avoid service on the grand assize. They might obtain royal grants of exemption from civil duties, they might bribe the sheriff not to summons them or they might not appear on the day of the grand assize.[21] Other knights were excluded from grand assizes; challenges by the parties, for instance, had this effect. For example in Lancashire in 1302, of the 13 knights whom the electors said were in the county, five were challenged by the parties.[22] It is also virtually certain that only knights with land were liable to service on the grand assize. The Statute of Westminster II set minimum landed qualifications for jurors in cases other than those involving the grand assize, and it seems to be implied that such qualifications already existed for knights of the grand assize.[23] This fact means that many of the landless knights who formed part of the *familia* of the great lords are unrepresented in the grand assize lists.[24] In 1220 in Herefordshire, Sir Robert Vernay was disqualified from acting as one of the four knights sent to check-up on a litigant who had essoined himself *de malo lecti* because he was 'from a household and [did] not have any land'.[25] It may well be that the specifications in the writ for arraigning a grand assize that 'legaliores milites' should be used was designed to exclude landless knights.[26]

There was another limitation on the number of knights who served on grand assizes. In 1293 it was noted in the plea roll of the Bench that Sir Thomas Gardino, who held the barony of Cogges in Oxfordshire,[27] had been made a knight of the grand assize but had come into court to point out that he ought not to have been put on to any assize or jury because he was a *baro* of the king.[28] And indeed it does appear that barons did not serve as grand assize electors or jurors.[29]

Another, although less significant, difficulty with grand assize lists is that, according to the Statute of Westminster II, knights from one county could act as grand assize electors or jurors in another county so long as they held a tenement in that county.[30] But it is my impression that, although such cases of grand assize jurors being drawn from other counties are not rare, neither are

[21] As, eg., in Somerset in 1238: JUST 1/174 m.22.
[22] CP 40/144 m.184d.
[23] *EHD*, iii. cl 38, p. 450.
[24] See G. A. Simpson, 'The *Familia* of Roger de Quincy, Earl of Winchester and Constable of Scotland', in *Essays on the Nobilty of Medieval Scotland*, ed. K. J. Stringer (Edinburgh, 1985), 102–30, esp. 120.
[25] *CRR 1220*, 157.
[26] *Bracton*, iv. 57.
[27] I. J. Sanders, *English Baronies* (Oxford, 1960), 37; *CIPM*, vii. no. 129; and see *CFR 1272–1307*, 280, for his relief.
[28] CP 40/101 m.16d.
[29] For the way in which barons had a different status from that of ordinary knights, see I. J. Sanders, *Feudal Military Service in England* (Oxford, 1956), 1–28.
[30] *EHD*, iii, cl. 28, p. 450.

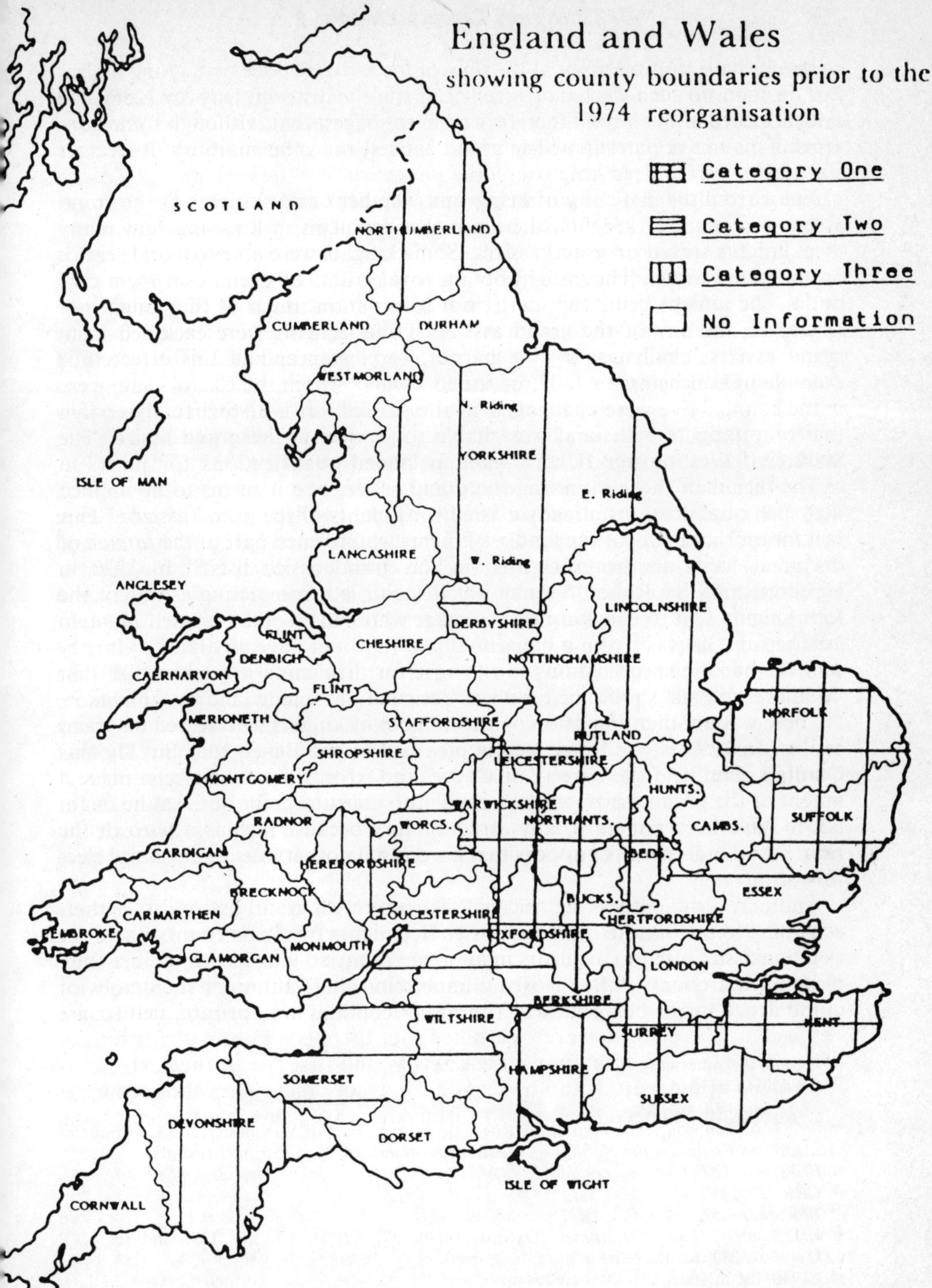

England and Wales
showing county boundaries prior to the 1974 reorganisation

they especially common.

The main source for grand assize lists is the eyre rolls. To this source can be added information from the eyre writ files, of which very few survive, and from the curia regis rolls which I have looked at in their published form up until 1242. For our purposes, only the Berkshire writ file of 1248,[31] a Kentish grand assize list from the curia regis rolls for 1227 and a Surrey list from the Bench records for 1258[32] have been found useful enough to supplement the evidence drawn from the eyres. An added attraction of the grand assize lists is that they usually name considerably more than 12 knights, usually around 16 or so. The jurors would then have been drawn from this pool of knights.[33]

Unfortunately the eyre rolls are themselves sometimes disappointing. In some of the eyre rolls only one or two lists or, often, no grand assize lists, occur. I have thought it best only to count knights where there are at least three grand assize lists in the eyre roll. This consideration, combined with the fact that only a limited number of eyre rolls have survived, means that it has proved possible to produce figures for only 27 counties in the period up until 1272.

The results are set out in the appendix.[34] As can be seen, I have presented only the number of grand assize knights as can be discovered from one eyre roll for each county. The appendix is, therefore, far from being exhaustive and excludes a large number of statistics which could be collected from a number of other eyres. However it seems unlikely that a more detailed study would significantly change the general arguments presented in this essay. The first column of figures in the appendix which needs to be noted is that of the number of knights per county. In themselves these numbers are of little use other than that they reveal the obvious fact that, in general, the bigger or more fertile the shire, then the greater its total number of knights. More interesting results occur when we divide the number of knights in each county by that county's total acreage. The figures produced, that is the average number of acres to each knight, show the relative density of knights in the 27 counties for which suitable information exists. In order to make the results of these calculations more intelligible, I have divided my counties into three groups and I have provided a map.

Category one represents the ten shires which were the most densely populated with knights, category two represents the next ten counties so populated and category three includes those counties where knights were thinnest on the ground. I have divided the shires into these three groups simply for convenience and in the belief that to create more than three groups could cause confusion. It should, however, be noted that there is no dramatic difference between the last few counties of one category and first few of the next.

Looking at the map, it can be seen that category one covers those counties on what might be called the London-Birmingham axis, along with Norfolk and

[31] *Roll and Writ File of the Berkshire Eyre of 1248*, ed. M. T. Clanchy (Selden Soc., xc, 1972 – 3), no. a31.

[32] *CRR 1227 – 30*, no. 42 (Kent); KB 26/160 m.6 (Surrey). The latter was pointed out to me by Dr Brand.

[33] Occasionally, the actual jurors are designated, eg. the Hampshire eyre of 1236: JUST 1/775 m.2. The list in the appendix includes all named jurors, whether or not their names were later deleted.

[34] The sixth column of the appendix is not supposed to indicate that knights actually possessed the stated number of acres.

Suffolk in the east and Kent and Surrey in the south. Category two embraces many of the more outlying shires which border the counties in category one. Category three includes the more peripheral shires. If this map is compared with estimates of the density of population and wealth of the English counties, then it can be seen that a broad similarity exists.[35] The greater the density of population and wealth in a county, then the greater its density of knights.

The usefulness of the figures presented in the appendix may be challenged by arguing that richer counties tended to hold more grand assizes per square acre than poorer counties so that, the argument goes, it is inevitable that richer counties will seem to have the greater density of knights. Yet this objection is unconvincing as it seems likely that the density of knights and the frequency of grand assizes were not related to each other but, rather, were both dependent on the same cause, this being the density of population and wealth in a county.

Apart from estimating the relative densities of knights in the shires, the grand assize lists can also be used to make a cautious estimate of the minimum number of knights in England at any one time. If we add up the total number of knights shown in the appendix then we reach a figure of 1539 knights, an average of 57 knights per county. This total figure may be put forward as a very rough indication of the minimum number of knights that there might have been in England at any one time. But it cannot be stressed enough that this figure is only an estimate and that it is, in many respects, unsatisfactory. It excludes the knights of 12 counties. Most of the shires for which information does not survive (like Cornwall and Lancashire) probably had relatively few knights, but other counties (like Cambridgeshire and Nottinghamshire) would probably have added significantly to the total sum of knights. Our total estimate is also unsatisfactory because it takes no account of any decline in the number of knights that might have occurred in the course of the century. Finally, it is a figure that, of course, includes only the knights of the grand assize.

Two main points may be made from the arguments and data presented in this essay: firstly, that the density of knights in the English shires tended, in general, to be aligned with the population and wealth of a county; and secondly, that the number of knights who were involved in the administration of local government at any one time was probably somewhere around 1000 – 2000. Although this number excludes barons, landless knights and those knights who successfully avoided grand assize service, it is difficult to believe that there could have been much more than 2000 knights in England at any one time. The order of magnitude for knightly numbers in the thirteenth century envisaged by Denholm-Young seems, therefore, to be roughly correct. This conclusion seems to be all the more convincing when it is remembered that my estimate has been arrived at by using a source which Denholm-Young overlooked.

35 See, amongst others, J .C. Russell, *British Medieval Population* (Albuquerque, 1948), 313; and *The Lay Subsidy of 1334*, ed. R. E. Glasscock (British Academy Records of Social and Economic History, n.s., ii, 1975), xxvii.

Appendix

County	Year of eyre	Nos. of grand assize lists	Nos. of knights	Total acreage	Average nos. of acres to each knight	References
Category One						
1. Bedfordshire	1227	18	51	302,942	5 940	*Roll of Justices in Eyre in Bedfordshire, 1227*, ed. G. Herbert Fowler (Beds. Hist. Rec. Soc., iii, 1916), nos. 169, 185, 186, 190, 193, 196, 197, 198, 200, 201, 204, 206, 208, 213, 214, 294, 320, 518.
2. Buckinghamshire	1227	10	60	479,360	7 989	*Calendar of the Roll of the Justices on Eyre, 1227*, ed. J. G. Jenkins (Bucks. Arch. Soc. Rec. Branch, vi, 1942), nos. 132, 134, 138, 142, 143, 256, 310, 311, 312, 313.
3. Suffolk	1240	15	101	948,269	9 388	JUST 1/818 mm.4, 4d, 13d, 17, 20, 20d, 26, 34d, 40d, 42.
4. Oxfordshire	1247	5	45	479,220	10,649	JUST 1/699 mm.8, 13, 17, 21, 24.
5. Warwickshire	1232	11	56	605,275	10,808	JUST 1/951A mm.8, 9, 9d, 11, 14d, 15d.
6. Northamptonshire	1202	7	59	638,612	10,823	*The Earliest Northamptonshire Assize Rolls 1202–3*, ed. D. M. Stenton (Northants. Rec. Soc., v, 1930), nos. 406, 439, 451, 463, 464, 467, 598.

Appendix (continued)

County	Year of eyre	Nos. of grand assize lists	Nos. of knights	Total acreage	Average nos. of acres to each knight	References
7. Surrey	1255	7	41	461,829	11,264	JUST 1/872 mm.7, 11, 13, 14, 17, 20; KB 26/160 m.6 (1258).
8. Leicestershire	1247	3	46	532,779	11,582	JUST 1/454 mm.8, 16d, 21.
9. Kent	1227	31	81	975,966	12,048	JUST 1/358 mm.1 (x6), 3 – 10, 11d, 14d, 15 (x3), (partly damaged); also *CRR 1227 – 30*, no. 42.
10. Norfolk	1257	16	108	1,315,064	12,176	JUST 1/567 mm.1, 1d, 2, 7d, 8d, 9, 9d, 10d, 22d, 23, 24d, 28d, 39d, 46 (x2), 47d.
Category Two						
11. Worcestershire	1255	5	37	458,352	12,387	JUST 1/1022 mm.1d, 2, 2d, 7, 19d, (partly damaged).
12. Berkshire	1248	3	36	479,360	13,315	*Roll and Writ File of the Berkshire Eyre of 1248*, ed. M. T. Clanchy (Selden Soc., xc, 1972 – 3), nos. 174, 372, a31.
13. Staffordshire	1227	4 (plus a knightly jury of enquiry)	55	741,318	13,478	JUST 1/801, mm.1 (x4), 15.
14. Hertfordshire	1248	4	29	404,523	13,949	JUST 1/318 mm.6d, 10, 14, 15d.

Appendix (continued)

County	Year of eyre	Nos. of grand assize lists	Nos. of knights	Total acreage	Average nos. of acres to each knight	References
15. Somerset	1243	7	69	1,037,642	15,038	*Somersetshire Pleas*, ed. C. E. H. Chadwick-Healey (Somerset. Rec. Soc., xi, 1897), nos. 421, 422, 423, 424, 425, 510, 587.
16. Derbyshire	1269	3	43	650,369	15,124	*Calendar of the Cases for Derbyshire from Eyre and Assize Rolls*, ed. C. L. Lugard (Barnston, Cheshire, 1938), 55 – 6, 157, 172.
17. Gloucestershire	1221	6	49	805,794	16,444	*Rolls of the Justices in Eyre, Gloucs, Wars, Staffs, 1221, 1222*, ed. D. M. Stenton (Selden Soc., lix, 1940), nos. 93, 111, 130, 132, 182, 184.
18. Shropshire	1203	6	48	861,000	17,954	*Pleas before the King or his Justices, 1198 – 1212*, III, ed. D. M. Stenton (Selden Soc., lxxxiii, 1967), nos. 770, 776, 777, 782, 783, 785.
19. Wiltshire	1249	5	47	864,101	18,385	*Civil Pleas of the Wiltshire Eyre, 1249*, ed. M. T. Clanchy (Wilts, Rec. Soc., xxvi, 1970), nos. 75, 77, 78, 226 (assuming knighthood), 334.
20. Essex	1254	8	53	979,532	18,481	JUST 1/233 mm.5, 12d (x2), 14, 18, 22, 30d, 33.

Appendix (continued)

County	Year of eyre	Nos. of grand assize lists	Nos. of knights	Total acreage	Average nos. of acres to each knight	References
Category Three						
21. Hampshire	1236	7	55	1,053,092	19,147	JUST 1/775 mm.1 (x2), 2 (x4), 3d.
22. Herefordshire	1255	4	28	538,924	19,247	JUST 1/300C mm.3d (x2), 9 (x2).
23. Lincolnshire	1202	17	138	2,705,293	19,603	*The Earliest Lincolnshire Assize Rolls*, ed. D. M. Stenton (Lincs. Rec. Soc., xxii, 1926), nos. 22, 61, 76, 82, 117, 134, 139, 145, 148, 157, 186, 187, 188, 196, 225, 266, 1175, 1207.
24. Devon	1238	11	85	1,671,364	19,663	JUST 1/174 mm.2, 3, 4, 8, 9d, 18, 18d, 19d, 22d.
25. Sussex	1248	3	33	932,409	28,254	JUST /909A mm.1d, 3, 4d.
26. Northumberland	1269	3	24	1,291,515	53,813	*The Early Assize Rolls of Northumberland*, ed. W. Page (Surtees Soc., lxxxviii, 1890), 137, 185–6, 192.
27. Yorkshire	1218–19	5	63	3,889,758	62,738	*Rolls of the Justices in Eyre*, ed. D. M. Stenton (Selden Soc., lvi, 1937), nos. 19, 207, 363, 365, 375.

Provision for the Families of the Montfortians disinherited after the Battle of Evesham

Clive H. Knowles

After the battle of Evesham, the victorious royal government first sought to crush the Montfortians by confiscating their lands, and then, by the terms of the Dictum of Kenilworth, obliged them to pay heavy fines for the recovery of their property.[1] Nevertheless, under both punitive policies, some measure of protection was extended to the families of the defeated rebels. To make such provision required finding the solution to several knotty legal problems, and trying to harmonize the terms of the legal settlement after the rebellion with the framework of the law.

The wave of pillage and confiscation which swept England after Evesham engulfed everyone associated with the defeated side. Not only the wives and widows but even the widowed mothers of rebels were plundered with impunity.[2] Their ruin seemed complete when, at the Winchester parliament of September 1265, Henry III confiscated the lands of his opponents and began to distribute them amongst his supporters. These grants were intended to be permanent, and each charter contained a clause expressly excluding all future action or claim belonging to anyone by inheritance in the land.[3] But the loyalists' venomous hatred of the rebels was not extended to their womenfolk. Possibly in the presence of the wives and widows of rebels killed in battle or captive in prison who had been specially summoned to Winchester, the king and council promulgated an ordinance making provision for their sustenance.[4] Though no text of this appears to have survived, its main provisions can be reconstructed from scattered references in the records. Wives and widows were assigned the lands and tenements of their own inheritance and marriage, and a varying proportion, between one-quarter and one-third, of the lands of the their husbands, to be held for life.[5] The ordinance may also have secured to the widowed mothers of rebels continued possession of the dower already allocated to them, on condition that, if the land was the right of a rebel son, it was to be handed over to a loyalist grantee on the widow's death.[6]

[1] For the resettlement in general, see F. M. Powicke, *King Henry III and the Lord Edward* (Oxford, 1947), ii, chs. 12, 13; C. H. Knowles, 'The Resettlement of England after the Barons' War, 1264–67', *TRHS*, 5th ser., xxxii (1982), 25–41. Unless otherwise stated, all manuscript references are to documents in the PRO.

[2] Eg., *CIMisc. 1219–1307*, nos. 656, 875, 936.

[3] Eg., *CChR 1257–1300*, 57–8.

[4] *Ann.Mon.*, ii. 366; *CR 1268–72, 263; CF. CIMisc. 1219–1307*, no. 928. The earliest reference to the ordinance is in Feb. 1266. See *CPR 1258–66*, 558.

[5] *CR 1264–68*, 199–200; below, note 11.

[6] Eg., *CChR 1257–1300*, 56; *Rotuli Selecti ad res Anglicas et Hibernicas spectantes*, ed. J. Hunter (London, 1834), 248.

At first, the royal ordinance could not be implemented systematically. The country was in turmoil, and it took time to survey the individual rebel's estates and establish beyond doubt those parts to which the wife or widow had a right.[7] So, pending further enquiries, the king made interim allocations to the womenfolk in tenancy 'for as long as it pleases the king.'[8] Amongst the first to benefit were those with highly-placed relatives who could intervene on their behalf.[9] Many wives and widows were already in possession of some lands by late September 1265.[10] From October onwards, as the number of grants multiplied, the elements which composed the ordinance one by one made their appearance. Earlier assignments made during pleasure were converted into grants for life. From November dates the first explicit grant to the wife of a rebel of all the lands of her inheritance, and from January 1266, when it became usual in assignments to give both the value of the grant and the total value of the rebel husband's lands, it is possible to identify the application of the sliding scale between one-quarter and one-third already described.[11]

The ordinance was still in force when the Dictum of Kenilworth, enabling the Montfortians to redeem their lands, was published in October 1266. Clause 31 confirmed to the wives and widows of rebels lands of their own inheritance and dowers of their first husbands, if any, free of redemption. Widows of rebels were to receive as dower issuing from the estates of their husbands that portion already ordained as theirs by the king.[12] In other words, the sliding scale of grants between one-quarter and one-third of the lands of the rebels was confirmed in the new decree.[13] Under the terms of the Dictum, dower granted to the widows of rebels was to be redeemed at their death; the same applied to that held by the mothers of rebels.

After the civil war ended in 1267 there were frequent disputes over the precise lands allocated to the widows of former rebels. Grantees were especially anxious to secure for themselves the chief manors of estates, to which the fees, and so possibly future wards and escheats, pertained. In 1268, John Giffard, the younger, who had been granted some of the lands of Robert fitz Nicholas, successfully pleaded *coram rege* that Smeetham (Essex), which had been allocated to Robert's widow, was the chief manor of the estate, and that other lands should be assigned to her in place of it.[14]

For their part, some widows tried to exempt certain lands from the redemption process on the grounds that these were of their free marriage.[15] Others, who had been widowed since the publication of the Dictum, claimed common law dower in lands allegedly alienated under duress by their husbands. In 1276 Elizabeth of Pembridge sought dower in the manor of Pembridge (Hereford)

[7] *CR 1264–68*, 130, 199–200; *CPR 1258–66*, 546, 558.

[8] *CR 1264–68*, 130.

[9] Eg., Roger de Somery, *CR 1264–68*, 130; *CPR 1258–66*, 497–8.

[10] *CIMisc. 1219–1307*, nos. 675, 769, 771, 777, 785, 853, 928.

[11] *CPR 1258–66*, 459–60, 462, 497–8, 541, but some grants 'during pleasure' continue to be recorded in late Oct. 1265: 467, 469, 471; *CR 1264–68*, 221; *CPR 1258–66*, 526, 529, 533, 550, 557, 558, 558–9, 564, 575, 582, 602, 644.

[12] *DBM*, 334–5.

[13] It was later believed that the sliding-scale had been laid down in the Dictum, eg., *CR 1268–72*, 135; *CFR 1272–1307*, 212; KB 27/134, m.16.

[14] *CR 1264–68*, 462; KB 26/185, m.16d.

[15] Eg., KB 26/189, m.28d.

which her late husband had transferred to Roger Mortimer in 1267.[16] When her son Henry was called to warrant the charter, he asserted that his father had made it in Mortimer's prison and had nothing in the land because Mortimer had seized it in time of war. Though Mortimer protested that it was impossible to invalidate the charter on the grounds that the father had no seisin at the time of making it, he eventually abandoned the claim of warranty and Elizabeth of Pembridge gave up her claim to dower in the manor. In return she received the manor of Stoke Lacy (Hereford), which she was to hold in dower until her death, when it would revert to the grantor. Mortimer's action was less generous than it might appear because he had obtained Stoke Lacy as security for the ransom of another former rebel, Adam le Despencer, and then refused to surrender it.[17]

Since dower land was only redeemable after the death of the widow, it is no surprise to find that there was a steady trickle of redemption cases down to the end of the thirteenth century and into the opening years of the next.[18] The last case we know of dates from 1302. More than thirty years earlier, in 1269, William de Huntingfield had recovered his lands from the grantee Geoffrey de Genevill, saving dower in the manor of Frampton (Lincs.), held by his mother Joan, which was to be redeemed at five years' valuation after her death.[19] Geoffrey could hardly have foreseen that the redemption process would still not be completed a generation later, for although William died in 1290, his mother lived another seven years.[20] When she died, her grandson Roger immediately took possession of Frampton without paying Geoffrey a redemption fine. He had still not received it in 1302.[21]

In dealing with the wardship of the heirs of rebels under age, the main problem that faced the compilers of the Dictum of Kenilworth was how to reconcile the conflicting claims of the chief lord and the grantee of the lands to that valuable right. Clause 15 tried to deal as fairly as possible with the interests of both parties whilst at the same time protecting the rights of the heir.[22] The chief lord of the heir of a rebel under age was to have the option of redeeming his lands from the grantee. If he exercised it, he was to recover all the usual rights pertaining to a wardship, including the marriage of the heir. When the heir reached his majority, he redeemed his inheritance from him. If the chief lord did not ransom the lands, the grantee replaced him and enjoyed all the rights of wardship until the heir came of age, when he was required to redeem from him in the usual way.

The records of the resettlement indicate that most chief lords believed that it was to their advantage to assert their right to wardships, even though this meant paying redemption fines which might not be refunded for many years. The dispute over the wardship of William of Birmingham's son illustrates this. Soon after the publication of the Dictum, Roger de Somery, William's lord,

[16] CP 40/17, m.88.
[17] *CPR 1258–66*, 425; *CR 1264–68*, 29–30; *GEC*, iv, 302 n.c.
[18] Eg., Isabella, widow of William of Birmingham, *CFR 1272–1307*, 212; *CCR 1279–88*, 319; KB 27/90, m.36d.
[19] *CR (Supplementary) 1244–66*, no. 378; *CPR 1266–72*, 390; *CR 1268–72*, 144–5; E 159/44, m.11.
[20] *CFR 1272–1307*, 286, 391.
[21] *CCR 1296–1302*, 610–11.
[22] *DBM*, 328–9.

offered to redeem the manor of Birmingham from the grantee, Roger de Clifford, because William's son was under age.[23] For many months Clifford ignored his plea and made waste contrary to the king's prohibition. Eventually, in February 1268, the justices of the special eyre *de terris datis* were commissioned to extend the land and apply the Dictum or, if they were unable to do this, refer the matter to the king. Later in the year Somery redeemed the manor, but was not reimbursed until after William's son came of age in 1283.[24]

The treatment of the families of the Montfortians raises several interesting questions. Why after Evesham were the wives and widows of rebels assigned a varying proportion of their husbands' forfeited lands? The different allocations may indicate the influence of particular families or foreshadow that later addition to the Dictum, recommended by the justice Martin de Littlebury, which distinguished between widows and wives *ne foveret inde rex inimicos*.[25] About the exceptional generosity of the provision there can be no doubt. Why was the treatment of the womenfolk under Henry III so much more humane than the fate of many of their counterparts under Edward II, who 'in addition to their loss of dower-rights, seem to have been deprived of both inheritance and jointure, . . . were given no allowance for their maintenance', and often ended up in prison?[26] One explanation is that the loyalists and rebels were closely bound together by ties of blood and marriage. Roger de Somery's step-son, Nicholas de Segrave, and son-in-law, Ralph Basset of Drayton, joined the rebel side, and both Philip Basset's sons-in-law fought for Montfort at Evesham.[27] The sympathetic way in which the triumphant loyalists dealt with the wives and widows of the rebels after Evesham parallels the way in which the Montfortians had protected the interests of their womenfolk after Lewes.[28] But the special solicitude of Henry III himself may also have played a part. In 1250 he had lectured the sheriffs assembled at the Exchequer on the need 'to give protection and speedy justice to widows and orphans', and his concern to alleviate their condition was acknowledged in the premature obituary of the king inserted in the Tewkesbury annals in 1263.[29] After Evesham, Henry displayed notable restraint in his dealings with the Montforts, offering an annuity to his widowed sister Eleanor, and agreeing to Louis IX making an award on the future of the family, always remembering their previous injuries to the realm.[30] In shaping royal policy towards the families of the rebels, Henry's own experiences as an orphan may have had an influence. It was left to his son Edward I to define the crime of levying war against the king and classify it as treason, with dire consequences for the families of those so accused.[31]

[23] *CChR 1257–1300*, 58; *CPR 1258–66*, 534.
[24] *CPR 1266–72*, 276; *CR 1264–68*, 522–3; *CChR 1257–1300*, 264.
[25] *Statutes of the Realm*, ed. A. Luders *et al.* (London, 1810), i. 18.
[26] C. D. Ross, 'Forfeiture for Treason in the Reign of Richard II', *EHR*, lxxi (1956), 567; N. Fryde, *The Tyranny and Fall of Edward II 1321–1326* (Cambridge, 1979), 63–4, 79; S. L. Waugh, 'The Confiscated Lands of the "Contrariants" in Gloucestershire and Herefordshire in 1322; An Economic and Social Study' (University of London Ph.D. thesis, 1975), 31–6.
[27] *GEC*, ii, 1; iv, 261; v, 435; xi, 603.
[28] *CPR 1258–66*, 334, 337, 354–5.
[29] M. T. Clanchy, 'Did Henry III have a policy?', *History*, liii (1968), 215–16; D. A. Carpenter, 'An Unknown Obituary of King Henry III from the Year 1263', in *England in the Thirteenth Century,* ed. W. M. Ormrod (Harlaxton, 1985), 51.
[30] *CPR 1258–66*, 678; *CPR 1266–72*, 140–1.
[31] J. G. Bellamy, *The Law of Treason in England in the Later Middle Ages* (Cambridge, 1970), ch. 3.

Rulers of Thirteenth Century Towns: The Cases of York and Newcastle upon Tyne

Edward Miller

Answers to questions about the sort of people occupying positions of power in thirteenth-century English towns are easy enough to find. Contemporary records tell us that responsible offices were held, or ought to be held, by *probi homines*, the 'better and more discreet' of the townsfolk. Alternatively, especially if the records are critical in tone, the leading townsfolk were *majores* or 'magnate burgesses' (as contrasted with *mediocres* or *minores*), or more bluntly, as at Newcastle in 1305, 'rich burgesses' inclined to 'sinister collusion among themselves'.[1] Urban ruling groups have also been described in terms of assumptions common to Marx and to nineteenth-century liberals. Medieval towns were 'non-feudal islands in a feudal sea'; each was a 'social unit more or less distinct from the surrounding countryside'; and town walls were frontiers marking the limits of a special sort of life, a bourgeois way of life led by bourgeois people. A town's rulers were also likely to be rich, but those at least of towns that had achieved any degree of maturity were likely by the thirteenth century to be bourgeois men, whose wealth derived from bourgeois enterprises differing markedly from the sources of wealth that made men rich in rural England.[2]

In order to test the validity of these assumptions we need to look at what individuals did and how individuals behaved, and for that purpose there is much to be said for restricting ourselves to a local context since there are practical limits to the number of individuals we can follow through the surviving records. Those records, of course, offer something less than a rounded view of thirteenth-century townsfolk. Many of the sources upon which students of urban history in later times rely most heavily are wholly or largely lacking for the thirteenth century. There is a consequent danger that our view of townsmen in that century will be biassed unduly towards activities for which there is evidence, in particular dealings in property. That danger can merely be kept in mind, together with the danger of forcing medieval facts into conformity with modern theory. The evidence we have will only take us so far, but at least it needs to be allowed to speak for itself.

[1] S. Reynolds, *Introduction to the History of English Medieval Towns* (Oxford, 1977), 123, 133; C. M. Fraser, 'Medieval Trading Restrictions in the North-East', *Archaeologia Aeliana*, 4th ser., xxxix (1961), 138. In the text most personal names have been modernized by omitting 'de' in names formed from place-names and giving the place-name in its modern form. Thus Richard de Emildon becomes Richard Embleton and so forth.

[2] M. M. Postan, *Medieval Economy and Society* (London, 1972), 213; Reynolds, ix; E. Ennen, *Die europaïschen Stadt des Mittelalters* (Göttingen, 1972), 11.

I

Town rulers, of course, need to be provided with a setting, for each town had its own individuality. York was an old town and one of the most populous in England. It was an important administrative centre, the seat of an archbishop and of the sheriff of the county, and even before the Scottish wars kings used it periodically as a kind of northern capital. County courts and the king's justices sat there, drawing in men from the shire who might also be customers for the city's goods and services, as were York's many religious institutions — the Minster, St. Mary's abbey, St. Leonard's hospital, a nunnery and a couple of priories even before the coming of the friars. All this helped to make York an important economic centre, a manufacturing town with a weavers' gild going back at least to Henry II's time, and a trading town set on rivers which supplemented the land routes into its hinterland and gave access to the Humber ports and the seas beyond. Economically, York was pre-eminent in the North and through much of the middle ages it ranked second or third among English towns.

Newcastle, by contrast, was a parvenu, a settlement which grew up at the gates of the Norman fortress guarding the crossing of the lower Tyne. Its origins were as military as its name and it never matched York as an administrative or an ecclesiastical centre. On the other hand, the well-known customs of the city as they were before Henry I was dead show how precocious Newcastle's urban development was. It appears in those customs as a community of burgesses who dealt in wool and hides and other commodities, who dyed cloth and sold cloth retail, and who lived in a place to which ships brought merchandise.[3] Within little more than a generation the fortress of the new castle had burgeoned into a town and a port; and it was as a town, and not least as a port, that it continued to develop in the twelfth and thirteenth centuries, so that in the 1290s the issues of the port were the major element of the town's revenues. Those issues included a levy on the coal bought and loaded in the port, and it had been said a few years earlier that the reason why the city's income was so much larger than it had been when King John fixed its payment to the Exchequer was 'because it was so increased by coals'.[4] Coal, however, was merely one contributor to Newcastle's general economic development in the thirteenth century, a development which still awaits detailed study although there are a few pointers to its direction and scale. In the reign of Henry II, Newcastle's contributions to royal taxes averaged only about one seventh of those of York, but by the 1330s Newcastle's taxable wealth may have been 80 per cent or more of the taxable wealth of York. This is a rough and ready measure, but it underlies the fact that by then Newcastle had attained a place in the front rank of English provincial towns.[5]

In spite of initial differences, therefore, York and Newcastle developed

[3] See *EHD*, ii. 970 – 1 for a translation.

[4] A. J. Lilburn, 'Pipe Rolls of Edward I', *Archaeologia Aeliana*, 4th ser., xxxvi (1958), 286 – 9; J. Brand, *History and Antiquities of Newcastle upon Tyne* (London, 1789), ii. 253.

[5] C. Stephenson, *Borough and Town: a Study of Urban Origins in England* (Cambridge, Mass., 1933), 225; *The Lay Subsidy of 1334*, ed. R. E. Glasscock (British Academy Records of Social and Economic History, n.s., ii, 1975), 219, 357. Unfortunately, Newcastle's payment in 1336 (it was excused in 1334) took the form of a fine. Its amount suggests an estimate of the town's taxable wealth of around £1333.

increasing economic similarities and there are also close similarities in the character of their ruling circles. In order to establish what these were, it is reasonable to concentrate attention in the first instance upon the men who, between John's reign and the death of Edward I, held the principal civic offices of mayor and bailiff. The list of office holders is not complete, especially for the earlier decades of the period, but the sample is reasonably large.[6] Mayors and bailiffs, of course, were not the sole members of a town's ruling circle, for charter witness lists show they were part of a somewhat larger group, including holders of other offices, regularly active in affairs. That larger group cannot be ignored, but mayors and bailiffs were men to whom their fellow citizens allocated special authority. To that extent they may be regarded as being representative of ruling circles as a whole.

These circles, in the first place, were not very large, especially when we remember that Newcastle had nearly 300 taxpayers (ie., heads of families of at least modest substance) in 1296 and that York had over 800 in 1327. By contrast, the known mayors of York in the period 1217 – 1307 numbered only 21 individuals from 18 families and the mayors of Newcastle 16 individuals drawn from a mere 8 families. In both towns some individuals emerge from obscurity, hold the mayor's office for a year or more, and then they and their descendants disappear from the leading ranks of townsfolk; other mayors came from families long active in the town without having previously held the mayoralty; but there were also some families whose members served repeatedly in that office. At York, John Spicer and then his son were mayors in at least seven of the years between 1273 and 1304, but the Selby family was the mayoral family par excellence. The first Hugh Selby seems to have been in office in a considerable number of the years between 1217 and 1245; his son John was mayor at least seven times in the period 1251 – 71; and John's son Nicholas at least four times in the 1280s. At Newcastle two families were, to an even greater extent, monopolists of the office: for in more than two years out of every three for which the mayor's name is known he was either a Scott or a Carliol, five members of each family holding office during the century. Re-election was also common, both of dynasts like the Selbys at York or like Henry Scott and Thomas Carliol at Newcastle, who were in office for 11½ and 9 years respectively, and of others — for John fitzRoger served for 6½ years at Newcastle and John Sampson for at least 8 years at York, while at Newcastle in 1305 Richard Embleton was beginning the first of his 23 years of mayoral service.

The ruling circle widens, of course, when we turn to the bailiffs, for there were three of them each year at York and four at Newcastle. At York we know the names of 95 bailiffs who between them had 133 years of service: they were drawn from about 70 families, but nearly half of them belonged to a mere 21 families, 12 of which belonged to the narrow ring of mayoral families. Again, re-election was common: Nicholas Selby, later to be mayor, served at least four terms as bailiff, as did Henry Holtby and Ivo Ousegate, while Robert Blund was elected six and John Coniston ten times. At Newcastle the ring was even smaller, with 66 known individuals providing 198 years of service. Many

[6] For Newcastle, C. Hunter Blair, 'Mayors of Newcastle upon Tyne, 1216 – 1399', *Archaeologia Aeliana*, 4th ser., xviii (1940), 1 – 3; and *Early Deeds relating to Newcastle upon Tyne*, ed. A. M. Oliver (Surtees Soc., cxxxvii, 1924), 200 – 15; for York, F. Drake, *Eboracum* (London, 1736), 359 – 67, which needs much supplementation from the records.

of them, therefore, served on a number of occasions and, perhaps inevitably, Scotts and Carliols were as prominent in the ranks of the bailiffs as among the mayors, 12 members of these two families providing at least 49 years of service. Equally inevitably, at the opening of the new century, Richard Embleton served for three years as bailiff as a preface to his career as mayor.

The governments of thirteenth-century York and Newcastle, then, were markedly oligarchical, and yet their oligarchies were never closed. The dynastic families (Selbys, Scotts, Carliols) are evident enough, and other families that provided fewer mayors were still consistent members of the ruling circles of their town: the Louths, earlier called Bretgates, and Sampsons at York, or the fitzRogers and de la Hayes of Newcastle. Richard Embleton, on the other hand, demonstrated how quickly a newcomer could climb the ladder of esteem. He first appears, almost certainly a recent immigrant from the Northumbrian village from which he took his name, exporting modest amounts of wool and modestly assessed to taxes in the mid-1290s. In the 1296 tax list, however, his name is next to that of a very rich man, Samson Cutler, whose daughter he may have married: by 1301 he was bailiff and he would soon be mayor and MP as well as by far Newcastle's greatest wool exporter.[7] Richard's eminence was in some ways exceptional, but others rose as rapidly in urban hierarchies. Gace de Chaumont's origins were probably remoter than even a Northumbrian village, for it is likely that he was an immigrant wine merchant from Anjou. Around 1250, however, we hear of him as a merchant of York, where he stocked the king's cellar and disposed of its surplus. In 1255 he was mayor of York and before he died about 1261 he had a manor in the Ainsty with which his descendants became so identified that the place was sometimes called Colton Chaumont.[8]

A high proportion of these leading citizens were clearly drawn from among the richer members of their communities. As at all times and in all places, of course, there were men who were assiduous in public service without possessing conspicuous wealth and also affluent men with no taste for office. On the other hand, office holders tended to need enough resources to afford periods of diversion from the business of earning a living, and a glance at the 27 men who were mayors or bailiffs of Newcastle in the years around 1300 confirms that they were in fact relatively wealthy. Twenty-four of them were assessed for the taxation of 1296 and the average value of their goods in Newcastle, ignoring any they had in country villages, was put at over £11 per head. That figure was three times the average for the tax-payers of the city as a whole. After at least seven of these 24 notables had died, too, 13 of the rest appear in the list of 'rich' burgesses drawn up in 1305, a list moreover from which Richard Embleton was omitted although he was certainly living and indubitably rich.[9]

The rich, of course, were seldom a monolithic interest in any town and contemporary events at York take us nearer to realities. It was alleged that Andrew Bolingbroke, MP in 1301, bailiff in 1303 and mayor in 1305, had organized a social gild intended to usurp jurisdiction over its members to their

[7] The significant evidence comes from the terms in which he endowed his chantries at Embleton and Newcastle: *CPR 1330–4*, 264; *A History of Northumberland* (Newcastle, 1893–1940), ii. 59.
[8] *CR 1254–6*, 131, 139; *CLR 1251–60*, 135, 242, 295; Drake, 388.
[9] Fraser, 147–50.

mutual advantage and to divert tax burdens from themselves to the poorer citizens. Clearly feelings were running high, for Bolingbroke was attacked with a drawn knife and nearly had his throat cut, and the matter of his clandestine gild was eventually brought before the justices of trailbaston in 1306. The trial has left a list of the 53 conspiring gildsmen, who obviously included some men of substance. At least 18 of them had held civic office or were to do so. Bolingbroke himself was a wine merchant, a property owner in the city and at Heworth, and rich enough to endow a chantry for his soul, and some of his associates, like John Fisshe and William Whitby, were wool exporters even though not on a very large scale. The gildsmen, however, were not coincident with the 'rich' men of York, for too many men of wealth and standing had no part in their association. They were, on the contrary, a faction, with leaders drawn from among the better off but with a following of more modest citizens, including men who became free of the city as a saddler, a poulterer, a girdler, a baker and a butcher. The advantages they sought were sectional and not class advantages.[10]

While rivalries for influence and advantage often divided town ruling groups, many ties also contributed to their solidarity. Business associations brought men together, as when Thomas Carliol joined with other leading Newcastle citizens, including Henry Scott, Richard de la Haye and John Fleming, to export wool. Then there were family and legal ties. Thomas Carliol probably married a Scott daughter and his sister married into the Pandon family, which in turn came to be connected by marriage with rising families like the Cowgates, Halliwells and Blagdons. Then, Walter Cowgate and Adam Galeway acted as feoffees for family settlements made by Nicholas Scott; Thomas Carliol was a pledge for Henry Scott; and Richard Embleton was the centre of a positive web of family relationships. He probably married successively a rich man's daughter and then the widow of John Scott, a dynast, and he married his own daughters into two of Newcastle's new rich families, the Actons and the Grapers.[11] Similar links between members of York's ruling circle are evident enough. Gilbert Louth, who was three times mayor, loaned money jointly with another mayor, John Spicer, who also acted as an executor of Gilbert's will. Gilbert, too, married a Warthill, a prominent property-owning family throughout the century. It was mere misfortune that Gilbert's wife lapsed into insanity and that the Warthill connection, in consequence of some feud the details of which are lost to us, led to his being suspected of complicity in a murder. In this case, family ties were perhaps too binding for Gilbert's comfort.[12]

[10] G. O. Sayles, *Scripta Diversa* (London, 1982), 65–80; M. C. Prestwich, *York Civic Ordinances, 1301* (Borthwick Papers, xlix, 1976), 19; *VCH, City of York*, 370; *CPR 1301–7*, 541; *Kirkby's Inquest*, ed. R. H. Skaife (Surtees Soc., xlix, 1867), 380.

[11] *CPR 1266–72*, 125; *CPR 1272–81*, 32; *CCR 1272–9*, 32–3; *CFR 1272–1307*, 12; *Early Deeds*, 72, 77 and nos. 218–19, 239, 269–73; *Feet of Fines: Northumberland and Durham*, II (Newcastle upon Tyne Rec. Soc., xi, 1932), nos. 107, 169–70; *Three Early Assize Rolls for the County of Northumberland*, ed. W. Page (Surtees Soc., lxxxviii, 1891), 393; *Hist. of Northumberland*, vii. 190.

[12] *CPR 1272–81*, 284; *CPR 1281–92*, 301; *CCR 1279–88*, 14; *Registers of John le Romeyn*, ed. W. Brown (Surtees Soc., cxxiii, 1913), no. 223.

II

More important than the fact that the rulers of towns were relatively wealthy, however, are the sources of their wealth. In very general terms these seem to have been principally trading profits and real property, although that does not imply that manufacturing craftsmen never figured in the ruling echelons of townsfolk. Craftsmen, after all, were often traders as well as makers, and in any case, at this time, enfranchised burgesses had much freedom to seize whatever economic opportunities came their way. Thus John fitzRoger, five times mayor of Newcastle in the 1270s, was apparently a dyer who also exported wool.[13] On the other hand, the famous bell-founder, Richard Tunnock, became bailiff of York in Edward II's time, although admittedly he was an exceptional craftsman: one of the richest of York taxpayers in 1327 and the only York citizen to have a chantry in the Minster (to which he gave the well-known bell-founders' window). He may, too, have been a goldsmith as well as a bell-founder and at York goldsmiths were probably the most prominent manufacturing craftsmen in the city's ruling circle, for, in addition to demand for their products from wealthy layfolk and religious, the York mints offered periodic employment for their skills. The Louth-Bretgate family, for example, was associated with the king's mint from before 1170, John Louth was the king's moneyer in 1217 and Jeremy Louth of Bretgate, a mid-century bailiff, was by craft a goldsmith. Henry Sperry, too, member of a family that produced at least six of York's bailiffs, was another goldsmith and one of the assayers at the York mint.[14]

A high proportion of office-holders, however, do seem to have been traders rather than makers. Some, but by no means all, were overseas traders, but distributive traders and middlemen between English producers and export merchants were also prominent; and very few of them were specialists, most being willing to turn an honest penny as opportunities offered. Inevitably the wool trade provided many of those opportunities, but Geoffrey Sainter, reeve of York at the beginning of the century, exported lead and hides as well as wool; and towards the century's close Peter Appleby sold furs to the lord of Oswaldkirk, bought wool in York as agent for a Fleming, exported wool on his own account and sent a ship to the Tyne with a cargo that included wine.[15] Robert Meek, one of Bolingbroke's conspirators and later mayor, was another versatile trader, a fishmonger who supplied the court but also a taverner who dealt in wine and with a wife who brewed ale commercially. Much earlier, John Sampson's father Alan, who was one of the York moneyers, also supplied Henry III with wine and sold cloth at St. Ives and Boston fairs.[16] Many Newcastle notables were men of the same sort, although court connections

[13] *Early Deeds*, nos. 18, 160, 223; J. Conway Davies, 'Wool Customs Accounts for Newcastle upon Tyne for the Reign of Edward I', *Archaeologia Aeliana*, 4th ser., xxxii (1954), 226.

[14] *History of York Minster*, ed. G. Aylmer, R. Cant (Oxford, 1977), 350–4; *Pipe Roll, 17 Henry II* (Pipe Roll Soc., xvi, 1893), 73; PRO, KR Memoranda Roll, 2 Henry III, m.3; John Rylands Library Latin MS 220, f.91; *Kirkby's Inquest*, 65n.; *Chronica Johannis de Oxenedes*, ed. H. Ellis (*RS* 1859), 297.

[15] *RLP*, 91; *Catalogue of Ancient Deeds*, no. A6264; N. S. B. Gras, *Early History of the English Customs System* (Cambridge, Mass., 1918), 240; *Rot.Parl.*, i. 28, 46; PRO, SC 6/1088/13; E 122/55/2; and JI 1/1085, m.45d.

[16] Prestwich, 19, 23–4, 26; PRO, E 101/366/1; *CR 1237–42*, 203; *CR 1242–7*, 262.

were less close until the war years late in the century. Thomas Carliol, who served at least nine terms as mayor in the 1260s and 1270s, exported wool on some scale in association with the Londoner, Thomas Basing, as well as with various Newcastle men; and he bought wool as far afield as North Yorkshire, arranging for its despatch overseas by merchants of Amiens and Florence. Peter Sampson, too, exported wool and hides and dealt in cloth. His partner, Peter Graper, exported wool and hides and bought iron from German importers for the king's castles in Scotland, and John Fleming exported wool and sold both cloth and wine at home.[17]

Trade, especially in these staples, enabled some individuals to acquire exceptional wealth and to do so remarkably quickly. Hugh Selby, the early thirteenth-century mayor of York, probably belonged to a family well established in the city, for it looks as though his father and grandfather were already active as wine merchants in the 1180s. Hugh, however, seems to have been a merchant on an altogether grander scale, shipping wool to Flanders and wine from Anjou and on occasion supplying wine to Henry III's court. Trade, in brief, is likely to have been the main source of the wealth that established the Selby dynasty so firmly in the city's life that as late as 1416 Alderman William Selby was still presenting a chaplain to 'old Hugh Selby's' chantry in St. William's chapel on Ousebridge.[18] Newer men than Hugh Selby, however, also achieved rapid social promotion. Richard Embleton, probably an incomer and still only a modest exporter in the 1290s, by 1308 was exporting one eighth of the wool that went out of Newcastle. He traded less as time went on, and mainly through agents or servants for grain and wine in times of scarcity or for army supply. But the 'sudden riches' he reaped from trade laid the foundations of the fortune that made him the outstanding citizen of Newcastle in the early fourteenth century.[19]

Trading profits both financed future trading and found their way into other forms of investment. While Peter Appleby sold goods on credit, others were straightforward lenders of money. Among York mayors, Adam Cerf, jointly with Alan Sampson, advanced cash to Roger le Peytevin of Towton, John Spicer and Gilbert Louth together made loans to Robert Percy, and Gilbert on his own accommodated various members of the Percy family. Thomas Carliol of Newcastle, too, loaned money to the lord of Warkworth, and Richard Embleton to Richard de Chartres and John of Trewick. But creditors were not of necessity countryfolk, for Gilbert Pandon provided his fellow inhabitants of Newcastle, Thomas and Alice Halliwell, with a certain sum of money in their great necessity.[20] Advances of goods or money may sometimes have

[17] *Three Early Assize Rolls*, 394–5; *Rotuli Hundredorum*, i. 132; F. Bradshaw, 'The Lay Subsidy of 1296', *Archaeologia Aeliana*, 3rd ser., xiii (1916), 286; Conway Davies, 226, 255, 263, 265, 284–6, 288; Fraser, 147; *CDRS*, ii. no. 1398.

[18] *Pipe Roll, 31 Henry II* (Pipe Roll Soc., xxxiv, 1913), 67; *CR 1227–31*, 355–6; *CR 1234–7*, 90–1, 205; *CR 1242–7*, 262; *Patent Rolls 1225–32*, 12, 320, 347–8; *York Memorandum Book*, ed. M. Sellars, II (Surtees Soc., cxxv, 1915), 51.

[19] Conway Davies, 259; C. M. Fraser, 'The Life and Death of John of Denton', *Archaeologia Aeliana*, 4th ser., xxxvii (1959), 305; *CPR 1307–13*, 95; *CPR 1313–17*, 281; *CPR 1321–4*, 207, 231; *CPR 1330–4*, 32, 378.

[20] *Yorkshire Inquisitions*, ed. W. Brown, I (Yorkshire Archaeological Soc., Rec. Ser., xii, 1892), 281; II (Yorks. Arch. Soc., Rec. Ser., xxiii, 1898), no. 59; *CPR 1281–92*, 301; *CCR 1279–88*, 49; *Northumberland and Durham Deeds* (Newcastle upon Tyne Rec. Soc., 1929), 77–9, 155; F. W. Dendy, 'An Account of Jesmond', *Archaeologia Aeliana*, 3rd ser., i (1904), 58; *Early Deeds*, nos. 226–7.

involved interest charges, for Peter Appleby was certainly said to have demanded payment 'in a usurious manner', but they also led to shifts in the frontiers of property. Gilbert Pandon's advance to the necessitous Halliwells put him in possession of three market stalls, initially for 12 years and eventually in perpetuity. Nor did property transfers of this sort stop at town walls. Thomas Carliol got Callaley and Yetlington for a seven year term for his loan to the lord of Warkworth; John of Trewick's debt to Richard Embleton paved the way for the latter's acquisition of Jesmond; and Gilbert Louth got Ormesby and Cargo Fleet as security for loans to William Percy of Kildale.

Trading profits invested directly in real estate or lending secured on real estate turned most leading townsmen into property-owners on some scale. Gilbert Louth and Richard Embleton are extreme, but not for that reason untypical, cases. Gilbert had much city property and was allowed a private oratory in his house in St. Mary's parish, Walmgate, but he also died seised of land in East Ness, Stillingfleet (where he was also patron of the parish church), Ormesby, Cargo Fleet and Newton under Roseberry. As for Richard Embleton, he was able to assign £10 yearly from his Newcastle rents to his chantry and he had interests in more than a score of northern villages stretching from Carham on the Scottish border down to Silksworth near Sunderland. Lesser men, if to a lesser degree, were men of the same sort. Peter Appleby had no country estates, but he did have four messuages, four tofts, a shop and 46s. 8d. rents in York, and also two messuages in Hull, the port through which much of his trade was conducted. Men who did not aspire to the office of mayor might still invest in the countryside; among many others, Adam Verdennell of York had property in Grimston and Heslington, and the Warthills, too, had interests in Heslington and leased land from the Selbys in Youlthorpe.[21]

Trading profits, therefore, go far to explaining the fluidity and openness of urban ruling classes, for they enabled men of enterprise and ability to climb quickly into positions of leadership. Ownership of property, on the other hand, was a means of storing wealth against future needs, sometimes to be realised quite quickly for new business investment and sometimes to hold savings for a man's old age. Thus Thomas Carliol, towards the end of his life, arranged for an annuity of £50 from his manor of Swarland and other holdings, and Adam Pandon was perhaps building up his pension fund when he let a plot in Pilgrim St. for 12s. yearly, land in Market St. for 44s. and other properties for like rents, although unhappily he fell upon hard times and had to sell these rents for a lump sum.[22] An income from property, finally, might be something of a necessity for those who assumed the more onerous civic offices, particularly if they did so repeatedly. In his later years Richard Embleton still sometimes sent his ships or servants to trade overseas, but he seldom ventured abroad himself and he no longer dominated the Newcastle wool trade. He was still among that town's rich men and near enough to being

[21] *CChR 1257–1300*, 222, 232; *CPR 1272–81*, 398, 458; *Feet of Fines for the County of York, 1272–1300*, ed. F. H. Slingsby (Yorks. Arch. Soc., Rec. Ser., cxxi, 1956), 42, 71; PRO, JI 1/1085, m.74; *Select Rentals and Accounts of Medieval Hull*, ed. R. Horrox (Yorks. Arch. Soc., Rec. Ser., cxli, 1981), 38, 136; *Yorkshire Lay Subsidy, 1301*, ed. W. Brown (Yorks. Arch. Soc., Rec. Ser., xxi, 1897), 105; *Register of Walter Gray*, ed. J. Raine (Surtees Soc., lvi, 1872), 90; *Year Books of Edward II: 7 Edward II*, ed. W. C. Bolland (Selden Soc., xxxix, 1922), 113–14.

[22] *Hist. of Northumberland*, vii. 387–8; *Early Deeds*, nos. 232, 236, 238–44, 246.

its perpetual mayor, but his wealth and influence were now grounded in his property in town and country.[23]

Proprietary interests, therefore, were often more important later rather than earlier in a man's life cycle, but they might also support a family's dynastic position even when its wealth received little reinforcement from the profits of trade. The Selby family is again a case in point. Hugh Selby, as we have seen, owed much of his fortune to commerce, but he also accumulated real estate. He had property in many parts of the city and also outside it at High Hutton, Escrick and, through marriage to a widow, at Osgodby.[24] At least at Osgodby he was succeeded by his eldest son, John, who also had interests in Fangfoss, Reedness, Acomb and Youlthorpe, as well, of course, as in York itself; and John in turn was succeeded by his son, Nicholas, who by then was claiming to enjoy the penalties for breaches of the assize of ale at Fangfoss and Youlthorpe *ab antiquo*.[25] For all their rural interests, however, John and Nicholas were repeatedly mayors of York. On the other hand, there is no mention of commerce in connection with either of them and there is likewise no evidence that Nicholas' heir, another Hugh, either traded or held civic office. His resources, when he came to arrange his affairs in 1338, consisted of city property and rents and the country estates, mostly acquired by his grandfather and great-grandfather, which had supported his father and grandfather in office. Meantime, Hugh's brothers were keeping up the family tradition of trade and office, to which in due course Hugh's son returned. The dynasty was sufficiently endowed, however, to stand a generation during which its main representative cared for neither.[26]

III

These glimpses of the economic resources of leading townsmen, on the other hand, tell us very little directly about their attitudes and mentalities; and much of the other evidence at our disposal is similarly inconclusive. About many of them, for example, it is not even easy to be sure what their background was. Many had names which point to an ultimately rural origin, but that origin might well be quite remote. No doubt the York Warthills and the Newcastle Blagdons had come at one time from the townships from which they were named, but most of those we encounter were born and bred in the towns in which their ancestors had settled. At the same time, everything points to a continuing stream of rural immigrants, of whom a small minority flourished mightily. Most were presumably of peasant stock, as Richard Embleton probably was, but a few came from the higher ranks of rural society. Peter Graper, Embleton's slightly older contemporary, appears to have been the heir

[23] *CPR 1313–17*, 281; *CPR 1321–4*, 207; *CPR 1330–4*, 378; Fraser, 'John of Denton', 306–7.
[24] *Feet of Fines York, 1232–46*, ed. J. Parker (Yorks. Arch. Soc., Rec. Ser., lxviii, 1925), nos. 984, 1056, 1227, 1237; D. & C. of York, Vicars' Chartulary, ff.8–9; PRO JI 1/1042, mm.5,9d.
[25] *Feet of Fines York, 1246–72*, ed. J. Parker (Yorks. Arch. Soc., Rec. Ser., lxxxii, 1932), nos. 1511, 1547; PRO, JI 1/1050, m.89; *Year Books of Edward II: 7 Edward II*, 113–14; *Notes on the Religious . . . Houses of Yorkshire*, I, ed. W. P. Baildon (Yorks. Arch. Soc., Rec. ser., xvii, 1985); *Placita de Quo Warranto*, 225.
[26] *Feet of Fines York, 1327–47*, ed. W. P. Baildon (Yorks. Arch. Soc., Rec. Ser., xlii, 1910), 120.

of a decaying gentry family from Colwell. By moving into town Peter reversed its declining fortunes, for by 1296 he was one of the wealthier Newcastle taxpayers and had re-established a rural base in Burradon.[27] Another somewhat younger contemporary, Richard Acton, again had rural roots, but as the younger son of a solid gentry family, the main line of which continued in possession of the township from which it took its name. Richard was already exporting wool in 1308 and he was still exporting when Edward III commandeered the wool of English merchants at Dordrecht in 1338.[28]

These scraps of family history do not suggest that there was any deep divide between town and country. Men of varying social ranks moved from villages to town and once there, if they had the requisite abilities and perhaps a little luck, were seemingly accepted and might even be conspicuously successful. Conversely, it does not seem to have been regarded as unnatural for townsmen to own property in country villages or for these 'bourgeois gentlemen' to assume many of the normal responsibilities falling upon gentlemen even while continuing also to be bourgeois. Nicholas Selby held his courts and collected their issues at Fangfoss and Youlthorpe like any other manorial lord, and we find Richard Embleton supervising the destruction of Harbottle castle, having custody of Dunstanburgh castle, and serving as keeper of the peace and assessor of the lay subsidy for the county of Northumberland.[29] Ultimately, moreover, Richard was killed in battle against the Scots at Halidon Hill, just as the mayor of York, Nicholas Fleming, was killed at Myton-on-Swale. Earlier, John Sampson had been keeper of Scarborough castle and had been maimed in Edward I's service at the siege of Stirling.[30]

In the light of his military record it is perhaps not surprising that John Sampson was knighted, but so were Gilbert Louth (probably because of the amount of income he received from land) and Nicholas Scott, who served as sheriff of Northumberland as well as mayor of Newcastle. The impression that the line between bourgeois and gentleman might well be indistinct is reinforced if we follow John Sampson's career a little further. In later life he was still involved in York's affairs, for his last term as mayor began in 1300 and soon afterwards he was alleged to have given refuge to the murderers of a servant of St. Leonard's hospital. That allegation landed him in gaol by the procurement of Walter Langton, Edward I's treasurer who was also master of the hospital. It cost John gifts of money and property to the hospital to secure his freedom. In addition to his city interests, however, John also built up a country estate, acquiring land at Aberford, Lotherton, Acaster Selby, Acaster Malbis and Appleton Roebuck — possibly sometimes through a measure of sharp practice, for it was suspected that he took advantage of the insanity of the previous holder to get hold of land at Lotherton and Aberford. That, however, was neither particularly gentlemanly nor particularly bourgeois behaviour; meantime, like any other country gentleman, he witnessed country charters (although sometimes as Sir John

[27] *Hist. of Northumberland*, iv. 292; ix. 45; *Northumberland Lay Subsidy of 1296*, ed. C. M. Fraser (Soc. Antiquaries Newcastle upon Tyne, Rec. Ser., i, 1968), 46, 64.

[28] Fraser, 'John of Denton', 305 – 6, 314; *CCR 1337 – 9*, 431; the account of the family in *Hist. of Northumberland*, vii. 365 – 6, needs some amendment.

[29] *Northumberland Durham Deeds*, 117; *CPR 1321 – 4*, 22; *CPR 1324 – 7*, 430; *CPR 1330 – 4*, 286, 358; *Hist. of Northumberland*, ii. 199.

[30] A. Gooder, *Parliamentary Representation of the County of York, 1258 – 1831*, I (Yorks. Arch. Soc., Rec. Ser., xci, 1935), 23 – 5; *CCR 1302 – 7*, 188, 280; *CDRS*, ii. no. 1949.

Sampson of York) and he was drawn into country feuds, some perhaps rooted in whatever the circumstances were that persuaded Richard Fauconbergh to sell Appleton Roebuck to him. In 1303 John, with his son and others, beat up an adherent of the Fauconberghs on the Appleton-Steeton road, and later that year John de Fauconbergh brought a party over from Holderness which for three days laid siege to John's house at Appleton. Evidently John Sampson had learned to live like a gentleman and it was probably symptomatic of his growing attachment to country life that when he got a licence for a private oratory, in 1309, it was for his house at Appleton.[31]

Ownership of property in the country, therefore, tended to draw townsmen back to the country where so many of them had their ultimate origins. John Sampson's descendants, like those of Gace de Chaumont earlier, played no further significant part in York life. Earlier still, the acquisition of Walton by the reeve of York, William Fairfax, and of Croft by his son-in-law, Robert Clervaus, had similar consequences. Robert Clervaus' son was a knight; the Fairfaxes of Walton had a long and distinguished future; and eventually the Clervaus of Croft provided themselves with a distinguished past, going back to a mythical ancestor who accompanied William the Conqueror to England. These bourgeois families became, in the clearest sense, country gentlemen, one of the classic forms of social promotion in early England.[32] At the same time, the completeness of their severance from the city must not be exaggerated. William Fairfax's heir and both the elder sons of Robert Clervaus married daughters of mayors of York; Robert's younger son, William, lived out his life as a citizen of York, and Sir Thomas Clervaus of Croft was still dealing in the York property market in the 1270s.[33] Roger Basy's descendants were equally faithful to an old connection. Roger's last service was to represent York in the 1295 parliament and his heirs were mainly associated with the estate he had acquired at Bilbrough. Roger's son and grandson, however, continued to have property in York. The son in his will calls himself citizen of York and the grandson styles himself Richard Basy of York, and as late as 1403 a Basy widow endowed a second chantry in the York church in which Roger had founded his chantry at the start of the fourteenth century.[34]

The Fairfax, Clervaus and Basy families, however, like the Chaumonts and the Sampsons, withdrew from York's active ruling circle; but rural investment, even on some scale, did not invariably diminish significantly participation in a town's affairs. That was true in the case of the Selby family at York and of their successor dynasts in the next century, the Langtons and the Graas; and at Newcastle it was equally true of the Carliols and the Scotts. The Carliols appear to have begun to invest in country property in the third generation or so, when in 1271 Thomas Carliol got Swarland manor and probably a freehold in Jesmond. Thomas's son and grandson inherited these estates, but both (as well as Thomas's younger son) served as mayor, MPs and collectors of

[31] *Records of the Trial of Walter Langton*, ed. A. Beardwood (Camden Soc., 4th ser., vi, 1969), 319–21; *Rot. Parl.*, i. 145; *CCR 1272–9*, 483; *Coucher Book of Selby*, ed. J. T. Fowler, I (Yorks. Arch. Soc., Rec. Ser., x, 1891), 326; PRO, JI 1/1107, mm.8,9d.

[32] *VCH, City of York*, 30–1, 45–7; T. Widdrington, *Analecta Eboracensia*, ed. C. Caine (London, 1897), 147; T. D. Whitaker, *History of Richmondshire* (London, 1823), i. 241.

[33] PRO, JI 1/1046, m.70d; *Kirkby's Inquest*, 178n.; *Yorkshire Deeds*, VII, ed. C. T. Clay (Yorks. Arch. Soc., Rec. Ser., lxxxiii, 1932), nos. 527–9, 533–6.

[34] *Coucher Book of Selby*, i. 330–1; Drake, 267; *CPR 1307–13*, 343.

customs for the city, and the grandson, even at the end of his life, still called himself Thomas Carliol of Newcastle. Only at this point, for lack of male heirs, did this line of Carliols disappear from both Swarland and Newcastle.[35] The rural interests of the Scotts, whose name is preserved in Scotswood and immortalized by the road that led to Blaydon races, were rather more suburban. The senior of the two lines into which the family divided had footholds in Backworth and Elswick, later extended into Seghill and Mason, by the mid-thirteenth century. This line was represented early in the fourteenth century by Nicholas Scott, the sheriff of Northumberland knighted by Edward II, but his grandson in the mid-century owned a ship taking hides and coal to Flanders and was one of the 12 men of Newcastle who deliberated upon responsibility for the felonious killing of John Denton. The junior line, meanwhile, was exploiting both the coal mines and the fields of Benwell, where it was established by 1296. For much of the fourteenth century, however, it provided Newcastle with bailiffs and the occasional MP; Richard Scott in the mid-century was sufficiently involved in the town's affairs to be accused of complicity in two murders there, and still styled himself Richard son of John Scott of Newcastle upon Tyne even in 1370.[36]

IV

The records of thirteenth-century York and Newcastle, then, are an endorsement of the contemporary view that towns were ruled by a small circle of *majores*, better if not more discreet than their fellows and most of them among the wealthier members of their communities. Much of their wealth, too, was derived from characteristically bourgeois vocations (trade, craft industry and finance), although ownership of real property was also an essential ingredient of their resources. On the other hand, when we draw too sharp a line between town and country, and in particular between bourgeois and gentlemen, we begin to fly in the face of medieval facts. It is not only that many townsfolk had more or less proximate rural roots (strong enough to move Richard Embleton to endow a chantry in his native village as well as another at St. Nicholas's in Newcastle), or that the pig was ubiquitous in towns, or even that many townsmen, not all of them outstandingly rich, invested in villages just as country landowners invested in urban real estate. There are other indications, too, of a certain uniformity in the mentalities of the leading elements in town and country. Townsmen like John Sampson and Richard Embleton joined knights and gentlemen not only in landownership but in war, and a few were advanced to knighthood or helped to administer shires as well as boroughs. In addition to Richard Embleton and Sir Nicholas Scott, the latter included the Newcastle bailiff Roger Higham, coroner of Northumberland, despite doubts

[35] Dendy, 156–7; *Hist. of Northumberland*, vii. 386, 390, 412; R. L. Baker, 'The English Customs Service, 1307–43', *Trans. American Philosophical Soc.*, n.s., li (1961), 60.

[36] *Hist. of Northumberland*, viii. 92, 115; ix. 37; xiii. 218, 239; *Feet of Fines: Northumberland and Durham*, ii. nos. 107, 169–70; J. Hodgson, *History of Northumberland*, II, ii (Newcastle, 1832), 4 n. 3(a); *Lay Sub., 1296*, 66; R. Welford, *History of Newcastle and Gateshead* (London, 1884), i. 126; *CPR 1334–8*, 285–7; A. MacDonald, 'Calendar of Deeds in the Laing Charters relating to Northumberland', *Archaeologia Aeliana*, 4th ser., xxviii (1950), no.37.

about his qualifications.[37] It is less surprising, therefore, that mayors were sometimes given the courtesy title of *dominus* even when they were not knights, and John Pandon's widow, the formidable Sybil Carliol, appears to have had no doubt about her right to be called the Lady Sybil.[38] The leading bourgeois families also behaved much like gentlemen in the niches they found for their cadet members and surplus daughters. John Sampson's brother was a pluralist rector and one of his sons was a canon of York, as was one of the sons of the first Hugh Selby, while a daughter of Roger Sperry of York became a nun at Hampole and Thomas Carliol's sister a nun at Lambley, a house of which Peter Graper's daughter was subsequently prioress.[39] Even marriage and feudal incidents could bridge the divide between town and country. Hugh Selby's and Richard Embleton's last wives appear both to have been from gentry families, and Henry Scott of Newcastle got the wardship and marriage of Nicholas Surtees, lord of the barony of North Gosforth and heir of a family settled in Teesdale since the time of Henry I. This was, no doubt, a business arrangement for which Henry paid dearly, but what is interesting is the absence of obvious incongruity in a bourgeois becoming the guardian of a gentleman.[40]

Testimony from York and Newcastle, in other words, suggests that lines of class demarcating thirteenth-century gentry and upper bourgeoisie ought not to be made too rigid. It is possible, of course, that they were exceptional towns, but there is nothing to show that they were unusually distinctive; and if they were not, what they teach us is that, despite the fact that they were centres of economic activities that were different from those absorbing the energies of most countryfolk, their ruling classes shared many of the attitudes of the dominant groups in the countryside around them. Perhaps there are also some pointers to a like conclusion if we look to the towns from a countryman's angle. Even in the late twelfth century the Yorkshire baron, Roger Mowbray, had close connections with a group of influential citizens of York; some of his charters were drawn up in the York house of one of them, William Tickhill; and when Roger granted land in Askham Richard to William, probably in return for a crusading loan, Roger spoke of him as a friend.[41] The absence of an impassable frontier between gentry and bourgeoisie in the thirteenth century, in other words, may have amounted to rather more than the relative freedom of the bourgeois to gain social promotion into gentility, for there seems in fact to have been a degree of common ground which, by the thirteenth century, was traditional. Perhaps this was not altogether surprising in a country in which the town of Cambridge's first gild was a gild of thegns and in which, long before the

[37] *CCR 1288–96*, 307; *CCR 1302–7*, 2.

[38] For the title *dominus*, eg. John Selby at York (D. & C. of York, Liber Albus, iii, f.59d) and Robert Mitford at Newcastle (*Hist. of Northumberland*, x. 420n.); and for the Lady Sybil, *Early Deeds*, no. 223.

[39] *Register of Walter Gray*, 108; D. & C. of York, Vicars' Chartulary, f. 27; *Register of William Greenfield*, ed. A. Hamilton Thompson, II (Surtees Soc., cxlix, 1934), no. 893; *Northumberland and Durham Deeds*, 74; *Hist. of Northumberland*, vii. 391.

[40] W. P. Hedley, *Northumberland Families*, I (Newcastle, 1968), 54–7.

[41] *Charters of the Honour of Mowbray, 1107–1191*, ed. D. E. Greenway (British Academy Records of Social and Economic History, n.s., i, 1972), xxx, 97–8, 248; *Early Yorkshire Charters*, ed. W. Farrer (Yorks. Arch. Soc., Rec. Ser., Extra Ser., 1914–16), i. no.547.

Normans came, the merchant who prospered was entitled to the rights of a thegn; nor was it altogether surprising in a country in which, in the future, knights and burgesses would come together in a parliamentary house that represented both the urban and the rural communities of the land.

The Place of Carlisle in the Commerce of Northern England in the Thirteenth Century

Henry Summerson

Carlisle has been neglected in studies of the patterns of commerce in medieval England. A paucity of source material, the result both of a series of fires which between 1251 and 1391 repeatedly ravaged the city and destroyed its muniments, and of Carlisle's sheer physical distance from those administrative and judicial centres, above all Westminster, whose activities generated the sort of documentary evidence invaluable to the historians of other towns and cities, is certainly one reason for this neglect. The fact that both the city itself and the region which supported it were undeniably impoverished and underpopulated by comparison with the towns and countrysides of most other parts of England is doubtless another. Urban life was slow to develop in the North-West, and at Carlisle, as in the burghs of southern Scotland, with which it has much in common, the early townsmen appear to have been outsiders, their places of origin attested by the *Vicus Flandrensis* and *Vicus Francorum* recorded there in the thirteenth century.[1]

Cumberland's natural disadvantages of terrain and climate, and of distance from centres of wealth and power, were compounded by political and administrative considerations. It was conquered territory, seized from Scotland in 1092, its possession disputed by successive Scottish kings for nearly 150 years afterwards. Carlisle's primary function in its early days was the maintenance of the border with Scotland, less than 10 miles away; the burgesses, so styled as early as 1130, were there as much to support the city's military and ecclesiastical establishments as to advance their own fortunes.[2] Their chances of achieving the latter were in any case still further restricted by the stroke of royal policy which at a very early date placed a substantial portion of Cumberland under forest law.[3] The existence of Inglewood forest, beginning at the very gates of Carlisle and extending as far south as Penrith, reduced the county's scope for arable farming and severely inhibited the development of what should have been Carlisle's natural hinterland.[4] The city's economic progress, though sufficient to enable it to pay a tallage of nearly £400 in 1210, was nonetheless slow and unspectacular.[5] Carlisle had a

[1] W. M. Mackenzie, *The Scottish Burghs* (Edinburgh, 1949), 36–8; Cumbria Record Office, Carlisle (hereafter CRO) D/Lons/L C11; Cartulary of Lanercost Priory (eighteenth-century transcript in library of Dean and Chapter, Carlisle), 82. Unless otherwise stated, all manuscript references are to documents in the PRO.

[2] *The Pipe Roll of 31 Henry I*, ed. J. Hunter (Record Commission, 1833), 142.

[3] *The Register of the Priory of Wetherhal*, ed. J. E. Prescott (London, Kendal, 1897), 26–7.

[4] See C47/11/1 no.16; C47/11/6 no. 28.

[5] *Pipe Roll 12 John* (Pipe Roll Soc., n.s., xxvi, 1949), 139.

fair by 1180 at the latest, yet in about 1200 it was still possible for two Cumbrian landowners to agree that the rent for property in Melmerby, north-east of Penrith, should be paid at the fair not of Carlisle but of Roxburgh, which was obviously still the principal venue for such arrangements in the Border counties.[6] Only when the Treaty of York in 1237 finally settled Carlisle's status as an indisputably English city, however, could its commercial role develop free from political constraints, against a background of growing population, expanding settlement and the emergence of other market centres to which the prospect of lasting peace in the Borders no doubt itself contributed.[7]

It was Carlisle's good fortune that, although peace inevitably meant a diminution of its supply role, the city nonetheless continued to fulfil non-commercial functions, from which its economic life certainly benefited. The castle was not deserted, although it was allowed to fall into a state not far removed from ruin, and there was still its garrison to be supported.[8] By 1237, moreover, Carlisle was the centre of a diocese, with a bishop increasingly likely to be resident in it, and also housed an important priory, a hospital and two friaries. The city was also the centre of Cumberland's secular administration, where the county court sat and the king's justices usually held their sessions. Such factors cannot be considered in isolation from economic ones. It is not just that catering for temporary or resident non-producers, in an economic sense, is bound to have stimulated the city's economic life, but that economic and religious contacts, in particular, often ran on parallel lines and may well have developed together. The geographical pattern of Carlisle's trade was naturally in large measure dictated by its means of access to other regions. There were roads to Newcastle through the Tyne gap (a journey made hazardous by 1256 by the operations of amateur coalminers), to York over Stainmoor, and into Scotland, either through Annandale or via Liddel and Castleton to Jedburgh, Roxburgh and beyond.[9] In Cumberland itself there were roads south to Penrith and Appleby and south-west to Cockermouth and Whitehaven, and there were also seaborne commercial ties with Ireland.[10]

Arable as well as pastoral farming was practised in north-west England. The royal demesnes round Carlisle castle produced corn, rye, barley and oats, with oats greatly predominating (as they did throughout the region), and their surpluses might be sold at the city's fair.[11] But it was pastoral farming which made the greater impact on Carlisle's economy, its principal products of livestock, wool and hides which are most commonly referred to as sold in the city. The wool of Cumberland was unquestionably marketed in Carlisle. A presentment made at the 1292/93 eyre, telling how the city bailiffs 'do not allow any outsider from the countryside to buy wool in the king's market in

[6] *The Register of the Priory of St. Bees*, ed. J. Wilson (Surtees Soc., cxxvi, 1915), 539 – 40; CRO D/Lons/L P25.

[7] C. M. L. Bouch, *Prelates and People of the Lake Counties* (Kendal 1948), 36 – 7.

[8] *Royal Letters*, ii. 124 – 5.

[9] G. V. Scammell, *Hugh du Puiset* (Cambridge, 1956), 215; *Three Early Assize Rolls for the County of Northumberland*, ed. W. Page (Surtees Soc., lxxxviii, 1890), 103; H. J. Lawlor, 'Notes on St. Bernard's Life of St. Malachy and his two sermons on the passing of St. Malachy', *Procs. of the Royal Irish Academy*, xxxv, C (1918 – 20), 230 – 64; G. W. S. Barrow, *Robert Bruce* (2nd ed., Edinburgh, 1976), 28.

[10] *Register of Wetherhal*, 16; *Register of St. Bees*, 103. For Ireland see below.

[11] E 372/105 m.20d; E 372/111 m.16d; E 101/505/5; E. Miller, 'Farming in Northern England during the Twelfth and Thirteenth Centuries', *Northern History*, xi (1976 for 1975), 9.

Carlisle, but hinder them and keep it for their own benefit. . .', points to an active wool market with Carlisle as its centre and with profits which were worth trying to monopolise.[12] Wool was also worked up into cloth in Carlisle, possibly at the beginning of the thirteenth century, for in 1202 cloth was reported as having been sold at Carlisle fair, though it need not have been made in the city, and certainly by the end of the century it had a fulling mill, and 28 people were named at the 1292/93 eyre as those who 'make cloths not in accordance with the assize and have sold them . . .'[13] Whether the cloth thus made served more than local purposes is not recorded — a good deal of it must have gone into the shops of the numerous city tailors — but there is no doubt that materials needed for processing wool and cloth were imported from outside the region.

This can be deduced not only from murage and pontage grants licensing the levying of tolls on woad, the most important of all dyestuffs, and on potash, the mordant most commonly used for fixing dyes, but, with greater precision, from an unfortunately unfinished plaint from the 1293 Northumberland eyre.[14] In this, Gilbert son of William of Carlisle sued against Simon de Tyndale of Newcastle for a debt of £33 owed by the latter for 36 dickers of hides bought from Gilbert in Carlisle on Palm Sunday 1292. Simon, said Gilbert, had agreed to pay £18 in cash, and to give him 36 quarters of woad for the other £18. Six quarters had already been handed over, so reducing the sum outstanding from £36 to £33. Simon did not deny the terms of the deal but claimed that the six quarters handed over had been only an earnest of future payment, to be made in full when he had actually seen and been satisfied with the quality of the hides. And when he had seen them, he had been so dissatisfied as to prefer to renounce the contract and lose his deposit rather than take the hides. This is a case which shows Carlisle to have been a place for the distribution of hides as well as of wool, and as such to have exchanged one primary product of its region for an import needed for the industrial treatment of another. It also points to wider contacts, between Carlisle and Newcastle and possibly beyond, since Simon de Tyndale's woad may well have come from the Continent, to which Newcastle obviously had much readier access than Carlisle. There is plenty of other evidence for contacts between the two towns. Both the bishop and priory of Carlisle had property in Newcastle where, by the late thirteenth century, the de Carleol family was practically running the town.[15] Peter of Penrith, a Carlisle juror at the 1278/79 eyre, sued Richard de la Heye, probably one of the bailiffs of Newcastle, at that eyre for detaining in Newcastle goods and chattels of Peter's to the value of £9 10s.[16] Relations were not, indeed, always easy. In 1255 Roger son of William of Newcastle paid 40s. for a writ of false judgment against Carlisle city court, and won his case, its offence costing the city £20, while in the aftermath of the 1292 fire four unknown carters from Newcastle 'loaded two carts with iron, cloth

[12] JUST/1/137 m.5.

[13] *Pipe Roll 4 John* (Pipe Roll Soc., n.s., xv, 1937), 243; JUST/1/137 m.26d; *Placita de Quo Warranto*, ed. W. Illingworth (Record Commission, 1818), 121.

[14] JUST/1/654 m.11.

[15] *The Register of John de Halton*, ed. W. N. Thompson (London, 1913), ii.55; *CPR 1258–66*, 118; C. M. Fraser, 'The Pattern of Trade in the North-East of England 1265–1350', *Northern History*, iv (1969), 59.

[16] JUST/1/133 m.31; JUST/1/130B m.12d; *Three Early Assize Rolls*, 367.

and bronze utensils, stolen when Carlisle city was burnt, and fled at once with the carts'.[17] The historian can feel more indulgent than could their contemporaries towards rogues whose lack of scruples so obligingly furnish him with evidence for cross-Pennine trading links and the means of transport used to maintain them.

It is less easy to be precise about Carlisle's links with Ireland. It is possible that contacts across the Irish Sea predated the English invasions, for there was a port at Whitehaven and a 'sceplending' on the river Waver by the 1150s. It is certain, however, that contacts were made as soon as the English occupation of Ireland began, with supplies being sent across from Cumberland for Henry II's expedition of 1171.[18] By the end of the twelfth century a roll of Dublin names could list 10 men as originating in Carlisle but then living in Dublin. Another three men from Carlisle were named as members of Dublin's gild merchant in 1226, while at around the latter date a *Vicus Hibernicorum* was recorded in Carlisle.[19] At the 1246 Cumberland eyre the failure of the tenant of a disputed toft in the city suburb to present himself in court was found to be due to his departure for Ireland before the issue of the writ.[20] It seems reasonable to suppose that movements of goods resulted from these movements of people, but evidence for the nature of Irish-Cumbrian commerce is very scarce. It seems clear, however, that Carlisle imported Irish grain, to compensate for Cumberland's deficiencies in this respect; indeed, such imports seem to be a particularly good example of the way commercial and religious links could be forged simultaneously and to their mutual benefit. Four Cumbrian monasteries, including Carlisle priory, came to have Irish daughter-houses, and they all used their Irish affiliations to maintain their own food supplies.[21] Thus, in 1235, the bishop and priory of Carlisle were licensed to buy food in Ireland, and by the end of the thirteenth century the priory had its own ship which it could send to Ireland to buy provisions there.[22] Carlisle castle, too, might draw on Irish supplies, as in 1222 when the justiciar of Ireland was instructed to send 500 quarters of wheat and 40 hogsheads of wine to provision it.[23] Such a shipment was probably exceptional only in its size, and it seems likely that traffic in foodstuffs across the Irish Sea was commonplace throughout the thirteenth century. It is not clear, however, where such cargoes were brought to land before the development of Skinburness at the end of the century. It could have been as far away as Whitehaven, where the abbot of St. Mary's of York had a ship in the 1270s, and which was connected to Carlisle by road. Or there may have been a landing-point on the Solway coast, from which goods could have been brought to Carlisle, as they were in the fourteenth century, either in carts or by water: though shallow, the river Eden was

[17] C60/52 m.11; *The Pipe Rolls of Cumberland and Westmorland 1222–1260*, ed. F. H. M. Parker (Cumberland and Westmorland Antiquarian and Archaeological Soc., (hereafter *CWS*) Extra ser., xii, 1905), 178; JUST/1/137 m.25.

[18] *Register of St. Bees*, 40–1; *The Register and Records of Holmcultram*, ed. F. Grainger, W. G. Collingwood (*CWS* Rec. ser., vii, 1929), no.72; *Pipe Roll 18 Henry II* (Pipe Roll Soc., xviii, 1894), 69.

[19] *Historical and Municipal Documents of Ireland A.D. 1172–1320*, ed. J. T. Gilbert (*RS*, 1870), 7–47, 84–6; CRO D/Lons/L C6.

[20] JUST/1/130A m.2d.

[21] W. T. McIntire, 'A Note on Grey Abbey and other religious foundations on Strangford Lough affiliated to the abbeys of Cumberland', *CWS Trans.*, 2nd ser., xli (1941), 161–73.

[22] *CPR 1232–47*, 113; *CDRI 1302–07*, no.249.

[23] *CDRI 1171–1251*, no.1055.

navigable by barges in the waters round Carlisle.[24]

The commercial nature of Carlisle's links with York is largely a matter of inference. Contacts between them, as one might expect, were long-established. It was the citizens of York, for instance, who in 1149 were able to tell King Stephen of the alliance made against him at Carlisle by King David I of Scotland, Ranulf of Chester and the future Henry II.[25] Again, the foundations of these links were at least partly ecclesiastical. The bishop of Carlisle, one of the metropolitan of York's few diocesan subordinates, was by 1282 retaining a proctor at the provincial court of York.[26] Wetheral priory, a dependency of St. Mary's of York, had property in Carlisle, and so too did St. Peter's hospital in York.[27] Trade followed, or perhaps accompanied, the crozier. Guy the merchant, a householder in Carlisle's Rickergate, was robbed in York in about 1229, while later in the century a few Carlisle men, including two cobblers and a butcher, settled there.[28] Several of Carlisle's inhabitants are in their turn recorded as taking their names from places in Yorkshire, less from York itself (though a William de Ebor' was included in a list of Carlisle's leading citizens in 1295) than from lesser communities coming within York's orbit: places such as Helmsley, Rillington, Malton, Pickering and Ripon.[29] The exact nature of the trade which presumably underlay these migrations is unrecorded, but since in 1251 Carlisle received a grant of murage 'in the form which the citizens of York have', the economies of the two cities were probably quite similar in kind, if hardly in scale.[30] Each was a centre for the distribution of both the produce and the needs of the region in which it was the dominant community, and no doubt its trade with the other helped each of them to fulfil this function.

As far as Carlisle is concerned, this function can be most clearly seen in its trade with Scotland and with the rest of Cumberland. These two should not really be considered in separation, since the English annexation of southern Cumbria in 1092 divided a region which was naturally a unity in language, social organisation and, when circumstances permitted, economic life. It should be admitted, however, that there was an element of compulsion in Cumberland's dealings with its county town. The tolls of which it was said in 1292 that they 'were taken throughout the whole county', which could mean in places as far apart as Egremont, Penrith and Kingsbridge in Liddel barony, suggest that as at Ayr in Scotland, Carlisle, at least on its market days of Wednesday and Saturday, had a monopoly of buying and selling which probably covered the whole of Cumberland. It also looks as if the city's officials had the task of safeguarding that monopoly by taking the appropriate tolls from defaulters who chose to take their goods elsewhere.[31] How effective such

[24] JUST/1/130B m.10d; E 101/14/31 f.3v; E 101/369/16 f.1.

[25] R. H. C. Davis, *King Stephen* (London, 1967), 107 – 08.

[26] *Register of John Halton*, i.31.

[27] *Register of Wetherhal*, 43 – 4, 173 – 81; *Early Yorkshire Charters*, ed. W. Farrer (Edinburgh, 1914), i. no. 175; *CChR 1300 – 26*, 93 – 4.

[28] *CR 1227 – 31*, 173; *Register and Records of Holmcultram*, nos. 6 – 8, 37 – 40; *Register of the Freemen of the City of York*, I, ed. F. Collins (Surtees Soc., xcvi, 1897), 2, 4, 6, 11.

[29] E 159/69 m.20; Lanercost Cartulary, 188 – 9; JUST/1/137 m.34; *CPR 1272 – 81*, 396; JUST/1/1277 m.30; KB27/71 m.5d.

[30] *CPR 1247 – 58*, 100.

[31] JUST/1/136 m.62d; JUST/1/133 m.28d; SC 8/268 no. 13386; *CIMisc*, iii. no.897; *Regesta Regum Scottorum* II, ed. G. W. S. Barrow (Edinburgh, 1971), no.462; A. A. M. Duncan, *Scotland: The Making of the Kingdom* (Edinburgh, 1975), 475.

measures were is unknown. A reference in 1292 to people leaving the city for Penrith 'with their loads of victuals and other things for sale', presumably bought in Carlisle, may be a reflection of the latter's role as regional entrepôt for the distribution of such commodities rather than the result of enforced trafficking.[32]

Scots needed no such constraints to bring them to Carlisle, where their presence as traders was all the more important to the city's economy because its hinterland to the South was so heavily restricted by the extent of Inglewood forest. Commerce was not the only cross-Border connection. Numerous landowners, lay and ecclesiastical, had property on both sides of the Border, the king of Scots among them, while several bearers of Scottish placenames, like Roxburgh, Berwick, Redpath, Galloway and Kirkcudbright, were to be found in late thirteenth-century Carlisle.[33] But once more such links served to reinforce commercial ones. Two Scottish monasteries, Jedburgh and Holyrood, had houses in Carlisle. A third, Melrose, transferred its house to its daughter-house of Holmcultram, while specifically reserving the right to accommodation for its men in it on the occasion of Carlisle fair.[34] Carlisle fair and market were magnets to draw Scots into England, with goods not always honestly come by. It is in transactions involving Scots that Carlisle can be most clearly seen as a venue for the sale of livestock, since it was at Carlisle fair that one Henry Scot was said in 1280 to have bought an allegedly stolen mare, in Carlisle market that four men some time before 1292 tried to sell two oxen and a horse subsequently found to have been stolen.[35] That the theft had been perpetrated in Scotland in no way deterred the city court from hanging three of the thieves. Men of Carlisle traded into Scotland: it was presented at the 1278/79 eyre that the lord of Liddel barony and his bailiffs would not 'allow the merchants of the city to pass through the middle of the vill of Liddel or elsewhere on his lands, going towards Scotland, unless they give tolls on their going and returning . . .' Scottish merchants certainly came to Carlisle.[36]

The most striking evidence for this is provided by another presentment made at the 1292/93 eyre, concerning a distraint made by the sheriff of Cumberland on Scottish merchants 'for a debt to a merchant from Gascony', which had resulted in the Scots leaving Carlisle. The citizens, afraid of losing their revenue from tolls, had given the sheriff 20s. 'to spare the lesser merchants from Scotland and distrain the greater'.[37] Clearly, a variety of Scottish traders came to Carlisle, ranging from men who were probably little more than peddlars to presumably substantial figures with the resources for dealing with a Gascon merchant. Such dealing probably took place in Carlisle, which may well have become a commercial rendezvous of some importance, able, at least on occasions, to attract French as well as Scottish traders. Of the goods recorded in other sources as imported into Scotland, the murage grant of 1261 suggests that corn, salt, fish, garlic, dyestuffs, leather, wine and cloth could have been bought in Carlisle.[38] Some of these goods would have been local

[32] JUST/1/137 m.5.
[33] *CIMisc.*, i. no.44; JUST/1/137 mm.24d, 25, 25d, 26d; JUST/1/131 m.12d.
[34] *CIMisc.*, ii. no.1146; E 136/17/29 m.7; *Register and Records of Holmcultram*, no.40d.
[35] CDRS, ii. no.183; JUST/1/137 m.26.
[36] JUST/1/133 m.28d.
[37] JUST/1/137 m.26.
[38] Duncan, 506 – 10; C 66/76 m.2.

produce; leather was made in the city as well as cloth, several tanners being recorded there. But wine could only have come from abroad, perhaps by the hands of Gascon merchants like that to which the Scots were indebted, while on at least one occasion dyes, though produced in England, were supplied from the Continent.

This is a case of considerable interest, since it shows how for Cumberland, as well as for southern Scotland, Carlisle could serve as a point for the distribution of foreign goods. An inquest in 1295 found that four Cumberland men had bought woad from two foreign merchants from 'Aunayse'.[39] None of these Cumbrian debtors seems to have been a Carlisle man, but they could easily have bought their woad in Carlisle. This is shown by another inquest into the debts owed to one of these same merchants, John Haungard. It was found that one William de Waverton had owed him £8, but had paid this off in stages and in various places: 40s. on the bridge over the river Wampool, 60s. in Newcastle, and 40s. in Carlisle on 15 August 1292, the day on which Carlisle fair opened.[40] Shown by the first inquest to have been a dealer in woad, John may have come regularly to Carlisle fair to sell his wares and collect his debts, a possibility suggesting once more that that fair had become of more than just local consequence, and so helping to explain why Scots and others came to trade with the city.

The evidence for Carlisle's trade in the thirteenth century is undeniably scanty and fragmented, but the impression here drawn from it — of a city serving as a centre for local and regional trade, and for the redistribution of goods sometimes brought there over very long distances — may perhaps be reinforced by two further considerations. The first is that in 1292, for all its natural disadvantages, Carlisle enjoyed an annual revenue estimated at £94 10s., a sum which compares favourably with York's £123 14s 9d. of the same date, — if Carlisle's revenue from tolls, £35 per annum, was distorted by its receipt of tolls from all over the county, it did not receive the toll of 1s. on each sack of wool entering and leaving the city which enriched York by over £50 —, and which suggests a genuine measure of prosperity to whch Carlisle's far-flung network of trade made an important contribution.[41] The second consideration is the role Carlisle was able to play in the organization of Edward I's Scottish wars. When we read of massive quantities of supplies coming to Carlisle from Ireland and then being distributed from there to strongpoints in southern Scotland, of commodities such as bronze, iron and canvass not only being purchased on the king's behalf in Carlisle market but also being brought in from the towns and villages of Cumberland by Carlisle citizens acting as middle men between local suppliers and the keepers of the king's stores, of the king's tents being carried to Carlisle from Newcastle, of money for wages and, at the very end of his reign, of medicines for the ailing Edward I being brought to Carlisle from York, what we see are surely the movements of people and goods over well-worn paths created by the pattern of regional trade, often moving now, indeed, at considerably greater speeds and in far

[39] E 106/3/8 no.2.
[40] E 143/4/2 no.14(2).
[41] *Placita de Quo Warranto*, 121; *VCH, City of York*, 35.

greater volumes, but in directions recognizably the same.[42] That pattern was not created by Carlisle, but during the thirteenth century Carlisle came to have its place in it, and without that city the pattern was not thereafter complete.

[42] M. C. Prestwich, *War, Politics and Finance under Edward I* (London, 1972), 122–4; E 101/5/22 mm.1, 1d, 4; *Liber Quotidianus Contrarotulatoris Garderobae anno regni regis Edwardi Primi vicesimo octavo A.D. MCCXCIX & MCCC*, ed. J. Topham (London, 1787), 71, 91–2; E 101/370/16 f.12.

Dublin in the Thirteenth Century:
The Making of a Colonial Capital City

J. A. Watt

It was in the medieval period that Gaelic Ireland underwent the first of those phases of colonisation which have so fashioned her historical development. It seems true to say that perhaps the most important single theme of medieval Irish history centres round the nature and consequences of two successive foreign settlements. The first was that of the Vikings which began around the mid-ninth century and lasted until the later thirteenth century when the Hiberno-Norse, as a distinct ethnic entity, drop out of the historian's view. The second was that of the Anglo-Normans which began in the last decades of the twelfth century and lasted at least until the seventeenth century when their lineal descendants, culturally distinguishable in Ireland as the 'Old English', were still substantial landholders.

To analyse what happened when different cultures, Gaelic, Scandinavian, Anglo-French, clashed and came to coexist in close and continuous direct contact is, it seems to me, the most challenging task that medieval Ireland presents to the historian. In this communication I want to try to tell a few paragraphs of that particular story or perhaps to draft the outlines of an important chapter of it.

I begin, then, at that point in time when Dublin, still essentially a Norse colony, despite partial integration into the polity of Gaelic Ireland and the hierarchy of the Irish Church, began its transformation into the foremost town of an English colony. But for that statement to be properly understood, I must say something about the word 'colony', which I have just used in two somewhat different ways in the same sentence.[1] Dublin had been a Norse colony in the sense that Scandinavians had left their home countries and settled permanently in a foreign land.[2] These migrant settlers formed themselves into communities, autonomous or semi-autonomous small city-states which were in no way subject to the country they had left. They were not in any dependant status of a mother country any more than, say, the European settlers in the Latin Kingdom of Jerusalem were administratively linked to a home country.

[1] Excellent semantic discussion by M. I. Finley, 'Colonies — an attempt at a typology', *TRHS*, xxvi (1976), 167 – 8. Irish historians have never hesitated to describe medieval Ireland as a colony and continue to do so, eg., R. F. Frame, *Colonial Ireland 1169 – 1369* (Dublin, 1981).

[2] Evaluation of the major excavations of Norse Dublin, which have changed fundmanentally our knowledge of the town, is far from complete. Discussion in L. de Paor, 'The Viking towns of Ireland', in *Procs. 7th Viking Congress*, ed. B. Almquist, D. Greene (Dublin, 1976), 29 – 37; H. B. Clarke, 'The topographical development of early medieval Dublin', *Journ. of the Royal Soc. of Antiquaries of Ireland*, cvii (1977), 29 – 51; P. F. Wallace, 'The origins of Dublin', in *Studies on early Ireland : Essays in honour of M. V. Duignan* (Dublin, 1982), 129 – 43.

The Anglo-Norman colonial process, however, was different from the Viking one in both degree and in kind. It was different in degree because the sheer numbers of immigrant settlers to the new English lordship were considerably greater; they spread very much more widely through the country and their social composition was very much more differentiated. The Anglo-Normans also expropriated very many more of the indigenous landholders than did the Vikings and confiscated very much more land. More significantly still, however, from the point of view of distinguishing the two colonising movements, was the fact that the Anglo-Norman settlement in Ireland remained a dependency of England. It is in this way that the Anglo-Norman colonising movement differed in kind from the Scandinavian one. The settled areas were formally incorporated into the metropolitan organisation of the country whence most of the settlers had come. For a new administration was established in Ireland, a replica of the English governmental system whose principles, procedures and personnel were subject to the closest control from England.[3] Thereby, no doubt, it was hoped to make of Ireland an extension of the power, wealth and prestige of the Crown. It was to be the new role of Dublin to be the seat of this new colonial administration and it is in that sense that I speak of it as becoming a medieval colonial capital city.

If there had been no considerable influx of settlers into Ireland in general and into the province of Leinster in particular, Dublin would have had no future as an English city. In fact, settlement was extensive and successful in all the fertile parts of Ireland. The Anglo-Norman settlement of Ireland,

> was no mere military occupation, supported by the settlement of English and French burgesses in a few large towns, but a part of that great movement of peasant colonization which dominates so much of the economic development of Europe from the eleventh to the fourteenth centuries, arising out of what can only have been a spontaneous growth of population and slackening as that growth slackens with the troubles of the fourteenth century.[4]

Details of the settlement process escape the historian. But its mark is plain to see on the map in the rash of English place-names denoting market towns and manorial villages in the fertile Dublin hinterland and in adjacent Kildare and Meath. The suffix *town* in conjuction with a personal name, as analysed by Professor Jones-Hughes,[5] is especially revealing in this context: names like Flemingstown, Julianstown, Painestown in co. Meath, or the seven different Johnstowns in co. Dublin. As the economy of the new colony boomed, so Dublin flourished. As the colonial administration increased its effectiveness and extended the range of its jurisdiction, so Dublin's place at the centre of government was consolidated. As more bishoprics became anglicised, so grew Dublin's importance in the life of the Irish Church.[6] Two themes in particular

[3] J. Otway-Ruthven, *A History of Medieval Ireland* (London, 1968), 144 – 90.

[4] J. Otway-Ruthven, 'The character of Norman settlement in Ireland', *Historical Studies*, v (1965), 77.

[5] T. Jones-Hughes, '*Town* and *Baile* in Irish Place-Names', *Irish Geographical Studies in honour of E. Estyn Evans*, ed. N. Stephens, R. E. Glasscock (Belfast, 1970), 244 – 58.

[6] J. A. Watt, *The Church and the Two Nations in Medieval Ireland* (Cambridge, 1970), chs. 2, 3.

need exploration if we are to follow systematically the changing Dublin scene in the first century or so after Henry II had taken formal possession of Dublin in late 1171 when, by and large, the English colony in Ireland was expanding to the maximum it was to achieve in the medieval period.

What needs to be said of the first of these themes, Dublin's importance in the civil administration which made it the colonial capital, can be said fairly quickly.[7] At the head of the administration stood the king's deputy, his *alter ego*, from 1185 throughout the thirteenth century, invariably entitled justiciar. He combined the roles of chief executive, chief justice and commander in chief. Dublin Castle was his headquarters. His court came in the course of the thirteenth century to sit usually in Dublin. Likewise fixed in Dublin, almost certainly from the earliest period and specifically from 1246, was that key department of government, the Exchequer. A fixed location for the Chancery has been harder to pinpoint, but Dublin is the only candidate in the field. As a professional judiciary came into operation in the first half of the thirteenth century, there emerged a court of common pleas fixed, from *c.*1248, in Dublin. When, in the second half of the thirteenth century, meetings of parliament became a feature of royal government in Ireland, though Dublin never monopolised its place of session any more than Westminster did of the English parliament, nevertheless it was the most frequently chosen place: 14 of the 22 parliaments of Edward I's reign met in Dublin. Dublin's place at the centre of government was threatened only once. From 1361 to 1394 the Exechequer and court of Common Bench were transferred to Carlow. The experiment was abandoned on the occasion of Richard II's first visit.

Certain aspects of my second theme, the evolution of the city itself in the thirteenth century, are equally straightforward. Perhaps the most obvious indicator of the anglicisation of Dublin, to the English historian, are the documents which register its consolidation as a royal chartered city.[8] The survival of charters and custumals has been such as to pose no great methodological problems in tracing the broad outlines of how, in the period 1171 – 1229, Dublin acquired all the elements of civic personality as that was understood by the law of England at that time. A series of charters embodied in formal legal terms all those rights and liberties with which the burgensic body wished to buy to promote and safeguard their corporate interests and which the lords of Ireland were prepared to sell. Close analysis of these charters reveals little exceptional about them; the burgesses of Dublin obtained for themselves most of those franchises which the chief towns of England were also obtaining for themselves in the same period. The general nature of these privileges (jurisdictional, fiscal, administrative) have been so often and so systematically scrutinized in the classic analyses of Maitland, Tait, Ballard and Bateson that it would be otiose for me here to examine the Dublin examples in any detail. Let it suffice to indicate broadly the main stages of their acquisition.

Sometime before Henry II left Ireland in 1172 he granted the city to his men of Bristol with all the liberties and free customs of that city. In a second

[7] In addition to Otway-Ruthven, *Medieval Ireland*, see H. G. Richardson and G. O. Sayles, *The Irish Parliament in the Middle Ages* (Philadelphia, 1952); G. J. Hand, *English Law in Ireland 1290 – 1324* (Cambridge, 1967).

[8] *Historic and municipal documents of Ireland*, ed. J. T. Gilbert (*RS*, 1870); G. Mac Niocaill, *Na buirgéisí, XII – XV aios* (Dublin, 1964).

charter of 1174 he granted them immunity from tolls and other exactions throughout his dominion in England, Scotland, Wales and France. Prince John, who became lord of Ireland in 1177, first confirmed his father's grants in 1185, and then in 1192 issued a charter which spelled out the franchises in detail, the model of Bristol continuing to be invoked. This charter he reissued in 1200 after he had become king. For the grant of an extended charter of 1215 we have a glimpse of the negotiations involved in such transactions. The then justiciar was Henry of London, archbishop of Dublin, himself of a family prominent in London municipal administration (he was the son of a London alderman; three of his brothers were in the successive years 1196 to 1200 sheriffs of London and one of them mayor, 1216 – 17)[9] negotiated for the king. John instructed the archbishop-justiciar:

> The burgesses of Dublin have offered us 200 *m.* to have their town at fee-farm by charter, including that section of the river that belongs to us. You may accept that sum, or the greater as shall seem to you most expedient for us and then they may send for our charter, which we will draw up as you may advise.[10]

The citizens got their *firma burgi* at their price, the king's part of the Liffey (a grant which soon plunged them into prolonged dispute with the Hospitallers at Kilmainham) and a comprehensive concession of much else. One further prized right was secured from Henry III in 1229; that of electing a mayor, an office which, in the early thirteenth century, was a novelty. London had set the fashion in 1191, to be followed quickly after 1200 by a dozen or more towns: York, for example, by 1213, Newcastle upon Tyne by 1216. With the purchase of the mayoralty came the definitive town constitution, again of a pattern similar to that granted to English towns in this period: 24 jurats (the town council) choose 48 young people who choose 96. The 96 are to guard the city from mischief and be answerable for mischiefs that arise through their neglect.

Thus in sum, by 1229, Dublin was virtually a self-governing city, *communa ciuium Dubliniensium*, the new city seal proudly proclaimed, with its own borough court, the Tholsel, with taxative, legislative, judicial powers, the position of its mercantile community both within and without the city protected by an array of privileges. It is no coincidence that the first Dublin custumal was drawn up *c.*1229. By the early fourteenth century, when the Dublin custumal known as the Chain Book received its final shape, we find the city government has drawn up a code of all the familiar English borough law, no doubt with local variants covering things like inheritance, legal procedure, alienation of land, election of officials, latrines, fouling the river, pigs in the streets, dog killing, immediate hanging of a robber caught redhanded 'whatever hour of the day it may be, before dinner or after', cucking stools, throwing an arsonist into the fire he had set alight, slocking, hanging a miller from the beam of his mill if he be attainted of robbery of grain or flour to the value of 4d., and so on, all with parallels in the

[9] E. St John Brooks, 'Archbishop Henry of London and his Irish connections', *Journ. Roy. Soc. Antiquaries Ireland*, lx (1930), 1 – 22.
[10] The text of the resultant charter is in *Historic and municipal documents*, 63 – 4.

custumals of English towns.[11]

The achievement of legal and constitutional independence is the first facet of anglicisation to be noted. We may see a second in its physical development. I know of no way of quantifying the population of thirteenth century Dublin which carries conviction. I have the impression that Dublin was the most populous of the new colonial towns of thirteenth century Ireland and that while it was a small town by the standard of the larger English towns, even excluding London, it did grow significantly in the thirteenth century. The evidence is patchy. The so-called Dublin White Book records the granting by the city of vacant lands within their jurisdiction to be developed by the grantee. The amount of new building (renovation of old churches and the building of new, foundation of new religious houses and of hospitals, civic buildings, stone houses for the new merchant class) is a significant pointer. A building programme which included a brand-new royal castle, a brand-new cathedral and four houses of friars could not be described as stagnant. The effect of all this development was to give Dublin the face of an English town. The nature of the Hiberno-Norse town conditioned the new shape and continued to show some of its features. But the new topography of Dublin proclaimed its Englishness in its street names: streets named after commodities produced and sold there — Le Sutter Lane (*vicus sutorum*, shoemakers' street), Skinner's Row (*vicus pellipariorum*), *vicus piscariorum* (Le Fishemet St., Fishamble St.), *vicus tabernorum vini* (Winetavern St.), *vicus cocorum* (Cook St.), *vicus figulorum* (Crock St., street of the potters); or after physical or constructional features — Bridge St., Castle St., Pipe St., Exchequer St., High St., Wood Quay, Le Hynd St., Cross Street; or on place names — *vicus rupelli* (Rochelistrete), must have housed merchants of La Rochelle; or on personal names — Picot's Lane, Bertram's Court (*curia Bertrami de Verdon*), Baggot's Rath, Doubleday's Mill, and so on; with the apparatus of English civil administration and justice — Tholsel, guildhall, high cross, pillory, cucking stool (not cuckold's stool as some have it), cistern etc.[12]

There is much in this anglicisation evidence to indicate that it is an essentially mercantile community that is improving itself. Two questions, then, remain. The first is: what can be said of Dublin's trading position in the thirteenth century? But it is the second which gets to the heart of the history of the city: who were the thirteenth century Dubliners? Quantifying Dublin's trade, the source of its prosperity, is about as difficult as estimating its population. Clearly there was a high degree of continuity between the commerce of Norse Dublin and of Anglo-Norman Dublin. The slave trade disappears from sight and nothing more is heard of trade with Scandinavia. But both Bristol and Chester took full advantage of the expanding English economy of the thirteenth century and their well-established links with Dublin worked to mutual advantage of all three. Trade with France also continued without interruption,

[11] *Calendar of the Ancient Records of Dublin*, I, ed. J. T. Gilbert (Dublin, 1889); *Borough Customs*, ed. M. Bateson (Selden Soc., xviii, 1904; xxi, 1906 [)]. *Slocking*: a Devon word for enticing away servants.

[12] There are excellent maps of medieval Dublin: P. J. Walsh, *Dublin c.840 to c.1540: the years of medieval growth* (Dublin, 1977); H. B. Clarke, *Dublin c.840 to c.1540: the medieval town in the modern city* (Dublin, 1978); H. B. Clarke and A. Simms, *Early Dublin 790 – 1170* and *Medieval Dublin 1170 – 1542*, in *A New History of Ireland* ix (Oxford, 1984), 36 – 7. See also, A. Simms, 'Medieval Dublin: a topographical analysis', *Irish Geography,* xii (1979), 25 – 41.

with Rouen, for example, as also with La Rochelle where, in 1221, Henry III was to ask the town authorities to respect the liberties which his men of Dublin had previously enjoyed in that town, and increasingly with Bordeaux which was to become in the thirteenth century the premier wine port for the lucrative English trade.

Also lucrative was the trade in Irish wools, woolfells and hides. For once there is evidence available to give at least some statistical backing to judgments about its significance. In 1275, Edward I imposed on the export of these commodities the so-called 'great custom'. There exist from that year to around 1340 precise figures for the substantial amounts exported and the considerable sums collected in each of the major Irish ports. Clearly this trade (destinations of the goods, incidentally, are not specified in the records) was of major importance in the economy of the colony. All the ports specified were flourishing because of the buoyancy of the agricultural economy which had developed in the newly planted market boroughs and manorial villages now busily exploiting Ireland's richest soil. New Ross and Waterford easily top the exporters' table, followed at not very far remove by Cork. These ports of the south-east linked the fertile lands of Kilkenny, south Tipperary, south-east Wexford and east Kildare with the markets of south-west England and of London too. Drogheda would appear to have profited more from the opening up of Meath and Louth than Dublin did from co. Dublin and North Kildare. Dublin was in fifth place, significantly behind the others as a major exporting town. Their trade was predominantly with Chester and with minor ports of the Dee and Mersey estuaries, with upstarts like Liverpool to whose start in the commercial world colonial Ireland was contributing, with Preston, and when Edward I warred with Scotland, with Skinburnness and Carlisle.[13] Who were the thirteenth century Dublin men? There are three aspects of the matter to be considered. Who were the new settlers? What of the existing town population, the Hiberno-Norse? And what of the majority population of Ireland; do the native Irish play any part in the growth of the colonial capital of their country?

Let me say at once, as preface to answering the first question, that there is not enough evidence to draw up the sort of fascinating merchant portraits that Gwyn Williams could compile in his study of *London: From commune to capital*. The evidence for the Dublin citizen is meagre. Essentially it consists of three lists of names of freemen and of new entrants to the merchant guild, some 2100 in all and from different dates in roughly the first half of the century.[14] They show no particular preponderance of Bristollians as Henry II's charter rather leads me to expect. Instead one has the impression of immigration of a widespread nature: certainly a preponderance from the south-west and south Wales, but also further along the west coast of England and into Scotland. London and the midlands figure quite prominently. There is a scattering from eastern England, from the Continent and from Ireland itself. They are relatively humble in status, men of modest craftsman-trader function rather than merchant barons. And they are mostly of the victualling, building and clothing trades. From a miscellany of sources it has been

[13] Most of this information is gleaned from the *CDRI*; see also, Mac Niocaill, *passim*.

[14] The lists are published in *Historic and municipal documents*, 3 – 48, 82 – 140. I have checked them against the original: Dublin City Archive, MS MR/2.

possible to compile a list of thirteenth century mayors and bailiffs.[15] That list reflects the freemen and guild lists so far as evidence of origin is concerned. The dignitaries are from (in alphabetical order) Beverley, Bristol, Chester, Chichester, Cornwall, Coventry, Durham, Exeter, Gloucester, Hereford, Leicester, Nottingham and Winchester. One mayor was from Poitou and three from Ireland itself: Bray, Castleknock, Callan.

The evidence for the fate of the Hiberno-Norse is both documentary and topographical. In Dublin, the creation of a separate town for the Hiberno-Norse, north of the river (*villa Ostmannorum*, or 'Oxmanstown' on the modern map), suggest expulsion and possibly inferior status. However, by judgments of Edward I in relation to the Waterford Ostmen, it was made clear that they laboured under no legal disabilities. Edward confirmed that Ostmen by charter of Henry II, which is not known in any original, ought to have English law. Ostmen were, so to say, Englishmen, as Irishmen were not.[16] Civic documents from Dublin indicate that Ostmanstown was rapidly assimilated into the English urban complex and was culturally indistinguishable from it.

For the relationship of the settlers with the native Irish, the situation is less clear-cut. Again, one aspect of the evidence is topographical. The district name 'Irishtown' was quite common in medieval Ireland and has survived as a town name in some places to this day: Kilkenny and Mullingar are examples. Now there is an 'Irishtown' on the modern Dublin maps. It is quite distant from the medieval city, situated where the Liffey flowed into the sea. In view of the other medieval examples of 'Irishtowns' it is natural to think of the Dublin Irishtown as a medieval creation. But I have not found any medieval reference to it. The earliest reference I have found is seventeenth century, so I am not drawing any inferences from Irishtown, Dublin. I am not going to argue, therefore, that the Dubliners, like their fellow settlers in Kilkenny and Mullingar, expressed the attitude of conqueror to conquered in the physical separation of Irish from English. Nevertheless this attitude of separation was embodied in the law. English law in Ireland differentiated between the legal capacities of English and Irish. There was not equality; the Irish had secondary status. Hence the concern of the Ostmen to have their 'English' status recognized. In broad terms, it can be said that an Irishman had something akin to villein status in English law.[17]

This did not, however, lead to the exclusion of native Irishmen from the commonalty of Dublin. The evidence for this is twofold. One sort comes from the English Chancery records. From the reign of Henry III down to the end of the century, a number of examples can be found of native Irishmen, living in Dublin, obtaining grants of the status at law of an Englishman for themselves, their families and descendants. We may see these grants of liberty, perhaps, as a cross between a serf's manumission and a medieval equivalent of naturalisation. Now these known examples all have non-Irish names (Carpenter and

[15] H. F. Berry, 'Catalogue of the mayors, provosts, and bailiffs of Dublin city, 1229 – 1447', *Procs. Royal Irish Academy*, xxviii (1909 – 10), C, no.2 (1910), 47 – 61. This catalogue has now been revised, *A New History of Ireland*, ix. 548 – 52.

[16] E. Curtis, *A History of Medieval Ireland from 1086 to 1513* (2nd ed., London, 1938), Appendix ii, 'The Ostmen after 1172', 403 – 7.

[17] Excellent analysis of the problem in Hand, 187 – 213.

FitzJohn are cases in point[18]) which means that our thirteenth century citizen lists must conceal some native Irishmen. Indeed in one case we have proof. For the Robert of Bray who was mayor in 1292 – 3 had been granted English law by Edward I some years earlier.[19] A daughter of Robert of Bray married Robert of Nottingham, who was mayor on seven occasions in the opening years of the fourteenth century. So native Irishmen and their families could achieve and maintain a position in the Dublin establishment. In practice, the towns, like the Church, operated a system of controlled entry of native Irishmen into the ranks of the colonists.

Despite the operation of this system, however, and the partial integration of English and Irish which it achieved, the prevailing attitude of both sides to the other in the country generally was one of mutual suspicion and hostility so keen as to make war endemic. The towns were of course especially tempting targets and were so chronically at risk as to feel themselves always living 'on the frontiers of the king's Irish enemies'. In the fourteenth century, when the balance of power between English and Irish began to tilt significantly in favour of the latter, the towns were especially hard hit.

Dublin, generally more secure than most, had its most traumatic experience early in the century with the invasion of Ireland by the Bruces. Edward Bruce, brother of King Robert I of Scotland, landed at Larne in May of 1315 'to expel the foreigners from Ireland', said the Annals of Connacht exultantly. Within a month, Edward had captured Dundalk and by September, Carrickfergus. He so impressed the northern Irish that in May 1319 they inaugurated him, in the traditional Irish manner, as high king of Ireland and invited Pope John XXII to recognize him as such. At the end of the year he was joined by his brother Robert and together with a large miscellany of Irish allies marched on Dublin. February 1317 saw them encamped just outside the city to the north-west at Castleknock. The citizens panicked. Mayor Robert of Nottingham arrested the earl of Ulster in St. Mary's abbey and imprisoned him in the castle for having brought the Scots down on them (he had not, though he was Robert Bruce's father-in-law); the only bridge over the river was broken, a substantial part of the western suburb (the Thomas St. area) was burned down, the bell tower of St. Mary's parish church was removed and the stone used to fortify the castle, and the Dominican friary was demolished to use its stone to construct a defensive wall. The Bruces, however, passed Dublin by. Robert went back to Scotland in May 1317 and Edward was killed in south Armagh in October 1318. Dublin had survived its worst threat.

There were to be other crises in the fourteenth century: the Great Plague, the transfer of the seat of government to Carlow, the constant threat of Irish attacks from the adjacent Wicklow hills. But Dublin was to emerge from that period a bit bloody, a bit bowed but tenacious, resilient and still recognizably the capital city of colonial Ireland, its Englishness, despite the national mix of its population, symbolized by the grant by Henry IV of the right of the mayor to have a sword borne before him in recognition of the city's services to the English Crown.

[18] *CDRI 1252 – 84*, nos. 2113, 2228.
[19] *CDRI 1285 – 92*, nos. 746, 748, 924.

Ireland and the Barons' Wars

Robin Frame

The subject of this paper can scarcely be said to have a historiographical existence at the moment. On the Irish side there are the general histories, almost nothing else.[1] They provide limited illumination; but they do draw attention to the quarrel that broke out in Ireland late in 1264 between the two most powerful settler families, the de Burghs (earls of Ulster) and the Geraldines of Offaly, who in the early fourteenth century were to become earls of Kildare. The dispute saw the Geraldine Maurice fitz Maurice seize Richard de la Rochelle, the Lord Edward's justiciar of Ireland. Some writers have hinted that the whole episode must have been connected with the tangled events in England during the period between Lewes and Evesham; but the nature of the link is not immediately apparent, and there has as yet been no close analysis. On the English side, Ireland barely figures at all: Jacob, Treharne and Powicke, for example, mention it only in the most incidental way.[2]

This state of affairs is an extreme manifestation of a more general phenomenon: the curious reluctance of historians of the thirteenth century to assign Ireland a coherent place among the Angevin dominions. There is not to my knowledge a single scholarly article on Anglo-Irish political relations between the death of King John in 1216 and the beginning of the Scottish wars 80 years later. The reasons for this neglect merit study in themselves; such an investigation would have to embrace, among other things, modern academic conventions on both sides of the Irish Sea, and the circumstances and attitudes that have created them.[3] The purpose of the present paper is more modest. It seeks to show that there is indeed a subject here, even at a moment in the thirteenth century when the sources are more than normally unpromising. For it is the virtual silence of contemporary witnesses, especially the royal records, which are in any case extremely scanty for much of the time that Edward held

[1] The best accounts are in A. J. Otway-Ruthven, *A History of Medieval Ireland* (London, 1968), 196 – 8; and H. G. Richardson and G. O. Sayles, *The Irish Parliament in the Middle Ages* (Philadelphia, 1952), 58 – 60. See also G. H. Orpen, *Ireland under the Normans, 1169 – 1333* (Oxford, 1911 – 20), iii. 241 – 4, 280 – 3, 297 – 8; E. Curtis, *A History of Medieval Ireland* (2nd ed., London, 1938), 150; J. F. Lydon, *The Lordship of Ireland in the Middle Ages* (Dublin, 1972), 121 – 2; M. Dolley, *Anglo-Norman Ireland* (Dublin, 1972), 156 – 7; and R. Frame, *Colonial Ireland, 1169 – 1369* (Dublin, 1981), 64, 85.

[2] E. F. Jacob, *Studies in the Period of Baronial Reform and Rebellion, 1258 – 1267* (Oxford, 1925), 6, 8, n.5; R. F. Treharne, *The Baronial Plan of Reform, 1258 – 1263* (Manchester, 1932), 77, 192, 334; F. M. Powicke, *King Henry III and the Lord Edward* (Oxford, 1947), ii. 487 – 90, and idem, *The Thirteenth Century, 1216 – 1307* (Oxford, 1953), 198; *DBM*, 51 – 3.

[3] See R. R. Davies, *Historical Perception: Celts and Saxons* (Aberystwyth Inaugural Lecture: Cardiff, 1979), 23 – 5.

Ireland, that has allowed English writers to avoid giving the Lordship more than a fleeting glance. The first recorded sign of official concern appears as late as February 1265, when the Montfort regime had heard about the magnate feuds and the capture of Rochelle.[4] The only obviously significant appearance of Ireland in the records before then relates to the abortive decision, taken at the close of the previous year, to exile Roger Mortimer and other Marchers there.[5] This proposal might itself be taken to indicate that for those in power in England, to send men to Ireland was the equivalent of placing them beyond the scope of the conflict.

Perhaps they did so regard it. But such a conclusion raises problems. Besides the king and the Lord Edward, a striking number of those at or near the centre of affairs in England had a significant Irish connection. The galaxy of successors to the Marshal lordship of Leinster included William de Valence, lord of Wexford, Roger Bigod, earl of Norfolk and lord of Carlow, successive Clare earls of Gloucester and lords of Kilkenny, Roger Mortimer, a landholder in Leix, and Simon de Montfort himself, for his wife's claim to her dower in Ireland — or compensation for it — was not the least of the matters in dispute between Simon and the king.[6] Then there were the husbands of the co-heiresses of the Lacy lordship of Meath: John de Verdon, who was captured at Lewes, and Geoffrey de Geneville, who was to play a crucial part in Ireland after the arrest of Rochelle. Among several others with Irish interests was John fitz Geoffrey, a former justiciar with lands near Limerick, who opposed the Lusignans in 1258. Although John died in the same year, his son John fitz John, who succeeded to his Irish lands, was prominent on the baronial side, and was to be with Earl Simon at Evesham.[7] This amounts to a considerable array. If Ireland was not merely on but beyond the fringe, we need to ask why.

The question becomes more insistent when the early decades of the century are recalled. At that time Ireland had been an integral part of the arena in which political dramas were staged, and precisely because of the nexus of landholding. King John had been drawn there in 1210 on account of the connection between his enemy William de Braose, recently lord of Limerick, Walter de Lacy, lord of Meath, and Hugh de Lacy, earl of Ulster, an alliance that may have involved William Marshal as well.[8] In 1234 the quarrel between the court and Richard Marshal had found its bloody *dénouement* on the Curragh of Kildare.[9] The natural character of the link with Ireland comes through in a well-known story in *L'Histoire de Guillaume le Maréchal*. During the crisis of 1216–17 John d'Erley suggested that his master might have to withdraw to Ireland with the young king; William replied that he would carry Henry on his

[4] *CDRI 1252–84*, no. 758; *CPR 1258–66*, 406–7. The editor of *CDRI* erroneously divided certain documents belonging to 5–6 May 1265 between 1265 and 1262 (nos. 727–8, 771–2: compare *CPR 1258–66*, 422–3). The mistake was pointed out in Orpen, iii. 282, n.3, but continues to mislead. See Otway-Ruthven, 198; Dolley, 155.

[5] *CDRI 1252–84*, nos. 753–5, 757, 760–1, 764, 768, 770; Powicke, *Henry III*, ii. 487–8; *DBM*, 51–3.

[6] Eg., *DBM*, 196–8; *CPR 1258–66*, 388–9, 418.

[7] D. A. Carpenter, 'What happened in 1258?', in *War and Government in the Middle Ages: Essays in Honour of J. O. Prestwich*, ed. J. B. Gillingham, J. C. Holt (Woodbridge, 1984), 115; *CDRI 1252–84*, nos. 289, 392–3, 410; *CDRI 1293–1301*, no. 638; *Calendar of Ormond Deeds, 1172–1350*, ed. E. Curtis (Dublin, 1932), no. 124.

[8] Orpen, ii, ch. xxi; Frame, 54–9.

[9] Orpen, iii. 60–75, remains the best account of this episode.

shoulders from island to island if need be.[10] And the Lordship does appear to have been considered as a refuge for the widowed queen and her younger son at this time.[11]

Why then was there apparently no prominent Irish angle to the troubles of 1258 – 65? One possibility is that we have been misled by the sparseness of the evidence and the lack of careful scrutiny of the fragments that do survive. There is, as I shall show, some truth in that. But the fact remains that there was no equivalent of 1210 or 1234. The explanation may be that the political links between England and Ireland had changed during the intervening years. From its earliest beginnings royal intervention in Ireland had been largely a matter of reacting to threats. The major stimulus to Henry II's expedition of 1171 – 2 was his alarm at the achievements of Strongbow and his associates.[12] John's visit in 1185 was partly provoked by — and may have foundered on — the power wielded by the first Hugh de Lacy.[13] It has been perceptively remarked that John's second expedition, in 1210, led to the enlargement of the royal stake in Ireland to a point where it could survive without further personal attention until 1394.[14] But it was a close-run thing: Henry III was all but brought to Ireland by the crisis involving Hubert de Burgh and the Marshals in 1233 – 4; indeed the chronicle of Walter of Guisborough solemnly describes a visit that never took place.[15] Until 1234, in short, royal authority in Ireland could be rivalled by that of one or more territorial magnates powerful both in the Lordship and in the world outside it.

Thereafter the balance quickly altered, biological accident as so often proving an efficient agent of structural change. The demotion of Hubert de Burgh and his line reduced the wider importance of their kinsmen in Ireland. Meath was divided between co-heiresses after the death of Walter de Lacy in 1241. In 1242 the death of Walter's brother Hugh without male heirs brought Ulster into the king's hands, where it remained for a generation. Even more important was the fragmentation of Leinster after the deaths of the last Marshals in 1245. Leinster had been no mere outer edge of the Marshal interests. It was too large, rich and secure for that — more secure than their Welsh lands could be in the time of Llywelyn ab Iorwerth: William Marshal II had used his Irish resources in his attempts to restore his position in South Wales in the early 1220s.[16] Although by the time of the Barons' Wars many more families had holdings — and valuable ones — in Leinster, for each the holding was recent, and usually formed a less weighty part of its entire landed wealth. This dissolution of earlier patterns of lordship may not have strengthened the English

[10] *L'Histoire de Guillaume le Maréchal*, ed. P. Meyer (Paris, 1891 – 1901), ii. 201.

[11] *CDRI 1171 – 1251*, no. 723.

[12] M. T. Flanagan, 'Strongbow, Henry II and Anglo-Norman Intervention in Ireland', in *War and Government*, ed. Gillingham, Holt, 62 – 77.

[13] W. L. Warren, 'John in Ireland, 1185', in *Essays presented to Michael Roberts*, ed. J. Bossy, P. Jupp (Belfast, 1976), 13 – 14, 22 – 3.

[14] C. A. Empey, 'The Settlement of the Kingdom of Limerick', in *England and Ireland in the Later Middle Ages: Essays in Honour of Jocelyn Otway-Ruthven*, ed. J. Lydon (Dublin, 1981), 18.

[15] *CDRI 1171 – 1251*, nos. 2048 – 50, 2052 – 4, 2058 – 9, 2084 – 6; *Documents on the Affairs of Ireland before the King's Council*, ed. G. O. Sayles (Dublin, 1979), no. 3; *Chronicle of Walter of Guisborough*, ed. H. Rothwell (Camden Soc., 3rd ser., lxxxix, 1957), 176.

[16] *Ann.Mon.*, iii. 61 – 2, 82 – 3; *Brut y Tywysogyon (Red Book of Hergest version)*, ed. T. Jones (Cardiff, 1955), 223; R. F. Walker, 'Hubert de Burgh and Wales', *EHR*, lxxxvii (1972), 472 – 6.

position in Ireland; but it made the royal authority there less vulnerable, partly because it meant that quarrels between the king and magnates in England would not be so directly and emphatically transmitted across the sea. Nevertheless the Barons' Wars did involve Ireland, as two examples will reveal. The first requires us to adopt an English point of view, the second an Irish; but together they form a single story.

An intriguing sentence in the Waverley annals appears to have passed unremarked. The annalist describes the battle of Evesham, and continues: 'at the same time barons and nobles of Ireland came to assist the Lord Edward, upon his summons, namely Sir Maurice fitz Gerald, Sir Maurice fitz Maurice [the leaders of the Geraldines, nephew and uncle], Sir Walter de Burgh, Sir Theobald Butler, and many others'.[17] There is no reason to doubt the truth of this statement. The names are correctly given. No English annals of the period strive to invent or inflate Irish matter, quite the reverse. Moreover, the Waverley annalist adds that Maurice fitz Gerald was sent with Hamo Lestrange on a disastrous sortie against Llywelyn ap Gruffydd at the time of the September council at Winchester, a detail which confirms that the Irish lords had arrived with troops.[18] Some confirmation of the story is to be found in the Chancery rolls, which suggest that Theobald Butler and Geoffrey de Geneville were indeed in England at least by October 1265, and that Walter de Burgh may well have been.[19] During 1266 there is indubitable evidence of Anglo-Irishmen playing a part in military and political affairs in England. In May and June Walter de Burgh was dealing with contrariants in the midlands.[20] Maurice fitz Maurice was expected around the same time; by early August he had arrived at Kenilworth where he witnessed a charter confirming a property-settlement connected with the marriage of Maurice fitz Gerald to Agnes, daughter of William de Valence.[21] Two lesser lords from Ireland lost horses at Kenilworth.[22] These scraps of information are sufficient to place it beyond doubt that Edward and Henry sought, and found, support in Ireland in their time of need.

That the royalists might receive backing from Ireland had struck contemporaries as likely. There is the curious advice given to the barons by a certain *Anglicanus fidelis*, probably in 1263, and included in the Tewkesbury annals; its recommendation that they should 'above all . . . guard the sea, and . . . find alliances for themselves in Ireland, Wales and Scotland' has an unmistakably defensive air.[23] The response of the Montfort government following the arrest of Rochelle and the collapse of order in Irish magnate society betrays a rising note of alarm. In February 1265 the archbishop of Dublin was appointed justiciar and instructed to see to the munitioning of the king's

17 *Ann.Mon.*, ii. 365.

18 *Ann.Mon.*, ii. 366; T. F. Tout, 'Wales and the March during the Barons' Wars', in his *Collected Papers*, II (Manchester, 1934), 85.

19 *CPR 1258–66*, 464, 467, 468, 493. P.491 shows the appointment of a 'Walter de Burgo' to hold an inquisition at Lynn in Norfolk. The de Burghs were a Norfolk family. See C. Ellis, *Hubert de Burgh* (London, 1952), 188–92. But there is no way of telling whether this was the earl of Ulster.

20 *CPR 1258–66*, 598, 602, 605 (where Walter is given his comital title).

21 *CPR 1258–66*, 585, 606; *CDRI 1252–84*, nos. 795, 798; *CDRI 1285–92*, no. 800; *CDRI 1293–1301*, no. 672.

22 *CR 1264–8*, 211, 212; *CDRI 1252–84*, nos. 801–2.

23 *Ann.Mon.*, i. 179–80; Treharne, 334.

castles.[24] In March, when further worrying news had been received, Roger Waspail was dispatched as a messenger to the archbishop, and given letters to Walter de Burgh and Maurice fitz Gerald instructing them to keep the peace.[25] Around the same time Henry and Edward were made to promise to get the recent peace-settlement (which involved Edward in surrendering Chester and other lands to Montfort and in promising neither to leave England nor to bring in aliens) accepted in Ireland as well as in Scotland and Gascony.[26] Early in May, Roger Waspail was himself appointed justiciar, and Rochelle, Geoffrey de Geneville, Walter de Burgh and Maurice fitz Maurice were summoned to court.[27] Then in June, after Edward's escape from captivity, yet another justiciar, the bishop of Meath, was appointed, Rochelle and Geneville were again called to England, and Walter de Burgh, Maurice fitz Gerald and Maurice fitz Maurice were commanded to send messengers with information about the state of Ireland. This, Earl Simon's last recorded communication with Ireland, also contains warnings against obeying, or releasing money to, Edward or his agents.[28] There is no sign that any of the three Montfortian justiciars in fact assumed office, or that the summonses to the magnates were other than futile.[29] The sense is of a shadow history, as the régime tried to respond to events about which it was imperfectly informed, and over which it had little control.

It may be possible to come closer to the substance rather than the shadow while remaining just on the hither side of mere surmise. The Worcester annals say that when Queen Eleanor was in northern France after Lewes, she busied herself in hiring alien troops, and also sent letters to Gascon and Irish lords demanding help for the king in England.[30] Her dealings with the Gascons were real enough.[31] One possible trace remains of her efforts to gather support in Ireland. On 17 November 1264, after the invasion scare of the autumn had subsided, the English government ordered the countess of Aumâle to release a ship belonging to St Mary's Abbey, Dublin, which had been seized by her bailiffs on the Isle of Wight. The ship had been returning from a trading journey to France. The mayor of Dieppe had put aboard it a knight who carried suspicious letters to the magnates of Ireland. The sailors, so it was claimed, knew nothing of these letters.[32] This provides a crumb of evidence for what the situation seems to demand: communication with Ireland from sources other than the Montfort government. The story acquires added significance when set against the little that is known about events in Ireland early in 1265. The lead was taken by Geoffrey de Geneville, who was never accorded a formal position by the Montfortians. Geoffrey's emergence is understandable. He and his brother-in-law John de Verdon were the only

[24] *CPR 1258–66*, 406–7; *CDRI 1252–84*, no. 758.
[25] *CR 1264–8*, 107; *CDRI 1252–84*, no. 766.
[26] Powicke, *Henry III*, ii. 489–90.
[27] *CPR 1258–66*, 422; *CDRI 1252–84*, nos. 727, 771–2.
[28] *CPR 1258–66*, 432; *CDRI 1252–84*, no. 776.
[29] H. G. Richardson and G. O. Sayles, *The Administration of Ireland, 1172–1377* (Dublin, 1963), 79–80.
[30] *Ann.Mon.*, iv. 452–3; Powicke, *Henry III*, ii. 461–2, 474, 476.
[31] J-P. Trabut-Cussac, *L'Administration Anglaise en Gascogne sous Henry III et Edouard I de 1254 à 1307* (Paris, Geneva, 1972), 28–9.
[32] *CR 1264–8*, 80–1 (misdated in *CDRI 1252–84*, no. 778).

magnates who seem to have divided their time at all equally between Britain and Ireland at this period.[33] Geneville's importance in Ireland even before the arrest of Rochelle is visible in his appearance among the six men — who included the justiciar, chancellor, treasurer and escheator — named as being present in June 1264 at the earliest Irish parliament of which there is clear record.[34] He was a courtier and 'foreigner' who retained lands in France. He had been overseas with King Henry in 1260.[35] More pertinently, his career in the British Isles had begun in the wake of the queen and her Savoyard entourage, with which he was closely associated.[36] Of all those who mattered in Ireland in 1264–5 he was the most likely to have had ready contact with royalist circles abroad.

An entry in the Irish pipe roll for 5 Edward I shows that Geoffrey had played one of the central roles belonging to the office of justiciar by raising an army against the Geraldines.[37] According to his own testimony in letters written in 1274, he and the other magnates had then agreed a series of ordinances, including one that guaranteed all men their lands as they had held them before the disturbances. This ordinance, apparently made at Dublin on 19 April 1265, was accepted as valid by Edward I's courts.[38] Plainly it was the reconciliation achieved by Geneville that made it possible for the magnates, of both factions, of the Lordship to be brought to Edward's service in the late summer. Since the exiguous record evidence down to June emanates from Edward's opponents, and then peters out altogether, we know nothing of how the expedition was arranged. But there are some tantalizing possibilities. Montfort's penultimate letters to Ireland, dated at Gloucester on 6 May and written before he knew of the settlement recently reached at Dublin, had been entrusted to Robert Burnell, Edward's clerk and future chancellor. If Robert reached Ireland, he must have found a situation very different from the one he had been led to expect. What role he might then have played is a matter for speculation.[39] Crucial to Edward's fortunes between May and August 1265 were William de Valence, the earl of Gloucester and Roger Mortimer, all of whom had interests in south-east Ireland. It is not impossible that William's lordship of Wexford was involved in the seaborne descent he made with John de Warenne on Pembroke early in May, an event that has been described as 'the turning-point of the royalist fortunes'.[40] Finally Geneville himself, as a Lacy co-heir, had strong Marcher connections. His castle of Ludlow was used by Edward and his friends during the days after his escape.[41] At the very least

[33] For John's movements between 1259 and 1263, see *CPR 1258–66*, 23, 86, 167, 218; *CR 1261–4*, 280–1; *CDRI 1252–84*, nos. 616, 671, 710, 731, 734.

[34] *Historic and Municipal Documents of Ireland*, ed. J. T. Gilbert (*RS*, 1870), 141.

[35] *CR 1259–61*, 285.

[36] J. R. S. Phillips, 'The Anglo-Norman Nobility', in *The English in Medieval Ireland*, ed. J. Lydon (Dublin, 1984), 95, 97 and n.

[37] *36th Report of the Deputy Keeper of the Public Records of Ireland, Appendix* (Dublin, 1904), 37.

[38] *Documents*, ed. Sayles, nos. 9, 10; *CDRI 1252–84*, no. 1163.

[39] He received a protection on 6 May and a respite of debts during his absence on 7 May. See *CPR 1258–66*, 422; *CR 1264–8*, 55–6; *CDRI 1252–84*, no. 727. There is nothing in the Chancery rolls to suggest that he was in England after that point.

[40] F. R. Lewis, 'William de Valence', *Aberystwyth Studies*, xiii (1934), 35.

[41] Powicke, *Henry III*, ii. 498. His lands in the March had been subject to baronial attack after Lewes. See *CR 1261–4*, 360–1.

we must allow for a network of news and rumour that quite escapes the historian.

How much difference the aid from Ireland made to the general outcome in 1265 and 1266 is impossible to say; had its impact been substantial, no doubt other English chroniclers would have remarked upon it. Nonetheless the Lordship is part of the scene, and in view of the peculiar sparseness of the sources it is reasonable that we should peer quite hard to find it. Its presence also underlines, even completes, a pattern. Among the strengths of the royalists in 1264 – 5 was the circle of support they enjoyed on and beyond the borders of England: they had the better of Earl Simon in the Welsh Marches, Scotland, France, Gascony and, it would seem, among the Anglo-Irish.

My second illustration demands both a change of standpoint and a movement back in time. It is a truism sometimes insufficiently valued that the Lordship of Ireland, like any part of a larger political structure, could be deeply affected by events whose dynamic lay elsewhere. On 15 July 1263 the Lord Edward made a spectacular grant: he gave Ulster to Walter de Burgh, who was already lord of Connacht, in return for the surrender of some lands in Tipperary.[42] In so far as they have thought about the motives and circumstances of this grant (and to be fair, its exact date has only been established relatively recently), historians have left the impression that it is to be understood against the background of the situation in the north of Ireland itself.[43] At first glance, there appear to be good reasons for thus viewing it. Between 1258 and 1260 Brian O'Neill, self-styled 'king of the kings of Ireland', had formed threatening alliances with Gaelic leaders in Connacht and elsewhere, creating a serious challenge to English authority.[44] At the same period Irish annals refer to intervention by Hebridean raiders and mercenaries.[45] And 1263 was to see an attempted assertion of Norwegian power in the area, when Haakon IV arrived in Scottish waters. An approach was made to Haakon by some northern Irish, and for a moment he toyed with the idea of campaigning in Ireland.[46] The revival of the lordship of Ulster might therefore be presented as a considered attempt to foster a solid English power in a vulnerable region; one writer has spoken of 'an acceptance of a devolutionary situation for the north of Ireland'.[47]

That some such calculation was present is possible. But the threat from

[42] *Handbook of British Chronology* (1961 edn.), 464; Otway-Ruthven, 196, n. 13; *Royal Letters*, ii. 331 – 2; *CDRI 1252 – 84*, nos. 860, 1520, 1548.

[43] For vagueness over the date, generally assumed to have been 1264, and/or the tendency to set the grant in a purely Irish context, see *Handbook of British Chronology* (1939 edn.), 335; *GEC*, xii. 2, 172 – 3; Orpen, iii. 266, 280; Curtis, 150; Dolley, 156; and, less forgivably, Frame, 31.

[44] See now K. Simms, 'The O Hanlons, the O Neills and the Anglo-Normans in Thirteenth-Century Armagh', *Seanchas Ardmhacha*, ix (1978), 78 – 82.

[45] *The Annals of Connacht*, ed. A. M. Freeman (Dublin, 1944), 126 – 7, 130 – 1; *Annals of Ulster*, ed. W. M. Hennessy, B. MacCarthy (Dublin, 1887 – 1901), ii. 324 – 5; and compare *CDRI 1252 – 84*, nos. 490, 652.

[46] *Icelandic Sagas*, ed. G. Vigfusson, tr. G. W. Dasent (*RS*, 1887 – 94), ii. 339, 349; iv. 351 – 2, 361 – 2; *Annals of Ulster*, ii. 332 – 3; *Annals of Connacht*, 140 – 1. See E. MacNeill, *Phases of Irish History* (Dublin, 1919), 332 – 3; A. A. M. Duncan and A. L. Brown, 'Argyll and the Isles in the Earlier Middle Ages', *Procs. Soc. Antiquaries of Scotland*, xc (1956 – 7), 212 – 13; A. A. M. Duncan, *Scotland: The Making of the Kingdom* (Edinburgh, 1975), 577 – 80.

[47] T. E. McNeill, *Anglo-Norman Ulster: The History and Archaeology of an Irish Barony, 1177 – 1400* (Edinburgh, 1980), 30.

O'Neill had been abruptly terminated by the Ulster colonists at the battle of Down in 1260. Haakon's flirtation with the Irish occurred some weeks *after* the grant to de Burgh. And was long-term thinking characteristic of Edward at this stage in any case? The grant may make better sense when set in a quite different context. Early in 1263 Edward had returned from overseas; he brought alien troops with him, and used them in an attempt to recover his position in Wales. During July he was involved in a fracas over Windsor Castle and in operations around Bristol.[48] On 13 July, two days before the grant of Ulster, Walter de Burgh was with him at Bristol, where he witnessed a charter by which Edward augmented an earlier grant of Ulster lands to Robert de Beaumes, one of his circle.[49] It is probable that Walter had raised troops in Ireland for Edward; certainly he will not have been at Bristol on his own. Quite apart from Edward's particular needs in 1263, the employment of Irish men and supplies was an established feature of Henry III's Welsh campaigns: they had been used as recently as 1256 – 7.[50] It seems likely that Walter's enrichment at this moment was prompted less by mature reflection on conditions in the remoter parts of Ireland than by his presence with his lord during a sticky period.

G. H. Orpen long ago argued that it was this grant which created the circumstances that led to the damaging quarrels of 1264 – 5. The de Burghs and Geraldines both had interests in the north and west of Ireland. De Burgh had now been greatly strengthened there. As lord of Ulster and Connacht he could claim overlordship of all the Geraldine lands, some of which had been held of the Crown.[51] Aspects of the affair need further study, not least the rivalry between the two Maurices over the Geraldine inheritance, which seems to have meant that their relations with Walter de Burgh were not exactly parallel; but in outline Orpen's analysis remains persuasive.[52] It relieves us of the need to search for a link between the Geraldines and Simon de Montfort, analogous to that between de Burgh and the Lord Edward, in order to explain their behaviour. Yet the possibility that such a connection developed cannot be dismissed out of hand.[53] The advancement of the de Burghs provided the Geraldines with a grievance at a time when the opponents of Henry and Edward were casting around for allies. One hint of such an alliance may survive. In September 1264 the English government issued instructions that the young earl of Gloucester, who was still in the baronial camp, should be given seisin of Kilkenny, and Earl Gilbert appointed agents to go to Ireland to receive it. Kilkenny appears to have been in the keeping of Walter de Burgh. Montfort ordered not only Richard de la Rochelle but also Maurice fitz Gerald and Maurice fitz Maurice to aid Gloucester in recovering his inheritance, as though he believed that the Geraldine lords might be counted upon should de Burgh prove recalcitrant.[54] The arrival of the earl's people may have been one

48 Treharne, 298 – 9, 304 – 6, 310 – 11; Powicke, *Henry III*, ii. 430 – 3, 439 – 40.
49 *CDRI 1252 – 84*, no. 1976.
50 J. F. Lydon, 'Three Exchequer Documents from the Reign of Henry III', *Procs. Royal Irish Academy*, lxv C (1966), 7, 14 – 18.
51 Orpen, iii. 241 – 4.
52 *The Red Book of the Earls of Kildare*, ed. G. Mac Niocaill (Dublin, 1964), no. 31; *CDRI 1252 – 84*, no. 563; *CPR 1258 – 66*, 432; Orpen, iii. 196.
53 Otway-Ruthven, 197 – 8.
54 *CPR 1258 – 66*, 350, 352; *CDRI 1251 – 84*, nos. 750 – 1 (where the sense is less clear).

more contribution to the instability in Ireland late in the year. At most, however, we may suspect a brief accommodation between the Geraldines and the Montfort government; there is no sign of a deep or prolonged commitment. Maurice fitz Gerald and Maurice fitz Maurice were to join the de Burghs in coming to Edward's service in 1265, before they can have known that Earl Simon's fate had been sealed at Evesham.

The grant of Ulster to Walter de Burgh was of great importance in both the short and the long term. If it was indeed a reward for Walter's help in 1263, it became an obstacle to further assistance from Ireland until Geoffrey de Geneville restored temporary harmony nearly two years later. The troubles it unleashed continued spasmodically until Edward I's ministers succeeded in encouraging a rearrangement of territorial interests between the families in the late 1290s.[55] But more than that, it altered the political map of the Lordship. There was no precedent for Connacht and Ulster being ruled together. On parchment they formed a vast territorial empire, the largest in the British Isles, amounting to potential lordship over some 40% of the land-mass of Ireland, and over several hundred miles of coast from Galway Bay round to Carlingford Lough. The practical control of the de Burghs over that empire remained far from complete, but it continued to expand and intensify until the Bruce invasion of 1315. They played a noteworthy part in the Anglo-Scottish wars from 1296 to 1333. And in the heyday of Walter's son, Earl Richard, Ireland came close to being a condominium, with authority shared between the earl in the north and west and the king's justiciar at Dublin.[56]

Much of this is so familiar to the historian of Ireland that it can seem almost in the nature of things. Perhaps it is going too far to suggest that on the contrary it was largely adventitious. But without the political crisis in England it is unlikely that Walter de Burgh's requests would have been so generously answered. Walter's aggrandizement can be set beside other traces of lavishness in Edward's patronage of Anglo-Irish lords in these years. The most notable was the promotion of John fitz Thomas, ancestor of the earls of Desmond, who was given the lordship of Desmond and the Decies in counties Cork and Waterford, together with the royal castle of Dungarvan, in fee-farm. This grant, like that of Ulster, was made at an interesting moment: it is recorded in a charter passed by Edward at Bermondsey on 7 November 1259, during a period of estrangement from his father.[57] It is not surprising that in 1268 Henry III was to send Henry of Almain to Ireland to investigate alienations made by Edward against the terms on which he had received his appanage in 1254.[58] Stephen Longespee, Edward's own justiciar, had initially refused to give John seisin; and John's grandson and heir had to fight a long political and legal battle before Edward as king confirmed the grant in 1292.[59] The situation foreshadows that of the 1320s, when turbulence in England led

[55] Otway-Ruthven, 205–7, 211.

[56] Orpen, iv. 141–58; Otway-Ruthven, 214–18; J. F. Lydon, 'An Irish Army in Scotland, 1296', *Irish Sword*, v (1961–2), 184–90; idem, 'Edward I, Ireland and the War in Scotland, 1303–4', in *England and Ireland*, ed. Lydon, 43–61; R. Frame, *English Lordship in Ireland, 1318–1361* (Oxford, 1982), 141–6.

[57] *CDRI 1252–84*, no. 629.

[58] *CDRI 1252–84*, no. 844; J. R. Studd, 'The Lord Edward and Henry III', *BIHR*, 1 (1977), 11.

[59] *CDRI 1252–84*, no. 1912 (p. 426); *CDRI* 1285–92, no. 1051.

to grants being made in Ireland which affected political balances there.[60] The difference is that sixty years earlier the Crown had more to give, and its actions could shape the Lordship more radically; whether Edward's generosity to Walter de Burgh should be regarded as moulding it for better or for worse is a question for another occasion.

This paper has touched in a preliminary fashion on one small corner of a subject that I hope to investigate more fully. Its implications are obvious, but perhaps worth stating. Ireland may not leap to the eye of the English historian of the thirteenth century, but it deserves a second look. For the Irish historian there is much that will make no sense when abstracted from the wider context to which it belongs. The real difficulty is revealed by those categories, 'English historian' and 'Irish historian'. Of course the distinction makes sense in some areas; but for the student of thirteenth-century politics and lordship it is profoundly unnatural. We face one of the more durable sections of the system of mental barriers that has been erected within the British Isles and along the Channel coast.[61] There is much work for many hands if it is to be demolished.

60 Frame, *English Lordship*, ch. v, and 332–3.

61 For a recent assault on another part of the system, see K. J. Stringer, *Earl David of Huntingdon, 1152–1219: A Study in Anglo-Scottish History* (Edinburgh, 1985), esp. ch. 9.

Some English Evidence of Attitudes to Crusading in the Thirteenth Century

Christopher Tyerman

When, sometime in the early thirteenth century, a Hampshire *crucesignatus*, William of Muntford, was raising money for his journey to the Holy Land, he described the crusade as 'my great business'.[1] He was in good company. All three English kings of the century took the Cross, as did hundreds if not thousands of their subjects. Men from England played prominent parts in crusades to the East in 1217–21, 1227–9, 1240–1, 1248–50 and 1270–2, their need for money having its effect on the land market, and hence the distribution of local power, their privileges posing legal problems, criminal and tenurial. Large sums were raised from inactive or non-*crucesignati* at regular intervals through taxation, vow redemptions, the sale of indulgences, gifts and legacies. In the familiar words of F. M. Powicke 'the business . . . of the Holy Land was a political and economic function of society'.[2] As this was also the century in which crusading was being consolidated by popes and canonists as an institution with wide spiritual and temporal application, it is perhaps worthwhile trying to see how the product was received by some of the customers, what underpinned their reactions and how far they accepted what the authorities, notably the papacy, were selling.

Unfortunately the crusade presents the historian with a moving target. For one thing active crusading was becoming increasingly Balkanised into a series of local campaigns against a shifting variety of opponents of the papacy. For another, involvement with the crusade operated at different levels. Most obviously there were those who actually set out to fight. Then there were those who redeemed their vows or bought indulgences, and increasingly in this century the administrative emphasis shifted from an appeal for men to an appeal for money, the growth of this market from the pontificate of Innocent III producing highly significant changes to the crusade movement by extending indirect participation as wide as possible. However, the motivation of the purchasers had no necessary connection with the specific object of fund-raising, although often it did, but rather with the benefits for sale, a respectable and available method of obtaining extensive remission of sins (or, on occasion, of legal punishment) and, as was to be demonstrated in later centuries, the popularity of the indulgences did not depend on active crusading.[3] A third

[1] *Cartulary of the Priory of St. Denys near Southampton*, ed. E. O. Blake (Southampton Rec. Ser., i 1981), 26, no. 39.

[2] F. M. Powicke, *The Thirteenth Century* (Oxford, 1953), 81. On privileges see J. A. Brundage, *Medieval Canon Law and the Crusader* (Madison, 1969). On finance see W. E. Lunt, *Financial Relations of the Papacy with England* (Cambridge, Mass., 1939–62), i.

[3] For England, see Lunt, ii. 525–620.

group comprised those, perhaps many, who from the Third Crusade, at least, took the Cross primarily to enjoy the temporal privileges associated with the status of being *crucesignatus*, notably legal protection.[4] In the thirteenth century most *crucesignati* never personally fulfilled their vows, their exposure to the crusade belonging firmly to domestic history. From domestic records the crusade emerges as an integrated feature of secular society as well as a popular spiritual exercise; in them, too, can be detected outline impressions of how people reacted to the crusade, not only in chronicles or the more obvious literary or academic works, but also in the records of justice, administration and the land market: episcopal registers, monastic cartularies and the multiferous rolls kept by the royal government. William of Muntford's 'great business', and contemporary attitudes to it, had a temporal as well as spiritual frame. Obviously, the evidence is limited by its bias towards those whose arrangements came to the attention of the courts, to those writers with axes to grind, and to a socially restricted group: propertied freemen, beneficed clergy or servants of the great. However, the social sample, at least, may be representative, for the vast majority of active English *crucesignati* either possessed disposable property or were employed by those who did. Finance prevented the indigent from going on crusade, or even buying remission, and the law prevented the unfree.

Traditional guides to medieval attitudes outside the schoolroom have been the chroniclers, but interpretation of their witness is controversial, never more so than when it concerns the most vociferous thirteenth-century commentator on contemporary attitudes to crusading, his own and others, Matthew Paris. Paris was anti-papal and a nationalist, but he was not a little Englander and he was an enthusiast for a certain form of crusading. His criticisms concentrated on two particular features of the administration of the crusade: creeping papal control of the English church and the misuse of crusade funds which this made possible, and, hence, some of the destinations for crusades proposed by the papacy. He drew attention to the confusion caused in the late 1240s by the conflicting crusade objectives, now the Holy Land, now Romania, now Frederick II, and he perhaps best encapsulated his attitude in the remarks he attributed to King Haakon of Norway, to the effect that the king was always willing to fight the enemies of the church but not all the enemies of the pope.[5] The positive side to Paris' opinions are here implied as well. His enthusiasm for campaigns against external enemies of Christendom, especially in the East, is evident in such passages as the obituary of Philip d'Aubigny, his praise of those who died on Richard of Cornwall's crusade or his eulogy on the fate of William Longsword at Mansourah in 1250.[6]

However, Paris' opinions have been dismissed as 'notoriously unreliable', especially where reactions to the anti-Hohenstaufen crusades are concerned.[7] Yet even if modern historians do not agree with him, some contemporaries

[4] The list includes King John (Gerald of Wales, *Opera*, ed. J. S. Brewer (*RS*, 1863), iii. 285); Hubert de Burgh (*Annals of Tewkesbury*, in *Ann.Mon.*, i. 86); and Bishop Philip of Durham (C. R. Cheney, *Innocent III and England* (Stuttgart, 1976), 254). See *CR 1237–42*, 95, for the effectiveness of crusader privileges in securing the release of a violent criminal, William Goscelin, from the Tower.

[5] *Paris*, iii. 287–8, 373–4; iv. 9, 133–4; v. 67, 73–4, 201.

[6] *Paris*, iii. 373; iv. 175; v. 150–4.

[7] N. J. Housley, *The Italian Crusades* (Oxford, 1982), 82.

did. The rectors of Berkshire argued in 1240 that the emperor was not a legitimate target for a crusade as he was not a heretic, that the pope should pay for the defence of his own patrimony, and that the goods of the church could be used for war only in very few cases, not, that is, against Frederick II. In 1255 the clergy of Lincolnshire rejected the proposed diversion of Holy Land money to the Sicilian enterprise and, in the same year, the clergy of Lichfield denounced this re-direction of funds 'since the reason for the levy which at first sight appeared pious now, it seems to us, is changed and is not pious'.[8] These clerical worries were exactly the same as Paris': jurisdiction, encroaching papal power, the misuse of Holy Land funds and crusades against Christians. Given the establishment by the papacy in England of a uniquely centralised and effective system for the extraction of ecclesiastical funds, this unanimity is not surprising: Paris and his colleagues squealed louder than some on the continent because they had more to squeal about.[9] Both opposition and support for the different goals of crusading was based on material unease, vested interests and intellectual traditionalism, and such reactions were not confined to the clergy. At Amiens in 1264 the baronial opponents of the Crown complained about the conversion of a crusade 'against the Saracens who are the foes of Christ's Cross into an attack on fellow-subjects of the same Christian religion', and the consequent misuse of money.[10]

Judged by such responses the papacy was being too radical in its wide application of crusade institutions and its development of the concomitant adminstrative machinery, and it appears that the lessons of opposition to the anti-Hohenstaufen crusades were learnt as crusades later in the century against Ghibellines or Aragonese were not preached in England where, after 1265, crusade appeals by the papacy concentrated on the relief of the Holy Land. Thirteenth-century Englishmen voted with their feet, only the eastern crusade attracting them in any significant numbers. Recruitment for the Albigensian campaigns was not aimed at England and English involvement in them was fortuitous.[11] In the Iberian peninsula, although some Englishmen were possibly among those Christians who captured Valencia in 1238 and re-populated Seville after 1248, there were no substantial forays against the Moors to compare with expeditions in the twelfth or fourteenth centuries, the Anglo-Castillian Crusade against Morocco in the 1250s remaining solely a diplomatic device.[12] Similarly, English crusaders in the Baltic, so familiar in the fourteenth century, are hard to find in the thirteenth: I can put a name to

[8] *Annals of Burton*, in *Ann.Mon.*, i. 265 – 7, 360 – 3.

[9] W. E. Lunt, *Papal Revenues in the Middle Ages* (New York, 1965), i. 41 – 2.

[10] *DBM*, 278 – 9.

[11] The legate, Robert de Courçon, was a native of Kedleston, Derbyshire, but only two men with close English connections, Walter Langton and Hugh de Lacy, played significant roles in the early Albigensian campaigns and they, as exiles from King John, were distinctly available. See Peter of Vaux-de-Cernay, *Historia Albigensis*, ed. P. Guébin, E. Lyon (Paris, 1926 – 39), i. 247, 253 – 4; ii. 129 – 32, 155; iii. 86 – 7; *La Chanson de la croisade albigeoise*, ed. E. Martin-Chabot (Paris, 1931 – 61), i. 93, 213; ii. 121, 175, 293; iii. 23, 75 – 7, 85, 93, 95, 121, 173, 175, 189, 213, 265, 293. Later, Poitou as well as Languedoc fell prey to Capetian aggrandizement, and cynicism of crusader motives appears in Roger of Wendover, *Flores Historiarum*, ed. H. Howlett (*RS*, 1886 – 9), ii. 305.

[12] *History of the Crusades*, ed. K. M. Setton, III (Wisconsin, 1975), 430; A. Mackay, *Spain in the Middle Ages* (London, 1977), 69.

only one, Robert de Morley (d. 1288).[13] Crusading against the Greeks, although frequently hitched to the needs of the Holy Land, consistently failed to capture English imaginations and it may not have been accidental that when Urban IV authorized preaching for expeditions to Greece and the Holy Land in 1263, his instructions to preachers in England only mentioned the Holy Land.[14] There was a persistent reluctance by Englishmen to respond to papal encouragement to support the anti-Hohenstaufen crusades, although it was recognized that the crusading status of the Sicilian enterprise was primarily a convenient, if inadequate, method of raising money. Even so, Henry III's enthusiasm, more a function of foreign policy than crusading ardour, was not universally shared. Although the papacy was selective in where it sought recruits and funds, not all Christendom being involved in all crusading appeals, nevertheless the English evidence indicates a considerable gap between papal desires and local wishes: in 1239 Richard of Cornwall swore a special oath to reinforce his refusal to be diverted from the Holy Land to Greece or Italy, and in 1247 Bishop Walter Cantelupe, in similar circumstances, secured a papal guarantee that no crusaders should be compelled either to redeem their vows if able to fight or to campaign against anybody but Saracens.[15] Such reactions could be influenced by non-crusading considerations of foreign policy or political advantage; however, as with the suspicious clergy, there appears an underlying reluctance to follow the Cross wherever the pope carried it.

Rejection of papal crusade plans did not imply any general decline in support for the ideal. Whilst it is difficult to find examples of Englishmen who had vowed to crusade elsewhere than the Holy Land, a trawl through the printed archives alone reveals hundreds of individuals who had taken oaths to go on 'the pilgrimage' or 'the journey' to Jerusalem or the Holy Land. Indeed, where the destination is specified, primarily in connection with essoins, property and inheritance cases, royal safe-conducts, licences permitting mortgages, the appointment of attorneys and many land charters, no other objectives are mentioned.[16] Of course, there may be a number of technical reasons for this. A crusade to the Holy Places earned a longer essoin and term of protection than other journeys, including simple pilgrimages to Jerusalem.[17] The

[13] This according to deponents at the Court of Chivalry in 1385/6. See *GEC*, ix. 210 and n. 4. For Henry III's institution of an annual pension for the Teutonic Knights in 1235, see Comte Riant, 'Privilèges octroyés aux Teutoniques', *Archives de l'Orient Latin*, i (1881), 418. Roger Bacon was sufficiently familiar with events in the Baltic to attack the campaigns of the Teutonic Knights on the grounds that they prevented the conversion of the Slavs. See *Opus Majus*, ed. J. H. Bridges (London, 1897 – 1900), iii. 120 – 2.

[14] The preaching campaigns of 1237 and 1246 and the attempt at a subsidy in 1262 all flopped. See Lunt, *Financial Relations*, i. 434 – 5, 436 – 7; *Flores Historiarum*, ed. H. R. Luard (*RS*, 1890), ii. 479; *Les Registres d'Urbain IV*, ed. L. Dorez, J. Guiraud (Paris, 1899 – 1958), nos. 392, 397, 466 – 8, 472.

[15] *Paris*, iii. 620; *Calendar of Papal Registers*, ed. W. H. Bliss, I (London, 1893), 234. For Richard's anti-papal and pro-Hohenstaufen entourage, see N. Denholm-Young, *Richard of Cornwall* (Oxford, 1947), 38 – 42; *Paris*, iii. 485.

[16] Full references would need a book. As a sample look at the citations in Brundage, *passim*.

[17] Glanvill, *Tractatus et Legibus et Consuetudinibus Regni Angliae*, ed. G. D. G. Hall (London, 1965), 16 – 17, 151; Henry de Bracton, *De Legibus et Consuetudinibus Angliae*, ed. T. Twiss (*RS*, 1882), v. 159 – 69; and John de Longueville, *Modus Tenendi Curias* (*c.*1307), in *The Court Baron*, ed. F. W. Maitland, W. P. Basildon (Selden Soc., 1891), 81. The last two sources draw a clear distinction between a general *passagium* and a simple pilgrimage to the Holy Land.

chances of lengthy absences, loss of communication and suspected or actual decease (all of which provoked litigation and hence records), were possibly greater with journeys to Palestine which were also perhaps more expensive; thus the need to sell or mortgage property could have fallen more acutely on Holy Land crusaders and so more of their transactions survive. Similarly, the fact that the few extant wills show that money was not bequeathed to Spain, Italy, Greece, or the Baltic may be due to traditional testamentary habits and the existence of a diocesan structure to collect Holy Land legacies, and, moreover, many testators had unfulfilled Holy Land vows.[18] But such explanations do nothing to diminish the cumulative impression of the overwhelming primacy of the Holy Land as opposed to the alternatives, especially as the social embrace of the sources is probably not unrepresentative: artisans, small landowners and parish priests to the greatest prelates and princes in the land; that is, all sections of the community with something to be sold, mortgaged, protected, inherited or bequeathed.

Such preferences do not, however, necessarily, reflect sentimental nostalgia or mass hysteria. Whatever the spiritual and social dividends, active crusading constituted a heavy and risky material investment which was recognized by the *crucesignati* themselves who placed the crusade in a secular order of priorities, private and public, as in Peter Langtoft's comment on the Scottish crisis of 1293:

> And if King Edward had gone towards Acre
> Greatly would the kingdom and royalty have been in peril.[19]

War was war, whether or not it was also holy, and thus reactions to the crusade were influenced by factors which determined the progress of any military enterprise. Political and diplomatic circumstances had to be favourable. Troops had to be organized like any others around the households of great men (Richard of Cornwall, Simon de Montfort, William Longsword or the Lord Edward) and to pay for them money had to be made available, not always a simple matter as the efforts of all four magnates mentioned to raise or raid funds illustrate. But just as Longsword needed capital to retain his paid knights and sergeants in 1249, so lesser men had to mortgage or sell land, often to the disadvantage of family and heirs.[20] In the history of the crusades, finance could be as significant as faith. Typical was Hugh de Neville's preoccupation, when drawing up his will at Acre in 1267, to secure payment and return fares for members of his retinue, a concern which was probably mutual.[21] Neville's escapism, as his mother might have put it, or Longsword's

[18] See, at random, *CRR*, viii. 297; *CR 1247–51*, 352; *CR 1256–9*, 485; *Register of Bishop William Ginsborough of Worcester*, ed. J. W. Willis Bund (Worcester Historical Soc., 1907), 283, 312, 388.

[19] *Chronicle of Pierre de Langtoft*, ed. T. Wright (*RS*, 1866–8), ii. 267. Cf. Henry III's similar sentiment in 1245 when trying to discourage recruits for Louis IX's crusade. See *Paris*, iv. 488–9, and hostility to his and Louis IX's crusades in the 1240s and 1260s.

[20] *Paris*, iii. 614, 635–6; iv. 7, 71; v. 1, 98–9, 131, 134–5; Lunt, *Financial Relations*, i. 432–4; S. D. Lloyd, 'The Lord Edward's Crusade 1270–2', in *War and Government in the Middle Ages: Essays in Honour of J. O. Prestwich*, ed. J. B. Gillingham, J. C. Holt (Woodbridge, 1984), 120–33.

[21] M. S. Giuseppi, 'On the Testament of Sir Hugh de Neville', *Archaeologia*, lvi (1899), 352–4.

enthusiasm, required careful planning and the direction of a traditionally hallowed cause: the plight of the Holy Land.

The primacy of the eastern *passagium* was dictated by the seriousness of the investment involved in crusading because only the Holy Land was spiritually, emotionally and in terms of social repute commensurate with the material outlay. The fundamental appeal of crusading had changed little: the spiritual goal was the remission of sins which was attained by the penitential exercise of the pilgrimage. All sources reveal that remission of sins, at least formally, remained central to the drive to fight for the Cross.[22] For the active crusader the path to remission was the characteristic pilgrimage, by which the crusade was distinguished from other holy or just wars. In consequence, the prominence of Jerusalem and the Holy Places was inevitable.[23] The failure of attempts to divorce crusading from Jerusalem in the attitudes of laymen is partly explained by this continued potency of traditional imagery, witnessed, for example, in stone by the chapel of the Holy Sepulchre in Winchester Cathedral, which may itself be associated with the crusade of Peter des Roches, and partly by long standing habits of patronage and spiritual investment, for instance in the Holy Land military orders.[24] Furthermore the very language used to conceal the separation of the ideal from its original objective was inadequate. One of the commonest euphemisms for the crusade was, fairly enough, the 'business of the Cross', a phrase which could be used, as in the anti-Hohenstaufen preaching of the 1250s, to deterritorialize the phenomenon and concentrate attention on a less earth-bound image of Christ.[25] Crusade sermons often accompanied a mass and their contents frequently emphasised general service to Christ and the mystical symbolism of the Cross.[26] The cult of the Holy Cross, stimulated by such imports as the Holy Rood of Bromholm, was widespread.[27] Yet the concentration on the Cross failed to distract attention away from the scene and physical reality of the Passion, possibly the reverse; and it evidently left active crusaders unconvinced that the *negotium Crucis* was the same as the *negotium papae*. There was thus a basic weakness in the policy of extending the crusade which in many other ways had proved so useful to kings and popes alike: the Holy Sepulchre could not be hidden in the shadow of the Cross. This was indeed implicitly recognized in papal bulls and by papal agents, whose main tactic to establish in the minds of the customers that the privileges being offered were the real thing was to equate them with those granted to crusaders

[22] Eg., Simon de Montfort in 1248 (*Paris*, v. 1); Giuseppi, 362.

[23] See, in general, F. H. Russell, *The Just War in the Middle Ages* (Cambridge, 1975).

[24] E. W. Tristram, *English Medieval Wall Painting: The Thirteenth Century* (Oxford, 1950), 163 – 6. Following the example of his early protector William Marshal, Henry III originally planned to leave his body to the Templars before deciding in middle age to bequeath it to Westminster Abbey. See *Foedera* I, i. 496.

[25] *Ann.Mon.*, i. 351, 353; *Monumenta Franciscana*, ed. J. S. Brewer (*RS*, 1858), 620, for Henry III asking the Dominicans to preach the *verbum crucis* in August 1255; cf. *Ann.Mon.*, i. 240; iii. 40 and *CPR 1247 – 58*, 507, for the king's injunction to continental subjects to assist the collector of the crusade tax in November 1255, 'for the love of the Crucified One whose business is principally engaged in this behalf', although the money was already destined for Sicily.

[26] 'Ordinatio de predicatione S. Crucis in Angliae', in *Quinti Belli sacri Scriptores Minores*, ed. R. Röhricht, *Société de l'Orient Latin*, ii (1879), vii – x, 1 – 26. The emphasis on the Cross is standard in thirteenth- and fourteenth-century western Europe. See also C. Morris, 'Dissemination of the crusading ideal in the twelfth century', *Studies in Church History*, xx (1983), 79 – 101.

[27] *Ann.Mon.*, iii. 56, 97; iv. 495; Wendover, ii. 274 – 6; *Gesta Abbatum Monasterii Sancti Albani*, ed. H. T. Riley (*RS*, 1867 – 9), i. 282, 291 – 2.

to the Holy Land. It was precisely the contrast between this sort of rhetoric and reality which, so Paris maintained, undermined the preaching against Manfred.[28]

In England, removed from the passions of Languedoc and Italy, only the Holy Land inspired miraculous signs in the Heavens (often, we may note, Crosses) or the literary dilemma of the crusader in love.[29] Paris even managed to extract national pride from deeds in the East: he made William Longsword into an English martyr and added his own gloss to Wendover's account of the crusade of the bishops of Winchester and Exeter in 1227 describing it as having been 'to the salvation and honour of many, especially of all Englishmen', an emotion echoed by Gregory X in 1272 when he wrote of the glory bestowed on the English people by the Lords Edward and Edmund in Palestine.[30] English authors took particular pride in the legends of Richard I. The ambassador from Bohemund VI of Antioch, who, in 1255, flattered Henry III that he was Richard's heir not only by hereditary right but in virtue, would have struck a chord with a king who a few years earlier, in his first enthusiasm after taking the Cross, had festooned his palaces with heroic images of Richard's combat with Saladin.[31] It was into Richard's shoes that the Lord Edward stepped after he had trod his footsteps in the Holy Land: 'behold he shines like a new Richard' was one enthusiastic contemporary comment.[32] The Richard I of legend inhabited a world of chivalric verities, central to which was the duty to recapture Jerusalem. The Holy Land was traditional and spiritually powerful and few Englishmen who considered the matter looked further, or nearer, for inspiration. For a variety of reasons, secular and spiritual, they were not converted to a papal view of the world or the crusade. Whether or not this conservatism in a European context was eccentric is another matter.

[28] *Paris*, v. 519 – 22, 536; and notice the papal attempts to concentrate on Manfred's Moslem mercenaries at Lucera: *Paris*, v. 681; *Ann.Mon.*, i. 350 – 3.

[29] Eg., during the recruitment for the Fifth Crusade and the 1227 crusade: *Ann.Mon.*, iii. 53; Wendover, ii. 323. Cf. *Paris*, iv. 345 – 6, for portents of disaster of the loss of Jerusalem, 1244. For a late thirteenth-century version of the common literary theme, see 'The Dialogue between Henry de Lacy and Walter Biblesworth on the Crusade', *Reliquae Antiquae*, ed. T. Wright, J. O. Halliwell (London, 1841 – 3), i. 134 – 6.

[30] *Paris*, iii. 127; v. 150 – 4; *Register of Archbishop Walter Giffard of York*, ed. W. Brown (Surtees Soc., 1904), 39 – 41.

[31] *Ann.Mon.*, i. 369 – 70; Tristram, 70 – 1, 132, 184 – 5, 215; *CLR 1245 – 51*, 362. Henry was also keen on pictures of the siege of Antioch and notice his display of Richard I's shield, perhaps tactlessly, at the Temple, Paris, in 1254. See *Paris*, v. 480.

[32] *Political Songs of England*, ed. T .Wright (Camden Soc., 1839), 128, in a poem celebrating Edward's accession.

The Social Context of Vernacular Writing in Thirteenth Century England: the Evidence of the Manuscripts.[1]

John Frankis

The social context of medieval vernacular literature has received a good deal of scholarly attention in recent years, but this has been particularly concentrated on the later period because evidence of all kinds becomes steadily more abundant after the mid-fourteenth century.[2] For the thirteenth century the evidence is more scanty and the whole position is less clear, and although various approaches have been adopted, much remains uncertain. There is for example still room for a study based on statements about entertainments at court or about the performances of singers and narrators (to avoid the controversial term 'minstrels') in great households; that the consideration of such familiar kinds of evidence might still lead to new conclusions has been demonstrated by Dr Bullock-Davies.[3] Another approach is reflected in the conjectures about poetic composition and performance that have grown out of the theory of oral-formulaic composition.[4] Different again is the approach exemplified in the late Professor Dobson's studies of *Ancrene Wisse*, in which the conclusions extend far beyond matters of social context, though that is involved too.[5] Something of the social context of thirteenth-century vernacular writing may also be deduced from a consideration of the manuscripts in which texts have been preserved, though it is in the nature of this material that the social context that emerges is almost exclusively clerical.

[1] This study aims to take into account a wide range of kinds of writing, but does not touch on business and administrative documents. For writing in the widest sense of the term, including the latter, see M. T. Clanchy, *From Memory to Written Record* (London, 1979).

[2] Important recent studies are R. F. Green, *Poets and Princepleasers* (Toronto, 1980); J. Coleman, *English Literature in History, 1350 – 1400* (London, 1981); *English Court Culture in the Later Middle Ages*, ed. V. J. Scattergood, J. W. Sherborne (London, 1983); P. R. Coss, 'Aspects of Cultural Diffusion in Medieval England', *Past and Present*, cviii (1985), 35 – 79. A narrower field is surveyed in A. Hudson, *Lollards and their Books* (London, 1985), and in *English Wycliffite Sermons* I, ed. A. Hudson (Oxford, 1983), introduction, esp. 189 – 202. The seminal study by M. B. Parkes, 'The Literacy of the Laity', in *Literature and Civilization: the Medieval World*, ed. D. Daiches, A. Thorlby (London, 1973), deserves special mention.

[3] C. Bullock-Davies, *Professional Interpreters and the Matter of Britain* (Cardiff, 1966); a general introduction to this aspect of literary study is J. Burrow, 'Bards, Minstrels and Men of Letters', in *Literature and Civilization*, ed. Daiches, Thorlby, 347 – 70.

[4] For the thirteenth century, see W. A. Quinn and A. S. Hall, *Jongleur* (Washington, D.C., 1981), which is centred in a stylistic analysis of *King Horn* and gives full references to the seminal studies of Parry, Lord and Magoun, as well as subsequent publications. The whole subject of oral tradition is notoriously problematic and the relevance of modern practices to the Middle Ages remains uncertain. See, eg., R. Finnegan, *Oral Poetry* (Cambridge, 1977); a rare survival from the thirteenth century is noted by R. A. B. Mynors, *A Catalogue of the Manuscripts of Balliol College* (Oxford, 1963), 242; see I. and P. Opie, *The Singing Game* (Oxford, 1985), 44 – 6.

[5] E. J. Dobson, *The Origins of Ancrene Wisse* (Oxford, 1976).

The overwhelming majority of manuscripts preserved from thirteenth-century England are in Latin, and a considerable majority of the manuscripts containing vernacular writing cannot be ascribed to any one particular milieu or place of origin; for texts in English, linguistic evidence may indicate a general geographical locality, which is important, but it can do little to illuminate the social context. For the period between the Conquest and 1200 there is even less evidence, so the position may be summarised very briefly: localisable vernacular manuscripts are exclusively clerical, especially those in English (some later copies of Old English homilies, the *Peterborough Chronicle* and, clearly clerical though not precisely localisable, the *Ormulum*), and even Anglo-Norman writing that we know to have been composed in the twelfth century for secular patrons, like Gaimar's *L'estoire des engleis* or Benedeit's *Voyage of St Brendan*, tended to be written by clerical authors and to be preserved in clerical manuscripts, often of later date, like BL Cotton Vespasian B.X from Durham Cathedral Priory (Benedeit) and BL Royal 13.A.xxi from the Premonstratensian Abbey at Hagnaby (Gaimar). The *Comput* and *Bestiaire* of Philippe de Thaun, dedicated to the second queen of Henry I, survive in a twelfth-century manuscript from the Cistercian Abbey of Holme Cultram (now BL Cotton Nero A.V.).[6]

There is a growing body of vernacular writing in both French and English after 1200, and the number of thirteenth-century manuscripts that can be ascribed to particular religious houses enables us to see that there was a concern for vernacular writing in many monasteries, especially in some of the great Benedictine houses. In some cases this was an inheritance from the Anglo-Saxon period: the pre-Conquest foundations had libraries that included manuscripts in Old English, and in some cases the study and copying of Old English texts continued into the thirteenth century: the case of Worcester is well known,[7] but one might also mention BL Cotton Vespasian A.XXII from Rochester Cathedral Priory, which contains thirteenth-century copies of homilies by Ælfric.[8] Continued interest in a range of kinds of vernacular writing may be illustrated from a few selected manuscripts, beginning with those from Benedictine houses. Perhaps the most extraordinary of these is BL Harley 978: this consists of thematically unrelated booklets, but with no signs that any of them ever circulated separately (ie., no dirt and wear on what would have been the outer leaves of independent booklets: on the contrary, there is perhaps some indication of linking between sections in the form of overlapping ruling of lines and the decoration of initial letters). The first and last sections contain indications that the manuscript was in use at Reading Abbey and there can be little doubt that these sections were compiled there;[9] the intervening sections are likely to have been at Reading too, though the actual place of writing is less certain; the mixture of hands is

[6] See J. Morson, 'The English Cistercians and the Bestiary', *Bulletin of the John Rylands Library*, xxxix (1956 – 7), 146 – 70; C. R. Cheney, 'English Cistercian Libraries', in his *Medieval Texts and Studies* (London, 1973), 328 – 45.

[7] Basic information is in N. R. Ker, *Medieval Libraries of Great Britain* (London, 1964), 205 – 15; Ker, *Catalogue of Manuscripts Containing Anglo-Saxon* (Oxford, 1957), lvi – lx and under separate manuscripts, esp. no. 398; the latter refers to the activities of the thirteenth-century scribe with the 'tremulous hand', who wrote glosses in several Old English texts.

[8] See Ker, *Catalogue*, xix; M. P. Richards, 'BL MS Cotton Vespasian A.xxii, the Vespasian Homilies', *Manuscripta*, xxii (1978), 97 – 103.

[9] B. Schofield, 'The Provenance and Date of *Sumer is icumen in*', *Music Review*, ix (1948), 81 – 6.

bewildering, but no more so than might be expected in a manuscript from a large religious house. The contents are varied: the first section contains music, mostly liturgical, but also including the famous 'Cuckoo Song', which is the only English text in the manuscript; a substantial central portion contains an important collection of Latin goliardic poems.[10] Other sections contain the French verse fables of Marie de France and, more surprisingly, her Breton lays; moreover, this is the only complete manuscript of all Marie's lays and is the basis of all modern editions. It is striking to find such courtly secular poetry, with traces of moral ambiguity and of paganism, preserved in a Benedictine abbey, and this may conceivably lend support to the theory, now generally abandoned, that the author of the lays was the Abbess of Shaftesbury.[11] A rather more conventional anthology is that in BL Arundel 292 from Norwich Cathedral Priory; here the contents are predominantly religious: the opening section contains English verse-translations of liturgical texts, short religious poems and the only extant copy of the Middle English *Bestiary*; the other contents are some Latin prose-texts (mostly religious, but also *Apollonius of Tyre*, the *Prophecies of Merlin* and some scientific material) and some Anglo-Norman poems, including a translation of the *Distichs of Cato*; the items added about 1400, including the famous poem on blacksmiths, do not concern us here, though they tell their own story about later medieval monasticism.[12] The Norwich manuscript thus reflects a fairly relaxed humane approach to piety, but not so alarmingly so as the Reading manuscript. More exclusively religious is Lambeth Palace MS 522 from St. Augustine's Canterbury, which contains only French writings, mostly Anglo-Norman, including Grosseteste's *Chasteau d'Amour*, St. Edmund's *Mirour de Seinte Eglyse* and a French verse *Gospel of Nicodemus*. This is a more obviously pious collection than either the Reading or the Norwich manuscript, and the use of the French language for religious literature is a long-recognized aspect of English monasticism.[13] Each of the main pieces in this manuscript is preceded by an illustration that relates in a general way to the following text and represents either the contemplative or the active aspect of the religious life; the contemplative figures, usually prostrate before the Cross or the Virgin, are generally Benedictine monks, but the active figures, shown preaching, are mostly friars, Dominicans in three cases and Franciscans in two: the implication, that the inhabitants of a Benedictine monastery might take a sympathetic interest in the activities of the newly-founded mendicant orders, is noteworthy.[14] Some other Benedictine manuscripts have thirteenth-century English

[10] Most of the Latin poems were printed in T. Wright, *The Latin Poems of Walter Mapes* (Camden Soc., old ser., xvi, 1841); see A. G. Rigg, 'Golias and other Pseudonyms', *Studi Medievali*, xviii (1977), 65 – 109. The contents of the manuscript are listed in C. L. Kingsford, *The Song of Lewes* (Oxford, 1890), xi – xvii.

[11] For references see C. Bullock-Davies, 'Marie, Abbess of Shaftesbury, and her brothers', *EHR*, lxxx (1965), 314 – 22, which sheds light on the abbess but does not strengthen the connection with the authoress of the lays.

[12] See E. Salter, 'A Complaint against Blacksmiths', *Literature and History*, v (1979), 194 – 215.

[13] See M. D. Legge, *Anglo-Norman in the Cloisters* (Edinburgh, 1950); Legge, *Anglo-Norman Literature and its Background* (Oxford, 1963). One may also note the widespread monastic use of French for works on estate-management, such as those by Walter of Henley and Grosseteste. See D. Oschinsky, *Walter of Henley* (Oxford, 1971), esp. the list of manuscripts on 51 – 5.

[14] The illustrations are accurately described in M. R. James, *A Descriptive Catalogue of the Manuscripts in the Library of Lambeth Palace* (Cambridge, 1932), 715 – 23.

poems added peripherally to Latin texts (eg., BL Royal 2.F.viii from St. Albans, and Bodleian Tanner 169 from Chester) and in these cases the English inscriptions are likely to have had a more or less private personal mnemonic function for some monastic reader.[15]

The monasteries of the Augustinian canons are also important for the encouragement of vernacular writing. This appears in the first instance in the fact that at least one house, Southwick Priory, acquired and preserved some Old English manuscripts. A pre-Conquest copy of the Old English Bede was obtained, directly or indirectly, from Winchester (now BL Cotton Otho B.x – xi), and a twelfth-century copy of other Old English texts (now BL Cotton Vitellius A.xv, part I) was also at Southwick by the late thirteenth century but is unlikely to have been written there.[16] An early Augustinian interest in vernacular writing may also appear in the fact that Osney Abbey held what is now the best manuscript of the *Chanson de Roland* (Bodleian Digby 23), while by 1180 the *Ormulum*, an English verse gospel-paraphrase, was being written by a man who identifies himself as a canon named Orm living under the Augustinian rule, but does not say at which monastery.[17] Vernacular manuscripts held by Augustinian houses in the thirteenth century include a French translation of Gregory's *Dialogues* at St. Frideswide's, Oxford (now Paris, BN f.fr. 24766), while the oldest extant collection of Welsh poetry, the Black Book of Carmarthen (now Nat. Lib. of Wales, Peniarth 1), was held by the Augustinian priory in Carmarthen. The *Ancrene Wisse*, a treatise of spiritual guidance for female recluses, one of the outstanding masterpieces of medieval English prose, was long thought on theological grounds to be of Augustinian origin and is now generally believed to have been composed in Wigmore Abbey in the early thirteenth century.[18] Finally, by the end of the century Peter de Langtoft, canon of Bridlington, was compiling his Anglo-Norman chronicle. One may note in passing that Augustinian literary activity in the English language continued vigorously to the end of the Middle Ages.[19]

The role of nunneries in fostering vernacular writing becomes more conspicuous in the later Middle Ages, but a striking early example is provided by BL Cotton Claudius D.iii, from the Cistercian nunnery at Wintney, which contains a thirteenth-century copy of the Old English translation of the Benedictine Rule. This is of particular interest in that the compiler evidently made no attempt to make or acquire a new translation, but copied an existing one in a form of language that may well have posed some problems of comprehension to the nuns who were to use it; it is one of the latest extant copies of an Old English text.[20] Other thirteenth-century manuscripts with vernacular texts from nunneries are Fitzwilliam, McClean 123, from the Fontevraut house

[15] See Carleton Brown, *English Lyrics of the Thirteenth Century* (Oxford, 1932), nos. 32.C, 63, 64.

[16] Ker, *Catalogue*, 230 – 4, 279 – 81 (nos. 180, 215).

[17] On the date and provenance of the autograph manuscript see most recently M. Parkes, 'On the presumed date of the manuscript of the Orrmulum', in *Five Hundred Years of Words and Sounds for E. J. Dobson*, ed. E. G. Stanley, D. Gray (Cambridge, 1983), 115 – 27.

[18] Dobson.

[19] Ker, *Medieval Libraries*, lists about a score of manuscripts in English or French, or with vernacular entries, from Augustinian houses. The contribution of Augustinian canons to writing in English surpasses the better publicised Franciscan contribution.

[20] M. Gretsch, 'Die Wintney-Version der *Regula Sancti Benedicti*', *Anglia*, xcvi (1978), 310 – 48, suggests that the text was copied from a manuscript from Winchester.

at Nuneaton, an important collection of religious poems in English and French,[21] and BL Egerton 2710 from the Benedictine nunnery at Derby, with contents exclusively in French.

Conspicuously absent from the foregoing list is any reference to the vernacular literary activity of friars: there are in fact no known thirteenth-century English manuscripts of mendicant origin with vernacular texts, a deficiency that can only be partly explained by the suggestion that vernacular texts used by Franciscans may have been written on rolls, which were much more perishable than books.[22] Among thirteenth-century manuscripts of unknown provenance, however, there are four, containing some of the most outstanding English poems from the period as well as a good deal of French material, which are often grouped under the heading of 'Friars' Miscellanies'. These are Trinity College, Cambridge B.14.39 (James Catalogue no. 323, henceforth cited as TCC 323), BL Cotton Caligula A.ix, Jesus College, Oxford 29 and Bodleian Digby 86. The discovery of the Franciscan contribution to vernacular writing, especially to religious lyrics, is largely due to a number of scholars in America in the first half of this century, notably Carleton Brown, R. L. Greene and R. H. Robbins; their work was of outstanding importance and as regards the period after 1300 it was reasonably firmly based.[23] The later Franciscan contribution to vernacular writing is obviously of great interest, and it is perhaps not surprising that the case was sometimes overstated, some poems and manuscripts being ascribed to Franciscans on rather inadequate evidence. Influential statements on the alleged Franciscan origin (or at least mendicant origin, for the Dominicans were, perhaps rather implausibly, drawn into the matter) of the Trinity, Caligula, Jesus and Digby manuscripts appeared especially in the 1930s and 1940s, and one would be content to let them lie in honourable retirement if they had not been resurrected for repetition in a number of recent publications.[24] Summarised briefly, the main arguments were as follows: TCC 323 was ascribed to Dominicans because it contains a laudatory anecdote about a *predicator*; Jesus 29 was held to be Franciscan

[21] B. Hill, 'Cambridge, Fitzwilliam Museum Manuscript McClean 123', *Notes and Queries*, ccx (1965), 87 – 90.

[22] B. Hill, 'The *Luue-Ron* and Thomas de Hales', *Modern Language Review*, lix (1964), 321 – 30. In support of Miss Hill's identification of Hales with the modern Halesowen one might note that Hailes, Gloucestershire, often suggested as Thomas's place of origin, is excluded by the fact that in Middle English *Hailes* and *Hales* were not homophones and there is no possibility that the spellings were interchangeable in the thirteenth century.

[23] Important publications on the Franciscan contribution to the composition and circulation of English poems, particularly religious lyrics, appeared in the introductions to Carleton Brown, xx – xxxiii; R. L. Greene, *Early English Carols* (Oxford, 1935), cxi – xviii, cxxi – xxxviii; and R. H. Robbins, *Secular Lyrics of the Fourteenth and Fifteenth Centuries* (Oxford, 1952), xvii – xviii; the latter summarised fuller statements published in *Modern Language Notes*, liii (1938), 239 – 45, and *Journal of English and Germanic Philology*, xxxix (1940), 230 – 8. From the late thirteenth and early fourteenth centuries come the Anglo-Norman writings of Nicholas Bozon, which constitute a major Franciscan contribution to vernacular literature.

[24] Especially D. L. Jeffrey, *The Early English Lyric and Franciscan Spirituality* (Nebraska, 1975), 205 – 8, but also D. Pearsall, *Old English and Middle English Poetry* (London, 1977), 94 – 102 (on 'Friars' Miscellanies'). D. Brewer, *English Gothic Literature* (London, 1983), 46, accepts the probable Franciscan origin of Digby 86 and, more tentatively, the likely Dominican origin of TCC 323. It may be mentioned that S. Wenzel, *Verses in Sermons: Fasciculus Morum and its Middle English Poems* (Cambridge, Mass., 1978), 90 – 3, is very cautious about the alleged Franciscan connection, while the scholarly study of J. B. Allen, *The Friar as Critic* (Nashville, 1971), scrupulously avoids alleged mendicant vernacular lyrics; cf. also Coss, 63.

because it contains one poem by a known Franciscan (the *Luve Ron* of Thomas of Hales); Caligula A.ix has so much in common with Jesus 29 that whatever applies to one was assumed to hold good for the other; and Digby 86 was alleged to be Franciscan because it includes a French prayer ascribed to St. Francis, has a calendar that includes the feasts of Dominic and Francis among other saints' days, and because it came to Digby from Thomas Allen, who is known to have acquired manuscripts from the Franciscan house at Oxford among other places. None of these arguments, of course, can carry much weight, and underlying most of them there seems to be a tacit assumption, no doubt encouraged by later fourteenth-century attacks on friars, that no-one but a friar would ever speak well of friars or take a sympathetic interest in their works or writings, so that any manuscript that contains commendation of friars or writing by friars was liable to be classed as the work of friars. Furthermore, other texts in such manuscripts might then be classed as mendicant compositions, and other manuscripts containing any of these texts, like the celebrated Harley 2253, were then said to be at least influenced or even dictated by friars. In this way a considerable body of alleged mendicant writings was compiled in order to boost the slender evidence summarised above. The argument that Jesus 29 must be a Franciscan manuscript because it contains a poem by Friar Thomas of Hales is best evaluated in the light of the fact that another work by him, an Anglo-Norman sermon, is uniquely preserved in a thirteenth-century manuscript from the Benedictine Abbey of Westminster (now St. John's College, Oxford 190).[25] Reference has already been made to the Benedictine interest in friars reflected in the illustrations of Lambeth 522, and one need only think of the enthusiasm for Franciscans reflected in such diverse forms as the patronage of Bishop Grosseteste and the commendation expressed by the author of *Ancrene Wisse*.[26]

Arguing the origin of a manuscript from the nature of its contents is not unreasonable, but it is full of pitfalls and any conclusions can only be tentative. This may be exemplified in Jesus 29: looking at its contents, one is struck by the one outstandingly anomalous text, *The Owl and the Nightingale*. Whereas the other pieces, English and French alike, are devotional texts that would appeal to any pious reader, *The Owl and the Nightingale* is uniquely learned, witty and urbane, full of jokes about music, poetry and ecclesiastical politics. Its appeal for preferment for Nicholas of Guildford indicates an origin in the world of the secular clergy, and the whole poem takes us much closer to Walter Map than to St. Francis. One might therefore be inclined to deduce that the men who copied *The Owl and the Nightingale* into the Jesus and Caligula manuscripts must surely have been secular clerics, and this deduction might seem to receive weighty, even overwhelming, support from the fact that the Caligula manuscript is dominated (194 out of 261 folios) by one long poem, Laȝamon's *Brut*, which declares itself to be the work of a secular cleric. That both manuscripts might be from the world of the secular clergy (perhaps parish priests, but more probably a college of secular canons or the familia of a bishop) seems intrinsically plausible, and it is therefore salutary that the researches of Miss Betty Hill have cautiously been directing our attention to

[25] M. D. Legge, 'The Anglo-Norman Sermon of Thomas of Hales', *Modern Language Review*, xxx (1935), 212–18.

[26] *Ancrene Wisse*, ed. J. R. R. Tolkien (EETS, ccxlix, 1962), 36, 213; and see the comments in Dobson.

the Premonstratensian Abbey at Halesowen (which accords well enough with the linguistic evidence).[27] In the absence of conclusive evidence it is wise to keep an open mind about the provenance of all four of these manuscripts, and moreover we limit our own capacity for observation if we treat all four manuscripts as being of the same kind simply because a small number of texts occurs in two or three of them and a very small number is common to all four. Certainly they have common features: they are all from the same period, *c.*1260 – 80, and on linguistic grounds may be assigned to the same general area (the south-west Midlands; more specifically, the diocese of Worcester, or perhaps the dioceses of Worcester and Hereford); they all contain a mixture of languages (English and French in Jesus and Caligula; English, French and Latin in the other two), and all are in some sense religious, though this point needs further explanation. Each, however, is also a highly individual collection with its own special nature. Jesus and Caligula have most in common, and may even in part have been copied from a common exemplar. They are both strikingly literary collections and should be classed as anthologies rather than as miscellanies; they cater for an interest in poetry, but the presence of Laȝamon's *Brut* and an Anglo-Norman prose-chronicle in Caligula gives it a historical dimension that Jesus does not have. It is not merely that the *Brut* would have been accepted as in some sense a record of history: a concern for the past of England is even more tellingly indicated in the apparent care with which at least one of the copyists preserved the linguistic archaisms of Laȝamon's text.[28] Caligula thus reflects a society that not only encouraged religious faith through the use of poetry, but also cared about its past and fostered legends that assert some sense of national identity. In both these manuscripts there are individual English poems that are close in spirit to the evangelical puritanism of the early Franciscans, but when the French pieces are taken into account the dominant tone of each collection is rather one of religious sobriety and conformity, with the further historical element in Caligula. On the other hand, Jesus and Caligula are relatively homogeneous collections when compared with the wide-ranging imaginative fertility reflected in BL Additional 46919 and BL Harley 913, two authentic Franciscan miscellanies from about half a century later, in which in fact a characteristic Franciscan element is not easy to isolate.[29] The most likely milieu for the production and readership of Jesus and Caligula seems to me to be the world of the secular clergy, but a house of regular canons would be equally conceivable.

TCC 323 is a different matter altogether. This too is an anthology, in one sense narrower in that all the contents are strictly religious, in one sense broader in that it contains both verse and prose in Latin, French and English.

[27] B. Hill, 'Oxford, Jesus College MS 29', *Notes and Queries*, ccxx (1975), 98 – 105, points to numerous correspondences beteween texts in the Jesus and Caligula manuscripts and works recorded in the catalogue of Titchfield Abbey, a daughter-house of Halesowen. Whether either manuscript was ever in Halesowen Abbey is not known, but either may well have been copied in that area from Halesowen manuscripts now lost.

[28] E. G. Stanley, 'Laȝamon's Antiquarian Sentiments', *Medium Aevum*, xxxviii (1969), 23 – 37; see 25 – 8 for the preservation of authorial spellings in Caligula.

[29] The fullest description of Additional 46919 is still that of P. Meyer in *Romania*, xiii (1884), 497 – 541; for Harley 913 see W. Heuser, *Die Kildare-Gedichte* (Bonn, 1904; repr. Darmstadt, 1965); both manuscripts are predominantly religious, but the former also contains texts on hunting, falconry and chivalry, and the latter various comic and satirical pieces.

Its most recent editor follows older opinion in taking it to be a preaching-book and cautiously concludes that it may be Franciscan.[30] Its nature as a preaching-book is, however, far from certain. One cannot deny that the texts in it might well be useful to a preacher, but the material is not obviously arranged in any systematic way. There is no trace, for example, of the alphabetic arrangement found in fourteenth-century preaching books like that of the Franciscan John Grimestone,[31] nor is there any apparent thematic arrangement. It seems in fact to be a rather haphazard collection, with various kinds of text being entered as they came to hand. Preaching a sermon from it could be a perplexing task: many of the texts are very long (like the Middle English verse-life of St. Margaret), extended works for reading aloud rather than sermons, and certainly not illustrations to a sermon. Some of the short vernacular poems admittedly resemble those in Grimestone's book or in the *Fasciculus Morum*, but these are only a small part of the whole. Reichl very reasonably argues that the large number of contributors (he distinguishes six major and six minor hands) points to compilation in a religious house, and clergy who had dealings with the laity are perhaps more likely compilers than members of an enclosed order, though the latter cannot be ruled out, particularly if one thinks in terms of a nunnery, but there seems no obvious reason for preferring a mendicant convent to a house of regular or secular canons.

Digby 86 is different again, and it is in many ways the most eccentric and revealing of the four manuscripts.[32] It is more truly a miscellany than the others, less exclusively a literary anthology. It begins with material for practical use (notes for the confessional, medical material, prayers, notes on prognostications, on the interpretation of dreams and on the signs of doomsday, and a calendar for religious use, very much the kind of material in fact that one finds in commonplace books of the later Middle Ages) but it goes on to become rather more literary, without quite losing sight of practicality in the form of interspersed prayers, proverbs and the like. The selection of literary texts is extraordinarily wide (the contents are roughly half French and a quarter each Latin and English), including verse and prose, religious and secular, from the pious to the scurrilous. It has more secular material than any of the other three manuscripts. Among the French contents, works of moral instruction like the *Doctrinal Sauvage*, of continental origin, stand side by side with fabliaux like the Anglo-Norman *Le Lai du Cor*, while the scurrilous *La Vie d'un Vallet Amerous* immediately precedes *Des Quatre Files Due*, an extract from Grosseteste's *Chasteau d'Amour*. The English pieces include numerous religious poems, as well as unique texts of the earliest extant English fabliau, *Dame Siriz*, and beast-epic, *The Fox and the Wolf*, a bird-debate on women, *The Thrush and the Nightingale*, and the remarkable poem on *The Names of a Hare*, which gives an unparalleled

[30] K. Reichl, *Religiöse Dichtung im englischen Hochmittelalter* (München, 1973), esp. 49–58.

[31] National Library of Scotland, Advocates MS 18.7.21, ed. E. Wilson, *A Descriptive Index of the English Lyrics in John of Grimestone's Preaching Book* (Oxford, 1973). See also H. G. Pfander, 'Medieval friars and some alphabetical reference-books for sermons', *Medium Aevum*, iii (1934), 19–29.

[32] The fullest published account is still in E. Stengel, *Codicem Manu Scriptum Digby 86* (Halle, 1871). My work on Digby 86, on which I am drawing here, has been made possible by a grant from the University of Newcastle upon Tyne Research Fund for the purchase of photostats of the manuscript.

insight into medieval rural superstition.[33] Emphasis on the variety of the material should not of course obscure the fact that the collection is predominantly religious, and it is especially the shorter English religious poems that link this manuscript with the others in the group, but these few shared poems should not lead us into classifying this extravagantly heterogeneous collection with the neat anthology for churchmen that we find in Jesus 29.

Carleton Brown, who first tentatively ascribed the Digby manuscript to friars in 1932, himself drew attention to the signatures that appear at various points in the margins and deduced from them that by the mid-fourteenth century the manuscript was in private lay hands.[34] In 1963, B. D. H. Miller amplified this in a carefully argued study to show that the manuscript had probably always been in lay hands and was likely to have been compiled for a lay household.[35] Miller's study ought to have put an end to the classification of Digby 86 as a 'friar's miscellany'; of course, one cannot rule out the possibility that some of the poems in it may have been transmitted by friars, but there is not positive evidence that this was so. Nevertheless, the manuscript still has in parts a distinctly clerical appearance. While the religious poems, saints' lives and works of meditation and instruction might appeal to any ordinarily pious reader, lay or clerical, the notes for the confessional, the psalms and prayers in Latin and especially the professional-looking calendar, also in Latin, all look like items for the practising cleric. So while accepting Miller's suggestion that the manuscript was compiled in and for a lay household, I would see the compiler (the manuscript is almost entirely in one hand) as a cleric, perhaps the local parish-priest, more probably a private chaplain in a manorial household, at any rate, a member of the secular clergy. Support for the suggestion that the compiler was a domestic chaplain to one of the Worcestershire families named in the marginal inscriptions may perhaps be seen in the fact that the contents of the manuscript indicate that he had a dual function, to provide both spiritual guidance and also what one might call book-based entertainment. That the secular pieces, as much as the religious ones, had a social function, rather than reflecting a purely private literary interest, is strikingly demonstrated by the Anglo-Norman poem entitled *Ragemon le Bon*.[36] This is the text for a parlour-game, a comic fortune-telling by the drawing of lots, and, as Långfors pointed out, the Digby version is decidedly ribald and even malicious by comparison with its continental French counterpart; so much so that it, or some very similar version, provoked a religious parody that is recorded in TCC 323. Moreover, where the French original is addessed to men, the Digby version is intended for mixed company: most of its stanzas, at least 40, are addressed to men, but the last 10 or 12 are addressed to women. One may note in passing that the fifteenth-century English version of the same

[33] Most of the texts here mentioned are unique to Digby 86, but the Anglo-Norman *Disciplina Clericalis* and the *Doctrinal Sauvage* are both preserved in a large number of manuscripts, while *The Thrush and the Nightingale* is also in the Auchinleck MS. The extract from Grosseteste is unique to Digby in this form.

[34] Brown, xxviii – xxxiii.

[35] B. D. H. Miller, 'The early history of Bodleian MS Digby 86', *Annuale Medievale*, iv (1963), 23 – 56.

[36] Edited together with its continental precursor and the religious version in TCC 323 by A. Långfors, *Un jeu de société du moyen age, Ragemon le Bon* (Helsinki, 1920).

game is addressed exclusively to women, a point with interesting social implications.[37] *Ragemon le Bon* thus gives us some insight into the society for whom the Digby manuscript was compiled: sexually mixed, though predictably male-dominated (the poem has familiar jokes about women and cuckoldry), requiring entertainment, somewhat naive and even coarse in taste, rustic rather than urban, at any rate lacking in the refinement and sophistication that one might expect to find in an aristocratic court (not to mention a Benedictine monastery, if one thinks of the contents of Harley 978), but on the evidence of other texts, fundamentally devout, responsive to spiritual guidance as well as to fun. Thus Digby 86, more than any other manuscript of the period, gives us an insight into what one might loosely call the upper middle class of thirteenth-century rural England.

What has emerged from the foregoing sketch of selected thirteenth-century manuscripts is a picture of the clergy, at that date the literate section of the community, mediating vernacular writings, partly to other clergy and partly to the laity; in the latter case religious instruction shades off into the provision of entertainment. Writing in French seems to have run somewhat ahead of that in English in the sense that the provision of texts for lay patrons and readers occurs at an earlier date for texts in the French language, whether Anglo-Norman or continental, than for those in English, and there may even have been some professional production of books with French texts for a lay readership before the end of the thirteenth century.[38] The first example of a professionally produced volume with English texts is presumably the Auchinleck Manuscript from the next century, *c.*1330–40. Whether any extant thirteenth-century manuscripts that include English contents were professionally produced for lay use is not known; in this, as in so many other matters, the important division is less that between clergy and laity, than that between regular clergy on the one hand and secular clergy and laity on the other, for the latter groups shared so much common experience of life. There is perhaps nothing unreasonable in the supposition that thirteenth-century manuscripts of romances and other secular poems in English were prepared for laymen by clerics, and Digby 86 probably provides the closest we can get to positive evidence of this; for similar texts in French the evidence of clerical origin is stronger, though the intended audience remains uncertain.

[37] Edited by Freudenberger, *Ragman Roll, ein spätmittelenglisches Gedicht* (Erlangen, 1909); both manuscripts of this poem are now available in facsimile: *Bodleian Library MS Fairfax 16*, ed. J. Norton-Smith (London, 1979), and *Manuscript Bodley 638: a Facsimile*, ed. P. Robinson (Norman, Oklahoma, 1982).

[38] Coss, 60–1 and n. 95. R. Vaughan, *Matthew Paris* (Cambridge, 1958), 159–81, gives information about the French religious texts, mostly saints' lives, composed by Matthew Paris for aristocratic readers. This does not of course constitute professional book-production (there seems to be no evidence of any related financial transactions), but it is presumably in some sense a precursor of the professional book-trade, which seems to have begun in England with the supply of texts in French for wealthy readers.

The South English Legendary: Constructing a Context

Annie Samson

Recent work has done much to qualify received views on the literacy of the laity and the place of English in the thirteenth century. A new model has now emerged of a society increasingly reliant in its organisation upon documents, and therefore with a much higher level of pragmatic literacy than was once assumed.[1] At the same time English has been demonstrated to be the first language of all but the very highest social groups rather than the despised medium of expression for the lower classes.[2] The distinctiveness of the regions has also been stressed, and interaction between the monasteries of the south-west Midlands and the local gentry in the diffusion of a vernacular culture persuasively argued.[3]

It is timely, then, to consider the place of the *South English Legendary* on this new map, since the work has been as puzzling to twentieth-century scholars as it was popular with later medieval audiences and readers.

The legendary is an extensive collection of saints' lives, usually combined with some pieces appropriate to a *temporale* (a collection of readings for the moveable and fixed feasts of the Church year). In all manuscripts except the first the items are arranged in calendar order. They are in English and have been defined as 'true instances of popular culture'.[4] The work is extant, either complete or in fragments, in some 45 manuscripts. Another 19 contain single items from it.[5] These date from the late thirteenth to late fifteenth centuries and none seems to reflect with particular closeness the original, which has been dated with varying degrees of assurance between 1260 and 1288.[6] Extant manuscripts produced up to the 1330s suggest that the work was initially confined to, though quite widely disseminated within, the south-west Midlands.

[1] M. T. Clanchy, *From Memory to Written Record* (London, 1979); M. B. Parkes, 'The Literacy of the Laity', in *Literature and Civilization: The Medieval World*, ed. D. Daiches, A. Thorlby (London, 1973), 555.
[2] Clanchy, 151.
[3] D. Pearsall, 'The Origins of the Alliterative Revival', in *The Alliterative Tradition in the Fourteenth Century* ed. B. S. Levy, P. E. Szarmach (Kent, Ohio, 1981); P. R. Coss, 'Aspects of Cultural Diffusion in Medieval England: The Early Romances, Local Society and Robin Hood', *Past and Present*, cviii (1985), 36.
[4] K. P. Jankofsky, 'Entertainment, Edification, and Popular Education in the *South English Legendary*', *Journ. of Popular Culture*, xi (1977), 706.
[5] M. Görlach, *The Textual Tradition of the South English Legendary* (Leeds, 1974), viii–ix; O. S. Pickering, M. Görlach, 'A Newly Discovered Manuscript of the *South English Legendary*', *Anglia*, c (1982), 109.
[6] B. D. Brown, *Southern Passion* (EETS, old ser., clxix, 1927), xi; Görlach, 37; T. J. Heffernan, 'Additional Evidence for a more Precise Date of the *South English Legendary*', *Traditio* (1979), 345.

The earliest (MS Laud 108) was copied before 1300 in a west Oxfordshire dialect.[7] The next (MS Harley 2277), produced around the turn of the century, appears to have originated in west Somerset. Two others of the early major manuscripts (MS Egerton 2891 and MS Corpus Christi 145), together with two fragments (MS Leicester City Museum 18D 59 and MS Nottingham University Mi LM 7/1), appear to have been copied in the same scriptorium *c*.1310–20.[8] They are in a west Berkshire dialect. MS Ashmole 43 was copied *c*.1330 and has been located in north-west Gloucestershire. After this period manuscripts proliferate and spread, though not evenly, further and further afield.[9]

The problems the work has presented are various: its original form, provenance, audience and the conditions under which it was read are still the subjects of uncertainty. These problems are clearly interrelated, and doubts about what might be called the context of the work compound, and are compounded by, difficulties in defining its genre, that 'internal substitute for context'.[10] With uncertainties about the form of the original, with no sufficiently close antecedents in Middle English to help us place it with any precision within the broad genre of hagiography, and no external indication of the purpose of the work, that 'inevitably circularity' which has been claimed as a feature of all interpretation has seemed more than usually intractable.[11] Thus context is hypothesised from hypothetical form, and form from hypothetical context in an inescapable round. Our new sense of thirteenth-century culture, however, together with a sharp eye to prevailing assumptions about the work may help us to define it and its context more closely.

Most of those who have worked on the legendary believe it to have been produced by a religious order (though secular clergy have also been suggested as possible originators) for either a lay audience or for nuns.[12] Most assume the work had some liturgical function and define it as a *liber festivalis*, a book of lections for the feasts of the liturgical year, and all seem to agree that it was designed for public delivery.[13] Unfortunately attempts to give these assumptions closer definition or to bring them into relationship with one another reveal them to be less than compatible, as the difficulty of defining the provenance of the work suggests.

On the face of it, it seems likely that the work was compiled by a member of one of the monastic orders. From what we know of the contents of such libraries as that of Ramsey Abbey, a monastic library might be assumed to have the relevant source materials to hand.[14] That four of the earliest surviving manuscripts seem to have been produced in the same scriptorium adds support to the idea, too, that the gap of around 40 years between them and the hypothetical original has to be remembered. However, it is hard to imagine the

[7] *The Early South English Legendary*, ed. C. Hörstmann (EETS, old. ser., lxxxvii, 1887).
[8] MS Corpus Christi is used as the base text by C. D'Evelyn and A. J. Mill for their edition, *The South English Legendary* (EETS, old ser., ccxxv–vi, ccxliv, 1956, 1959).
[9] See Görlach, map, 305.
[10] J. A. Burrow, 'Poems without Contexts', *Essays in Criticism*, xxix (1979), 6.
[11] E. D. Hirsch Jr., 'Objective Interpretation', in *On Literary Intention*, ed. D. Newton-de Molina (Edinburgh, 1976), 26.
[12] For a summary of views see Görlach, 45.
[13] Hörstmann, vii; B. Boyd, 'New Light on *The South English Legendary*', *Texas Studies in English*, xxxvii (1958), 187; Heffernan, 345.
[14] Görlach, 24.

circumstances under which a monastic order would use for liturgical purposes a vernacular text so decidedly popular in tone. The tentative suggestion that the work was compiled for the use of Benedictine nuns seems ruled out since the legendary addresses an audience in the outside world, and one which needed theological terms explaining.[15] Because the legends differ so much in length (and some of them are very long) it is unlikely that they were compiled for use in regular church services, either by a monastic order or by secular clergy.[16] If they were compiled by friars for the purpose of preaching, then one might expect less emphasis on narrative and more on instruction, and the distance of the legends from sermon form has been noticed.[17]

Speculation about the provenance of the legendary, then, has necessarily taken into account, and has generally foundered upon, the assumptions that the work had a liturgical function and was therefore designed for public delivery. However, if it is difficult to envisage a context in which the work was used, then we need to re-examine the grounds for the assumption that it was intended as a *liber festivalis*, and this re-examination will involve considering anew the closely related, though not quite identical, question of the kind of audience for which it was designed. If the work is a *liber festivalis* then that form presupposes public delivery to a sizeable audience, theoretically at least. However, the work might have been intended for public delivery without having had any liturgical function at all.

The supposition that the legendary was, from its inception, a *liber festivalis*, seems to rest upon the calendar order of all extant manuscripts save the earliest (MS Laud 108), on traces of liturgical influence detectable in individual legends, and on those features which have been taken to imply that the work was designed for public performance.

Whether or not the original version of the legendary had, or was intended to have, a calendar order is clearly crucial to the question of whether we are to take it as a *liber festivalis*; but to assume a calendar order entails accounting for the differences between Laud and its successors.

MS Laud 108 is a miscellany. According to the numbering, in a fifteenth century hand, its first seven items have been lost. In its present state it begins with the Life and Passion of Christ (8) and the Infancy of Jesus (9). These are followed by the saints' legends (10 – 67) appearing in Hörstmann's edition, *The Early South English Legendary*. Other material includes the romances *Havelok* (71) and *King Horn* (72) and then, in a later hand, the legends of St. Blaise, St. Cecilia and St. Alexius, which are also included in Hörstmann's edition.[18] It is generally held that the romances were combined with the legendary in the late fourteenth century.

Laud's version of the legendary differs from those of MS Harley 2277 and MS Corpus Christi 145, and indeed from any other complete copy, in a number of respects. It is, first, very much shorter, containing only 59 items as opposed to the 92 items of Harley and the 107 items of Corpus Christi. Also, items appropriate to a *temporale* are almost completely absent from it, though

[15] For Benedictine nuns see Görlach, 47. D. A. Lawton, 'Middle English Unrhymed Alliterative Poetry and the *South English Legendary*', *English Studies*, lxi (1980), 390.
[16] Brown, xciii.
[17] Görlach, 49.
[18] Boyd, 187.

no version of the legendary contains a complete *temporale*. Most significantly, it alone is not arranged in calendar order, though traces of such an order appear about a third of the way through, preceded by a few unique lines, usually described as a prologue, which seem to suggest that a calendar order was intended:[19]

> Al þis bok is i-maked of holi dawes : and of holie mannes liues
> þat soffreden for ore louerdes loue : pinene manie and riue,
> þat ne spareden for none eiȝe : godes weorkes to wurche:
> Of ȝwas liues ȝwane heore feste fallez : men redez in holi churche.
> þei ich of alle ne mouwe nouȝt telle : ichulle telle of some,
> Ase euerech feste after oþur : In þe ȝere doth come.
> Hörstmann, *Early South English Legendary* (*ESEL*), 177, ll.1 – 6)

These differences between Laud and later manuscripts have been accounted for in two ways. The early view, propounded by Hörstmann, was that the legendary was indeed a *liber festivalis* and that Laud represented a stage in its evolution.[20] However, given the monastic provenance he also hypothesised, these twin assumptions seem somewhat contradictory, for there is little or nothing within the work which a monastery would be unlikely to possess or to be able to acquire quickly. Even supposing there were such problems, it is hard to imagine a scribe in a scriptorium not resorting to a booklet system of production if the calendar order were intended from the outset.

In fact, Laud's statement of intention and abortive practice became accepted as evidence that the next earliest manuscript (MS Harley 2277) better represented the intentions of the work's compiler. On this view, which has been substantially accepted for the last 50 years, Laud is to be regarded as disordered.[21] However, this later reconstruction of the textual history of the work is even more difficult to accept than Hörstmann's, for although some disarrangement of Laud's quires seems to have occurred when the manuscript was rebound, *c.*1350 – 1400, no textual critic, so far as I know, has suggested that its physical composition is relevant to the arrangement of its contents.[22] But if Laud itself shows no disorder we have to assume either a physically disordered exemplar, and disordered in such a way as to deny its original compiler's intentions, or a scribe for Laud who deliberately departed from exemplar and calendar order. There is no evidence for either of these assumptions, and in the second case we would have a new set of intentions to take into account.

A more satisfactory explanation for Laud's 'prologue' and the arrangement of the following eight items offers itself if we take into account the admittedly obscure relationship between the *South English Legendary* and Jacobus de Voragine's *Legenda Aurea*, an extensive compilation of saints' legends and *temporale* pieces, produced *c.*1255 – 70, and like our legendary arranged in

[19] Hörstmann first defined the lines thus. However, since Laud lacks its first seven items we may well have lost a different statement of intention.
[20] Hörstmann, viii.
[21] M. E. Wells, '*The South English Legendary* in Its Relation to the *Legenda Aurea*', *Procs. Modern Language Assoc.*, li (1936), 337.
[22] For a description of the manuscript see Görlach, 88.

calendar order, though the *Legenda Aurea* follows the liturgical year, beginning on 29 November. A close connection between the two works is no longer claimed, and Manfred Görlach, who has done much to clarify the subject, defines the influence of *Legenda* on legendary as only marginal.[23] Nevertheless, he occasionally identifies its use as source material in his discussion of individual legends.[24] He claims that its influence begins to show itself intermittently from Matthew (21). Item 28 is the 'prologue' from which the abortive calendar order starts.

Given that there seems to be no connection between *Legenda* and legendary until item 21, it may be that the scribe of Laud came upon the former as he was copying from an exemplar that conformed to no calendar order and began to use it when its individual items seemed an improvement on those of his original. At the same time he might have felt that the order of the *Legenda* was a good one and decided to adopt it. If he were already a considerable way into his work, however (and the point at which the *Legenda*'s influence is first discernible suggests this[)], the project could well have emerged as less than practicable. On this hypothesis, we may well find recorded in Laud the first tentative attempt at a calendar order.

It may be relevant, too, that the calendar order, where it exists, begins in all manuscripts on 1 January and not on 29 November, the beginning of the liturgical year. While it has been claimed that this practice was common in legendaries produced in England, the *Sanctorale* of the Hereford Breviary suggests that service books were not so arranged.[25]

Possibilities and probabilities do not convert into certainties however, so my real point is a negative one: that the calendar order of manuscripts subsequent to Laud provides no support for assuming that the legendary had any kind of liturgical use.

Unsupported by calendar order, the relationships perceived between the work and the liturgy seem fairly tenuous. Liturgical sources, concentrated between January and June, have been detected for one layer of the early compilation, but a liturgical source does not imply a liturgical *function* and it would be natural for a compiler to use such material, whatever his purposes.[26]

Moreover, references within the work which have been taken to support its liturgical use seem to imply that those reading the legends are *not* in church:

> Her of at seint Petres tid me singþ at holy chirche
> (*SEL*, 249, l.63)

and

> Me singþ a Myhelmasse day in holy churche also
> (*ESEL*, 304, l.165)

Laud's 'prologue', too, shares this feature, and, moreover, implies that the legendary is made for continuous reading:

[23] Görlach, 25; and idem, *The 'South English Legendary', 'Gilte Legende' and 'Golden Legend'* (Braunschweig, 1972).

[24] Görlach, *Textual Tradition*, 131.

[25] Heffernan, 348. *The Hereford Breviary* II, ed. W. H. Frere, L. E. G. Brown, (Henry Bradshaw Soc., xl, 1910), 51.

[26] Görlach, *Textual Tradition*, 14.

þei ich of alle no mouwe nouȝt telle : ichulle telle of some

(*ESEL*, 177, l.5)

The arguments, then, for taking the work as a liturgical text are not compelling, or even very satisfactory. At the same time, a comparison of the selection of saints in Laud with those noted in extant ecclesiastical calendars provides some evidence against the assumption.

Notwithstanding differences between, and inconsistencies within, various Uses, there is a body of saints almost universally venerated which one would expect to find in Laud if it were intended as a liturgical text.[27]

A comparison of the contents of Laud with those of the thirteenth-century Calendar of the Hereford Breviary and, where this is defective, with the Breviary's *Memorie Feriales*, reveals a striking lack of coincidence. The legendary not only ignores some major feasts, it also provides lives for saints whose days were observed as feasts of only three lessons (as opposed to the six and nine allotted to more important saints), or even by no more than a memorial.[28] Moreover, there does not appear to be any closer coincidence between the legendary and York and Sarum Uses.[29]

More interestingly, Laud has often extensive legends for some saints not in the Hereford Calendar, and who appear only infrequently in other Calendars and service books. Patrick, Brendan, Mary of Egypt and Dominic, for example, are not in the fourteenth-century Hereford Ordinal, or the *Ordinale Exoniensis*, a good indicator of pre fourteenth-century Sarum Use.[30] Also, no single Calendar of the other four Calendars I consulted contains them all, so it is unlikely that Laud was following any particular local practice.[31]

Laud's selection of saints, then, does not reflect liturgical priorities; major saints are absent and marginal ones given considerable attention. Moreover, it is usual within the legendary to conflate into one Life the stories appropriate to the different feasts of any individual saint, and this process seems to have taken place in the earliest layer of the work, which has been claimed to show the strongest liturgical influence.[32]

It is perhaps indicative, too, that the *temporale*, probably grouped separately in early copies of the work, is incomplete in all versions, lacking such important feasts as Christmas, Ascension and Pentecost. If, as has been claimed, 'the feasts and fasts of the church year were seldom regarded as of great importance' in the developing work, it becomes even more unlikely that the work

[27] R. W. Pfaff, *New Liturgical Feasts in Later Medieval England* (Oxford, 1970), 1, outlines these inconsistencies.

[28] Frere and Brown, ii. xiv, 11; eg., for August Laud is without Peter, Stephen, the Assumption. It has, however, the minor feasts of Oswald and Hippolytus.

[29] Frere and Brown, iii. xxxii.

[30] *Ordinale Exoniensis*, ed. J. N. Dalton, I (Henry Bradshaw Soc., xxxvii, 1909), xxvii. See Görlach, *Textual Tradition*, 13, on the importance of the *Ordinale*.

[31] F. Wormald, *English Benedictine Kalendars after A.D. 1100*, II (Henry Bradshaw Soc., lxxxi, 1946), 21, Evesham Abbey, Worcs. (thirteenth and fourteenth century): no Patrick, Francis or Dominic; 39, St. Peter's Abbey, Gloucs. (twelfth century with thirteenth and fourteenth century additions): no Mary of Egypt, Brendan, Dominic, Francis; 91, Muchelney Abbey, Somerset (*c.*1300): no Mary of Egypt, Brendan, Dominic; J. B. L. Tolhurst, *The Monastic Breviary of Hyde Abbey, Winchester*, V (Henry Bradshaw Soc., lxxi, 1934); Kalendarium (*c.*1300): no Brendan, Francis, Mary of Egypt.

[32] Görlach, *Textual Tradition*, 18.

had a liturgical use.[33]

If the work did not have a liturgical function, what are we to make of the claims that it was designed for public performance? Do we have to envisage a public, non-liturgical context for it? I do not think so, for once the assumption of liturgical use is seriously questioned, the remaining evidence that the work was intended for a large, communal audience is remarkably tenuous. It consists of the occasional injunction to its audience to pay attention, and the bidding prayers at the end of each legend, but while these prayers presuppose a community of believers sharing the same practices, there is little about them to suggest a community whose members are necessarily physically present to one another. The prayer at the end of *Katherine* seems to come closer than most to communal prayer:

> Ihesu crist for þe suete loue : of seinte Katerine
> graunti us þe Ioye of heuene: and schilde us from helle pine.
> Amen amen, segge we alle : for is holie tyme.
>
> (*ESEL*, 101, ll.302–4)

Such devices are common in medieval literature, part of a convention of writing as though the poet were speaking directly to an audience, a reinforcement, if one likes, of the myth of presence. Seemingly spontaneous direct addresses to an audience define themselves, of course, as illusion within an already written text and are a part of the work's fiction. The creation of fictional audience and situation is a device for governing how the work will be received and is not to be taken as reflecting directly any extra-textual reality.

If the devices I have discussed offer no support for the idea of public performance, other features of the work might seem to tend against it.

The widely different lengths of the legends (they range from 58 to 2478 lines) suggest at the very least that there could have been no regular occasion for their reading. Moreover, although it is dangerous to impose our notions of the acceptable on a society so much more trained to listen than ours, the scientific, cosmological detail of *Michael III*, or the theological debate in *Katherine* hardly seem designed for delivery to the large *lewede* audience so aften assumed. Even more than these two legends, however, that of *Thomas a Becket* seems to stretch that hypothesis to its limits. The life is very much longer than any other in the collection (2478 lines as opposed to the 803 lines of *Michael* and the 736 lines of *Brendan*, the two next longest), too long, it seems, to be delivered upon a single occasion. More tellingly, its blow by blow account of the conflict between church and state seems likely, despite all Becket's undoubted popularity, to appeal primarily to those with a fairly active interest in political machinations. The legend, indeed, illuminates nicely the necessity for Henry VIII's Act in Council of 1537 by which Becket was condemned as 'a rebel and a traitor', and his image and story systematically erased from church and book.[34] The work is primarily political history, its bias against the Crown buttressed by its hagiographical cast and framework.

[33] O. S. Pickering, 'The Expository *Temporale* Poems of the *South English Legendary*', *Leeds Studies in English*, x (1979), 1; see also Pickering, 'Three *South English Legendary* Nativity Poems', *Leeds Studies in English*, viii (1975), 105.

[34] *The Golden Legend*, ed. A. Aspland (Holbein Soc., London, 1877), 35.

These three legends, then, and they are among the more extended, seem to presuppose a relatively informed, cultured readership with considerable breadth of interest. Their detail, and the extent of *Thomas* suggests, too, individuals or small homogeneous groups as readers or listeners.

If the work was not designed for liturgical use, or for public performance to a large *lewede* audience, for whom was it intended? And what were the conditions under which it was read? As I have suggested, some of the content seems to presuppose a moderately cultured and informed audience, yet at the same time the work's assumption of an audience outside a religious order, and its popular tone, have been variously pointed out.[35]

Here, I think, we have to interrogate the text a little more closely. The work is, by definition, hagiographical, but hagiography is a broad term so that we need to consider, not so much the genre of the work, but its location within that genre. And that consideration must take into account the fact that the legendary has no precisely similar antecedents in Middle English literature.

Its nearest Middle English forebears are, I think, the poems in the *Katherine* group, a small collection of female saints' lives extant in two manuscripts: MS Bodley 34, which contains also *Sawles Warde* and *Hali Meiòhad* and dated *c.*1210, and MS Royal 17 Axxvii, from which *Hali Meiòhad* is absent. The Latin source for the life of Juliana, one of the poems of the group, is extant in MS Bodley 285, a collection of saints' lives in Latin written *c.*1200–50, possibly in Ramsey Abbey.[36] Comparison of the *Katherine* group with the *South English Legendary* helps to define the tone of the latter more precisely. If one sets the different versions of Juliana's temptation by the devil side by side (*Iuliene* (emended text), 27, and *ESEL*, 64) the legendary emerges as non-devotional, its interest in narrative and event, in the charting of extremity, and charting it so as to evade the human suffering it purports to depict.[37] By contrast, the cadences of Juliana's prayer, in direct speech, give weight to her earlier and continuing heroic stance, make her capacity to see through the devil's disguise credible.

The legendary's emphasis shows itself not only in its style of writing, but in Laud's selection of those saints who are so marginal to the liturgy. Brendan's journeys, Patrick's purgatory, the sexual and penitential exploits of Mary of Egypt are present to gratify appetities other than the purely devotional. This is hagiography rubbing shoulders with romance for most of the time, and occasionally with history and science.

Although he would see the influence of one genre upon the other as becoming marked only in the fourteenth century, Dieter Mehl has already pointed out the fluidity of the boundary between romance and hagiography in English writings.[38] But a variety of associations between romance and religious literature in general seem to show themselves somewhat earlier. Thus, *c.*1300, we have the English romance *Guy of Warwick*, and a work based on Alcuin's *Die Virtutibus et Vitiis* associated with the romance under the title

[35] Brown, xciii; Jankofsky, 706.

[36] S. R. T. O. d'Ardenne, *þe Liflade ant te Passiun of Seinte Iuliene* (EETS, old ser., ccxlviii, 1961), vii.

[37] Laud 108 is without *Juliana.*

[38] D. Mehl, *The Middle English Romances of the Thirteenth and Fourteenth Centuries* (London, 1968), 17.

Speculum Gy de Warewyke. Both appear in the Auchinleck manuscript, *c*.1330.[39]

That saints' legends, romances, religious manuals were read by roughly similar audiences may perhaps be inferred from their appearance in the same libraries and manuscripts. The 40 volumes given by Guy de Beauchamp, earl of Warwick, to Bordesley Abbey in 1306 demonstrate the wide reading habits of at least one thirteenth-century educated Englishman.[40] The works listed include saints' lives, courtly romances, didactic and historical literature. One of the titles is particularly telling: 'volume del Romaunce de Aygnes'.[41]

If we turn to works in English, the *South English Legendary* itself appears bound with romances in two manuscripts: with *Havelok* and *King Horn* in Laud 108, in King's College, Cambridge MS 13 with the fourteenth-century *William of Palerne*. Both works are written in what is arguably the same hand.[42] These combinations, of course, because of their lateness, can do no more than suggest the possibility of a common readership for legendary and romances in the thirteenth century.

However, similarities in subject matter and treatment between secular romance and religious teaching abound. Many of the most notable female saints have affinities with the stereotypical romance heroine (high birth, beauty, desirability) and their persecution often seems to stem as much from the unrequited lust of the powerful as from their adherence to the Christian faith. Their faithfulness to the love of Christ and disdain for earthly suitors finds, perhaps, a secular analogue in the *danger* in which the romance heroine holds her suitors. The resemblance between virgin saint and romance heroine expresses itself in visual terms, too, the saint depicted in glass or paintings with the long golden hair and high forehead of the ideal beauty.

The Prologue to the Corpus Christi manuscript makes its connection with romance clear. Christ is portrayed as the heroic king defending his kingdom; the saints are his knights, their exploits the subject of the work:

> Men wilneþ muche to hure telle . of bataille of kynge
> And of kniȝtes þat hardy were . þat muchedel is lesynge
> Wo so wilneþ muche to hure . tales of suche þinge
> Hardi batailles he may hure . here þat nis no lesinge
> Of apostles & martirs . þat hardy kniȝtes were
>
> (*SEL*, 3, ll.59–63)

Here we have the work offered as a substitute for romance; like romance it will deal with heroic deeds and will satisfy the same audience. The only difference suggested is that the exploits the legendary deals with will be true.

In *Handlyng Synne*, begun according to its author in 1303, we have what in some ways seems to be an equivalent, though the work with its jaunty, simple rhymes and its appetite for the titillating and scandalous story seems somewhat downmarket of the legendary.[43] Although Robert of Brunne is teaching the

39 *The Auchinleck Manuscript*, ed. D. Pearsall, I. Cunningham (London, 1977).
40 Clanchy, 60.
41 M. Blaess, 'L'Abbaye de Bordesley et les livres de Guy de Beauchamp', *Romania*, lxxviii (1957), 511.
41 Lawton, 392.
43 *Robert of Brunne's 'Handlyng Synne'*, ed. F. J. Furnivall (EETS, old ser., cxix, 1901).

main points of doctrine as outlined in Peckham's *Constitutiones* of 1281, his appeal, too, is to an audience with a taste for marvels:

For lewde men y vndyr-tǫke
On englyssh tunge to make þys boke.
For many ben of swyche manere,
þat talys and rymys wyl bleþly here;
Yn gamys, & festys, & at þe ale,
Loue men to lestene troteuale:
þat may falle ofte to vylanye,
To dedly synne, or oþer folye;
For swyche men haue y made þis ryme
þat þey may weyl dyspende here tyme

(ll.43 – 52)

Both the *South English Legendary* and *Handlyng Synne*, then, in their statement of their purposes, in their content, and through their literary relations seem to suggest (and this is after all predictable) that there is a much less rigid division between the secular and the religious in the thirteenth century than our systems of categorisation sometimes make allowance for. Thus, to identify an audience for a certain kind of secular work will be to define one for many religious works as well.

As I noticed at the beginning of this paper, lay literacy has come to seem more widespread in the thirteenth century than was once believed. M. B. Parkes has argued for the pragmatic literacy of a wide sector of society, and Michael Clanchy, as well as illustrating an increasing reliance on documents of all kinds, has also shown convincingly that French was a second language, even among the more aristocratic.[44] But if there was widespread pragmatic literacy among the laity who spoke English as a first language, then we are only a step away from inferring a demand for vernacular literature of all kinds.

Peter Coss recently seems to have taken that step most successfully in his discussion of the cultural diffusion of romances.[45] If we posit the same kind of audience for the legendary as he has done for the romances, then we have a work written initially for regional gentry and perhaps secular clergy, and designed either for individual reading or for reading in the chamber, rather than as entertainment of the hall or public instruction in church.

In the light of Derek Pearsall's contention that the monasteries of the south-west Midlands were the guardians and transmitters of alliterative poetry, and D. A. Lawton's claim that the legendary is a precursor of that poetry, and from what we know of monastic libraries, it seems sensible enough to assume a monastic provenance for the work.[46] The *Iuliene* legend of the *Katherine* groups suggests strongly that such monastic translation was already being undertaken.[47] Although the coupling of the *Katherine* group with *Hali Meiòhad* indicates a readership of nuns, it seems likely that the Fourth Lateran

[44] Clanchy, 151.
[45] Coss.
[46] Pearsall; Lawton.
[47] d'Ardenne, xviii.

Council (1215) gave the necessary incentive to production of the legendary, just as it gave rise to Peckham's *Constitutiones* and the subsequent manuals of instruction which were their direct consequence. *Handlyng Synne* is, after all, clear evidence that such works were produced by religious orders at the turn of the century.

If I am right in my reading of the text and context of the legendary, then the gain is considerable. If the work is not anchored to the liturgy then its selection of saints, and the changes in that selection over a period of time, are likely to reveal something of the values and attitudes of the group for whom it was written. We shall have, too, mapped out a little more clearly for our inspection some of the interconnections between the secular and religious literature of the period.